Alleviating Poverty in Nigeria through the Improvement of the Labour Conditions in the Informal Economy

European University Studies

Europäische Hochschulschriften
Publications Universitaires Européennes

Series XXIII
Theology

Reihe XXIII Série XXIII
Theologie
Théologie

Vol./Bd. 932

PETER LANG
Frankfurt am Main · Berlin · Bern · Bruxelles · New York · Oxford · Wien

Samuel Rapu

Alleviating Poverty in Nigeria through the Improvement of the Labour Conditions in the Informal Economy

A Socio-ethical Enquiry

PETER LANG
Internationaler Verlag der Wissenschaften

Bibliographic Information published by the Deutsche Nationalbibliothek
The Deutsche Nationalbibliothek lists this publication in the Deutsche Nationalbibliografie; detailed bibliographic data is available in the internet at http://dnb.d-nb.de.

Zugl.: Frankfurt, Philo.-Theol. Hochschule Sankt Georgen, Diss., 2012

F 42
ISSN 0721-3409
ISBN 978-3-631-62606-1

www.peterlang.de

This work is dedicated to all the poor people in Nigeria who are deprived of the just remuneration of their labour. May their labour never be in vain.

CONTENTS

FOREWORD

The idea behind this dissertation was conceived within the context of my parish pastoral ministry. My encounter with people afforded me the opportunity to be a part of their life. An essential part of the parish pastoral ministry was to visit the parishioners who could no longer come to the church. One of such visits made a striking impression on me. It was a visit to a family whose members I noticed were no longer coming to morning masses as they used to do. It was discovered during the visit that their absence from the church was due to the fact that the man of the house had been critically ill and the entire family was on the blink of total collapse.

The man in question was a farmer who, before he became ill, though not a rich man, could at least produce what was sufficient to meet the basic needs of the family. His wife supported the family financially by selling beans pies (popularly know as *akara*) and bread at the roadside. This woman had no capital of her own except her frying-pots and her labour. She got every other thing she needed for her business on credit – loaves of bread, oil, beans, etc. As is always the case with businesses of this nature, this woman was expected, to pay back on a daily basis what she got on credit. Getting new supplies on credit depended strictly on her ability to pay back previous ones. She kept faithfully to the terms of the business and was able to make some profits until her husband took ill. With the family pressure at the time of her husband's illness, she could no longer keep to the terms of the business deal and so lost the benevolence of her creditors. The couple had children who at that critical moment were not old enough to support the family especially in the farm work. All of these meant for this family a total loss of every source of livelihood.

During my visit I was told that what the woman needed in order to go back to her business was only one thousand, eight hundred naira (N1,800.00), an equivalent of about fifteen dollars ($15). And indeed as soon as she got that amount of money and resumed her business, the fortune of the family became bright once more. It was like giving the family a new breath of life.

There are many Nigerian families in this same or similar situation. The majority of them are working or engaged in one occupation or the other. In spite of this, they continue to groan under the heavy weight of poverty as a result of the unfavourable conditions in which they live and work. These are the people who make up what is referred to in this work as the informal economy.

It is indeed not difficult to see how hardship and misery have become the common features of the average families in Nigeria. At the same time one is confronted with the stark reality that Nigeria as a nation is endowed with abundant resources. In the face of these conflicting realities, one cannot but ask: Why is there so much misery in a nation that is so abundantly blessed with resources? Why must people work so hard and still live in abject poverty? What has gone wrong in Nigeria? What could be the possible way out of the problem of poverty that confronts the nation?

ACKNOWLEDGEMENTS

My profound gratitude goes first and foremost to God almighty. "What I am now, I am through the grace of God." (1 Cor. 15:10).

My gratitude goes also to Aid to the Church in Need and to the Catholic Diocese of Fulda, Germany for partly financing this project. I would also like to specially thank my bishop, Most Rev. Dr. Michael Elue for giving me the permission to proceed on further studies and also for his immense support. Special thanks also to His Grace, Most Rev. Dr. Augustine Akubeze, the then chairman of the Further Studies Commission. Thanks also to someone who was like a father to me, the late Bishop Emmanuel Otteh.

My sincere appreciation goes also to my moderator, Prof. Dr. Bernhard Emunds and to the second Moderator, Prof. Dr. Josef Schuster S.J. for their faithful guidance. Thanks also to the entire staff of the Nell-Breuning institute, especially Markus Demele and Wolf-Gero Reichert. I also express my in-depth gratitude to the numerous authors whose works I have consulted for this dissertation.

I am indeed indebted to my brother-priests and colleagues from whom I was privileged to draw inspiration at various stages of my doctoral programme: Rev Fr. John Nwanze, Rev. Prof. Dr. Patrick Isichei, Right Rev. Msgr. Dr. Peter Uzor, Rev. Dr. Pius Benson, Rev. Dr. Clement Akinselonyi, Rev. Dr. Hubert Opara, Rev. Dr. Jude Okocha, Rev. Dr. Blaise Okpanachi, Rev. Dr. Ifeanyi Emejulu C.S.Sp, Rev. Frs. Augustine Aghogba, Vincent Jijingi, Augustin Nkwain, Joseph Abitiya, Norbert Uchuno, Charles Uganwa, Dominic Chukwudi, Pascal Nduka, Leonard Biachi, Peter Nkadi, Valentine Dimude, Mike Ashibuogwu, Thaddeus Ajayi and Stephen Okojie.

Many thanks also to the following persons and groups of persons for the immense contributions and support given to me in the course of writing this work: the Irish province of the Society of African Missions, the Mary Ward Sisters in Bad Homburg, Dr. Emeka Ani and family, Sr. Mary-Stelphin Nwachukwu DMMM, Maria and Sven Nyqvist, Regina Schönberger, Rosa Gleißner, Angilika and Reinhold Pöl, Gelinde Gleißner and late Alfons Gleißner, Johanna Frank, The entire lay faithful of St. Robert Parish Heringen, Mr. Edward Hugo, Sr. Calice DMMM, Sr. Ugochi Ozurumba, Sr. Julitta Okeke DDL, the DDL Sisters in Frankfurt and Sossenheim communities, Sr. Nula Edozien OLA, Sr. Somkenechi Onyenankeya DMJ, Sir and Lady Odabi and family, Chief Mike E. Arinze KSM, Mrs Margaret Gbenoba, Barbara Flugel, Harry Braun, Hildegard and Joseph Flugel, Mr. Christopher C. Onwuka and to the entire members of my immediate and extended family.

ABBREVIATIONS

ACGS	Agricultural Credit Guarantee Scheme
ADP	Agricultural Development Programmes
AEP	Agricultural Employment Programme
ATO	Alternative trading organization
BLP	Better Life Programme
BOFI	Banks and Other Financial Institutions
BWI	Bretton Woods Institutions
CB	Community Banks
CBCN	Catholic Bishops Conference of Nigeria
CBD	Central Business District
CBN	Central Bank of Nigeria
CBO	Community Base Organization
CET	Common External Tariff
CLS	Core Labour Standards
CST	Catholic Social Teaching
DFRRI	Directorate of Food, Roads and Rural Infrastructure
DWA	Decent Work Agenda
DWCP	Decent Work Country Programme
ECA	Excess Crude Account
ECOSOC	Economic and Social Council
ECOWAS	Economic Community of West African States
EFCC	Economic and Financial Crimes Commission
EPZ	Export Processing Zones
FCPE	Free and Compulsory primary Education
FDI	Foreign Direct Investment
FEAP	Family Economic Advancement Programme
FSP	Family Support Programme
FTF	Fair Trade Federation
G10	Group of 10

G7	Group of 7
GDP	Global Gross Domestic Product
GNI	Gross National Income
GNP	Gross National Product
GSM	System for Mobil Communications
HIPC	Heavily Indebted Poor Countries
HIV/AIDS	Human Immunodeficiency Virus/Acquired Immunodeficiency Syndrome
HPI	Human Poverty Index
ICFTU	Confederation of Free Trade Unions
ICLS	Conference of Labour Statisticians
ICP	International Comparison Programme
ICPC	Independent Corrupt Practice and other Related Offences Commission
ICT	Communication Technology
IGA	Income-Generating Activities
ILC	International Labour Conference
ILO	International Labour Organization
IMF	International Monetary Fund
IPEC	International Programme on the Elimination of Child Labour
JDPC	Peace and Development Commission
LEEDS	Local Government Economic Empowerment and Development
MDG	Millennium Development Goal
ME	Micro-enterprise
MFI	Microfinance Institution
MNE	Multi-national Enterprise
MSE	Micro and Small-Scale Enterprise
NAC	National Action Council
NAPEP	National Poverty Eradication Programme
NDE	National Directorate of Employment
NDF	National Development Frameworks
NDIC	Nigeria Deposit Insurance Corporation

NEEDS	National Economic and Empowerment Development Strategy
NEITI	Nigeria Extractive Industries Transparency Initiative
NGO	Non-governmental Organization
NIC	Industrialized Countries
NLC	Nigerian Labour Congress
NTC	Nigerian Tobacco Company
OECD	Organization for Economic Co-operation and Development
OFN	Operation Feed the Nation
PAP	Poverty Alleviation Programme
PBN	People's Bank of Nigeria
PHCN	Power Holding Company of Nigeria
PRS	Poverty Reduction Strategy
PRSP	Poverty Reduction Strategy Paper
PWC	Post-Washington Consensus
RBDA	River Basin Development Authorities
RBP	Rural Banking Programme
RES	Rural Electrification Scheme
SAP	Structural Adjustment Programme
SE	Small Enterprise
SEEDS	State Economic Empowerment and Development Strategies
SNA	System of National Accounts
SPWP	Special Public Works Programme
SWF	Sovereign Wealth Fund
UN	United Nations
UNDP	United Nations Development Programme
UNESCO	United Nations Education, Scientific and Cultural Organization
USCB	United States Catholic Bishops
VSD	Vocational Skills Development Programme
WAI	War against Indiscipline
WCL	World Confederation of Labour
WIDER	World Institute for Development Economics Research
WTO	World Trade Organization

GENERAL INTRODUCTION

Poverty has been a recurrent topic in international discussions, within which many approaches and strategies have been proposed for dealing with the social problem it constitutes. In the fields of academic pursuits, many theories aimed at dealing with the problem of poverty have also been propounded.

In recent times, the global efforts at combating the menace of poverty have been intensified under the coordination of the various agencies of the United Nations Organization. Notable among these institutions committed to the alleviation of poverty are the Bretton Woods Institutions and the International Labour Organizations.

In Nigeria, several efforts have also been made by successive governments and non-governmental organizations (NGO) including the Church to combat the menace of poverty in the nation.

The pervasiveness of poverty in Nigeria despite the many poverty alleviation programmes that have been embarked upon raises a question about the suitability and effectiveness of the programmes with regard to the causes of the problem. There is therefore a need for a proper examination of the causes of poverty and the evaluation of the entire system for dealing with poverty in the nation. This dissertation derives its relevance from this perceived need. The entire project is therefore a critical enquiry into the problem of poverty in Nigeria. Being an enquiry, it raises some basic questions about human suffering in the nation. Such questions include: What is the nature of poverty in Nigeria? Who are the poor people in Nigeria? What are the causes of poverty? What efforts have been made and are being made to overcome the problem of poverty? How successful are these efforts? What else could be done in order to deal with the problem of poverty in a more sustainable way? The ethical orientation for making this evaluation will be derived from the social teaching of the Catholic Church.

This Dissertation is permeated with the conviction that the wealth of a nation lies not in robust economic indices but in well developed human resources available in that nation. In other words, economic progress does not translate automatically into real wealth and poverty alleviation in a nation. In order to effectively deal with poverty, any particular nation, no matter how rich it may be in natural resources, needs to create a favourable condition that enables its citizen to participate actively in wealth creation and receive a fair share of the wealth produced in the nation. This requires functional and reliable socio-economic systems and structures that ensure that every citizen who can work is not only give the opportunity to do so but also empowered to work productively in conditions that befit his or her dignity as a human person. This conviction underscores the central position given to human work in this dissertation and the particular attention paid to the need to improve the labour conditions in the informal economy where majority of poor people are working to earn their living.

The main argument in this work is therefore that the pervasiveness of poverty in Nigeria is as a result of structural failures that cause the formal economy to continually dwindle while the informal economy rapidly expands, creating atypical jobs. This trend must be reverted if the menace of poverty in the nation must be overcome in a sustainable way.

We believe that most Nigerians are capable of actively shaping their lives and are eager to influence the development of their nation in a spirit of patriotism, if given the opportunity. Targeting the people in the informal economy would amount to empowering the majority of poor people who are still capable of changing their living and working situations and contributing meaningfully to the socio-economic development in the nation, if given the opportunity to do so. Improving their working and living conditions would amount to putting them in the position to overcome poverty and contribute meaningfully in the generation of more wealth in the nation. Poverty eradication strategies must be holistic and all-embracing, and therefore cannot afford to neglect the informal economy where the majority of the poor people are working.

Our ultimate goal in this work is not to produce a new national Poverty Reduction Strategy Paper (PRPS) but rather to broaden the debate on poverty alleviation by probing deeper into some of the dimensions that have received insufficient attention and in the light of the Catholic social teaching, recast the debate so as to facilitate a wider focus and coherent strategy for a sustainable poverty alleviation in the nation.

To achieve this goal, this dissertation is predominantly descriptive, analytic and prescriptive. The descriptive approach entails the definition of some basic terms and general overview of the prevailing political and socio-economic situations. This prepares the ground for the analytical aspect which involves making an ethical evaluation and judgement that eventually provide the basis for making recommendations for sustainable poverty alleviation in Nigerian.

Following this approach, this dissertation is divided into seven chapters. The first three chapters are mainly descriptive. From a global dimension, the first chapter examines the concept of poverty. It is an attempt to understand what it means to be poor and how poverty exists in our world today. It takes a look at the various types of poverty, its measurement and its major causes. The concept of 'working poverty' is also closely examined since the reality for most poor people is that they must work, often in bad conditions and at works that trap them in poverty.

Chapter two is an overview of the informal economy as a universal phenomenon. It formulates a conceptual framework by defining what the informal economy is and what it is not. It takes a look at the size and importance of the informal economy and identifies some groups of informal economic actors that deserve special attention. It also describes, on a general note, the conditions of work in the informal economy and the factors that shape and reshape theses conditions. This chapter is indeed an encounter with the poor people at the very spot where the majority of them work and earn their living. It attempts to provide a deep understanding of the conditions in which the poor live and work and the factors that shape and reshape these conditions. The outcome of the enquiry will be useful in answering the question: Why are people poor even though they are working? The answer to this question is necessary in determining which strategy and policy actions are needed for a more effective and sustainable poverty alleviation.

The third chapter concentrates on poverty and the informal economy in Nigeria. It starts by examining how poverty exists in the nation, using economic and social indicators. The political, economic and social circumstances in the nation are examined with a view to understanding how they have impacted on the human development and the overall well-being in the nation. Thereafter, an in-depth consideration is given to the informal economy where most of the poor in Nigeria work and earn their living. Major aspects of Nigeria's informal economy that are examined include its historical emergence, size and current trends, the different categories of workers and the various types of labour relationships in it, its contributions to the national economy and the various challenges that confront it. Attention is also given to how the prevailing socio-economic and political circumstances have influenced and still influence the ability of the poor to use their labour (the most valuable if not the only asset they have) to contribute meaningfully to wealth creation, have a fair share of the increased availability of public and private resources and participate fully in the life of the society.

The next three chapters (chapters four, five and six) constitute the analytical part of this work. The fourth chapter surveys the Catholic social teaching (CST), with a view to formulating an ethical orientation for evaluating the poverty alleviation efforts both at national and international levels. It starts by articulating what constitutes the CST and goes on to show what implications some fundamental and social principles have in relation to poverty. A closer look is taken at how poverty and its causes are conceived in the social teaching of the Church. The chapter concludes with an articulation of the guidelines for poverty alleviation offered by the Church in her social teaching. These guidelines also identify some important measures for global socio-economic reforms for poverty alleviation.

Chapter five is an evaluation of the past and current poverty alleviation efforts. This aims at finding a political concept for responding to the impulses from the Catholic social teaching and for implementing the guidelines it offers for dealing with the problem of poverty. Although a wide range of poverty alleviation approaches are analyzed in this chapter, more attention is however given to the economic growth approach attributed to the Bretton Woods Institutions (BWI) and the labour-intensive growth approach of the International Labour Organization (ILO). International discussions on poverty and its alleviation have been dominated in recent times by these two approaches.

The sixth chapter takes a critical look at current and past efforts at alleviating poverty in Nigeria, especially by the government and the Nigerian Church. This is done in the light of the ethical impulses from the Catholic social teaching and the insights gained from the analysis in chapter five.

In the seventh chapter, which constitutes the prescriptive part of this work, concrete recommendations are made for a sustainable alleviation of poverty in Nigeria. For precision sake, the recommendations are limited to reform measures at the national level towards developing an integrated poverty alleviation strategy and for improving the labour conditions in the informal economy.

The last part, which is the general conclusion, contains a résumé of the entire work and a discussion of some major challenges for the Nigerian Church towards poverty alleviation in the nation.

CHAPTER ONE
The Problem of Poverty

Introduction

Poverty is a global phenomenon. It proves to be the oldest but yet unresolved social problem. It has been and is still being studied and interpreted from different perspectives – social economic, political, and religious. Consequently, there have been contrasting views about its nature, types, measurement and causes. Against this background, this chapter explores the important aspects of poverty with a view to gaining a good understanding of how it exists in our world today.

1.1 Conceptual Framework

1.1.1 Definition

Poverty has many faces, changing from place to place and across time, and has been described in many ways. This multifaceted nature of Poverty was acknowledged by world's heads of states at the Copenhagen World Summit of Social Development in 1995. Poverty, they observed, has various manifestations, including lack of income and productive resources sufficient to ensure sustainable livelihoods; hunger and malnutrition; ill health; limited or lack of access to education and other basic services; increased morbidity and mortality from illness; homelessness and inadequate housing; unsafe environments; and social discrimination and exclusion. It is also characterized by a lack of participation in decision-making and in civil, social and cultural life.[1]

Amartya Sen defines poverty from the viewpoint of "capability" to function in the society. Base on his argument that well-being emanates from a capability to function in society, Sen postulates that poverty arises when people lack key capabilities, and so have inadequate income or education, or poor health, or insecurity, or low self confidence, or a sense of powerlessness, or the absence of rights such as freedom of speech.[2]

In recent times, poverty has been increasingly defined in terms of social exclusion and lack of participation. Accordingly, poverty exists when the margin of self-expression is drastically reduced and the people concerned are denied equal chance of participation in the activities and living conditions of the society. The

---

1 United Nations, Report of the World Summit for Social Development, (Copenhagen: March 1995), para. 19.

2 Amartya Sen, Development as Freedom. (New York: Oxford University Press, 1999), especially pp. 87 – 110.

term social exclusion is therefore used to emphasise the processes which push people to the edge of society, limit their access to resources and opportunities and curtail their participation in normal social and cultural life, leaving them with a feeling of being marginalised, powerless and discriminated against.

Other common terms associated with poverty are vulnerability[3] and inequality. Vulnerability connotes a situation in which peoples' personal well-being is put at risk because they lack sufficient resources; a situation in which they are at risk of being in debt, suffering poor health, experiencing educational disadvantage and living in unbefitting housing and environment. Vulnerability is therefore defined as the risk of falling into poverty in the future, even if the person is not necessarily poor now. It is often associated with the effects of "shocks" such as a drought, a drop in farm prices, or a financial crisis.[4] It can simply be referred to as poverty in potency.

Inequality lays emphasis on the distribution of attributes, such as income or consumption, across the whole population. In the context of poverty analysis, inequality requires examining if one believes that the welfare of an individual depends on their economic position in relation to other people in society. It can therefore be said that poverty, or rather being really poor, is related to but distinct from inequality and vulnerability.[5]

In an attempt to capture the different aspects of poverty, the United Nations Organization takes a broader look at the phenomenon and states:

> Fundamentally, poverty is a denial of choices and opportunities, a violation of human dignity. It means lack of basic capacity to participate effectively in society. It means not having enough to feed and cloth a family, not having a school or clinic to go to; not having the land on which to grow one's food or a job to earn one's living, not having access to credit. It means insecurity, powerlessness and exclusion of individuals, households and communities. It means susceptibility to violence, and it often implies living on marginal or fragile environments, without access to clean water or sanitation.[6]

---

3 For further readings on 'vulnerability', see the following documents: Stefan Dercon, Income Risk, Coping Strategies and Safety Nets, Background paper for World Development Report 2000/2001, (Washington, D.C.: World Bank, 1999); Margaret Grosh and Paul Glewwe, eds., Designing Household Survey Questionnaires for Developing Countries: Lessons from 15 Years of the Living Standards Measurement Study. (Washington, D.C.: World Bank, 2000); Robert Holzmann and Steen Lau Jorgensen, Social Protection as Social Risk Management: Conceptual Understandings for the Social Protection Sector Strategy Paper, Social Protection Discussion Paper 9904, (Washington, D.C.: World Bank, 1999); Saurabh Sinha and Michael Lipton, Damaging Fluctuations, Risk and Poverty: A Review, Background paper for World Development Report 2000/2001, (Washington, D.C., Brighton: Sussex University, Poverty Research Unit and World Bank, 1999).

4 World Bank, Introduction to Poverty Analysis: Poverty Manual, All, JH Revision, (Washington, D.C.: World Bank Institute, 2005), p. 10.

5 Ibid., p. 9.

6 United Nations, World Summit for Social Development Agreements, §19, at: http://www.un.org/esa/socdev/wssd/text-version/agreements/poach2.htm 30.02.2011. For a similar definition, see: European Commission, Joint Report on Social Inclusion 2004: People are said to be living in poverty if their income and resources are so inadequate as to preclude them from having a standard of living

In sum, poverty can simply be defined as deprivation and lacks. There are however conflicting opinions as to what constitutes this deprivation. In other words, there is no unanimity concerning what one should lack in order to be considered a poor person. This has given rise to different concepts of poverty and different ways of measuring it.

1.1.2 Types of Poverty

There are two important types of poverty, namely, *absolute poverty*, also referred to as "extreme poverty" (a life situation in which the physical existence of a human being is endangered because of a situation of deficiency or deprivation) and *relative poverty*, sometimes referred to as "moderate poverty" (when the socio-cultural minimal standards are not attained or attainable in a given life circumstance).

Absolute poverty occurs when people lack the basic amenities for survival. It is defined as "a condition characterised by severe deprivation of basic human needs, including food, safe drinking water, sanitation facilities, health, shelter, education and information. It depends not only on income but also on access to services."[7] Absolute poverty is most common in developing countries but exists also to a lower extent in the so-called developed nations. In some European countries, for instance, the homeless people and the Roma in some settlements, still experience extreme poverty. Absolute poverty is not defined in relation to societal circumstance. It refers to a set standard which is the same in all countries and which does not change over time.

Relative poverty exists when some people's way of life and income is so much worse than the general standard of living in the country or region in which they live that they struggle to live a normal life and to participate in ordinary economic, social and cultural activities of the society. Relative poverty makes reference to a standard which is defined in terms of the society in which an individual lives. What this means will vary from country to country, depending on the standard of living enjoyed by the majority.

With regard to poverty alleviation, the concept of relative poverty in international discussions remains however controversial. Many experts do not subscribe to it as a good approach in dealing with global poverty. Some are of the opinion that relative poverty has more to do with 'inequality' rather than with poverty. Many international organizations committed to poverty alleviation focus

considered acceptable in the society in which they live. Because of their poverty they may experience multiple disadvantages through unemployment, low income, poor housing, inadequate health care and barriers to lifelong learning, culture, sport and recreation. They are often excluded and marginalised from participating in activities (economic, social and cultural) that are the norm for other people and their access to fundamental rights may be restricted.

7 United Nations, Report of the World Summit for Social Development, op. cit., para. 19.

more on absolute poverty. In line with this, our focus in this work will also be on absolute poverty which of course is more prevalent in Nigeria and obviously has more relevance to poverty eradication in developing nations. This buttresses the fact that in a situation where absolute and relative poverty co-exist, it is absolute poverty which is by far the more serious issue.

Distinctions are also made between *objective poverty* and *subjective poverty*. The existence of objective poverty is determined by experts with the help of established Standards irrespective of what the people concerned think about themselves. On the contrary, subjective poverty exists when the person concerned declares him or herself to be poor.

Concerning the social implication of poverty, it is important to ascertain whether the poverty situation has to do with *structural (persistent) poverty* or *transitory (temporal) poverty*. This index-linking of comparison has become of particular importance in recent studies, since for the majority of people living in poverty, the duration of poverty is limited to a couple of years.

1.2 Measuring Poverty

The importance of the measurement of poverty is to know who is poor, how many people are poor, and where the poor are located. The measurement of poverty is also necessary in order to keep the poor on the agenda, monitor and evaluate projects and policy interventions that are geared towards the poor and evaluate the effectiveness of institutions whose goal is to help the poor. The measurement of poverty therefore takes into due consideration the socio-cultural and socio-economic composition of the society. Since poverty has many dimensions, it has to be looked at through a variety of indicators - levels of income and consumption, social indicators, and indicators of vulnerability to risks and of socio/political access. Three things are required in computing a poverty measure. First, one has to choose the relevant dimension and indicator of well-being. Second, one has to select a poverty line, that is, a threshold below which a given household or individual will be classified as poor. Finally, one has to select a poverty measure to be used for reporting for the population as a whole or for a population subgroup only.[8]

1.2.1 Measurement by Income and Consumption

A common method used to measure poverty is based on incomes or consumption levels. Two approaches are involved – income approach and consumption

8 Cf. Aline Coudouel et al., Poverty Measurement and Analysis, Poverty Reduction Strategy Paper, (Washington, D.C.: The World Bank, 2004). Available also at: http://siteresources.worldbank.org/INTPRS1/Resources/383606-1205334112622/5467_chap1.pdf. See also: World Bank, Introduction to Poverty Analysis: Poverty Manual, All, JH Revision, (Washington, D.C.: World Bank Institute, 2005), pp. 10-13.

approach. Both however arrive at the same result. The income approach places emphasis on whether households or individuals have enough resources to meet their needs. This is the most conventional view – poverty is seen largely in monetary terms – and is the starting point for most analyses of poverty. Following this approach, poverty is then measured by comparing an individual's income with some defined threshold below which they are considered to be poor. An income-related example of absolute poverty would be living on less than $X per day.[9]

The consumption approach involves asking whether people are able to obtain a *specific* type of consumption good, e.g. whether they have enough food to eat, whether they have shelter, whether they have health care, or whether they have access to education. The analyses that adopt this approach naturally go beyond the more traditional monetary measures of poverty: nutritional poverty might be measured by examining whether children are stunted or wasted; and educational poverty might be measured by asking whether someone is illiterate, or by the amount of formal schooling they have received.

Sample surveys are a common method for obtaining information on consumption and income. With these sample surveys, households are made to answer detailed questions on their spending habits and sources of income. Such surveys are conducted more or less regularly in most countries. These sample survey data collection methods are increasingly being complemented by participatory methods, in which case people are asked what their basic needs are and what poverty means for them.[10] Based on these approaches, a person is considered poor if his or her consumption or income level falls below some minimum level necessary to meet basic needs. This minimum level is usually referred to as the "poverty line".

Poverty lines: A poverty line can be defined as the monetary cost to a given person, at a given place and time, of a reference level of welfare. People who do not attain that level of welfare are deemed poor; and those who do are not.[11] What is necessary to satisfy basic needs varies across time and societies. Therefore, poverty

---

9 Cf. Jonathan Haughton, Handbook on Poverty and Inequality, (Washington, D.C.: World Bank, 2009).

10 The origin of this income measurement of poverty, a method which the World Bank has been using since 1990 in estimating global income poverty, is traced to the English man Seebohm Rowntree. Rowntree's method contained in his classic study of poverty in the English city of York in 1899 bears much semblance to the World Bank's current estimation of global income poverty. Rowntree used a method that involved conducting a survey covering nearly every working-class family in York to collect information on earnings and expenditures. He then defined poverty as a level of total earnings insufficient to obtain the minimum necessities for the maintenance of "merely physical efficiency," including food, rent, and other items. He calculated that for a family of five, the minimum weekly expenditure to maintain physical efficiency was 21 shillings, 8 pence; he proposed other amounts for families of different size and composition. Comparing these poverty lines with family earnings, he arrived at his poverty estimate. For details, see: Benjamin Seebohm Rowntree, Povert: A Sturdy of Town Life, (London: Macmillan and CO., 1901), pp. 295-296.

11 D. O. Ajakaiye and V. A. Adeyeye, Concepts, Measurement and Causes of Poverty, (CBN ECONOMIC & FINANCIAL REVIEW, VOL. 39 N0. 4).

lines vary in time and place, and each country uses lines which are appropriate to its level of development, societal norms and values. The international poverty in the past was approximated to $US 1 per day (in 1985 purchasing power dollars) for absolute poverty. The new World Bank estimates, which reflect improvements in internationally comparable price data having considered the cost of living in developing countries, set a new poverty line of US$1.25 a day for absolute poverty and US$2 for *moderate poverty*.[12] The estimates are based on the results of the 2005 *International Comparison Programme* (ICP), released in 2008.[13] The $1.25 per day poverty estimate is however useful only as indicators of global progress, not to assess progress at the country level or to guide country policy and program formulation. In analysing poverty at the national level, each country uses the Country-specific poverty lines. This reflects what it means to be poor in each country's situation and irrespective of international price comparisons.[14]

A distinction is sometimes made between "absolute poverty line" and "relative poverty line". While a relative poverty line varies with average expenditure, the absolute poverty line maintains a fixed "real value over time and space. It is widely argued that for the purposes of formulating anti-poverty policies, a poverty line should always be absolute in the space of welfare. This guarantees that the poverty comparisons made are consistent in the sense that two individuals with the same level of welfare are treated the same way.[15]

The method of measuring poverty based on income or consumption has both strengths and weaknesses. It has been noted that the advantage of measuring poverty based on income lies in the fact that it is based on nationally representative samples; it allows inferences about the conditions and evolution of poverty at the national level. Moreover, since household surveys collect information beyond monetary income or consumption, the approach makes it possible to obtain a broader picture of well-being and poverty, investigate the relationships among different dimensions of poverty, and test hypotheses on the likely impact of policy interventions. Converting information on income or consumption collected in household surveys into measures of wellbeing requires many assumptions. Poverty estimates are however very sensitive to these assumptions. Moreover survey design varies between countries often making comparisons difficult. Another shortcoming of income and consumption data collected at the household level is that they cannot

---

12 Moderate poverty is used normally by the World Bank to classify those whose income is lees than US$2 a day but not less US$1.25 a day.

13 The research behind these new estimates is contained in the research paper: Shaohua Chen and Martin Ravallion, The Developing World Is Poorer Than We Thought, But No less Successful in the Fight against Poverty. (Washington D.C.: World Bank, 2008).

14 World Bank, World Development Report 2000/2001: Attacking Poverty, (New York: Oxford University Press, 2001), box 1.2.

15 D. O. Ajakaiye and V. A. Adeyeye, Concepts, Measurement and Causes of Poverty, (CBN ECONOMIC & FINANCIAL REVIEW, VOL. 39 N0. 4).

reveal inequality within the household. This means that they can understate overall inequality and poverty.[16]

1.2.2 The Human Poverty Index (HPI)

From a human development perspective, poverty means more than the lack of what is necessary for material well-being. Above the poverty of income, more importance is placed here on the poverty of choice and opportunity which focuses on the causes of poverty and is believed to lead directly to strategies of empowerment and other actions to enhance opportunities for everyone. In the capability concept, the poverty of a life lies not merely in the impoverished state in which the person actually lives, but also in the lack of real opportunity due to social constraints (as well as personal circumstance) to lead valuable and valued lives.

The *Human Development Report 1997* introduced a human poverty index (HPI) in an attempt to bring together in a composite index the different features of deprivation in the quality of life in order to arrive at an aggregate judgment on the extent of poverty in a community.[17] The HPI concentrates on the deprivation in the three essential elements of human life[18] reflected in the Human Development Index HDI: longevity, knowledge and a decent standard of living. Income is not included as one of the elements. The (HPI-1) is derived separately for developing countries and the (HPI-2) for a group of select high-income OECD countries. This separation was made in order to better reflect socio-economic differences and also the widely different measures of deprivation in the two groups.

1) The first deprivation relates to *survival*: the likeliness of death at a relatively early age and is represented by the probability of not surviving to ages 40 and 60 respectively for the HPI-1 and HPI-2.
2) The second dimension relates to *knowledge:* being excluded from the world of reading and communication and is measured by the percentage of adults who are illiterate.
3) The third aspect relates to a *decent standard of living*, in particular, overall economic provisioning. This is represented by a composite of three variables -the percentage of people with access to health services and to safe water, and the percentage of malnourished children under five.[19]

---

16 World Bank, World Development Report 2000/2001, op. cit., pp. 16-18. Cf: Lawrence Haddad and Ravi Kanbur, "Are Better-off Households More Unequal or Less Unequal?" Policy Research and External Affairs Working Paper 373, (Washington, D.C.: World Bank, 1990).

17 United Nations Development Programme, Human Development Report 1997, (New York: Oxford University Press, 1997), p. 17.

18 In addition to these three indicators, the HPI-2 also includes social exclusion, which is the fourth dimension of the HPI-2. It is represented by the rate of long term unemployment.

19 Ibid., p. 18. For details on the computation of the HPI, see: United Nations Development Programme, Human Development Report 2007/2008, Technical note 1, (New York: Oxford University Press, 2008).

The HPI is however not without limitations both in data and in concept. Like the income-based measurement, it falls short of capturing the totality of human poverty.

As a follow-up to *Human Development Report 1997,* the *World Development Report 2000/2001: Attacking Poverty* broadens the notion of poverty to include vulnerability and exposure to risk—and voicelessness and powerlessness. All these forms of deprivation, according to this report, severely restrict what Amartya Sen calls the "capabilities that a person has, that is, the substantive freedoms he or she enjoys to lead the kind of life he or she values."[20] It assembles comparable and high-quality social indicators for education, health, access to services and infrastructure. It also includes the development of new indicators to track other dimensions, for example, risk, vulnerability, social exclusion, access to social capital as well as ways to compare a multi-dimensional conception of poverty, when it may not make sense to aggregate the various dimensions into one index.

1.3 Working Poverty

Having surveyed the concept of poverty in General, the time is ripe to be more specific by taking a look at poverty among workers or workers who are poor. It is considered necessary to examine the concept of working poverty because the reality for most of the world's poor is that they must work – often for long hours, in poor working conditions and without basic rights and representation – at work that is not productive enough to enable them to lift themselves and their families out of poverty.[21] There is therefore a strong conviction that the lack of opportunities for the poor and their precarious work conditions have contributed immensely to their impoverishment and continue to curtail their ability to stay out of poverty. "In fact, the majority of the poor of working age receive inadequate incomes from their labour, which leave them and their families below the poverty line."[22]

The concept of working poor brings us closer to the target of this work, although we may have to go a step further in order to reach the targeted group of workers in more concrete terms. We will be concerned here with a concept that has gained popular acceptance in describing workers who are poor – "working poor". Research works on "working poverty" deal with two objects of study, namely employment and poverty that have been usually studied separately.

---

20 Cf. Amartya Sen, Development as Freedom, op. cit.: Amartya Sen expounded the view of development as freedom and analysed poverty in terms of various forms of "unfreedom" that prevent people from realizing and enlarging their capabilities. His approach to development is broad and integrated, encompassing both civil and political liberties and economic and social rights as primary goals of development and the principal means of progress.

21 ILO, World Employment Report 2004–05: Employment, Productivity, and Poverty Reduction, (Geneva: International Labour Office, 2005), p. 26.

22 Ibid, pp. 23-24.

1.3.1 Definition

Who are the working poor? They represent a group of persons in society who, in more ways than one, may be falling through those cracks which represent the failure of the economic system.[23] These are working people living in poverty. Steven Kapsos defines them as "individuals who both fall below an accepted poverty line and who participate in the labour market."[24] They should however not be thought of only in terms of employed labour. The self-employed who are poor are also included in this category of workers. For this reason the working poor have been more specifically defined as "...individuals engaged in either paid or self employment who belong to households with an adult equivalent per capita household expenditure (or income) that falls below a specified poverty line."[25]

The International Labour Organization (ILO) also defines the "working poor" as "individuals who are working but who also fall below an accepted poverty line."[26] The ILO includes the whole family in the concept of working poverty. In this way, a person is counted as working poor only if that person is unable to lift himself or herself *and his or her family* above the poverty threshold. This means that somebody who earns only 50 cents a day would not be considered as working poor if somebody else in the family earns enough to make sure that each family member lives on more than US$1 a day. Conversely, somebody might earn as much as, for example, US$5 a day but with a family consisting of, say, 10 members (9 of them not working) each member would be living on less than US$1 a day. Such a person would still be counted as working poor.[27]

Family income, although very important, is however not enough to determine whether one belongs to the working poor or not. In addition to low income, the working poor are usually denied other fruits of their labour and good working conditions. We therefore argue that the family income of $1 or $1.25 a day does not necessarily lift workers out of absolute poverty, it is also important that other basic benefits of a decent work be guaranteed. Without going into detailed discussion on this issue, suffice it to state that we do not intend in this work to approach the issue of working poverty purely on the basis of income alone to the exclusion of other labour market indicators. And so, the working poor will be conceived as working people living in poverty; individuals engaged in either paid or self employment. They are involved in works that not only provide an insufficient level of income

---

23 ILO, Statistical Report on the working poor in the Caribbean, a report by the Labour Market and Poverty Studies Unit, Department of Economic, The University of the West Indies St. Augustine, Trinidad and Tobago, (Geneva: International Labour Office, 2006), p. 1.

24 Steven Kapsos, Estimating growth requirements for reducing working poverty: Can the world halve working poverty by 2015? Employment Strategy Papers 2004/14, Employment Trends Unit, Employment Strategy Department (Geneva: International Labour Office, 2004), p. 2: The poverty lines used in the paper are $1 and $2 per day.

25 ILO, Statistical Report on the working poor in the Caribbean, op. cit., p. 2.

26 ILO, "Key Indicators of the Labour Market": Poverty, working poor and income distribution KILM 20

27 ILO, World Employment Report 2004–05, Op. cit., p. 26.

but also lack social security, good working conditions, voice and representation and other basic rights at work.

The following statements are therefore true about this category of workers: the working poor have very low productivity, *resulting in low income. In terms of human development gaps,* the working poor are less likely than formal workers to have access to social services and more likely to have low levels of health, education and longevity. *In terms of social exclusion,* the working poor are more often excluded, than formal workers, from state, market and political institutions that determine the 'rules of the game' in these various spheres. And excluded from the mainstream, they have a high risk of plunging into poverty and.[28]

The term working poverty helps also to distinguish the poor who are working from inactive or passive poor and paupers who survive basically on charity or government aid. The working poor are productive people who engage their human potentials in economic activities in order to survive. Some of them may have access to some sort of government support which in most cases is not enough for a decent life. The majority of them however have no access to any form of government aid. This distinction is important for policy interventions, as it helps to identify specific target groups.

The distinction also helps to clarify one of the commonest misperceptions about poverty, namely: People are poor because they have no work or because they do not want to work. The solution most likely to be proposed under the influence of this misconception is: Give them work to do or make them to work. This pattern of thought and approach to poverty has always found expression in human history even in our own time.[29] This explains why policy makers and policy executors often concentrate almost only on job creation at the expense of job quality improvement.

It should also be borne in mind that while poverty in the developed world is often associated with unemployment, the extreme poverty that exists throughout much of the developing world is largely a problem associated with persons who are employed or involved in one or other forms of labour. Recent researches on the concept of the “working poor” in developing economies further confirm that the majority of people in poverty must work in order to survive and support their families in a context where no efficient social protection schemes or social safety nets exist. For these poor workers, the problem is typically one of poor labour conditions, which usually culminate in low income and productivity, lack of protection and right, poor working environment, various forms of abuse and exploitation at work and miserable conditions of living. The working poor also referred to as vulnerable workers will be treated in subsequent chapters of this work as the informal worker.

---

28 Cf. Martha Alter Chen et al., Mainstreaming informal Employment and Gender in Poverty Reduction: a Handbook for Policy-makers, (London: Commonwealth Secretariat, 2004), p. 12.

29 We will return to this point in discussing the different approaches to poverty alleviation in chapter five.

1.3.2 Trends and Estimates

1.3.2.1 Global Estimates

Available estimates of the working poor are based mostly on income. According to the ILO, there were approximately three billion people living on less than two dollars per day—at least 1.39 billion of them were employed in 2003. About 550 million of those lived in extreme poverty—on less than one dollar per day.[30] There were an estimated 1.38 billion $2 per day working poor in 2004, with lower and upper estimates of 1.24 and 1.6 billion. This means that over 48 per cent of the world's workers (and over 57 per cent of the developing world's workers) were at that time not earning enough to lift themselves and their families above the $2 per day moderate poverty line. The strong global gross domestic product (GDP) growth recorded in 2006 led to a stabilization of labour markets worldwide, with more people in work. The share of working poor in total employment decreased from 54.8 per cent in 1996 to 47.4 in 2006.[31]

The challenges facing different regions of the world remained relatively unchanged by the end of 2007. Apart from the rather low impact of growth on job creation, attention was also drawn to another concern: the ongoing (but, already slightly decreasing) growth did not have an impact sufficient to reduce the levels of working poverty, especially in the poor regions of the world. Despite working, more than four out of ten workers did not earn enough to lift themselves and their families above the US$1 a day poverty line.[32]

Estimates of the share of workers in extreme poverty suggest that up to an additional 7.0 per cent of workers were at risk of falling into poverty between 2008 and 2009. This would translate into an additional 215 million workers. At the US$ 2 a day poverty line, it is estimated that up to additional 5.9 per cent of workers (185 million workers) were at risk of falling into poverty between 2008 and 2009.[33]

In the most recent report, one out of every five workers in the world is estimated to have been living with their family in extreme poverty (less than US$ 1.25 per person per day) in 2009, down sharply from a decade earlier.[34] The share of workers living with their families below the US$ 2 a day poverty line is estimated at around 39 per cent, or a total of nearly 1.2 billion workers worldwide.[35]

---

30 ILO, World Employment Report 2004–05, op. cit., p. 24.

31 ILO, Global Employment Trends Brief, January 2007, (Geneva: International Labour Office, 2007), p. 1.

32 ILO, Global employment trends: January 2008, (Geneva, International labour Office, 2008), p. 10.

33 ILO, Global employment trends: January 2010, (Geneva: International Labour Office, 2010), p. 22

34 This improvement is attributed mainly to the stable progress recorded in recent years in eastern Asia, especially in China and India, in terms of reduction in total poverty. Cf.: ILO, Global Employment Trends 2011: The challenge of a jobs recovery (Geneva: International Labour Office, 2011), p. 23.

35 ILO, Global Employment Trends 2011: The challenge of a jobs recovery, (Geneva: International Labour Office, 2011), p.23.

1.3.2.2 Sub-regional Estimates

Sub-Saharan Africa has the highest incidence of working poverty of all developing regions. Around 55 per cent of all people employed are not earning enough to lift themselves and their families above the US$1 a day poverty line. This share had decreased slightly during the late 1980s, but since 1990 it stayed continuously at a level as high as 55.8 per cent. In terms of US$2 a day working poverty, the same stagnation took place since 1990, leaving the working poor share in total employment at just below 90 per cent in 2003.[36]

In 2004 there were around 140 million $1 working poor and over 220 million $2 working poor in sub-Saharan Africa. Each of these figures is approximately two times the region's levels in 1980. The high share of working poor and total poverty is likely to persist given the region's high unemployment rates, insufficient capacity for job creation, rapidly expanding labour force and huge overall decent work deficit.[37]

The incidence of working poverty continues to grow in 2006 at both the US$1 a day as well as the US$2 a day level. Only a gradual decrease has been recorded in the share of working poor in total employment. Moreover, more than eight out of ten people earned too little to lift themselves and their families above the US$2 a day poverty line; and five out of ten were not able to lift themselves and their family out of extreme poverty of US$1 a day.[38]

Despite a decrease of 4.3 percentage points in the share of working poor at the US$1 a day level from 1997 to 2007, more than half of those employed still do not earn enough to lift themselves and their families out of poverty. 85.4 per cent of those employed in 2007 were still living on less than US$2. The situation remained critical despite the positive economic trend in the past few years; these numbers have continued to grow.[39]

In the 2010 Global Employment Trends, estimates of extreme working poverty range from stagnation at the 2008 level of 57.7 per cent of the employed, to an increase of 10.0 percentage points.[40] The general feeling in the year 2011 is that sub-Saharan Africa has rebounded from the global economic crisis, although the region has not yet fully returned to pre-crisis rates of economic growth. The region remains characterized by very high working poverty rates.

The global estimates and trends presented so far show that working poverty though a serious challenge is on the decrease on the global front. They however indicate and project a deteriorating state of employment and a growing rate of poverty among worker (working poverty) and total poverty in sub-Saharan Africa.

---

36 Cf. ILO, World Employment Report 2004–05 op. cit., p. 60. See also Steven Kapsos, Estimating growth requirements for reducing working poverty: Can the world halve working poverty by 2015? op. cit., p. 22.

37 ILO, World Employment Report 2004–05, op. cit., p. 64.

38 ILO, Global Employment Trends Brief, January 2007, op. cit., p. 3.

39 ILO, Global employment trends: January 2008, op. cit., p. 16.

40 ILO, Global employment trends: January 2010, op. cit., p. 24.

The general trends reveal a severe lack of decent employment opportunities in the developing world. This lack poses a constraint for further development as poor people cannot contribute to overall demand, nor can they invest in the education, well-being or health of their children to make sure that they can escape the poverty trap.[41] This issue remains of grave concern for human development and the alleviation of poverty.

The incidence of poverty is believed to be higher among the working poor. As earlier observed, the reality for most of the world's poor is that they must work – often for long hours, in poor working conditions and without basic rights and representation – at work that is not productive enough to enable them to lift themselves and their families out of poverty.[42] Indeed the majority of the working poor who are employed are in low-productivity, low-income and survivalist-oriented activities in the mainly informal smallholder or subsistence agricultural sector – a sector characterized by seasonal underemployment. Most of these smallholders do not earn enough to sustain a decent living.[43]

Most analyses recoded in various reports illustrate the strong relationship between working poverty, vulnerable employment and labour productivity. This has led to the conclusion that at least each person working, but earning less than US$1 per day per family member is either underemployed (working less than desired) or has a very low productivity job (working long hours, but not efficiently because of lack of education or equipment) and is, therefore, an underutilized worker. And having considered the condition of the unemployed, the discouraged and those who would work if given the opportunity to do so, it becomes clear that economic growth and social development could be much higher if everyone was given the chance of a decent job. This conclusion underscores the need for addressing the problem of working poverty in order to alleviate poverty in a sustainable way.[44]

1.4 Causes of Poverty

Just as poverty is multifaceted, so also are its causes. Many factors have indeed been identified as the causes of poverty, ranging from natural, social, religious, economic and political factors. In this section, factors that do not warrant socio-ethical judgement will not merit much attention. Some of them that fall within this category include ignorance of the mind, disease, natural catastrophe, dishonesty, birth control and population growth. Attention will be directed to the socio-economic and political factors that are considered to have much relevance to working poverty.

---

41 ILO, World Employment Report 2004–05, op. cit., p. 73

42 Ibid, p. 26.

43 ILO, Global Employment Trends 2004: Overview, (Geneva: International Labour Office, 2004), p. 21

44 ILO, Global employment trends: January 2008, op. cit., p. 39.

From a social ethical point of view, the causes of poverty could be reduced to the deficiencies and anomalies in institutions, systems and structures of the society. Poverty is indeed a direct consequence of social and economic processes that interact and frequently reinforce each other in a way that exacerbate the state of deprivation in which people live.[45] Thinking along this line, Muhammad Yunus writes:

> It is the institutions that we have built, and feel so proud of, which created poverty. It is the concept we developed to understand the reality around us, which contributed to the creation of poverty, made us see things wrongly, and took us down a wrong path, causing misery for people. It is our policies born out of our reasoning and theoretical frame work, with which we explain interactions among institution and people that caused this problem for many human beings. It is the failure at the top, rather than lack of capability at the bottom which is the root cause of poverty.[46]

We wish therefore to treat poverty as a structure problem that emanates mostly as a result of bad governance. Bad governance, in this sense, encompasses the anomalies in institutions, systems and structures of the society. In addition to the issue of governance at national level, we will examine how colonialism and governance of global economic integration in recent times have contributed to poverty especially in developing countries.

1.4.1 Bad National Governance

Governance here refers to the institutional environment that influences the way the affairs of the State, private business, and civil society are structured and administered. The nature and quality of these institutional and stakeholder interactions and the outcomes are the predominant governance issues that have direct consequences for the welfare of a nation and its citizens. Weak and bad governance has been identified as the prime cause of poverty. Unaccountable and unresponsive state institutions, absence of the rule of law, lack of protection against violence, extortion and intimidation, and lack of civility and predictability in interactions with public officials are huge failures in governance that prevent people, especially workers, from taking advantage of new economic opportunities or engaging in activities outside their immediate area of security. Constraints arising from threats of physical force or arbitrary bureaucratic power make it difficult for them to pursue their economic goal, to engage in public affairs, to make their interests known, and to have them taken into consideration.[47]

The absence of strong institutions governed by rule of law, and processes that enable stakeholders to negotiate productively among themselves and collectively

---

45 Cf. World Bank, World Development Report 2000/2001, op. cit.

46 Muhammad Yunus, Eliminating poverty through market- based social entrepreneurship, published by the Global Urban Development Magazine on the website: http://www.globalurban.org/Issue1PIMag05/Yunus%20article.htm, accessed on 22.06.2011.

47 See for example, World Bank, World Development Report 2000/2001, op. cit., pp. 35 & 36.

secure socially just outcomes is indeed an integral aspect of bad governance that often results in high rates of poverty. The persistence and pervasiveness of poverty in several countries have been linked to the lack of popular participation in governance and decision-marking as well as weak institutional base. This has led, among other things, to poor accountability, lack of transparency in resource allocation, weak programme implementation and monitoring.[48]

Bad governance is also an attribute of a weak State which often fails in its duty to deliver the essential services to its population and provide basic infrastructure needed to build a virile business environment. The inability of governments to provide adequate physical, natural, and financial assets makes people especially vulnerable to negative shocks. The inability of the State or community to develop mechanisms to reduce or mitigate the risks that poor people face is also identified as another underlying cause of vulnerability. Some of these mechanisms include public health interventions, trustworthy law enforcement agency and a fair legal system, public work schemes in times of stress, micro-credit to tide people through the aftermath of an adverse shock, social networks of support and insurance, famine relief in extreme circumstances.[49]

Deficiencies in the governance of the labour market are other major sources of poverty especially among workers. Poverty manifests itself when individuals are unable to generate sufficient wealth from their labour to maintain a minimum standard of living; a situation that also renders them vulnerable and excludes them from participating meaningfully in social life. The extent of poverty, therefore, can be viewed as an outcome of the functioning of labour market.[50]

Labour market deficiencies limit naturally job growth and absorption capacity in the formal economy and in this way it generates unemployment and underemployment. [51] The most abundant resource of the poor is their labour. Unemployment and underemployment contribute therefore in no small measure to people's inability to utilize their labour maximally and thus be able to earn enough income that can keep them out of poverty.[52] This occurs mostly as a result of low investment in human capital development. Investment in people can boost the living standards of households by expanding opportunities, raising productivity, attracting capital investment, and increasing earning power: Where this is lacking, the standard of living of households is usually drastically reduced due to limited opportunities, reduced capital investment and low earning power. It is indeed true that structural unemployment and underemployment are usually due to lack of skills and low educational qualification. People with low skills and poor educational qualification often are highly susceptible of job loses, and often end up

48 D. O. Ajakaiye and V. A. Adeyeye, Concept, Measurement and Causes of Poverty, op. cit.

49 See for example, World Bank, World Development Report 2000/2001: Attacking Poverty, op. cit., p. 37.

50 Cf., ILO, Key Indicators of the Labour Market: Poverty, working poverty and income distribution KILM 20.

51 D. O. Ajakaiye and V. A. Adeyeye, Concept, Measurement and Causes of Poverty, op. cit.

52 Cf. ibid.

in low income jobs As long as they are there, the possibility of rising above the poverty line remains quite remote.[53]

The problems encountered by people, especially those in the working age brackets, as a result of labour market deficiencies goes however beyond unemployment and underemployment. Labour market deficiencies also have some adverse effects on the general conditions of work. The majority of people in poverty must work in order to survive and support their families often in a context where no efficient social protection schemes or social safety nets exist. For these poor workers, the problem is not directly unemployment. The problem for them is rather typically one of poor employment *quality,* including low wages and productivity. [54]

Wrong policies are other major deficiencies in governance that produce negative labour market outcomes and generate poverty. Some of these policies include monetary policies that adversely affect cost and people's access to credit, fiscal policy which results in retrenchment, lay-offs and exchange rate policy which raises the domestic cost of production in an import dependent production system. Many economies of the world are often plunged into poverty often due to wrong policy response to macroeconomic disequilibrium recorded mostly in the balance of payments that occur usually as a result of expansive aggregate demand policies, terms-of-trade shocks, and natural disasters. Policy failures account for poverty largely because they constrain people of working age from using their greatest asset, "labour". As a result of policy failures, workers are often rendered vulnerable to job losses resulting from job-cut-backs in the public sectors or from the winding up of industries adversely affected by shifts in relative prices and from a host of other resultant effects.[55]

Wrong economic policies also contribute immensely to low economic growth performance. Low economic growth performance, especially over along period of time, is in turn a direct causal factor of poverty in any nation. No nation with such economic performance can escape poverty. Low growth hinders, for example, the employment generation and expansion of an export base desirable for creating wealth both for the citizens and for the entire nation. Conversely, through rising employment, increased labour productivity and higher real wages it generates, growth, especially when accompanied with equitable distributions, helps peoples and a nations to escape poverty.[56] The high incidence of poverty in the developing countries, mostly in Africa, has been consistently linked with the low economic growth attained in these regions over a long period of time.[57]

---

53 Ibid.

54 Cf. ILO, Key Indicators of the Labour Market: Poverty, working poverty and income distribution KILM 20

55 D. O. Ajakaiye and V. A. Adeyeye, Concept, Measurement and Causes of Poverty, op. cit.

56 Ibid.

57 See for example, World Bank, World Bank, World Development Report 2000/2001, op. cit.

1.4.2 Colonialism

Some development scholars have identified colonial history as an important contributive factor to the impoverishment of peoples in some parts of the world today. It is argued that in most countries with a history of colonization, the colonizers structured local economies mainly to facilitate the expropriation of resources for their (colonizers) own economic growth and development. A concise historical survey is therefore undertaken here to shows how colonial economic and political patterns formed the foundation of the poor economic development and the impoverishment of economies in Africa.

Highlights of the African economy in the pre-colonial era are useful for appreciating the harm that was done in the colonial era. The earliest economies in Africa were based on hunting fishing and gathering of food. They were predominantly characterised by movement. As livestock and crops became domesticated, population became sedentary. Specialization was then made possible as people began to produce surplus food and commodities for exchange in the market and so trade and commercial networks were developed. Economies in Africa were interdependent and based on long-distant trade long before contact with the Europeans in 1400s.[58] Trade was initially restricted mainly to food crops ivory, timber, gum, and wax. Other commodities such as slaves, mangrove tree poles, iron and gold were later introduced into the market.

In the 19th century, the British succeeded in gaining political dominance over the coast of eastern Africa. It was however soon clear that the colonialists did not come to assist African countries to develop economically. Their mission was for the benefit of European economies. The European traders who relied on intermediaries to reach the hinterland began to establish permanent trading posts called factories or shipboards.[59] As the plantations were developed in the "New World" of the 1600s, the demand for slaves rose, reaching its peak in the 1800s. The devastating social and economic effect of the slave trade on Africa, starting with the loss of productive human labour to the resultant redistribution of the population of the continent was recorded as follows:

> Many of those who were not captured died during raids or went into hiding to escape being caught. Agricultural production must have decreased, in part because of the difficulty of farming during the raids. In addition, the strongest young men and women were forced to leave their farms or disappeared on their own initiatives until danger subsided. Health was also affected as a result of new diseases such as cholera and smallpox, which were introduced by the movement of people through the continent. Susceptibility to disease also increased, resulting from the poor diets and reduced food

58 Basil Davidson, Africa: History of a Continent, (New York: Macmillan, 1972), p. 84.

59 Raph Austen, African Economic History: Internal Development and External Dependency, (London: James Currey, 1987), pp. 81-84

consumption that occurred with the disruption of agriculture. This surely lowered productivity for physical reasons as well as for psychological reasons.[60]

The expansion of the industrial revolution, which continued in the 19th century led to the eventual end of the illegal trade in slaves but also to an increase in the demand for the raw materials that were needed to sustain industries in Europe. Only as it became clear that the colonies would soon seek independence did European countries begin to guide some of their colonies toward the goal of developing their own economies. In doing so they began to establish a few domestic industries (usually fledging import-substitution industries for simple-to-produce goods such as matches, plastic shoes, beer and soft drinks and textiles) in addition to continuing production of primary commodities for export. These efforts were minimal, however, and did little to make African economies self-sufficient. By the 1960s, the colonial administrations were being dismantled rapidly across the continent – but many economic ties to the former colonial powers remained.[61]

The development plans the colonial powers drew up for their colonies at the eve of the official end of colonialism were naturally bound to fail. One of the reasons for this being that during the colonial era, physical infrastructure was minimally designed mainly to produce and export primary commodities to Europe and support the colonial administrations. The educational system was also designed to serve this purpose. Human resources were lacking in the areas of management and public administration, especially in the aspects of running a government or operating large-scale business or industry.

Although many countries at that time were still agrarian, agriculture was neglected in the development plans in favour of industrial development. The craze for industrialization impacted negatively on the economies and led to rural-urban migration. Job opportunities were however insufficient for the migrating population. This brought about the rapid spread of informality in the years following the independence. It is not surprising that despite the fact that many African Nations have gained political independence, economic independence has however remained illusive and evasive.

1.4.3 Deficiencies in Global Economic Governance

The cause of poverty in general and working poverty in particular can also be examined within the context of the processes of globalization that have taken place within the past few decades. Globalization refers to "an intensification and acceleration of cross-border interaction which actually or potentially links all individuals, institutions and states into a complex structure of mutual but frequently

60 Virginia DeLancy, The Economies of Africa. In: Understanding Contemporary Africa, ed. April A. Gordon and Donald L. Gordon, (London: Lynne Reinner Publishers, Inc. 2007), p. 111.

61 Ibid., p. 114.

imbalanced dependencies."[62] As a complex process with a wide range of aspects that penetrate virtually all areas of life and has become an everyday reality, globalization manifests "economic, ecological, socio-cultural and political characteristics which can be observed in their interactions."[63] Although globalization is multi-dimensional, "it is the economic dimension of globalization – the integration of domestic economies with the world economy and the inevitable consequential increase in the economic interdependence of the countries through trade and free factor movements and flow – that is perceived to constitute the heart of the globalization process."[64] For the purpose of consistency, attention will however be given here to the socio-economic and political dimensions.

It is a widely accepted view that the key characteristics of globalization have been the liberalization of international trade, the expansion of Foreign Direct Investment (FDI), and the emergence of massive cross-border financial flows which have brought about increased competition in global markets. It is also widely acknowledged that this has come about through the combined effect of two underlying factors: the policy decisions to reduce national barriers to international economic transactions and the impact of new technology, especially in the sphere of information and communications.[65] Another distinctive feature of the current process of globalization relates to changes in migration patterns. This globalization process largely limits the cross-border movements of people. "While goods, firms and money are largely free to criss-cross borders, people are not."[66]

As a complex phenomenon, Globalization has had far-reaching effects that are often viewed from two extreme positions. At one extreme are the mainstream economists represented by neoclassical economists who often emphasize only the benefits of the free flow of goods, capital ideas across the international boundaries and downplaying the social problems that arise from it. They perceive globalization as an irresistible and benign force for delivering economic prosperity to people throughout the world. At the other extreme are the hardcore opponents of globalization who often perceive it as a source of all contemporary social ills.[67] In all, from one extreme, globalization is considered to be unavoidably necessary for economic prosperity and from the other extreme it is viewed as the trigger of global poverty and insecurity.

---

62 German Bishops' Conference, The many faces of globalization: Perspectives for a humane world order, Study of the Groups of Experts "World Economic and Social Ethics" and the church agencies Adveniat, Caritas International, Misereor, Mission Aachen, Missio München and Renovabis, (Bonn: Deutche Kommision Justitia et Pax, 2000), p. 12.

63 Ibid

64 United Nations Development Programme, Nigeria Human Development Report 2000/2001 Millennium Edition, (Lagos: UNDP, 2001), p. 2.

65 World Commission on the Social Dimension of Globalization, A Fair Globalization: Creating Opportunities for All, (Geneva: Internaational Labour Office, 2004), § 132.

66 Ibid, § 134.

67 Cf. ibid., § 131.

Indeed, "the impact of globalization can be both negative and positive and differs by context, by industry and trade, and by employment status."[68] There is enough evidence that globalization has set in motion a process of a far-reaching positive change that has impacted on the lives of many people. It is believed to have created a world that is more interconnected than ever before. This growing interdependence is supposedly noticeable not only in economic relations – trade, investment, finance and the organization of production globally – but also in social and political interactions among organizations and individuals across the world. It is further believed that the growing interconnectivity is nurturing the conviction among people across the world that they are all part of a global community. It is also argued that the global market economy has the potency of producing great productive capacity, which, if properly managed, can deliver unprecedented material progress, generate more productive and better jobs for all, and contribute significantly to reducing world poverty. These are however yet to materialize globally.[69]

The major negative side of globalization is perhaps that it has led to the rise of poverty in many parts of the Globe. The current impoverishment of people in the Third World countries, especially in Sub-Saharan Africa is particularly linked to the globalization process that has been witnessed in the last couple of decades. How globalization has generated poverty in these countries is clearly seen mostly in the imbalances created within the process. Unbalanced patterns in investment, trade, and labour markets are indeed prime sources of today's socio-economic turbulence.[70] Wealth is no doubt created, but too many countries and people are not sharing in its benefits. These people and countries have little or no voice in shaping the process. Globalization has not met their simple and legitimate aspirations for decent jobs and a better future for their children. Many of them live in the limbo of the informal economy without formal rights and in a swathe of poor countries that subsist precariously on the margins of the global economy.[71]

Among those who are working, the very few people who have benefited most from globalization are mainly those associated (as shareholders, managers, workers or sub-contractors) with successful multi-national enterprises (MNEs) and with internationally competitive national enterprises. More generally, only those endowed with capital and other assets, entrepreneurial ability and education and skills that are in increasing demand have benefited. Other groups of workers have

---

68 Marilyn Carr and Martha Alter Chen, Globalization and the Informal Economy: How Global Trade and Investment Impact on the Working Poor, (WIEGO, 2001) p. 1. Available online at: http://www.wiego.org/papers/carrchenglobalization.pdf.

69 Cf. World Commission on the Social Dimension of Globalization, A Fair Globalization: Creating Opportunities for All, op. cit., p. x.

70 World Commission on the Social Dimension of Globalization, A Fair Globalization: The Role of the ILO, Report of the Director-General to the World Commission on the Social Dimension of Globalization (Geneva: ILO, 2004), p. 5.

71 World Commission on the Social Dimension of Globalization, A Fair Globalization: Creating Opportunities for All, op. cit., p. x.

however been adversely affected by trade liberalization and the relocation of production to lower-wage economies – primarily those without assets, the illiterate and unskilled workers and indigenous peoples.[72]

It is argued, for instance, that the increased mobility of capital associated with globalization gives employers more bargaining power over the workers, or rather, favours capital more than it favours labour. And as economies adjust to greater openness, labour markets are producing simultaneously higher rates of job creation, dislocation and destruction. These labour-related developments have of course so many negative impacts on workers.[73]

At the same time, increasing international competition for markets and for foreign direct investment (FDI) has generated pressures to increase labour market flexibility and erode labour protection. Hence, in spite of the benefits of FDI and the fact that workers in foreign firms often earn more than those in local firms, there have been growing concerns over the inadequate quality of the employment that has been generated in developing parts (economies) of the global production system. This is particularly true of employment in firms acting as sub-contractors to MNEs in labour-intensive industries such as garments and footwear.[74]

The indigenous peoples in the developing nations are usually rendered vulnerable and have suffered severely because their integration into the global economy often occurs without their free and prior informed consent and without adequate protection of their rights, livelihoods, and culture. In cases like this, investments in extractive industries, mega-hydroelectric dams, and plantations have led to massive dislocations, disruption of livelihoods, ecological degradation, and violation of their basic human rights. Particularly affected are those associated with uncompetitive enterprises, mainly the small and medium-sized enterprises that had a limited capacity to adjust to a rapid liberalization of the global economy. Impoverished producers of importables, whether in the urban informal economy or in agriculture, have been particularly vulnerable to the influx of cheap imports and sharp changes in the relative prices and availability of inputs. Such producers are also unable to seize the new economic opportunities that have been generated because they lack capital and access to credit, information and extension services.[75]

The social problems that emanated in the process of globalization and are responsible for the impoverishment of nations and peoples are however not due to globalization *per se* but rather due to deficiencies in its "governance"[76] both at the

72 Ibid., §§ 208 & 209.

73 Ibid., § 251.

74 Ibid., § 210.

75 Ibid., § 211.

76 Governance as related to globalization is the system of rules and institutions established by the international community and private actors to manage political, economic and social affairs. A litmus test of (good) governance, at both the national and global level consists in how far it (governance) has been able to further values such as freedom, security, diversity, fairness and solidarity. It also consists in how it has been able to ensure respect for human rights, international rule of law, democracy and participation, promote entrepreneurship and adhere to the principles of accountability, efficacy and subsidiarity. Cf.

national and international levels.[77] The observation made by the ILO Director-General highlights the basic deficiency in the governance of global economy: "The absence of an appropriate framework for the governance of markets in general, and labour markets in particular, creates an environment of insecurity which prevents the accumulation of physical, financial, human and social capital."[78] To this end, low economic growth in most poor nations and the impoverishment of workers can rightly be attributed to ineffective, inappropriate and misguided legal and institutional frameworks and improper and ineffective implementation of policies and laws. The attainment of economic growths that are pro-poor is obviously hindered by the absence of commercial policies that stimulate business expansion, an efficient, accountable public administration free from corruption and a strong educational system. All of these have to do with governance.

A host of interlocking problems that hinder economic development and full integration of most developing countries into the global economy are traceable to poor governance at the national level. These countries are reputed for their lack of the basis for good governance, which is a well-functioning democratic political system that ensures representative and honest governments responsive to the needs of people. They also lack the formal institutions required for the efficient and equitable functioning of a market economy. But what they lack most, in concrete terms, is a sound financial system that mobilizes savings and promotes investment, the regulation of markets to prevent abuse and anti-competitive behaviour, mechanisms for ensuring transparent and socially responsible corporate governance, an effective system for delineating property rights and for the enforcement of contracts, labour market institutions, including appropriate legal frameworks, freedom of association, and institutions for dialogue and bargaining required to protect the fundamental rights of workers, provide social protection and promote sound industrial relations. The absence of such institutions has continually hindered the attainment of stability and sustainable economic growth. And without them many developing countries will remain highly disadvantaged in access to global markets. The overall result in most of these nations has been low gross national product (GNP) and alarming growth in unemployment, inequality and poverty.[79]

Furthermore, in their quest for success in the global economy, most developing countries have adopted economic policies that have often involved far-reaching liberalization of trade, investment and finance. These policy options, which are

---

World Commission on the Social Dimension of Globalization, A Fair Globalization: Creating Opportunities for All, (Geneva: ILO, 2004), § 335.

77 World Commission on the Social Dimension of Globalization, A Fair Globalization: Creating Opportunities for All, opt. cit., p. xi.

78 ILO, Working out of Poverty, Report of the Director-General, (Geneva: International Labour Office, 2003), p. 72.

79 World Commission on the Social Dimension of Globalization, A Fair Globalization: Creating Opportunities for All, op. cit., § 242.

usually associated with collateral liberalization of the domestic economy involving privatization, a reduction in the role of the State in economic management and regulation, and a general expansion in the role of the market, failed in many of the countries due to lack of due consideration for the pre-existing policy and institutional environment, and the state of the economy and of the external economic environment at the time the policies are applied.[80] Indeed policies adapted for facilitating integration into the markets were sometimes applied in ways that undermined the important role of the State in managing the process of integration into the global economy, and in ensuring that it meets both economic and social objectives. This role includes the provision of classical public goods which have positive externalities such as health, education, and law and order; the supervision of markets and the correction of market deficiencies and failures; the correction of negative externalities such as environmental degradation; the provision of social protection and safeguarding the vulnerable; and investment in areas of public interest where private investment is not forthcoming. Another important role of the State lies in limiting the impact of globalization on income inequality, through progressive taxation, wage policies, social programmes and other mechanisms.[81]

Non-accountability, non-transparency and other corrupt practices, especially among public servants and public administrations,[82] are other major aspects of poor governance at the national level that create an unfavourable environment for doing business and hinder many developing countries from full integration into the global economy and the attainment of the economic growth capable of leading a country and its people out of poverty.[83]

At the global level, the current structure and processes of governance manifest vast inequality in the power and capacity of different nation States. This inequality reflects itself primarily in the economic power of different nations. The industrialized countries with far higher per capita incomes, which translate into economic clout in negotiations to shape global governance, have become the source of much-needed markets, foreign investments, financial capital and technology. This underlying inequality in economic power translates into bargaining strength in negotiations that poor countries are often unable to resist.[84]

The problems posed by these structural inequalities are reflected further in the democratic deficit in global governance. The reality on the ground actually reveals that Global governance is not fully based on democratic and participatory decision-making processes that lead to fair outcomes. The governance structure of the post-

80 Ibid,, §§ 246 & 247.

81 Ibid., § 249.

82 This is not to say that corruption is restricted and practice only within the domain of public service and administration. However, it can be argued that the enormous abuses and corruption recorded in the private sectors were possible because of poorly functioning systems and deficiencies in public administration, in other words, due to poor governance.

83 World Commission on the Social Dimension of Globalization, A Fair Globalization: Creating Opportunities for All, op. cit., § 224.

84 Ibid., § 340.

war world, centred on the United Nations and the Bretton Woods institutions continue to be defined by the victorious powers, despite significant developments that have taken place in the global scenario and remarkable achievement made by other nations since after the end of war.[85] These inequalities are further compounded by the many important decisions on global governance which are taken outside the multilateral system. Limited membership groups of rich nations such as the Group of 7 (G7), the Organization for Economic Cooperation and Development (OECD), the Basle Committee, and the Group of 10 (G10) within the IMF continually take important decisions on economic and financial issues with a global impact.[86]

The creation of a system of rules governing the global economy that has been prejudicial to the interests of most developing countries, especially the poor within the comity of nations, is a major flaw in global governance that has contributed to the uneven social and economic impact of globalization responsible for low growth and poverty in many parts of the world.[87] There has been a clear lack of fair rules for trade, capital, technology flows and for dealing with unstable commodity prices, and greater access to markets needed to provide more policy space for developing countries, especially the least developed. There is also lack of fair rules for basic social protection, respect for core labour standards, adequate adjustment assistance for workers and a true global commitment to employment creation as the best way of eradicating poverty. [88]

The evolving system of multilateral agreements and rules manifests a bias in agenda setting towards measures to expand markets. Contrary to this, measures to achieve a more balanced strategy for global growth and full employment have received only but inadequate attention. In addition to this, there is a far less emphasis on policies to help developing countries to cope with the strains of adjustment and to strengthen their capacity to thrive in a competitive global economy. Less attention is paid to the development of their technological capacities in an increasingly knowledge-based global economy. The goal of full employment and achieving decent work for all also receives low priority in current international policies.[89]

The failure to check the indiscriminate use of agricultural protectionism to boost some industrialized economies to the detriment of some other weaker economies in the Third World is another major weakness in global governance. Agricultural protectionism does not only upset the aim of globalization, it is also a major obstacle to the reduction of poverty. It is on record, that agricultural

85 Ibid., § 341.

86 Ibid., § 348.

87 Ibid., § 353.

88 World Commission on the Social Dimension of Globalization, A Fair Globalization: The Role of the ILO, op. cit., p. 5.

89 World Commission on the Social Dimension of Globalization, A Fair Globalization: Creating Opportunities for All, op. cit., § 354-356

subsidies in the industrialized countries are now estimated to amount to over US$ 1 billion per day, while 70 per cent of the world's poor live in rural areas and subsist on less than US$1 a day.[90] Related to this problem of agricultural protectionism is that of the falling prices for non-oil commodities. Many developing countries still depend on non-oil commodities, especially agricultural commodities, for more than half of their export earnings. Yet world prices of these major export commodities continue to fall in real terms. This fall is particularly significant in the case of cotton, coffee, rice, tin, cocoa and sugar.[91]

There are also a host of wrong policies in global economic administration that hinder growth and increase the incidence of poverty in developing nations. A good example concerns the policies associated with economic liberalization. It is often argued that trade liberalization policies being pursued under the World Trade Organization and other allied international organizations have contributed to the enlargement of the informalization of labour and production in recent times. Trade liberalization increases competition for formal firms. To remain competitive, these formal firms try to reduce costs by cutting worker benefits, replacing permanent workers with part-time labour and subcontracting parts of production to the informal enterprises, including home-based workers. Some formal firms may even be forced to lay off workers, who would subsequently seek employment in the informal economy where they are often confronted with hard labour conditions.[92]

Most serious issue is the pace and sequencing of the liberalization process. At a time in the past, a "big bang" approach to liberalization was advocated and widely applied. This involved liberalization across the board, carried out simultaneously. Today, after much harm has been done to many developing economies, it is generally acknowledged that this was a grievous mistake. It is now a well known fact that the supporting institutions and regulatory frameworks required for a market economy need to be developed gradually, and require strong public administrative capacity.[93]

Another major critique against policy measures for liberalization is that sometimes trade policies are formulated in a way that enthrones liberalization as an end in itself, whereas liberalization is only but a means for achieving ultimate objectives such as high and sustainable growth, full employment and the reduction of poverty. As such, trade policies should be framed with these ends in mind and be evaluated accordingly. The "absolutization" of liberalization has of course had

90 Ibid., § 374.

91 IMF: International Financial Statistics Yearbook, various issues, cited in Oxfam, Rigged Rules Double Standards, (Oxford: Oxfam International, 2002), p. 44.

92 United Nations Economic and Social Council, Role of the Informal Sector in Poverty Reduction, E/ESCAP/CPR(3)/1 2 October 2006, § 20

93 World Commission on the Social Dimension of Globalization, A Fair Globalization: Creating Opportunities for All, op. cit., § 248.

grave consequences for inclusive integration and equitable distribution of the benefits of globalization.[94]

Apart from inequality, lack of fair rules and wrong policies mentioned here, lack of competent institutions is another teething problem in the current governance of global integration. Not only that global markets lack appropriate institutions for public supervision which, in many countries, provide national markets with legitimacy and stability, the mechanisms for ensuring coherence in global governance as a whole are either weak or non-existent. This reflects itself more in global decision-making. Negotiations on global issues often take place in disjointed and parallel sectors such as trade, finance, health, social affairs and development assistance. In pursuing global goals, each individual international organization so concentrates on its specific mandates that it loses sight of the fact that actions taken in one field affect outcomes elsewhere.[95]

The absence of global mechanisms and policies for ensuring socio-economic security is another noticeable deficiency. One of the major roles that are meant to be performed by the multilateral agencies, voluntary organizations and bilateral development cooperation programmes is to galvanize and mobilize funds which should be channelled towards reducing poverty, providing social security and meeting the needs of vulnerable people. This role has unfortunately not been fulfilled at the global level due to non availability of funds. The role, as it were, is now expected to be fulfilled at the national level by each individual State. While in rich countries, a significant proportion of national revenue is allocated to fulfilling these social needs, most developing countries must linger at the edge of social collapse since it is no more within their capacity to finance the socio-economic security needs of their citizens.[96]

1.5 Conclusion

By way of concluding this chapter, let us articulate the salient points. The chapter examined the concept of poverty in general and working poverty in particular. Poverty, it was discovered, is fundamentally a violation of human dignity. It is a denial of choices and opportunities – not having the land on which to grow one's food or a job to earn one's living, not having access to credit. It means also susceptibility, insecurity, powerlessness and lack of basic capacity to participate effectively in the society. In its absolute form, it means not having access to the basic necessities of life – not having enough to feed and cloth a family, not having a school or clinic to go to (cf. 1.1.1 – 1.1.2).

The measurement of poverty is required in order to ascertain who is poor, how many people are poor, and where the poor are located. It is also necessary in order

94 Ibid., § 370.

95 Ibid., § 352.

96 Ibid., § 357.

to keep the poor on the agenda, monitor and evaluate projects and policy interventions that are geared towards the poor and evaluate the effectiveness of institutions whose goal is to help the poor.[97] Because the understanding of poverty goes beyond monetary calculations, its measure goes beyond income to include other indicators of human development such as opportunity and empowerment (cf. 1.2).

The concept of working poverty was closely examined since the reality for most poor people is that they must work often in bad conditions and at work that is not productive enough to enable them to lift themselves and their families out of poverty. The working poor are therefore working people living in poverty; individuals engaged in either paid or self employment. They are involved in works that not only provide an insufficient level of income but also lack social security, good working conditions, voice and representation and other basic rights at work.

Available evidence reveals that working poverty is indeed a serious social challenge, especially in the developing nations and particularly in Sub-Saharan Africa, where a deteriorating state of employment and a severe lack of decent employment opportunities have been generating high incidence of poverty among workers (cf. 1.3).

In examining the cause of poverty, we attempted to answer the question: Why are people, especially the working people, poor? Poverty, it was discovered, is a direct consequence of social and economic processes that interact and frequently reinforce each other in a way that exacerbate the state of deprivation in which people live.

At the very heart of the problem is the issue of governance or rather bad governance that generates unjust structures. Bad governance encompasses the anomalies in institutions, systems and structures of the society that produce those social and economic processes that interact and reinforce each other in a way that exacerbate the state of deprivation in which people live. Some major aspects of bad governance identified include, the absence of strong institutions governed by rule of law, lack of physical structures and essential services, labour market deficiencies and bad economic policies. These failures in governance prevent people, especially workers, from taking advantage of new economic opportunities or engaging in activities outside their immediate area of security. They particularly produce unfavourable business atmosphere, generate unemployment, underemployment and precarious work conditions. But above all, they prevent the poor from using the most valuable if not the only resources they have – their labour – to earn enough income that can keep them out of poverty (cf. 1.4.1).

How colonialism contributed to the impoverishment of nations and peoples, particularly in African, manifested itself in the way the colonialists governed the nations they colonized and in the way economic activities were organize in the colonial era. The colonial masters had no interest in the development of the local

97 Aline Coudouel et al., Poverty Measurement and Analysis, Poverty Reduction Strategy Paper, op. cit.

people. Local economies were structured and organized mainly to facilitate the expropriation of resources for their own economic growth and development (1.4.2).

Having examined the cause of poverty within the context of the processes of globalization that have taken place within the past few decades, it was particularly discovered that globalization has led to poverty in developing countries mainly due to poor governance of the processes of global integration. While on the one hand, unstable national political systems and poor governance continue to hindered internal economic and human development and full integration into the global market, global governance, on the other hand, marred by unfair rules and policies, fails to deliver equal participation and equitable distribution of the gains accruing from the integration of global economy. Within this global socio-economic order, increased competition and unbridled quest for profit thrive unhindered and steadily give rise to the deregulation of labour through Off-shoring, outsourcing and downsizing. The bitter consequence of all this has been the high rates of unemployment, the informalization of labour and production and high incidence of poverty among low and unskilled workers, especially in Sub-Saharan African countries (1.4.3).

CHAPTER TWO
Informal Economy in General

Introduction

In this chapter attention is turned to the informal economy. The decision to examine the phenomenon of informality is predicated on the belief that there is a very high likelihood that people who constitute the working poor work mostly in the informal economy.[98] This is also with a view to understanding better the condition in which the poor live and work. This whole endeavour, it is believed, will further provide more answers to the question: Why are people poor even though they are working? Understanding the condition in which the poor work and the factors that shape and reshape these condition is undoubtedly necessary for knowing what policy actions to recommend for a more effective and sustainable poverty alleviation strategy

2.1 Conceptual Framework

Informality is a complex phenomenon that cannot be covered with one simple definition. It does not belong to a single unit of study. It is a dynamic process which includes many types of economic and social activities. It is indeed by its very nature difficult to study, define and measure. For this reason, there abound so many terminologies describing the same phenomenon, such as: "traditional", "informal", "underground", "second", "cash", "parallel" black sector/economy etc.

Further confounding any attempts to define this category of economic activities is the fact that most of the activities are temporal in nature. Mogensen is therefore right when he observed that informality is a phenomenon that "develops all the time according to the "principles of running waters": it adjusts to changes in taxes, to sanctions from the tax authorities and to general moral attitudes, etc."[99]

Different scholars and researchers at different time have defined it in different ways, each highlighting a particular aspect of the phenomenon. Accordingly, the definitions vary depending on the angle from which each author wants to look at the phenomenon. These definitions are too numerous to be covered in this work. One commonly used working definition refers to it as "all currently unregistered economic activities which contribute to the officially calculated (or observed)

98 ILO, World Employment Report 2004–05: Employment, Productivity, and Poverty Reduction, (Geneva: ILO, 2005), p. 26.

99 Gunnar V. Mogensen, et al., The informal economy in Denmark: Measurement and results, Study no. 3, Copenhagen: The Rockwool Foundation Research Unit, 1995.

National Product."[100] Another definition describes it as "market-based production of goods and services, whether legal or illegal that escape detection in the official estimates of Gross Domestic Product."[101]

2.1.1 Initial Concept: Informal Sector

The term or rather the concept of the "informal sector" was first popularized by the ILO in the early 1970s when it was used to refer mainly to survival activities of those working in the marginal or peripheral segments of the economy. In its Kenya Mission Report in 1972, the ILO defined informality as a "way of doing things characterized by (a) ease of entry; (b) reliance on indigenous resources; (c) family ownership; (d) small scale operations; (e) labour intensive and adaptive technology; (e) skills acquired outside of the formal sector; (g) unregulated and competitive markets".[102]

At the 1991 International Labour Conference (ILC), the "informal sector" featured as a major topic for tripartite debate. In the 1991 Report of the ILO Director-General to the International Labour Conference, it was defined as:

> very small-scale units producing and distributing goods and services, and consisting largely of independent, self-employed producers in urban areas of developing countries, some of whom also employ family labour and/or a few hired workers or apprentices; which operate with very little capital, or none at all; which utilize a low level of technology and skills; which therefore operate at a low level of productivity; and which generally provide very low and irregular incomes and highly unstable employment to those who work in it.[103]

In 1992, the ILO Bureau of Statistics prepared a report on "Statistics on Employment in the Informal Sector." These statistics formed the basis for discussion at the International Conference of Labour Statisticians (ICLS) the following year. Consequently, in 1993, the 15th ICLS adopted an *international statistical definition* of the "informal sector". The informal sector was defined in terms of characteristics of the enterprises (production units) in which the activities take place, rather than in terms of the characteristics of the persons involved or of their jobs. Hence informal sector "encompasses the total of all informal enterprises

---

100 Cf. Edgar L. Feige, The Underground Economy and the Currency Enigma, in G. Fiorentini and S. Zamagni (eds), The Economics of Corruption and Illegal Markets, The International Library of Critical Writings in Economics, (Cheltenham, UK: Edward Elgar Publishing Limited, 1999).

101 J.D. Smith, Market motives in the informal economy, in: Gaertner, W. and Wenig, A. (eds.): The economics of the informal economy, (Heidelberg: Springer Publishing Company, 1985), pp. 161-177: For more definitions covering different aspects, see: Esther K. Ishengoma and Robert Kappel, Economic Growth and Poverty: Does Formalisation of Informal Enterprises Matter? (Hamburg, Germany: GIGA German Institute of Global and Area Studies, 2006).

102 Cf. ILO, Employment, Incomes and Equality: A Strategy for Increasing Productive Employment in Kenya, (Geneva: International Labour Office, 1972).

103 ILO, The dilemma of the informal sector, Report of the Director-General (Part 1), (Geneva: International Labour Office, 1991), p. 4.

… and is distinct from the employment relationship dimension."[104] This definition was subsequently imbedded in the revised International System of National Accounts (SNA) in 1993. It was to serve statistical purpose, by providing a guide to experts in compiling their national statistical data on informal sector in order to be consistent with the framework of the System of National Accounting and provide for a separate accounting of Gross Domestic Production (GDP) in the informal sector.[105]

With regard to the production units in question, the term "*enterprise*" was used in a broad sense. "It covers not only production units which employ hired labour, but also those that are owned and operated by individuals working on their own account as self-employed persons, either alone or with the help of unpaid family members. The activities may be undertaken inside or outside the enterprise owner's home, and they may be carried out in identifiable premises or without fixed location. Accordingly, self-employed street vendors, taxi drivers, home-based workers, etc., are all considered as enterprises."[106]

For statistical purposes, a *sector* "groups together similar kinds of enterprises which, in terms of their economic objectives, functions and behaviour, have certain characteristics in common".[107] It groups together similar kinds of production units, which in terms of economic objectives, functions and behaviour have certain characteristics in common. Ralf Hussmanns observes that the result of this however is not necessarily a homogeneous set of production units. For this reason, it may be necessary to divide a sector into more homogeneous sub-sectors for the purposes of analysis and policy-making.[108]

The 15th ICLS (1993) defined *informal sector enterprises* (*informal enterprises*) as "private unincorporated enterprises whose size in terms of employment is below a certain threshold to be determined according to national conditions (usually five to ten workers), and/or which are not registered under specific forms of national legislation, such as factories or commercial acts, tax or social security laws, professional groups regulatory acts, or similar acts, laws or regulations established by national legislative bodies (as distinct from local regulations governing trade licences or business permits)." [109]

Consistent with the enterprise approach, *employment in the informal sector* comprises all persons who, during a given reference period, were employed in at

104 ILO, Decent work and the informal economy, Report VI, International Labour Conference, 90th Session, Geneva, 2002, (Geneva: International Labour Office, 2002), p. 126.

105 Ralf Hussmanns, Informal Sector and Informal Employment: Elements of a Conceptual Framework, a paper presented at the Fifth Meeting of the Expert Group on Informal Sector Statistics, Delhi, September 2001.

106 Ralf Hussmanns, Statistical definition of informal employment, guideline endorsed by the Seventh International Conference of Labour Statisticians, 2003, p. 4.

107 ILO, Decent work and the informal economy, Report VI, International Labour Conference, 90th Session, Geneva, 2002, (Geneva: International Labour Office, 2002), p. 125.

108 Ralf Hussmanns, Statistical definition of informal employment: op. cit., p. 4.

109 ILO, Decent work and the informal economy, op.cit., p. 125.

least one informal enterprise, irrespective of their status in employment and whether it was their main or a secondary job[110]

The 15th ICLS fine-tuned its definition of the informal sector by adopting a number of recommendations regarding the scope of informal sector surveys and the statistical treatment of particular situations at the borderline between the informal and other sectors. These recommendations include:

1) The exclusion from the informal sector of units which are exclusively engaged in the production of goods or services for own final consumption or own fixed capital formation (e.g. construction of own houses) of households;
2) The exclusion of agricultural activities from the scope of the informal sector, for practical reasons;
3) The inclusion or exclusion of enterprises engaged in the production of professional or technical services rendered by self-employed persons (doctors, lawyers, accountants, architects, engineers, etc.) on the same basis as other enterprises; and
4) The option to include/exclude paid domestic workers engaged by households in/from the informal sector, depending upon national circumstances and the intended uses of the statistics[111]

The Conference of Labour Statisticians recognised however that an enterprise-based definition would not capture all dimensions of informal employment, nor is it sufficient to cover all informal economic activities which after all cannot be

---

110 ILO, Resolution concerning statistics of employment in the informal sector, adopted by the Fifteenth International Conference of Labour Statisticians, January 1993.

111 Ralf Hussmanns and Farhad Mehran, Statistical definition of the informal sector: International standards and national practices, a pdf document available at: http://www.gdrc.org/informal/huss0772.pdf: The 15th ICLS did not totally prohibit the inclusion of private unincorporated enterprise engaged in agricultural and related activities, if they met the criteria of the informal sector definition. It however recommends the exclusion of agricultural and related activities from the scope of informal survey, suggesting that measuring them separately would be good for practical data collection. We subscribe in this work to the argument that the activities of persons engaged in the own-account production of good for own final use by their household should not be considered as informal work because they do not produce goods for batter or trade, e.g. backing of bread for house consumption. This however is not applicable to those engaged in subsistent agriculture, as this would mean treating the millions of subsistent farmers in developing nations as non-workers. One cannot deny the fact that the activities of these farmers also have some economic implications although they do not, as it were, produce mainly for trade or batter. Those involved in subsistent agriculture must be treated as informal workers, for it is through these activities that they earn their living. They do not have any other source of income. Their activities are quite different from the activities of those who from time to time or as a hobby bake bread for family consumption or those who plant tomatoes in their garden for family consumption. These of course cannot be referred to as informal workers.

reduced to a sector. The Conference therefore observed that further work was needed on the employment-based dimension of informality.[112]

2.1.2 New Concept and Expanded Definition

In recent years, activists and researchers have worked with the international organizations, especially the ILO, to broaden the concept and definition of informality. The intention was to incorporate the whole of informality, as it is manifested in industrialised, transition and developing economies and the real world dynamics in labour markets today, particularly the employment arrangements of the working poor.[113] This has also led to the rethinking of the nomenclature 'informal sector' and the search for a term that would better capture the broadened concept of informality.

At its 90th Session (June, 2002), the International Labour Conference (ILC) adopted a resolution containing Conclusions concerning Decent Work and the Informal Economy. This marked a new dimension in addressing the topic – a topic which has generated much controversy over the past 30 years. Emphasis was therefore shifted from enterprises that are not legally regulated to employment relationships that are not legally regulated or protected. Consequently, the term "informal sector" was declared to be "an inadequate, if not misleading term to reflect these dynamic, heterogeneous and complex aspects of a phenomenon which is not, in fact, a "sector" in the sense of a specific industry group or economic activity".[114] The term "informal economy" was then introduced to encompass the expanding and increasingly diverse group of workers and enterprises in both rural and urban areas operating informally.[115] The preference for the term "informal economy" against "informal sector" was supported with the argument that the workers and enterprises in question do not fall within any one sector of economic activity, but cut across many sectors.[116]

Following its formal adoption, the term "informal economy" was defined as "all economic activities by workers and economic units that are – in law or in practice – not covered by formal arrangements. Their activities are not included in the law, which means that they are operating outside the formal reach of the law; or they are not covered in practice, which means that- although they are operating within the formal reach of the law, the law is not applied or not enforced; or the law discouraged compliance because it is inappropriate, burdensome, or imposes

112 Cf. Ralf Hussmanns, Informal Sector and Informal Employment: Elements of a Conceptual Framework, op cit..

113 Martha Alter Chen et al, Mainstreaming Informal Employment and Gender in Poverty Reduction: A handbook for Policy-makers and Other Stakeholders, (London: Commonwealth Secretariat, 2004), p. 21.

114 ILO, Decent work and the informal economy, op. cit., p. 2.

115 Ibid.

116 ILO, Resolution concerning decent work and the informal economy ILC90-PR25-292-En.Doc. para. 3.

excessive costs."[117] Clearly, this expanded definition focuses on the nature of employment, in addition to the characteristics of enterprises, and includes all types of informal employment both inside and outside informal enterprises.

In a review of the 2002 ILC conclusions, Lin Lim points out that another outstanding feature of the new conceptual framework is that it depicts a continuum of production and employment relations.[118] In this way, it discards the idea that there are distinct formal and informal "sectors" without direct links and insists that there are "linkages, grey areas and interdependencies between formal and informal activities."[119] The new conceptual framework therefore views formal and informal enterprises and workers as co-existing along a *continuum*, with decent work deficits most serious at the bottom, unprotected, unregulated, survivalist end, but also existing in some formal jobs as well, and with increasingly decent conditions moving up towards the formal protected end.[120] Highlighting these dynamic linkages between formal and informal activities is essential for policy concerns that aim at enhancing positive linkages between the formal economy and the informal economy and for ensuring that there is decent work all along the continuum. With the observations made here, the issue should no longer be whether informal workers or informal units have direct ties with the informal economy – clearly they do – but whether those ties are benign, exploitative or mutually beneficial.[121]

Following the endorsement of the new conceptual framework by the ILC in 2002, it was also adopted in 2003 by international statisticians at the 17th

---

117 Ibid.: Note that the emphasis here with reference to the coverage by the law is on formal law, i.e., the formal law is not fully applied to them. This does not mean that there are no rules or norms regulating the activities of workers or enterprises. People engaged in informal activities have their own "political economy" – their own informal or group rules, arrangements, institutions and structures for mutual help and trust, providing loans, organizing training, transferring technology and skills, trading and market access, enforcing obligations, etc. What is not clear is what these informal rules or norms are based on and whether or how they observe the fundamental rights of workers.

118 Lin Lim, Highlights of the ILC conclusions, presentation to the Turin Workshop on the Follow-up to the ILC Conclusions on Decent Work and the Informal Economy, ILO International Training Centre, Turin, 10-12 February, 2003.

119 ILO, Resolution concerning decent work and the informal economy, para. 3.

120 This settles the wave of thinking described as "dualist". It subscribes to the notion that the informal sector is comprised of marginal activities – distinct from and not related to the formal sector – that provide income for the poor and a safety net in times of crisis. According to this school of thought, informal activities have persisted over the years largely due to a slow rate of economic growth and/or a faster rate of population growth that has hindered the creation of enough modern job opportunities that would absorb surplus labour. Some economist in this school of thought had argued that the informal economy in developing countries would disappear once these countries achieved sufficient levels of economic growth and modern industrial development. The informal economy has however continued to growth even in some countries that have recorded considerable economic growth recorded in many countries. For more on the different view on the informal economy, see: Kristina Flodman Becker, The Informal Economy: Fact Finding Study, (Stockholm, Sweden: Swedish International Development Agency, 2004), pp. 3, 52.

121 ILO, Decent work and the informal economy, op. cit., p. 38.

International Conference of Labour Statisticians (ICLS). Based on this new expanded concept, the ICLS on its part defined "informal employment" as follows.

> The total number of informal jobs, whether carried out in formal or informal enterprises, or the total number of persons engaged in informal jobs during a given reference period. It comprises the activities of own-account workers and employers in informal enterprises; the activities of all contributing family workers (whether working in formal or informal enterprises); the employment of all employees in informal jobs in formal enterprises, informal enterprises or households; members of informal producers' cooperatives; and the activities of persons engaged in the own-account production of goods for own final use by their households.[122]

The 17th ICLS acknowledged, however, that "the relevance and meaning of informal employment varied among countries, and that therefore a decision to develop statistics on it would depend on national circumstances and priorities."[123]

This conceptual framework endorsed by the 17th ICLS relates the enterprise-based concept of employment in the informal sector in a coherent and consistent manner with a broader, job-based concept of informal employment. 'Employment in the informal sector' and 'informal employment' are therefore two concepts that should not be confused. Both of them are measures that are useful for analytical and policy- making purposes, and they refer to different aspects of the 'informalisation' of employment and to different targets for policy making. They should not be used interchangeably. In their application, however, the two concepts need to be defined and measured in such a way that they are consistent and that one can be clearly distinguished from the other.[124] Each of them is considered still useful. It is believed that while an enterprise-based definition of the informal economy might be useful in statistical terms - for example, in calculating national accounts - an employment-based approach is useful in policy terms - for example, in considering who to target and how to finance social protection policies.

It is also necessary to note that the employment-based definition of the informal economy is particularly good for promoting a work-centred approach to poverty reduction and economic development, if used by national statisticians in collecting employment data and by national policy makers in designing policies. The work-centred-approach to poverty reduction is one that focuses on the needs and constrains of the working poor as workers not only as citizen or as members of poor household and disadvantaged communities.[125] This is the approach that is most favoured in this work.

---

122 Ibid., p. 127

123 ILO, Guidelines concerning a statistical definition of informal employment, endorsed by the Seventeenth International Conference of Labour Statisticians, November-December 2003.

124 Ralf Hussmanns, Defining and measuring informal employment, a paper prepared for the United Nations Economic and Social Council, 18-20 February 2004, Bangkok, p. 2, accessed from: http://.unescap.org/stat/sos1/sos1_11e.pdf.

125 Martha Chen , et al, Informality, Gender and Poverty: A Global Picture, in: Economic and Political weekly, May 27, 2006, p. 2133. Available at:

It is however necessary to add that even though the term "informal sector" has been found inadequate for designating informalization, we do not intend to completely eliminate its use in this work. Since its discovery almost four decades ago, the term "informal sector" has been found useful by academics and development experts alike. It is used in a number of international labour standards and observations by the ILO Committee of Experts on the Application of Conventions and Recommendations. It is also used in official statistics and in national policies and practices. Moreover "informal economy is yet to find universal acceptance. Many notable authors (e.g., Esther K. Ishengoma and Robert T. Kappel) and some international institutions such as the World Bank and the United Nations Economic and Social Council still maintain the enterprise approach and so retain the term "informal sector". For these reasons, "informal sector" will be retained wherever it appears in an instrument or official observation. We are of course not oblivious of the fact that the term "informal sector" could have misleading connotations when used in some contexts. It is however hoped that the definitions and clarifications offered so far and of course later would be of significant help to avoid such ambiguities.

2.1.3 Some Misconceptions about the Informal Economy

As observed earlier in the opening page of this chapter, the informal economy has been a concept that is largely misunderstood and confused with other economic activities. For a deeper understanding and for the avoidance of such misconceptions, we wish therefore in this short section to do a kind of differentiation of the informal economy from what it is not but often presumed to be. Keeping in mind the definitions we have made above, the informal economy is different from the following:

2.1.3.1 Black or Criminal Economy

By definition, the informal economy is understood to be outside the world of regular, stable, and protected employment and outside the world of legally regulated enterprises. This distinguishes it immediately from the formal economy which is within a legally regulated environment. The informal economy should however not be confused or conflated with the criminal economy. Although production and employment arrangements in the informal economy are sometimes semi-legal or illegal, the informal economy nevertheless produces and distributes legal goods and services. In contrast, the criminal economy deals exclusively in illegal goods and services and harbours, for example, people who are involved in drug trafficking and money laundering and people involved in smuggling. There are, of course, isolated cases of *criminal activities* in the informal economy. There could also be deliberate tax evasion. This is however true only of a small part of a

---

http://www.wiego.org/publications/EPW/Chen%20Vanek%20Heintz%20Informality%20Gender%20and%20Poverty.pdf.

larger whole. These points are clearly emphasized in the Conclusions made at 90th Session of the International Labour Conference concerning decent work and the informal economy:

> In some (...) countries, the term "informal economy" is considered synonymous with the "underground", "shadow" or "grey" economy. However, the majority of workers and enterprises in the informal economy produce legal goods and services, albeit sometimes not in conformity with procedural legal requirements, for example where there is non-compliance with registration requirements or immigration formalities. These activities should be distinguished from criminal and illegal activities, such as production and smuggling of illegal drugs, as they are the subject of criminal law, and are not appropriate for regulation or protection under labour or commercial law. There also may be grey areas where the economic activity involves characteristics of both the formal and informal economy, for instance when formal workers are provided with undeclared remuneration, or when there are groups of workers in formal enterprises whose wages and working conditions are typical of those existing in informality.[126]

2.1.3.2 Reproductive or Care Economy

The reproductive or care economy – comprises unpaid domestic work and care activities – is neither a part of nor the same as the informal economy. This is because the informal economy is defined as part of the market economy: that is, as producing goods and services for sale or some other form of remuneration.[127]

2.1.3.3 Micro and Small-Scale Enterprises (MSEs)

A grievous misconception that often finds expression among academics, researchers and policy makers is the view that the micro and small-scale enterprises (MSEs) and the informal economy are one and the same phenomenon.[128] Many of them equate the informal economy with the micro and small-scale enterprises (MSEs). It is therefore not surprising that some author use the concepts 'informal sector/informal economy' and "micro and small-scale enterprises interchangeably.[129] This reductionist conception is not only misleading, it also has negative consequences for policy formulation in the sense that it reduces the scope of informality/informalization to what is obviously a part of the whole. Policies based on this conception are consequently not far-reaching and produce limited results.

Another faulty conceptualization is clearly noticeable in the strict dichotomy between the informal economy and the small-scale enterprises, which places the MSEs outside the informal economy and treats both of them as two separate or

126 ILO, Conclusions concerning decent work and the informal economy, para. 5

127 ILO, Women and Men in the Informal Economy: A statistical picture, (Geneva: International Labour Office, 2002), p, 12.

128 Jantjie Xaba et al., The informal Sector in Sub-Saharan Africa, (Geneva: International Labour Office, 2002), p. 25.

129 Cf. Hans Dieter Seibel, Coping with Scarcity:Microenterprise Strategies in Nigeria, (Saarbrücken, Verlag für Entwicklungspolitik 1996), pp. 1 10

distinct phenomena. Sethuraman, one of the early proponents of the view argues as follows: "Perhaps the distinguishing feature between the informal sector unit and the small enterprise is their orientation: whereas the former is motivated primarily by employment creation, the latter is concerned primarily with profit maximization."[130]

This comparison gives immediately the impression that two separate entities that do not have anything to do with each other are being taught of – the informal sector and the small enterprise. Thinking of the small enterprises and the informal economy enterprises as two distinct subject areas is no longer compatible with current categorization of the informal economy, as we will see later in this chapter in 2.3.1.

One can however say without prejudice that, in all, the informal economy "is dominated by a large number of small scale production and service activities that are sole proprietors, partnerships, co-operatives, and even private limited liability companies."[131] This of course means that there is a link between the MSEs and the informal economy but the MSEs are not equivalent to or synonymous with the informal economy. There is also a consensus among authors that in many developing countries, most informal workers are engaged in the MSEs, and that most MSEs are informal. Because of this prominent position the MSEs occupy in the informal economy, they therefore deserve further treatment at this point.

What then are the MSEs? Generally speaking, there is no universally acceptable definition of MSEs. There is a considerable fuzziness about what the concept denotes. Different countries, institutions and individuals define them in various ways based on some parameters. May Nwoye identifies such parameters to include: (1) total investment cost, (2) size of work force, if labour leaders would decide, (3) level of turn-over, (4) operational environment.[132] Other important parameters include the net profit (balance sheet), private ownership and mode of operation. While some authors further differentiate between micro and small-scale enterprises, others treat both simply as one and the same phenomenon. Christaan Haan identifies three types that throw more light on the nature of the MSEs, especially in Africa: *Income-Generating Activities (IGAs), Micro-enterprises (MEs), Small enterprises (SEs).*

The *Income-Generating Activities* are the predominant type of MSEs, especially in rural areas. They refer essentially to pre-entrepreneurial, subsistence type of self-employment, and function as 'the employer of the last resort'. These business units constitute an important source of household income supplementing

130 S.V. Sethuraman, The Urban Informal Sector in Developing Countries: Employment, Poverty and Environment, (Geneva: International Labour Office, 1981), p. 13.

131 Joseph O. Dada, Harnessing the Potentials of the Informal Sector for Sustainable Development: Lessons from Nigeria, p 15, a pfd. document available at: http://unpan1.un.org/intradoc/groups/public/documents/AAPAM/UNPAN025582.pdf.

132 May-Ifeoma Nwoye, Small Business Enterprises: (How to start and succeed), (Benin-City, Nigeria: Benin Social Science Series for Africa, 1994), p. 15.

farming incomes. Usually they involve part-time, seasonal activities, based on traditional technologies, local materials and local markets. Examples of IGAs include: seasonal trading and hawking, pig and poultry raising and many traditional craft activities.[133]

The *Micro-enterprises* are rated slightly higher than IGAs, in the sense that they work with a few family workers, apprentices and sometimes one or a few (up to 10) permanent workers. Their technology is a mix of traditional and more-modern-but-obsolete techniques and equipment. They lack access to capital, have modest technical skills and lack management. They are more linked with markets and part of their production inputs are 'imported', and they serve local and nearby markets, for which reason they are more found in larger villages, rural towns and regional centres. Some of them have some potential for growth, or at least for the development of entrepreneurial skills. Some examples of MEs are: small shops, metal working, carpentry, tailoring, and various forms of repair services (e.g. radio & TV, cars, household appliances).[134]

The *Small enterprises* can be defined as firms with roughly 10 to 20 (sometimes 50) workers. They make use of non-traditional or 'modern' technologies in at least some of the productive aspects of the transformation process. Their products and services range from simple to complex, and similarly span a range of consumer types. The marketing pattern may be somewhat complex, reflecting innovation in raw material procurement and in output sales. SEs are often on the margin of being formal: they are usually registered with the local government and tend to be paying some taxes. In terms of location, the SEs are more urban- than rural-based. Some examples of small enterprises are: sawmills, garment assembly, motorised transport, construction and medium-scale industrial agro-processing.[135]

133 Hans Christiaan Haan, Training for Work in the Informal Sector: New Evidence from Eastern and Southern Africa, (Turin, Italy: ILO International Training Centre, 2001), p. 29

134 Ibid., p. 29.

135 Ibid., pp. 29-30: For further reading, see: Jeffrey Ashe, The PISCES II experience: local efforts in micro-enterprise developmen.t, (Washington: USAID, 1985); USAID/IMPACT Associates, Micro- and small enterprises in Uganda: report of the National Baseline Survey, consultancy report prepared for USAID, Kampala 1995: Michael Farbman and Adam Lessik, The impact of classification, in: Antoinette Gossens et al., Small enterprises, new approaches, proceedings of the Workshop "Small Enterprise Development, in search of new Dutch approaches, Ministry of Foreign Affairs/Dept. of Netherlands Development Cooperation, 1989.

Differentiation of the main MSE-segments with more details[136]

Income-generating activities	Micro-enterprises	Small enterprises
• Mixed with household economy	• Mixed with household economy, but shifting towards separation	• Separate from household economy
• Self-employment (with some help from family members)	• Up to ten workers (mostly: family workers, apprentices)	• Numbers of workers: 11-50
• Little no fixed assets (less than USD 500)	• Moderate fixed assets (less than USD 10,000)	• Fixed assets up to USD 100,000
• Traditional, manual technologies	• Mixed but obsolete technology	• More modern technology
• Profits for household consumption	• Profits used for household consumption and reinvestment in firm	• Profits used for re-investment in the firm
• Diversification to increase household income and/or to minimize risk	• Strategy: specialization to increase household income	• Strategy: specialization to increase profits

Although this categorization of the MSEs may not lead to clear-cut distinctions as there are obviously grey areas and overlap, they however highlight the heterogeneity of the informal enterprises and provide some useful insights to the different support needs of the distinguished segments. This further stresses the fact that policy interventions aiming at these enterprises and the workers in them must be multi-dimensional. The differences in them should play a major role in designing training programmes, in policy formulation, in the support interventions and underlying strategies.

2.2 People in the Informal Economy

2.2.1 Categorization

Because of its heterogeneous and complex nature, the informal economy could to be viewed from different perspectives. The scope of this work permits only the listing of few examples as follows: From a *labour categories/employment* status perspective; from an *industrial classification* perspective (trade, services, manufacturing, construction and transportation); from a *rural/urban divide* (rural

136 Hans Christiaan HAAN, Training for Work in the Informal Sector: New Evidence from Eastern and Southern Africa, (Turin, Italy: ILO International Training Centre, 2001).

informal economy and urban informal economy; from the standpoint of *urban spatial structure*: those in the Central Business District (CBD) and those in suburban areas; from a *location perspective*: those who are location-specific and those who are not; from a *zoning perspective*: those located in proper business locations and those in home-based enterprises; according to *size classification*: 1 persons unit (own-account workers), 2–4 persons units (micro enterprises), 5–9 persons units (small scale enterprises); from a *migratory status* (native, recent migrants and long-term migrants); from the viewpoint of *employment quality*: normal jobs and misemployment (begging, prostitution and scavenging); from the viewpoint of *income/employment enhancing potential*: enterprises/work with growing market demand that reflects high-income elasticity of demand and those with low-income elasticity of demand (rickshaw services).[137]

Based on these perspectives, people in the informal economy have been classified in diverse ways. We wish however to limit ourselves to the categorization based on employment/work. The main segments of informal employment, classified by employment status, are therefore as follows:

a) *Self-employment in informal enterprises:* workers in small unregistered or unincorporated enterprises, including:
   i) Employers: A more entrepreneurial class of employers who invest their own capital in running informal enterprises and who hire others and may not, therefore, contribute their own labour;
   ii) Own account operators: Owner operators of single-person units or family businesses or farms who do not hire others and who contribute both their own capital and labour to the enterprise;
   iii) Unpaid family workers: Family workers who work in family businesses or farms without pay; they contribute their own labour but may or may not contribute their own capital;
b) *Wage employment in informal jobs:* workers without legal protection for formal or informal firms, for households, or with no fixed employer, including:
   i) Employees of informal enterprises and formal enterprises;
   ii) Other informal wage workers such as:
   - Casual or day labourers: Wage workers with no fixed employer who sell their labour on a daily or seasonal basis;
   - Temporary workers who get work through an agency;
   - Part-time workers for a fixed employer, and unregistered or undeclared workers;
   - Domestic workers: Wage workers who work for families especially as cleaners and baby setters;

137 For details, cf. A.T.M. Nurul Amin, The Informal Sector in Asia from Decent Work Perspective, a working paper on the informal economy, (Geneva: International Labour Office, 20002).

- Some workers who are neither fully dependent wage workers or fully independent self-employed: disguised wage workers such as industrial outworkers for formal or informal firms (and their intermediaries) who work on a sub-contract for a piece rate but are responsible for all non-wage costs of production; and dependent contractors such as commission agents who sell goods on a commission for others or taxi and truck drivers who work for a company that owns the vehicles they drive.[138]

2.2.2 Most Vulnerable Groups

By vulnerable groups we mean those people who find it hard to enter the labour market and who suffer from some sort of discrimination and are more exposed to the vicissitudes of the labour market. The mere fact of being a woman, a young person or an immigrant; the fact of having some kind of disability or belonging to certain ethnic groups can be a limitation to participation in the labour market.[139] This implies that women, young people, immigrants, the disabled and those racially or ethnically discriminated against encounter more difficulties and limitations with regard to entering the labour market in quality job posts, with a fair salary, social security, etc. In order to understand labour markets in developing countries, it is important to recognise the multi-segmented nature of the informal economy, especially as it affects these vulnerable groups. Understanding the work arrangements, and associated costs and benefits of different segments of the informal economy, especially the vulnerable people, is necessary for addressing the problem of poverty. A closer look at the cases of women and children will help us to appreciate the difficulties faced by the vulnerable groups.

2.2.2.1 Women

Women have higher unemployment and underemployment rates and more participation inside informal economy. Women generally have less access to quality jobs within the informal economy compared to men. They are concentrated in the more precarious forms of employment in which earnings are low.

> Within the informal economy, women are concentrated in works associated with low and unstable earnings and with high risks of poverty. Outside of agriculture, women are more likely than men to be own account workers, domestic workers, unpaid contributing workers in family enterprises and industrial outworkers. A significant proportion of women working in agriculture are also unpaid contributing workers on the family farm.[140]

---

138 Cf. Martha Chen, et al, Informality, Gender and Poverty: A Global Picture, op. cit., p. 2132.

139 A list of documents and publications that expose the situation of these vulnerable groups in some countries and a review of the programmes, policies and successful experiences that have addressed these issues and can serve as a guide to the future action-taking of countries are available on the website: http://www.cinterfor.org.uy/public/english/region/ampro/cinterfor/temas/informal/grupos/index.htm#1.

140 Martha Alter Chen et al., Progress of the World's Women 2005: Women, Work and Poverty, (New York: UNIFEM, 2005), p. 9.

Within employment categories, women's hourly and monthly earnings are generally lower than men's. A gender gap in earnings can be seen across almost all employment categories. There are however few exceptions among public sector employees in certain countries, such as El Salvador, and in a country like Egypt where most of women's employment involves unpaid work on family enterprises and the few women who do participate in paid employment tend to be highly educated. In these exceptional cases, women's average hourly earnings can be higher than men's.[141]

Women work fewer hours on average in paid work than do men. This is partly attributed to the fact that women spend long hours in unpaid household labour. Because women are usually responsible for unpaid household work, women can be restricted to own-account or home-based employment, even if they have to work longer hours and earn less than they would in other types of employment.[142]

2.2.2.2 Children and Young People

With the growth of informal activities, there has been a rise in the number of child workers. The ILO and some other international organizations distinguish between child work and child labour, with the latter term being used to describe less acceptable practices. The ILO uses the concept "hazardous" to distinguish between "work" and "labour" with characteristics such as: working at too young an age; working for hours that are too long; working under strain; working on the streets; working for inadequate pay; working without stimulation; assuming too much responsibility; and being subject to intimidation.[143]

Child labour in the informal economy usually remains out of reach for most official institutions. Children are mostly employed in low productivity and poorly paid jobs, hardly ever covered by social security. Most cases of child labour are found in the informal economy, often in the most hidden and hazardous forms of work, including forced labour and slavery. Children are the most vulnerable to all the negative aspects of informality. Drawing from the figures provided by the International Programme on the Elimination of Child Labour (IPEC), the ILO document on decent work stipulates that out of the estimated 211 million working children in the world between the ages of 5 and 14 years, at least 111 million are involved in hazardous and exploitative work. Sub-Saharan Africa accommodates the highest number of working children: roughly 29 per cent of children in the 5 to 14 age group are working.[144]

One of the factors responsible for the increase in the number of children engaged in child labour is economic crisis. In time of economic crisis, families attempt to adjust to the financial difficulties by allowing children to go into child

141 Ibid.

142 Ibid

143 Jantjie Xaba, et al., Informal Sector in Sub-Saharan Africa, op. cit., p. 15.

144 ILO, Decent work and the informal economy, op. cit., pp. 25-26.

labour. Girls start working at an earlier age. They are usually paid less for the same job done by their male counterparts. They are more vulnerable than boys, as they usually work longer hours mostly in hidden and unregulated sectors where they are particularly exposed to exploitation and abuse, including slavery, sale and trafficking, debt bondage, serfdom and child prostitution.

Other factors blamed for the expansion of child labour are poverty, wars and deadly diseased like the HIV/AIDS pandemic which leave many children orphans and force them to drop out of school and go into economic activities at the early stages of their lives. Many of these children end up in child labour in the informal economy. Some go into begging, while others take to minor crimes as a means of surviving.

This short discussion on the vulnerable groups in the informal economy draws attention to the fact that there is need to give special consideration to the peculiar condition of this group of people while formulating policies and intervention actions for improving labour/work condition in the informal economy.

2.3 Size and Contributions of the Informal Economy to Economic Development

Mapping the informal economy so as to comprehend its size, composition, economic importance and evolution is always an extremely difficult exercise. International comparability is also impossible as different definitions have been used by different countries.[145] A number of factors have further contributed to making these exercises so difficult. While many countries have reportedly undertaken a survey on employment in the informal sector,[146] only very few countries among them have done so on a regular basis.[147] Furthermore, only two or three countries are reported to have collected the data that provide for measures of informal employment outside informal enterprises.[148] In addition to this, available data are far from being comprehensive and up-to-date. They also fall short of being accurate in reflecting the actual numbers of workers and enterprises in the informal economy. While many countries exclude agriculture from their measurement of the informal economy, some measure only the urban informal economy.[149]

145 Ibid., p. 10.

146 That is, not employment in the informal economy as a whole but only the employment in informal enterprises.

147 Martha Alter Chen et al, Mainstreaming Informal Employment and Gender in Poverty Reduction: A handbook for Policy-makers and Other Stakeholders, op. cit., p. 25.

148 Ibid.

149 Ibid.

These constraints notwithstanding, and in the absence of reliable data collected directly, other indirect methods[150] have been used to estimate the size and composition and the contributions of the informal economy on regional basis. The findings from such methods have been put together in a number of works and the available estimates can be summed up as follows.

Informal employment comprises one half to three quarters of non-agricultural employment in developing countries: this is further specified as follows: 48 per cent in North Africa; 51 per cent in Latin America; 65 per cent in Asia; and 72 per cent in sub-Saharan Africa. It is believed that if South Africa is excluded, the share of informal employment in non-agricultural employment would rise to 78 percent in sub-Saharan Africa.[151]

In all developing regions, self-employment comprises a greater share of informal employment (outside of agriculture) than wage employment.[152] The informal economy accounts also for 60% of the urban employment in Africa, 40-60% in Asia and 40% in Latin American and in the Caribbean. Its share of new jobs in African is 93% and 83 in Latin American and in the Caribbean[153]

Estimates of the contribution of the informal sector (i.e. not the informal economy, as a whole, but rather only the informal enterprises) to the GDP indicate that informal enterprises have really contributed significantly to non-agricultural GDP.[154] The average share of the informal enterprise sector in non-agricultural official GDP ranges from a low of 27% in Northern Africa to as high as of 41% in Sub-Saharan Africa. In Latin America, the contribution of informal sector enterprise to GDP stands at 29% and 41% in Asia.[155]

According to Kristina Flodman Becker, the terms 'informal sector' and 'informal economy' were not used in developed countries in the collection and classification of labour statistics. The most common term reportedly used is 'non-standard work', which refers to all work that is not regular, stable and protected.[156] The three categories of non-standard or atypical work – self-employment, part-time work and temporary work – accounted in the 1990s for 30 per cent of overall employment in 15 European countries and 25 per cent of total employment in the United States.[157]

---

150 For a detailed discription of the direct and indirect methods, please see: Kristina Flodman Becker, The Informal Economy: Fact Finding Study, (Stockholm, Sweden: Swedish International Development Agency, 2004), pp. 15-17.

151 Martha Alter Chen et all, Mainstreaming Informal Employment and Gender in Poverty Reduction: A handbook for Policy-makers and Other Stakeholders, op. cit., p. 26.

152 Ibid, p. 27.

153 Cf., Jacques Charmes, Estimations and Survey methods for the Informal Sector, (Versailles, France: University of Versailles, 2002)

154 Cf. ILO, Women and men in the informal economy: a statistical picture, op. cit.

155 Kristina Flodman Becker, The Informal Economy: Fact Finding Study, op. cit., p. 19.

156 Ibid., pp. 28-29.

157 Ibid., p. 29.

In about half of the countries included in popular estimations across the regions, the share of informal work in total employment is higher for women than for men. Women are believed to be more involved in those informal activities that are undercounted, such as paid domestic activities in private households and home work. Women are also believed to be more than men in small-scale economic units where their economic contributions are invisible and therefore not counted.[158]

2.4 The Conditions of Work in the Informal Economy

In order to understand the nature of work in the informal economy, it is good to first take a look at the nature of the informal enterprises in which most of them work. The state of these informal enterprises is highly precarious. They are generally characterized by ease of entry; reliance on indigenous resources; family ownership; small scale of operation; labour-intensive and adapted technology; skills acquired outside the formal school system; and unregulated and competitive markets.[159] Since informal enterprises are usually not registered and recognized, they are excluded from or have limited access to public infrastructure and benefits. They have to rely on informal, often exploitative institutional arrangements, whether for information, markets, credit, training or social security. They are highly dependent on the attitudes of the public authorities and susceptible to the strategies of large formal enterprises. They are placed at a competitive disadvantage because they do not have the type of influence which those in the formal economy are often able to exert – the influence which sometimes violates an essential feature of a market economy, i.e. free and equal access to markets based on efficiency rather than influence.[160]

The working conditions of informal workers are generally as precarious as those of the informal enterprises in which the majority of them work and earn their living. Informal workers and operators are termed "informal" mainly because they share one important characteristic: *they are not recognized or protected under the legal and regulatory frameworks.* This however is not the only defining feature of work in the informal economy. "Work in the informal economy is also characterized by small or undefined work places, unsafe and unhealthy working conditions, low levels of skills and productivity, low or irregular incomes, long working hours and lack of access to information, markets, finance, training and technology."[161]

Informal workers and entrepreneurs are also said to be generally characterized by varying degrees of vulnerability borne more by women, migrant, ethnic

158 ILO, Decent work and the informal economy, op. cit.,, p. 12.

159 ILO, Employment, Incomes and Equality: A Strategy for Increasing Productive Employment in Kenya, op. cit., p. 6.

160 ILO, Decent work and the informal economy, op. cit., p. p. 3.

161 ILO, Resolution concerning decent work and the informal economy, § 9.

minorities, less educated and child labourers. Owing to the fact that informal workers and operators are not recognized under the law, they receive little or no legal or social protection and are rendered incapable of enforcing contracts or having security of property rights. They are rarely able to organize for effective representation and have little or no voice to make their work recognized and protected. They are excluded from or have limited access to public infrastructure and benefits. There are usually involved in employment relationships that are generally highly unstable and casual. It is therefore not surprising that productivity among them is low and their incomes are very unstable, low and irregular.

2.4.1 Security Gap

The situation of informal workers and entrepreneurs is also described in terms of the seven essential securities which are often denied them: *Labour market security, employment security, job security, work security, skill reproduction security, income security* and *representation security.*

Income security is "a major determinant of other forms of labour-related security".[162] It represents adequate actual, perceived and expected income, either earned or in the form of social security and other benefits. It encompasses the *level* of income (absolute and relative to needs), *assurance* of receipt and *expectation* of current and future income, both during working life and in old age or disability retirement. Classic income security protection mechanisms include a minimum wage machinery, wage indexation, comprehensive social security, and progressive taxation.[163] Income security therefore consists of adequacy, continuity, fairness in relation to needs and by comparison with the income of others, and assurance of compensation in case of income loss beyond the recipient's control. Income security is guaranteed by income protection and low degree of income inequality. Issues concerning income security invariably take into cognisance not just the level on income, but most importantly the protection of income and the degree of income inequality.

Representation security at work is based on the freedom of workers and employers to form and join organizations of their own choosing without fear of reprisal or intimidation. Freedom of association and the right to organize constitute a fundamental human right. It is also a key enabling right. If workers or employers are denied the possibility of organizing, they will not have access to a range of other rights at work.[164]

Representation security includes both individual representation and collective representation. *Individual representation* is about individual rights enshrined in

---

162 ILO: Economic security for a better world, (Geneva: International Labour Office, 2004), p. 296.

163 ILO, Social-Economic Security Programme, Definitions: What we mean when we say "economic security", a pdf document available at: http://www.ilo.org/public/english/protection/ses/download/docs/definition.pdf.

164 ILO, Decent work and the informal economy, op. cit., p. 71.

laws as well as the individuals' access to institutions. *Collective representation* means the right of any individual or group to be represented by a body that can bargain on their behalf and which is sufficiently large, sufficiently independent and sufficiently competent to do so. Cooperative societies and independent trade unions with the right to collectively bargain over wages, benefits, and working conditions as well as to monitor working practices and strike have been the typical forms of guaranteeing representation security.[165]

Skill reproduction security denotes workers' access to basic education as well as vocational training to develop capacities and acquire the qualifications needed for socially and economically valuable occupations. Lack of skills no doubt is a problem of labour that leads to, among other things, low productivity and income. Skills security puts into consideration not only the level of skills but also and more importantly the suitability of the skills for the jobs to be performed.[166]

Labour market security is guaranteed when there are ample opportunities for adequate income-earning activities. It has a structural component, in that it represents the types and quantity of opportunities. Furthermore, it has a cognitive side, as it also features expectations that opportunities are or will become adequate. Labour market security is guaranteed by availability of enough income-earning opportunities, or where the supply of workers matches the demand for them.[167]

Employment security is protection against loss of income-earning work. For wage and salary workers, employment security exists in organizations and countries, in which there is strong protection against unfair or arbitrary dismissal and where workers can redress unfair dismissal. For the self-employed, it means protection against sudden loss of independent work, and/or business failure. Typical forms of enhancing employment security have been protection against arbitrary dismissal, regulations on hiring and firing, and imposition of costs on employers for failing to adhere to rules.[168]

Job security signifies the presence of niches (a place, employment, status, or activity for which a person or thing is best fitted) in organizations and across labour markets allowing the workers some control over the content of a job and the opportunity to build a career. Job security is not synonymous with employment security. Whereas employment security refers to the opportunity of a worker to continue working in an enterprise, job security refers to the worker's ability to pursue a line of work in conjunction with his or her interests, training and skills. Job security can become a reality if only there is labour market security.[169]

Work security denotes working conditions in organizations that are safe and promote workers' well being. Classical "occupational health and safety" provisions shielding workers from occupational hazards, diseases, and injuries are

165 ILO, Social-Economic Security Programme, op. cit.

166 Ibid.

167 Ibid.

168 Ibid.

169 Ibid.

an integral part of work security. However, work security goes beyond this in addressing the modern scourges of stress, overwork, absenteeism, and harassment.[170]

2.4.2 Decent Work Deficit

The most meaningful and more concrete way to look at the situation of those in the informal economy is in terms of *decent work deficits*. Decent work deficits in the informal economy are considered specifically in four areas; employment, right, representation and social protection. Decent work deficit in the informal economy means that "poor-quality, unproductive and unremunerative jobs that are not recognized or protected by law; the absence of rights at work, inadequate social protection, and the lack of representation and voice are most pronounced in the informal economy, especially at the bottom end among women and young workers."[171]

Rights deficit: The informal economy is where most jobs have been created in recent years, but it is also where the greatest problems with regard to workers' rights are found. The informal economy is where the workers' rights are in greatest deficit in terms of freedom of association, collective bargaining, child labour, forced labour and discrimination at work.

While it could be said that workers' rights are at least formally recognized in most countries and that some protection exists against the worst forms of abuse they are exposed to, this however is not the case in the informal economy, where workers are hardly "recognized as workers and most of the times face the employer as individuals. Fear is pervasive: fear of losing one's job, however bad, fear of losing security, however fragile. The lack of legal protection of workers' rights in the informal economy is therefore an overriding issue." It is generally believed that the right gap in the informal economy exists and persists due to inappropriate or inapplicable labour legislation.[172]

Employment deficit: This is the situation that people cannot find work or conduct business in the formal economy. Their inability to find work in the formal economy compels them to take up informal jobs in the informal economy, since they cannot afford to be openly unemployed.[173] Employment in the informal economy is however highly unstable volatile precarious. In the foregoing discussion, it is already clear that jobs in the informal economy in comparison with those in the formal economy are seriously deficient in terms of workers' rights, proper working conditions, legal and social protection, representation and voice. In addition to this, "in many informal sector micro-enterprises, a clear

170 Ibid.

171 ILO, Decent work and the informal economy, op. cit., p. 4.

172 Dan Gallin, Organizing in the Global Informal Economy, a paper posted at: http://www.globallabour.info/en/2007/09/organizing_in_the_global_infor.html, accessed on 01.03.2011.

173 ILO, Decent work and the informal economy, op. cit., p. 95.

employer/employee relationship is lacking. Labour relations are based on casual employment kinship or personal and social relations rather than contractual arrangements with formal guarantees"[174]

Representational deficit: "People in informal work represent the largest concentration of needs without voice, the silent majority of the world economy."[175] Mostly, women and youth, who make up the bulk of informal workers, are especially without voice – whether for pursuing their employment interests through collective bargaining or for lobbying with politicians and bureaucrats on issues such as access to infrastructure, property rights, environmental concerns and social security. Even in places where informal workers and operators have the right to organize, they are rarely organized and hardly have their own membership-based organizations to represent their interests. Some initiatives undertaken to mobilize and organize themselves have been mainly at the grass-roots or community level, in self-help groups or in trade-based associations. Such associations are however fragile in nature, structurally constrained, limited in effectiveness and hardly officially registered and recognised. In most cases, they are not affiliated to established national or international organizations of employers, chambers of commerce, trade unions or cooperatives.[176]

Representational gap: has been identified as an important reason for the inadequate legal and social protection for informal entrepreneurs and workers and for their lack of access to productive assets, capital and product markets, training systems, public services and amenities. For "without effective freedom of association, they are not able to exercise countervailing power to make their work recognized, protected, formal and decent."[177]

The organizational and representational deficit in the informal economy, especially the limited coverage of the informal organizations and their range of services and activities is traceable not only to the denial of the rights to organize, but also to the "irregularity and instability of their members' employment and incomes. Their daily struggle for survival, their lack of managerial and technical skills, and their limited ability to mobilize assets from external sources…."[178] Some other major constrains to effective organizing of informal workers or incorporating existing informal organizations into recognized organizations include:

- Interest and needs among the various groups of informal workers are highly heterogeneous

---

174 Valentina Forastieri, Implementation of Working Conditions and Environment in the Informal Sector through Safety and Health Measures, a working paper available at, http://www.ilo.org/public/english/protection/safework/sectors/informal/inform1.htm#wcond.

175 ILO: Reducing the decent work deficit: A global challenge, Report of the Director-General, (Geneva: International Labour Office, 2001), p. 64.

176 ILO, Decent work and the informal economy, op. cit., p. 72.

177 Ibid., p. 73.

178 ILO: World Labour Report 1997-98: Industrial relations, democracy and social stability, (Geneva, International Labour office, 1997), pp. 216-217.

- The needs and worries of informal workers also differ significantly from those catered for by the existing official unions. Ethnic, family and kinship ties, for instance are stronger among informal workers than among formal workers. Unlike the formal workers whose basic need are often met, the informal workers find themselves often so caught up in the daily struggle for survival that they hardly find the time or see the need to join in collective action,
- The highly precarious nature of their working conditions and employment relationships means often that they would risk their source of livelihood to join or participate in the activities of a union. It sometime means unbearable intimidation and reprisals for them
- There are also legal and institution barriers to trade union organizing in the informal economy;
- Most informal workers, especially the home-workers and farmers in the interior, are highly inaccessible to unionists
- Their inability to cope with financial and other obligations make them unattractive as potential member of unions
- Inexperience on the part of union members and lack of tested strategies for organizing informal workers
- The traditional bias that make it difficult the see operators in the informal economy as real workers.[179]

Social protection deficit: Social protection includes public social security schemes and also private or non-statuary schemes, such as mutual benefit societies and occupational pension schemes. All sorts of non-statutory schemes, formal or informal, are included under the definition of social protection. The concept also covers concerns with food provision, housing, sanitation, income generation and employment generation. Social protection is considered to be an indispensable part of government social policy and an important tool in the prevention and alleviation of poverty. In fact work cannot be decent and workers cannot have human dignity without adequate social protection.[180]

Unfortunately, despite the fact that most workers in the informal economy are most at risk and therefore most in need of social protection, they have little or no social protection and receive little or no social security, either from their employer or from the government. Beyond traditional social security coverage, workers in the informal economy are without social protection in such areas as education, skill-building, training, health care and childcare, which are particularly important for

179 Cf. ILO, Promoting gender equality: A resource kit for trade unions, Booklet 4: Organizing the unorganized: Informal economy and other unprotected workers, (Geneva: International Labour Office, 2001).

180 Amuda Shrestha, Social Protection in the Informal Economy, a paper presented in the National Consultation Workshop "Identifying Challenges of Informal Economy for Trade Unions" organised by DECONT on 15-16 May 2004 at Lalitpur. Available at: http://www.nepaldemocracy.org/institutions/Informal_Economy.htm.

women workers.[181] The lack of social protection is therefore a critical aspect of workers in the informal economy. It has been further compounded by the problem of compliance and governance in terms of contribution to the social security and protection from adverse working conditions.[182]

An integral and important aspect of social protection that deserves special attention is the occupational safety and health standards in the informal economy. This concerns the working condition or the working environment in which the informal operators and worker live and work. A major reason why social protection is especially critical for informal workers is that they are much more likely than formal workers to be exposed to poor working environments, low safety and health standards and environmental hazards.

The conditions under which most informal workers operate are indeed precarious and unsafe. For the homeworkers, their home and workplace are one and the same place. "The distinction between working and living conditions often becomes blurred and both are related to broader problems of poverty and underdevelopment."[183] For informal workers who operate in open spaces or in locations not legally recognized for the purpose and with no right of ownership, their occupational safety and health problems are also linked to their lack of access to sanitary facilities, potable water, electricity or waste disposal.[184]

The exposure to poor working environments, low safety and health standards and environmental hazards has definitely devastating consequences on the health and productivity as well as the general well-being and quality of life of informal workers and their families. In spite of this, it continues to exist in a remarkable measure because those involved are often not even aware of the risks they face, and, if they are, they do not know how to avoid them. The problem is therefore aggravated by inadequate technical and managerial skills of informal operators.[185]

Institutional responses to these problems are often weak in many developing countries partly because national and local authorities do not have adequate knowledge of the state of occupational safety and health standards in the informal economy and partly because of lack staff and resources. Policy intervention is also hindered by lack of adequate information on occupational accidents and diseases arising from hazardous working conditions which could be used for the identification of priority areas of prevention. Difficulties encountered in gaining access to informal workers, especially those that work within the privacy of their homes, is another major obstacle to institutional response and policy intervention.[186]

---

181 ILO, Resolution concerning decent work and the informal economy, § 10-

182 Amuda Shrestha, Social Protection in the Informal Economy, op. cit.

183 Valentina Forastieri, Implementation of Working Conditions and Environment in the Informal Sector through Safety and Health Measures, op. cit.

184 ILO, Decent work and the informal economy, op. cit., p. 76.

185 Ibid.

186 Ibid.

2.5 Factors Responsible for Informality and its Expansion

A number of factors are believed to be responsible for the expansion of the informal economy and for the harsh condition of work in it. We will however concentrate on the important economic and political factors such as governance, poor economic performance and non-pro-poor economic growth and the flexible specialization and global chains in recent decades. The link between poverty and informality will be treated separately.

2.5.1 Governance: Weak Legal and Institutional Frameworks

Informality which encompasses the precarious state of enterprises and condition of work in the informal economy is principally a governance issue. As in the case of poverty, the factors responsible for the growth of informality is traceable to inappropriate, ineffective, misguided or badly implemented macroeconomic and social policies often developed without due consultations; the lack of conducive legal and institutional frameworks; and the lack of good administration for proper and effective implementation of policies and laws.[187]

Three types of legislation and regulations that are of basic importance include: commercial or business regulations governing the establishment and operation of enterprises; the laws pertaining to property rights, which could affect the ability to transform assets into productive capital; and labour legislation governing employment relationships and the rights and protection of workers.[188]

Informality often emerges as a result of the inability of operators to comply with difficult, irrelevant or prohibitive rules and regulations. This is particularly so where rules and regulations that impact on economic activities and determine transaction costs are unpredictable, not cost effective and do not provide the requisite business information.[189] According to S. de Silva, such transaction costs include: obtaining a licence to conduct a business; acquisition of title to land or acquiring a lease; access to training, credit facilities; enforcement of contracts and access to the law; obtaining telecommunication, electricity and other utilities such as water; obtaining information on, and access to, market information, raw materials, prices, potential customers and sources of supplies of goods and services; labour and social charges; and tax costs, etc.[190] It is often the poor formulation of these laws and regulations that make them burdensome and give room for "corrupt and inefficient bureaucracies that increase transaction costs, discourage compliance, impede economic participation and encourage endemic corruption, thus preventing entrepreneurs from participation in the formal economy."[191]

187 ILO, Conclusions concerning decent work and the informal economy, para. 14.

188 ILO, Decent work and the informal economy, op. cit., p. 27.

189 Ibid.

190 S. de Silva: The informal economy: Issues and challenges, draft paper, 2001, as cited in: ILO, Decent work and the informal economy, op. cit., p. 28.

191 Ibid.

High cost of compliance with commercial or business regulations governing the establishment and operation of enterprises compels economic actors to avoid them and consequently remain informal. Most owner operators of informal enterprises operate semi-legally or illegally often because the regulatory environment is too punitive and cumbersome. In addition to this, many activities in the informal economy do not generate enough output, employment or income to fall into existing tax brackets. There is no doubt that owner operators would be willing to pay the costs of registration and pay taxes if they were to receive the incentives and benefits of formality (enjoyed by registered businesses). Indeed the cost of remaining illegal is so high that no one would under normal circumstances want to remain in it. Martha Alter Chen and the co-writers drive the point closer home when they observed that operating outside the statutory legal framework is seen to have more costs than benefits for most informal workers. Most self-employed and wage workers in the informal sector are deprived of secure work, workers' benefits, social protection and representation or voice. The self-employed, they further argue, would have to take care of themselves and their enterprises as well as their employees (if they hire others) or unpaid contributing family members (if they run a family business). In addition to this, they often face competitive disadvantage vis-à-vis larger formal firms in capital and product markets. This is also the case with the informal wage workers who would have to take care of themselves as they receive few (if any) employer-sponsored benefits. Both groups receive little (if any) legal protection through their work or from their governments.[192]

Laws governing property rights and titling of the assets of the poor have also been identified as another major cause of informality in several developing countries.[193] The absence of an appropriate system of property rights and the titling of the assets of the poor in the informal economy deter the generation of productive capital needed for business development.[194] Hernando de Soto argues that although the poor do sometimes hold assets, these assets represent "dead capital" because they are held in forms not recognized by the legal system and hence cannot be used to generate productive capital that the poor can use for formal economic activities.[195]

In many nations of the world labour legislation often does not take into account the realities of modern organization of work. Inappropriate definitions of employees and workers may have the adverse effect of treating a worker as self-employed and outside the protection of labour legislation.[196]

---

192 Martha Alter Chen et al, Mainstreaming Informal Employment and Gender in Poverty Reduction: A handbook for Policy-makers and Other Stakeholders, op. cit., p. 25.

193 ILO, Decent work and the informal economy, op. cit., p. 28.

194 ILO, Conclusions concerning decent work and the informal economy, para. 18.

195 Cf. Hernando de Soto, The mystery of capital: Why capitalism triumphs in the West and fails everywhere else, (New York, Basic Books, 2000).

196 ILO, Conclusions concerning decent work and the informal economy, para. 14.

Inappropriate legal and administrative frameworks that do not guarantee and protect freedom of association make it difficult for workers and employers to organize and pursue their employment interests through collective bargaining or to lobby policy-makers on issues such as access to infrastructure, property rights, taxation and social security.[197] Similarly, the absence of good public policies prevents people, especially those in the informal economy from investing in their education and skills needed to boost their own employability and productivity, and from making sustained contributions to social security schemes.[198]

Governance however has a meaning that goes well beyond government and law. It extends to the controlling, directing or regulating influence of the set of institutions and policies that determine the functioning of an economy and a society.[199] The institutional structures and procedures at national and local levels play a crucial role in encouraging formality or informality – they determine how laws and regulations are implemented, the transaction costs of compliance with legislation and regulations. The institutional structures and procedures in most third world countries are often very weak. This gives room for improper formulation and implementation of legislations and regulations guiding these transactions and other economic activities. Weak institutions that are corrupt, that hinder equitable access to all potential clients, that are not transparent and consistent in the application of rules and regulations, that do not protect and enforce contractual obligations that respect the rights of workers, usually discourage greater compliance with both business and labour regulations and inhibit the attainment of decent work for all.

2.5.2 Poor Economic Performance and Non-pro-poor Economic Growth

It is a common belief that a decline in economic performance as well as "Non-pro-poor Economic Growth" impacts negatively on labour market and worsens general labour conditions. Economic performance at any given time has an overwhelming influence on the employment status and relationships of available work force which in turn shape and reshape the general work condition in the informal economy. Over the years firms in the formal economy adjust to decline in economic growth by retrenching employees in order to cut down their operating costs. The retrenched workers are left with no option other than to accept informal jobs or start their own informal businesses.[200] The ILO report 2004 indicates that the expansion of the

197 Ibid., para. 17

198 Ibid., para. 19

199 Anne Trebilcock, Decent and the Informal Economy, discussion paper presented at the EGDI–WIDER Conference on Unlocking Human Potential – "Linking the Informal and Formal Sectors" in Helsinki, 17-18 September 2004.

200 Robert Kappel and Esther K Ishengoma, Economic Growth and Poverty: Does Formalisation of Informal Enterprises Matter? A working paper written for GIGA Research Program: Transformation in the Process of Globalization, Munich, April 2006, p. 10, at http://mpra.ub.uni-muenchen.de/1456/ The

informal economy and the deteriorating employment situation in many developing countries in Sub-Saharan Africa, Latin America and the Caribbean are associated with low Gross Domestic Product growth rates (GDP) as a result of decrease in economic growth rate.[201]

An increase in the economic growth rate of a country does not however automatically result in the movement of workers from the informal economy to the formal economy.[202] It is argued that economic growth can even contribute to the growth of the informal economy and the deterioration of the labour conditions in it unless it is pro-poor, meaning if it is accompanied by improvements in formal employment levels and income distribution.[203]

Economic crises and unfavourable economic restructuring naturally contribute enormously to decline in economic performance which in turn promotes the spread of informality.[204] These economic crises are witnessed in various ways in different parts of the world. While some nations have experienced little or no growth in recent decades, others have concentrated on capital-intensive growth, resulting in "jobless growth". Since in both situations not enough jobs are created for all those seeking work, people are forced to find employment or to create their own work in the informal economy.

Some nations have worsened their problem by pursuing some harmful patterns of economic growth. For instance some developing nations have paved the way for decline in economic performance by neglecting the agricultural sector and adopting policies favouring foreign investment, large companies and manufacturing industries when most of their population is still in rural areas and still largely dependent on agriculture. Some other countries experience "high-tech" growth, but

---

following materials will make an interesting reading: G. Ranis and F. Stewart, V-Goods and the Role of the Urban Informal Sector in Development, in: Economic Development and Cultural Change, Vol. 47, No. 2, 1999, pp. 259-288; Victor Tokman, Integrating the Informal Sector into the Modernisation Process, in: SAIS Review, Vol. 21, No. 1, 2001, pp. 45-60.

201 ILO, Global Employment Trends, (Geneva: International Labour Office. 2004), also at http://kilm.ilo.org/GET2004/DOWNLOAD/trends.pdf.

202 As was witnessed in some East Asian countries, despite high GDP growth rates (over 7 percent) an increase in unemployment was unfortunately recorded at the same time. According to the United Nations report, in the 1990s China underwent the highest economic growth rate (GDP per capita annual growth rate of 9.5 percent) yet between 1996 and 1999 experienced a 28 per cent decrease of employment in state owned enterprises, a more than 50 percent decrease of female workers in urban collective enterprises and a 41 per cent increase of own-account workers and employees in micro-enterprises. Cf. United Nations Development Program, Human Development Report 2001 (New York: Oxford University Press, 2001)

203 Cf., Kristina Foldman Becker, Fact finding study: The Informal Economy op. cit.

204 In the economic crisis that took place in Latin America in the 1980 it became evident that employment in the informal sector tends to grow during periods of economic crises. This was further confirmed by the economic crisis in Asia few years later, during which numerous people who lost their formal jobs especially in the former East Asian Tiger countries tried to find jobs or create work in the informal sector. For more on this, see: Victor Tokman, ed, Beyond Regulation: The Informal Economy in Latin America (Boulder, Colorado: Lynme Riermer Publishers, 1992); Eddy Lee, The Asian Financial Crisis: The Challenges for Social Policy (Geneva: International Labour Office, 1998).

at the same time create some sort of imbalance in which the demand for highly skilled labour relegates most of those without such skills to the informal economy.[205]

There is indeed no doubt that the measures adopted by a nation in response to an economic crisis can increase or reduce the effects of the crises in the nation, especially with regard to the informal economy. There is a consensus among researchers that the stabilization and structural adjustment policies of the 1980s and 1990s, which in many countries resulted in growing poverty, unemployment and underemployment, contributed to the spread of the informal economy and deterioration of work conditions. Economic restructuring and the downsizing of enterprises that results from it, especially in the transition and developing economies, but elsewhere as well, also compelled the many retrenched workers in the formal economy to move into the informal economy thereby expanding the informalization of production and labour. The privatisation of state owned enterprises resulted in job-retrenchment; while trade liberalisation contributed to the contraction and closure of some formal enterprises which were unable to compete given the availability of cheap imports. As social security systems in the majority of developing countries are poor, retrenched people are forced into self- or wage-employment in the informal economy as alternative sources of income.[206] For instance, the restructuring of state owned enterprises in China, where some nine million workers were laid off in urban areas, has been an important reason behind government policies to promote flexible informal employment as the most important means of solving employment pressures.[207]

2.5.3 Flexible Specialization and Global Chains

By flexible specialization here, we mean a system in which firms embark on the decentralization of production and the organization of work along the lines of non-permanent or irregular labour relationships, i.e. forming smaller, more flexible specialized production units, some of which remain unregistered or informal. In this way, the use of a regular workforce based in a single large registered factory or workplace gradually gives way to the decentralized system of production. This is one of the methods adopted by many formal enterprises in their bid to cut costs and improve competitiveness. These firms are increasingly operating with a small core of wage employees with regular terms and conditions (formal employment) based in a fixed formal workplace and a growing periphery of "non-standard" or "atypical" and often informal workers in different types of workplaces scattered

205 ILO: Decent work and the informal economy, Report VI, International Labour Conference, 90th Session, (Geneva, International Labour Office, 2002), p. 29.

206 Robert Kappel and Esther K Ishengoma. Economic Growth and Poverty: Does Formalisation of Informal Enterprises Matter? A working paper written for GIGA Research Program: Transformation in the Process of Globalization, Munich, April 2006, p. 11, at http://mpra.ub.uni-muenchen.de/1456/.

207 ILO, Decent work and the informal economy, op. cit., p. 30.

over different locations. These measures often include outsourcing or subcontracting and a shift away from regular employment relationships to more flexible and informal employment relationships.[208] The use of sub-contracting agencies of firms leaves the workers hanging, not knowing who their real employer is. This kind of employment relationship makes it also difficult to organize the workers. It also cheapens labour and leads to the deterioration working conditions.

There are some empirical evidences that link increases in informal employment to trade policy. It has been particularly argued that the trade liberalization policies being pursued under the World Trade Organization in the process of globalization have contributed in no small measure to the emergence and expansion of the informal economy. "Trade liberalization increases competition for formal firms, and to remain competitive, these formal firms try to reduce costs by cutting worker benefits, replacing permanent workers with part-time labour or subcontracting to the informal sector, including home-based workers. Some formal firms may even be forced to lay off workers, who would subsequently seek employment in the informal sector."[209] It is further observed that although globalization and trade liberalization have created new employment opportunities mainly in the export sector of developing economies, new jobs are not necessarily being created in the formal sector, and it is possible that informal employment also expands.[210]

Kate Meagher reports that due to flexible employment relationships, workers in Sub-Saharan Africa have been made to work longer hours, demand no formal wages and have minimal overheads. She further observed that formal distributors and manufacturers simply use informal operators in exploitative ways to extend their market to a wider public, and even into rural areas.[211] This, according to Meagher, is what experts call global commodity and value chains.

These value chains "involve the full range of activities and stakeholders who are involved in bringing a product from conception, sourcing of raw materials, marketing, distribution and delivery to the final consumer.[212] They demonstrate clearly how the formal and informal economies are linked across the borders of many countries and also locally, influencing decent work for workers depending on which segment of the chain they are in. The lower down the chain, the more likely employment relationships are to be informal and the larger the decent work gaps. The lower part of the chain is unfortunately dominated by informal workers and operators of informal enterprises.

There are, in all, both direct and indirect linkages between informal workers and formal businesses, given that the informal economy includes the full range of

---

208 Ibid., p. 35.

209 United Nations, Economic and Social Council, Poverty and Informal Sector: Role of the Informal Sector in Poverty Reduction, E/ESCAP/CPR(3)/1 2 October 2006, § 20.

210 Ibid, § 21.

211 Kate Meagher, Crisis, Informalisation and the Urban Informal Sector in Sub-Saharan Africa, Development and Change, Vol. 26, 1995, p. 13.

212 Jantjie Xaba, Pat Horn and Shirin Motala, Informal Sector in Sub-Saharan Africa, op. cit., p. 20.

"non-standard" wage employment that flexible specialization has given rise to, such as sweatshop production, homeworkers, industrial outworkers, temporary and part-time work and unregistered workers. A setting like this makes the employment relationships very complicated. There exist therefore many disguised wage employees in the informal economy who may not even be aware of who their ultimate "boss" is, but who are clearly dependent on someone for the inputs, equipment, work location and sale of the final products. They do not also know that someone has certain responsibilities for ensuring decent work for them.[213]

As a result of these factors, a higher percentage of people working in the informal economy, compared to those working in the formal economy, are poor.[214] These conditions expose them to informality which means precarious work without legal recognition and protection, without social protection and without representation and voice. The result of it all is poor working and living conditions and low productivity and income. Under such a condition, it is extremely difficult to escape poverty.

2.6 Linkages between Poverty and the Informal Economy

There is no simple relationship between working in an informal enterprise and being poor so that one can say that all who are working in informal enterprises are poor. Certainly, not all jobs in the informal economy yield low incomes. In fact some people in the informal economy, especially the self employed earn more than unskilled or low-skilled workers in the formal economy. Similarly there is no direct relationship between working in a formal enterprise and escaping poverty so that one can say convincingly that all who are working in formal enterprises are not poor. But one must bear in mind that working in a formal enterprise does not always mean working formally or being in formal employment. Consequently, working in the formal economy is no guarantee for escaping poverty. Apart from some of the part-time workers, casual workers, sub-contractors, home workers already mentioned, many other workers in the formal public and private sectors are indeed trapped in absolute poverty. This is often the case in many developing and transition countries, where remuneration in the civil service and state-owned enterprises is not enough to keep worker above the poverty line.[215]

One point that however cannot be denied is that a greater share of the working poor is concentrated in the informal economy, and most of them are women.[216] There is indeed a consensus among scholars that there exists at least some sort of

213 ILO, Decent work and the informal economy, op. cit., p. 38.

214 Martha Alter Chen et al, Mainstreaming Informal Employment and Gender in Poverty Reduction: A handbook for Policy-makers and Other Stakeholders, op. cit., p. 25.

215 Cf. ILO, Decent work and the informal economy, op. cit., p. 31.

216 For details on the linkage between poverty and informal economy, see: United Nations Economic and Social Council, Poverty and the Informal Sector: Measurement Issues, (E/ESCAP/CPR(3)/2)/14 November 2006.

causal relationship between being poor and working informally. The commonest assertions along this line are, firstly, that poverty makes most people to go into the informal economy and secondly most people in the informal economy remain poor mostly because of the living and work conditions in it.

Indeed poverty is an element that contributes to the expansion of the informal economy.[217] It forces most people to take up unattractive jobs in the informal economy, and the low incomes that such jobs yield, thereby creating a vicious cycle of poverty. In a state of poverty, one cannot afford to remain unemployed, and any job seems to be better than no job. Since in many developing countries wages in the public sector are insufficient to support a family, formal workers or family members are therefore forced to supplement their incomes by finding work in the informal economy.[218]

Poverty also prevents real opportunities and choices for decent and protected work. Low and irregular incomes (and often the absence of public policies) prevent people from investing in the type of education and skills needed to boost their own employability and productivity, and from making sustained contributions to social security schemes. And because of the inability to acquire basic education (primary and secondary) often needed to function effectively in the formal economy, in addition to a lack of recognition of skills garnered in the informal economy, the poor people often encounter serious barriers of entering the formal economy where there is a higher likelihood of earning enough for the living.[219]

The implication of the links between poverty and the informal economy is that measures to deal with the problems of the informal economy and to provide decent work for those currently engaged in it are essential to eradicate poverty.[220] The view that the informal economy helps to eliminate poverty should however be taken with caution. Such a view encourages the creation of job opportunities in the informal economy instead of creating more new jobs in the formal economy and helping people in the informal economy the move into the formal economy. There is however no doubt that the work in the informal economy helps the poor to cushion the scourging weight of poverty. This is an aberration that should not be allowed to become the norm.

2.7 Conclusion

As clearly stipulated in the introduction, this chapter aims mainly at gaining an understanding of the circumstances in which the working poor work and live. It is, in other words, encountering the poor people at the very spot where the majority of them work and earn their living – in the informal economy. The knowledge gained

217 Kristina Foldman Becker, The Informal Economy: Fact Finding Study, op. Cit., p. 10.

218 ILO, Decent work and the informal economy, op. cit., p. 31.

219 ILO, Conclusions concerning decent work and the informal economy, para. 14.

220 ILO, Decent work and the informal economy, op. cit., p. 32.

from this, it is believed, will be very crucial in further answering the question: Why are people poor despite the fact that they work? It will also be a useful guide in the concluding chapter in recommending policy actions to be taking to attain sustainable poverty alleviation.

We started by formulating a conceptual framework that includes defining what the informal economy is and what it is not. Informal economy was defined as all economic activities by workers and economic units that are – in law or in practice – not covered by formal arrangements. Their activities are not included in the law, which means that they are operating outside the formal reach of the law; or they are not covered in practice, which means that- although they are operating within the formal reach of the law, the law is not applied or not enforced; or the law discouraged compliance because it is inappropriate, burdensome, or imposes excessive costs (cf. 2.1.1 – 2.1.2).

Based on this definition, the informal economy was differentiated from (1) criminal economy that is associated with criminal business activities such drug trafficking, money laundry etc, (2) reproductive or care economy comprising unpaid domestic work and care activities that do not strictly speaking qualify as economic activities, and (3) micro and small-scale enterprises that are major constituents of the informal economy but not synonymous to it (cf. 1.2.3).

The informal economy comprises all business units and activities in the informal enterprises (informal sector) and all informal jobs in informal and formal enterprises (informal employment). People and activities in the informal economy as a whole therefore include: (a) Self-employment in informal enterprises – employers, own account operators, and unpaid family workers, (b) Wage employment in informal jobs – employees of informal enterprises and formal enterprises and other informal wage workers such as casual or day labourers, temporary workers, part-time workers, domestic wage workers etc (cf. 1.3.1).

The vulnerable and most disadvantaged groups in the informal economy include woman, young people, immigrants and people with disability. These are people who find it hard to enter the labour market and who suffer from various forms of discrimination and are more exposed to the vicissitudes of the labour market (cf. 1.3.1).

The size and contributions of the informal economy to the entire economy accord it a special significance in development matters. Its size ranges from as low as 25 per cent of total employment in the United States to as high as 72 per cent of non-agricultural employment in sub-Saharan Africa. Its share of new jobs in African is 93% and 83 in Latin American and in the Caribbean. The average share of the informal sector enterprise (i.e. not the informal economy, as a whole, but rather only the informal enterprises) in non-agricultural official GDP of developing countries ranges from a low of 27% in Northern Africa and 29% in Latin America to a high of 41% both in Sub-Saharan Africa and in Asia (cf. 1.4). A useful implication that can be drawn from these estimations is that the informal economy should not be neglected in a development issue such as poverty alleviation.

Taking a look at the conditions of work in the informal economy, we discovered that informal work is predominantly precarious and characterized by decent work deficits which includes, rights deficit – informal workers do not fully enjoy rights at work; employment deficit – informal workers are not gainfully employed; representational deficit – informal workers do not have voice; social protection deficit – informal workers are not enlisted in official social protection schemes (cf. 1.5).

Next, we tried to find out which factors are responsible for informality (the unfavourable labour condition in the informal economy) and its expansion. These factors basically include governance – weak legal and institutional frameworks; poor economic performance and non-pro-poor economic growth; and flexible specialization and global chains in production and labour (cf. 1.6).

Finally we looked at the links between poverty and informal economy and discovered that poverty makes people to enter the informal economy with the hope of earning a living. But instead of earning a decent living, the hard condition of work in the informal economy traps them in poverty (cf. 1.7). This permits us to close this chapter as follows: "The vast majority of the poor work, but only few are able to work their way out of poverty. This is because most of them are engaged in the informal economy, where they are likely to face (decent work deficits) lower incomes, greater financial risks, lower standards of human development and greater social exclusion compared to better-off workers, especially those who work in the formal economy."[221]

221 Martha Alter Chen et al, Mainstreaming Informal Employment and Gender in Poverty Reduction: A handbook for Policy-makers and Other Stakeholders, (London: Commonwealth Secretariat, 2004), p. 12.

CHAPTER THREE

Poverty and the Informal Economy in Nigeria

Introduction

In this chapter our focus shifts from poverty and informal economy in general to poverty and the informal economy in Nigeria. The first task would be to examine how and why poverty exists both among the working population and in the nation as a whole. This will warrant examining the political economic and social circumstances in the nation with a view to understanding how they have impacted on the human development and overall wellbeing in the nation. Thereafter, an in-depth consideration will be given to the informal economy where most of the poor in Nigeria work and earn their living. This is with a view to ascertaining how the prevailing socio-economic and political circumstances which determine the condition in which the poor work and live also affect the ability of the poor to use their labour (the most valuable if not the only asset they have) to contribute meaningfully to wealth creation, have a fair share of the increased availability of public and private resources and participate fully in the life of the society.

The relevance of the entire undertaking in this chapter is predicated on the conviction that the ability of a nation to keep itself and its citizens out of poverty depends squarely on its capability to use the resources it has to produce enough wealth to meet at least the basic needs of the entire population. Enough wealth can however be produced when the citizens of the nation are given the opportunity to develop their potentials and be able to use them productively to transform the available resources in the nation into wealth. This implies that wealth does not fall from heaven; the wealth of a nation is produced by the citizens. The first *Human Development Report* of the United Nations Development Programme (UNDP) expresses this in simple terms, "people are the real wealth of a nation".[222]

And so, in looking at the problem of poverty in Nigeria the important questions that should be asked are: How much wealth is produced in the country? How is it produced? How do prevailing social, political and economic circumstances in the nation affect the people's ability to participate in the creation of wealth and their chances of receiving a fair share of the wealth produce in the nation?

222 United Nations Development Programme (UNDP), Human Development Report 1990, (New York, Oxford: Oxford University Press, 1990), p, 9.

3.1 Poverty in Nigeria

3.1.1 An Overview: Paradox of Poverty in Wealth

Nigeria is endowed with enormous economic potentials. It has a vibrant private sector, highly motivated entrepreneurs, vast and fertile agricultural land, and a large domestic market. It is the seventh-largest oil exporter in the world (2 million barrels per day) and is richly endowed with other natural resources as well. Despite this rich endowment in human and natural resources, Nigeria's economic and social development remains far below the minimum expectations of the population.[223] The economy of the nation has failed to meet even the basic needs of the people. More than half the population lives in absolute poverty. The disparity between abundance of resources and the increasing poverty is a clear indication of a skewed distribution of Nigeria's wealth.[224] Experts refer to this ugly situation as the "paradox of plenty" or the "curse of oil."[225]

The country's economic and social indicators have slipped to well below the average for developing countries. Apart from having very low income, many Nigerians do not have access to the basic amenities of life such as food, shelter and clothing. They also lack access to medical facilities, electricity, water and other social services and physical infrastructure.[226] This state of deprivation results for many Nigerians in political powerlessness and exclusion from social life – a condition in which the poor do not belong to any organized group and cannot promote their course politically and influence governmental policies.[227] Social exclusion is therefore often perceived by the poor in Nigeria, among others, as a state of being unwelcome in a community and neighbourhood.[228]

The total poverty head count in Nigeria rose from 27.2 per cent in 1980 to 65.6 per cent in 1996, an annual average increase of 8.83 per cent in the 16-year period. It however declined between 1996 and 2004 by an annual average of 2.1per cent to

223 International Monetary Fund, Memorandum on Economic and Financial Policies of the Federal Government of Nigeria for 1999, available at: http://www.imf.org/external/np/loi/1999/022299.htm, accessed on 30.04.2011.

224 UNICEF-Nigeria, The Nigerian situation, accessed from: http://www.unicef.org/nigeria/1971_2199.html, accessed on 26.03.2009.

225 United States Library of Congress - Federal Research Division, Country Profile: Nigeria, July 2008, p. 10. A pdf document also available at: http://memory.loc.gov/frd/cs/profiles/Nigeria.pdf.

226 Cf. World Bank, Nigeria: Voice of the Poor – A Country Synthesis Report on Consultation with the Poor, 2000/2001.

227 Sani Lawal Malumfashi, The concept of poverty and its Dimensions, in: Mustapha C. Duze et al. (eds), Poverty in Nigeria: Causes Manifestations and Alleviation Strategies, (London: Adonis & Abbey Publishers Ltd, 2008), p, 6.

228 World Bank, Nigeria: Voice of the Poor, op cit., p. 22.

54.4 per cent.[229] It is believed that in 2008, about 54 percent of Nigeria's population were living on less than US$1 a day.[230]

The 2010 UNDP Human Development Index ranked Nigeria 15th among countries with low human development and 142nd among 169 nations of the world. The human poverty index value was estimated at 0.423, the life expectance at birth at 48 years, and the gross national income (GNI) per capita (PPP 2008 $) at 2,156. Nigeria's low ranking which has been the trend for decades clearly shows how backward Nigeria has been in terms of the volume of wealth produced in the land and in terms of human development.

Available facts on two important indicators of poverty – education, and occupation – reveal the following: (i) The higher the educational attainment, the lower the incidence of poverty.[231] Those without education account for most of the poor and an overwhelmingly large fraction of people in absolute poverty.[232] (ii) Households whose heads are farmers have the highest likelihood of being poor.[233] But as we would see later, it is not only farmers that run the risk of being poor but also many other informal workers whose jobs are less productive and rewarding in terms of remuneration and general welfare.

Nigeria has indeed a high incidence of working poverty. According to Nomaan Majid, Nigeria had, as at 1986, a working poor estimation of 49.1 per cent of the nation's working population. In 1997, this figure rose to 72.4 per cent of the nation's entire working population. Nigeria is further said to have a 6.38 working poor annual growth and a 3.59 working poverty rate annual growth.[234] Later estimations revealed that the population of the working poor in Nigeria living under US$1.25 a day has grown to 64.4 per cent and that of those living under US$2 to about 83.9 per cent of the nation's entire working population.[235] However, going by the most recent estimations, the share of the working poor of the total employment for US$1.25 stands at 57.3% and at US$2 the share stands at 78.2.[236]

---

229 United Nations Development Programme (UNDP), Human Development Report Nigeria 2008 – 2009 Achieving growth with equity, (Abuja, Nigeria: Development Programme, Nigeria, 2009), p. 12.

230 United States Library of Congress - Federal Research Division, Country Profile: Nigeria, op. cit., p. 12..

231 United Nations Development Programme (UNDP), Human Development Report Nigeria 2008 – 2009, op. cit., p. 66.

232 World Bank, Nigeria Poverty in the Midst of Plenty: The Challenge of Growth with Inclusion: A World Bank Poverty Assessment, (World Bank, Population and Human Resources Division Western Africa Department Africa Region, 1996), para. 29.

233 United Nations Development Programme (UNDP), Human Development Report Nigeria 2008 – 2009, op. cit., p. 66.

234 Cf. Nomaan Majid, The size of the working poor population in developing countries, an Employment Paper 2001/16 for the employment sector of the Employment Strategy Department, (Geneva: International Labour Office, 2001).

235 Cf. ILO, Key Indicators of the Labour Market: Poverty, working poverty and income distribution KILM 20

236 ILO, Key Indicator of Labour Market: Working Poverty, Table 20b, Working poverty (national estimates): For more on these data, please visit: http://kilm.ilo.org/KILMnetBeta/default2.asp.

3.1.2 Causes of Poverty in Nigeria

For the purpose of constituency, the treatment of the major causes of poverty in Nigeria will be limited to the examination of some important political, social and economic factors.

3.1.2.1 Political and Administrative Factors

Nigeria, Africa's most populous country with an estimated population of 140 million, is located in the Western part of Africa, bordered by Republic of Benin to the west, Republic of Niger to the north, the Republic of Cameroon to the east and the Atlantic Ocean. The nation's terrain varies from coastal swamps and tropical forest in the south, to savannah and semi-desert in the north. The Jos Plateau in the centre and the mountains along the eastern border are the highest points in the country. The River Niger, the third longest river in Africa, reaches the sea through an extensive Delta of mangrove swamps. Another important river is the River Benue. Nigeria has a total area of 923,768 sq. km and overall population density in 2006 was about 139 people per square kilometre.[237]

Nigeria attained the status of an independent country within the Commonwealth on October 1. 1960. The post-colonial politics in Nigeria was dominated by prolonged brutal military rule. In fact, more than half of Nigeria's over fifty years of independence was spent under military dictatorship. It is therefore no exaggeration to say that much of "the nation's leadership in the several decades following independence was determined by coup, not by election, and by military, rather than civilian, government."[238] It is on record that compared with other African countries, Nigeria, since its independence, has witnessed more violent changes in government that saw the emergence of leaders who obviously did not have the interest of the nation at heart. Describing these leaders as a wasted generation, John Odey writes:

> A generation of military leaders who had no respect for the law and the constitutional provision of the land, who flouted court orders with impunity, installed the reign of anarchy and baptized it into a culture with insane decrees, set up their own parallel organization in the name of task force with the aim of intimidating, molesting and cowing innocent citizens to submission, is a waste generation.[239]

The first military coup plunged the entire nation into a thirty-month civil war that spanned from July 1967 to January 1970. In the period after the war, Nigeria still witnessed other violent military takeovers. The nearly thirty years of military dictatorship have robbed the nation the opportunity of fully developing its potential and denied the citizens their political rights and compromised the respect for

---

237 Cf. United States Library of Congress - Federal Research Division, Country Profile, op. cit. p. 16.

238 Ibid., p. 4.

239 John Okwoeze Odey, The Parable of a Wasted Generation, (Enugu: Snaap Press, 2000), p. 51.

human rights and the development of the human person. Much of the nations resources were plundered and mismanaged during this period.[240]

Years of military rule, with fiscal neglect and mismanagement have indeed contributed in no small measure to the high incidence of poverty in Nigeria. George Ehusani sums up the wider effects of bad military leaders on the development of the Nigerian people as follows:

> The majority of Nigerians have been stripped naked by corrupt, selfish, greedy and callous elite.... The majority of Nigerians have suffered untold hardship at the hands of a succession and despotic rulers, decadent administrators, visionless leaders and reckless managers. They have been humiliated, pauperized and reduces to a state of destitution by the combined forces of military dictatorship, political subterfuge and economic profligacy. Nigerians have lost their individual and collective pride to the excesses of indigenous conquerors who seem to recognise no order except that established by mammon.[241]

Today, Nigeria is a democratic federal republic with a presidential system of government. The current constitution which is modelled after the United States constitution provides for a separation of powers among executive, an elected legislature, and an independent judiciary. Executive power is vested in the president, who is simultaneously chief of state and head of government.[242]

Nigeria is divided administratively into the Federal Capital Territory (Abuja) and 36 states, which are grouped into six geo-political zones: Each state is governed by an elected governor and a House of Assembly. The number of delegates to the House of Assembly is based on population (three to four times the number of delegates each state sends to the federal House of Representatives) and therefore varies from state to state within the range of 24 to 40. The 36 states are further divided into 774 local government areas. Each Local government is governed by a council headed by an elected chairman and his chancellors.[243]

Despite the enthronement of democracy in the nation, Nigeria has continued to experience enormous political challenges. The political situation in the nation continues to reflect "institutional fragility and some fundamental weaknesses in the management of resources and governance (both economic and political). According to Richard Joseph[244]: No one will describe Nigeria, in large part, as a well-governed country, or contend that the way in which many public institutions are administered – which is essentially what governance means – contributes positively to its

---

240 Sofo C.A. Ali-Akpajiak and Toni Pyke, Measuring Poverty in Nigeria, (Oxford: Oxfam GB, 2003), p. 2.

241 George Omaku Ehusani, A Prophetic Church, (Ede: Provincial Pastoral Institute Publication, 1996), p. 7.

242 Cf. United States Library of Congress - Federal Research Division, Country Profile: Nigeria, op. cit., p. 17.

243 Ibid., p. 18.

244 Richard Joseph is John Evans Professor of International History and Politics at Northwestern University. Former fellow of The Carter Centre, Atlanta, he focuses on African governance, political economy, and democratization. He is quite familiar with the political, social and economic trends in Nigeria having conducted extensive researches in the country.

development.[245] These weaknesses in governance inhibit the effectiveness of distributional policies and mechanisms while promoting rent-seeking behaviours and corruption."[246]

Nigeria has been having difficulties coping with coordination in governance. The federalism which the nation adopted is yet to find a firm footing due to lack of a strong framework for the intergovernmental cooperation, which is essential, if not inevitable, for coordinating the overlapping economic and political responsibilities among tiers of government and channelling efforts towards achieving the goals of human development.

The current political situation in the country exhibits many deficiencies in public bureaucracy. Many organs of government still find it difficult to effectively discharge their statutory mandates. The ineffectiveness of those of them that are supposed to regulate private sector firms has given room for the breach of standards to become the norm rather than the exception. Cumbersome processes and transactions have been introduced in some crucial areas such as obtaining legal title to property, starting a business, enforcing contracts. All of these have contributed to the absence of a favourable business environment in the nation.[247] Consequently, Nigeria's rating in "Doing Business Indicators" has remained unimpressive. The situation continues to deteriorate with every passing year. Going by the ranking of the World Bank, Nigeria slipped from 134 in 2010 to 137 in 2011. The indicators put into consideration in the rating include, starting a business, dealing with construction permit, registering business, getting credit, protecting investor, paying tax, trading across borders enforcing contracts and closing a business.[248] Bad leadership, a high rate of corruption and infrastructural gap in the nation are undoubtedly responsible for the bad rating Nigeria as a nation has received.

Deficiencies also exist in the area of distribution of revenues and fiscal functions among the different levels of government – federal, state and local governments. Apparently some jurisdictions are saddled with some responsibilities they do not have the resources to handle. This, according to K.S. Adeyemi, "explains why the major commercial centre of the country, Lagos, is decaying with adverse consequences for the cost of doing business and the image of Nigeria as an investment destination."[249]

---

245 Richard Joseph, Economic Transformation and Developmental Governance in Nigeria: The Promise of the Obama Era, Paper present at the Inaugural BusinessDay Scholars in Society Forum in Lagos, Nigeria in May 2909.

246 United Nations Development Programme (UNDP), Human Development Report Nigeria 2008 – 2009, op. cit., p. 13.

247 K.S. Adeyemi, Economic Policy reform in Nigeria: Achievements and Challenges, an unpublished paper, accessible at: http://www.valuefronteira.com/vf/images/UnionBank/economic%20policy%20reforms%20in%20nigeria.pdf.

248 See the World Bank's Doing Business website and online database: www.doingbusiness.org.

249 K.S. Adeyemi, Economic Policy reform in Nigeria: Achievements and Challenges, op. cit.

The consolidated revenue is so shared that the 36 states, the Federal Capital Territory as well as 774 local governments receive about 45 per cent of consolidated revenue while the federal government controls the rest. However, the federal government does not have statutory powers to control the sub-national governments for the purposes of macro stabilization. Apart from this, areas such as primary and secondary education, primary and secondary healthcare services, rural roads and infrastructure, water and sanitation and community services, with direct implications for human development, are assigned to these lower tiers of government in Nigeria. The federal government is nevertheless expected to provide services in some of the areas where the sub-national governments have responsibilities. This has often given rise to conflict, wastes and inefficiencies therefore highlighting the need to adopt a cooperative approach to governance that will ensure the adequate provision of physical infrastructure and social services and the attainment of the goals of human development in the nation.[250]

3.1.2.2 Socio-economic Factors

The arching problem of governance which has contributed to the incidence of poverty in Nigeria reflects itself further in the poor provision of physical infrastructure and social and financial services which in turn impacts negatively on the general level and wellbeing in the nation. There is no doubt that the level of development, the quantity of wealth, the ability of the people to participate meaningfully in the creation and distribution of wealth and the overall wellbeing in a nation are conditioned by the availability, accessibility and quality of physical infrastructure and social and financial services (power supply, transport, communication, education, health care, social welfare scheme, credit facilities) in the nation. The ability to check the rate of poverty incidence in a nation depends therefore on the creative interplay and effective management of these sectors of the economy. The high incidence of poverty in Nigeria has consequently been partly attributed to poor attitude and low expenditure by the government on these sectors.[251] Closely related to these socio-economic problems are those of corruption social inequality and bad patterns of economic development in the nation.

3.1.2.2.1 Physical Infrastructure

Nigeria is indeed a nation with a wide infrastructural gap. The major infrastructural gap has been in areas such as power, road and rail transportation, and information technology. Decades of underdevelopment have resulted in the deterioration of public infrastructure in the country, thereby imposing large transaction costs on businesses and reducing the competitiveness of the Nigerian private sector. Currently, the nation ranks poorly on several indicators of infrastructural access,

250 United Nations Development Programme (UNDP), Human Development Report Nigeria 2008 – 2009, op. cit., p. 103.

251 For a comparative and tabular illustration of these points see: Ngozi Okonjo-Iweala and Philip Osafo-Kwaako, Nigeria's Economic Reforms: Progress and Challenges, a working paper, (Washington, DC: The Brookings Institution, 2007), table 2, p. 6.

cost and quality. Not only are the road and rail networks small, about 50 per cent of the federal roads is perennially in poor condition and rail enjoys only about 5 per cent of the freight market.[252]

With regard to energy, the current installed power generation capacity of 6,000 mw and the available energy output of 3,000 mw is nothing but a far cry from the actual demand for power in the nation estimated at above 10,000 mw.[253] A moderate comparison further shows how critical the problem in Nigeria's power and energy sector is. Per capita power consumption in Nigeria was estimated at 82 kilowatts (kW) compared with an average of 456kW in other sub-Saharan African countries and 3,793kW in South Africa.[254] This accounts for constant power outage and load shedding in the nation. A situation like this obviously renders the investment environment highly unpredictable. It was recently reported that the Governor of the Central Bank of Nigeria, Sanusi Lamido Sanusi, disclosed that bankers often shy away from granting loans to both the agriculture and manufacturing sectors in Nigeria because of the inadequate and epileptic power supply by Power Holding Company of Nigeria (PHCN), the municipal electricity company of the nation. The bankers, it was further revealed, expressed fear that the loans that they would have advanced to businessmen would likely end up as non-performing loans because PHCN was not performing optimally.[255]

An infrastructural gap as a result of deficiency in governance is also noticeable in the area of information and communication technology ICT. The telecommunications sector has indeed been poorly developed. Costs of installation and tariff structure are also very high. Computer penetration remains low. Access and use of internet are limited to a few privileged people who are mainly in the urban centres. The loss to the economy has been quite enormous, since the nation is denied the full benefits of ICT.[256] The citizenry especially the poor are also denied access to information and thus limited in their ability to develop their potential sources of livelihood.[257]

In sum, the general infrastructural gap in Nigeria has crippled corporative investment in the nation, especially as companies are forced to generate their own power and provide their own infrastructure. This has undoubtedly imposed

---

252 Ibid

253 United Nations Development Programme (UNDP), Human Development Report Nigeria 2008 – 2009, op. cit., p. 15.

254 Ngozi Okonjo-Iweala and Philip Osafo-Kwaako, Nigeria's Economic Reforms: Progress and Challenges, op. cit., p. 5.

255 Daily Independent (Lagos), Nigeria: Giving Fillip to Agric Sector, 15 March, 2011.

256 Cf. United Nations Systems, Nigeria: common Country Assessment, (Abuja: United Nations Systems, 2001).

257 Sofo C.A. Ali-Akpajiak and Toni Pyke, Measuring Poverty in Nigeria, op. cit., p. 64.

significant extra costs on businesses and reduced their competitiveness in an increasingly global market[258]

3.1.2.2.2 Financial Services

Financial services in Nigeria have also been rated poor. The poor and low income segments of the population are reportedly underserved with financial services. They often lack access to credit, which makes it difficult for them to start a business or expand one. It is also noted that a large share of savings is not channelled into productive investments in Nigeria. Banks are generally reluctant in providing credit to firms in the real sector, especially the business units owned by the poor. Weak financial intermediation[259] capacity in the nation has also undoubtedly hindered investment as firms especially Small and Medium Enterprises which provide work to greater percentage of the working population have been forced to rely on expensive alternative private sources of finance.[260] This of course has grievous repercussions for productivity and earnings in the affected segments of the economy.

3.1.2.2.3 Social Services

The situation is not different in the area of social services. Nigeria's education system has been in shambles, with high pupils-to-teacher ratios and poorly furnished classrooms. The deficiency in the education system which reflects itself more concretely in Nigeria's poor performance in literary and school-enrolment indicators is viewed by many observers as a major obstacle in the development of the people, especially with regard to labour mobility. An important causal factor of the problem of education in Nigeria is the inadequate budgetary allocation it receives compared to other sectors.[261]

Progress in improving the quality and standard of education in the country has also been hampered by problems such as lack of adequate and qualified manpower, poor environments of learning and overcrowding, lack of teaching and learning materials, illegal fees in most educational institutions, poorly designed curricular, weak machineries for supervision, absence of infrastructural facilities, recurrent strikes by teachers and lecturers who often demand regular payment and increment in salaries and better treatments, etc.[262] These problems do not only hamper performance they also make education inaccessible und too expensive especially for the poor people in Nigeria.

---

258 United Nations Development Programme (UNDP), Human Development Report Nigeria 2008 – 2009, op. cit., p. 37.

259 Financial intermediation is a means of facilitating the channelling of funds between lenders and borrowers. Through this process, funds are transferred from people who have deposited their excess funds (savers) to those who need more money for their business transactions (borrowers)

260 United Nations Development Programme (UNDP), Human Development Report Nigeria 2008 – 2009, op. cit., p. 19.

261 Sofo C.A. Ali-Akpajiak and Toni Pyke, Measuring Poverty in Nigeria, op. cit., p. 19.

262 Ibid., p. 18.

Nigeria's health care has also deteriorated over the last few decades due to neglect, poor funding and leadership.[263] Also contributing to the decline in the health sector is the collapse of institutional capacity as a result of the continuous migration of Nigeria's qualified professional to other nations that offer better remuneration for their services and also the poor motivations of those who decide to remain in the country.[264] In terms of access to safe water and sanitation, only 40 per cent of Nigeria's population reportedly have access to either portable water or sanitation. The situation is however critical in the rural areas.[265] All of these have resulted in poor health care delivery, rendering public-health care services inaccessible and too expensive for most of the poor. In fact, no nation with such a poor health record can produce enough wealth to keep itself and its citizens out of poverty. For an unhealthy nation is an 'unwealthy' nation. People certainly need to be healthy in mind and body in order to produce wealth for the community in which they live.

Provision of Social Security services is another area of social development gap in Nigeria. It is a well known fact that Nigeria does not have any form of State social security system.[266] What this implies is that the Nigerian government, either alone or in collaboration with non-governmental organizations (NGOs), is yet to put in place a programme that seeks to provide a guaranteed minimum level of income or other forms of support for the population of the country as a whole, or for specific groups, such as the poor, unemployed, underemployed, elderly and disabled people.[267] Less than 1 percent of the population older than sixty years received pensions. In rural areas, older people are customarily catered for by their children, grandchildren, spouses and siblings. There is however the feeling that this traditional practice of caring for parents is beginning to erode under harsh conditions of scarcity and shrinking resources in urban areas.[268]

Having felt the need for a social security policy to combat poverty in the nation, the Yar'Adua government set up in 2009 a National Working Committee on Social Security Policy for Nigeria. The committee headed by former Head of State, General Yakubu Gowon was charged with the responsibility of making recommendations for the implementation of a social security system with a view to combating poverty in the nation. Four months after its inauguration, the committee presented its recommendations. The honourable Minister of Labour, who received the report on behalf of the President, promised a speedy implementation of the recommendations. He reiterated the desire of the Yar'Adua's government to

263 Cf. Anthony Hodges, Children's and Women's Rights in Nigeria: A Wake-up Call, Situation Assessment and Analysis, (Lagos: UNICEF/National Planning Commission, 2001).

264 Ibid.

265 Sofo C.A. Ali-Akpajiak and Toni Pyke, Measuring Poverty in Nigeria, op. cit., p. 14.

266 Cf. Helen Chapin Metz, ed. Nigeria: A Country Study. Washington: GPO for the Library of Congress, 1991. http://countrystudies.us/nigeria/51.htm.

267 Louis I. Okoroma, Nigeria: Mass Suffering - Will Social Security End It? Leadership (Abuja), 30 August, 2009, available at http://allafrica.com/stories/printable/200908311201.html.

268 Cf. Helen Chapin Metz, ed. Nigeria: A Country Study, op. cit.

provide a system that will safeguard the welfare of the people, noting that the essence of government is to provide security and welfare for its citizens. This strong assurance was conveyed with the following words: "I want to assure you, even though it took us 49 years to do it, and it took the committee four months to put the policy together, the government will implement it and this will be done in four months".[269] Four months have however come and gone and nothing concrete has been done.

Furthermore, while Nigerians await the new social security system promised by the government, scepticism has been expressed from different quarters about the feasibility of such a programme. The doubts are not unconnected with the harsh socio-economic realities in the nation – the high level of unemployment and underemployment in the country, corruption, illiteracy, infrastructural gap, low production capacity, to mention but a few. It was reported, for example, that the National Chairman of one of the political parties, the National Action Council (NAC), Dr. Olopade Agoro, opposed the calls for social security in the country on the grounds that the country is not ripe for it and that the state of the Nigerian economy cannot sustain a social security system. Agoro further argued that for any country to put in place a successful national social security system there must be employment opportunities for the citizens. In his words, "You cannot put social security in a country where about ninety percent of the population are unemployed. It is achievable if the leadership of the country establish working industries that will ensure employment for the citizens."[270] Against this backdrop, Agoro insisted that the best social security that government can put in place is to reduce the widening gap between the rich and the poor by balancing the disparity in lifestyles, income and expenses of the poor and the rich to make the domestic situation conducive for social security.[271]

Honourable Sunny Moniedafe, a member of an opposition party, though not opposed to the need for a social security system, however pointed out that the government must first address some basic problems such as the absence of a good database of the number of the poor and underprivileged as well as a reliable population statistics and census result.[272]

No matter how one would like to look at the issue, one obvious point is that the absence of a social security system has a strong implication for the pervasiveness of poverty in the nation. There is no way a nation like Nigeria with the harsh socio-economic environment already mentioned in this chapter can afford to keep itself and its citizens out of abject poverty if it does not pay proper attention to the welfare and well being of its citizens.

Nigeria has however a functioning pension scheme which has undergone series of reforms. Crushed under the weight of poor administration, inadequate funding,

---

269 Louis I. Okoroma, Nigeria: Mass Suffering - Will Social Security End It? op. cit.

270 Ibid.

271 Ibid.

272 Ibid.

and fraud, the old scheme that was introduced in 1994 was abolished and in June 25, 2004, a new social insurance system based on the defined contribution approach came into existence. This was in accordance with the Pension Reform Act of 2004. The new system, which is managed by the National Pension Commission, requires members of the military to contribute 2.5 percent of their wages and the military to contribute 12.5 percent on their behalf, while public- and private-sector workers and their employers contribute each 7.5 percent.[273] There is however no mechanism put in place to insure that this scheme is properly extended to the many workers outside the formal employment in the public and private sectors.

3.1.2.2.4 Social Inequality and Income Gap

Inequality is another social problem closely associated with poverty in Nigeria. Concerns about inequality have been strong in Nigeria. Its prevalence has indeed been very high. Inequality in Nigeria implies that opportunities for upward mobility are very limited; it means few decent jobs, poor income and low purchasing power for workers; it also means poor infrastructure and institutional failure in key sectors, including education, health and transportation.[274]

Available studies show that despite its vast resources, Nigeria continues to rank among the most unequal countries in the world. Between 1985 and 2004, inequality in Nigeria worsened from 0.43 to 0.49, placing the country among those with the highest inequality levels in the world. The high incidence of inequality also reflects widening income gap and access to economic and social opportunities between genders; growing inequality between and within rural and urban populations; and widening gaps between the federating units' economies.[275]

The wide income gap or inequality in wages and salaries in Nigeria is a moral issue that has a direct implication for poverty in the nation. Of particular importance is the problem of minimum wage that lingers on in public discussions without any clear solution in view. Although, there was an agreement in 2000 between President Olusegun Obasanjo and the labour unions for a minimum pay of N7,500 for employees of the federal government, constitutionally, the national minimum wage remained N5,500.00 per month. The Nigerian Labour congress described as a 'scandalous inequality', this situation in which the minimum wage constitutionally remains N5,500 while, for instance, a Permanent Secretary or a Chief Executive of a parastatal who are political appointees receives as and when due the sum of ₦1,348,105.50 as monthly pay.[276]

Recently, the federal government approved an upward review of the national minimum wage from N5,500 in 2000 to N18,000 (an equivalent of about US$120)

---

273 United States Library of Congress - Federal Research Division, Country Profile: Nigeria, op. cit., p. 10.

274 United Nations Development Programme (UNDP), Human Development Report Nigeria 2008 – 2009, op. cit., p. 17.

275 Ibid., p. 11.

276 Nigerian Labour Congress, Economic Crises and Credible Electoral Reforms: Mobilizing for Positive Change, 2009 May Day Speech by Nigerian Labour Congress.

which is a far cry from the N52.200[277] demanded by organized labour. Against this backdrop, the so-called new minimum wage has been described as nothing but a 'starvation wage', given the prevailing harsh economic realities.[278]

The state governments have however shown a dogged attitude towards the implementation of this new minimum wage, thereby making the hope of the poor for a just wage for their labour even dimmer. This blatant refusal by the State Governments to implement with immediate effect the new minimum wage has been viewed by the Nigerian Labour Congress as sheer neglect of the workers' welfare.[279]

Even when the new minimum wage is fully implemented, its impact with regard to reducing income gap in the nation will be very minimal as there are obvious indications that it will not be applicable to all workers and not mandatory for all employers of labour. A spokesman of the president of Nigeria was reported to have confirmed this in an exclusive newspaper interview when he said: "Any organization, whether private or public, that employs more than 50 persons will be compelled to pay the N18, 000 minimum wage; and everybody - all the relevant agencies, would have to be prepared."[280] This means in essence that the many workers in the small and medium enterprises will not benefit from the new salary package, since these business units do not normally engage up to fifty workers.

The high incidence of inequality in Nigeria is indeed a clear manifestation of structural injustice that emanates from deficiencies in governance in general but particularly an absence of sound redistribution policies.[281] Nigeria has indeed for a long time condoned a systemic structure of inequity. It is only such a structure, it is argued, that can permit just 20 per cent of the population to possess 65 per cent of national assets while as much as 70 per cent of the same population languish in different degrees of poverty.[282]

3.1.2.2.5 Corruption

Another pointer to structure injustice and social decadence in Nigeria is the prevalence of corruption which has continued to drain the wealth of the nation and generate poverty. Corruption is often related to non-transparency, misappropriation of public funds, wasteful public investment, lower government revenues, and lower quality of public infrastructure. Nigeria has for many years been counted among the

---

277 For details on how this amount was arrived at, please see. Nigeria Labour Congress, Demand for the Review of the National Minimum Wage and General Wage, 2009: This document is also available at: http://www.nlcng.org/minimum%20wage.pdf.

278 Nigerian Labour Congress, Press Conference on the New National Minimum Wage Addressed by the President of the Nigeria Labour Congress, Comrade Abdulwahed I. Omar after the Meeting of the Central Working Committee of Congress at the Main Auditorium of Labour House on Friday January 14, 2011.

279 Nigeria Labour Congress, Policy Document, available at: http://www.nlcng.org/policydoc.pdf.

280 See "Leadership" of Wednesday, 30 March 2011.

281 United Nations Development Programme (UNDP), Human Development Report Nigeria 2008 – 2009, op. cit., pp. 11-12.

282 Ibid., p. 47.

most corrupt nations of the world. The 2010 Transparency International Corruption Perception Index ranked Nigeria 134th among the nations of the world. Compared with the rankings of the previous year in which Nigeria occupied the 130th position, it becomes clear that the rate of corruption in the nation is on the increase.

Nigeria generates a reasonable amount of wealth from oil. Unfortunately, instead of being invested in furthering economic and human development in the nation and in provision and improvement of physical infrastructure and social services, the oil wealth has rather been squandered, mismanaged and stolen by a corrupt few who have "infected the moral fabric of the society, contributing to group rivalries and a loss of national direction"[283] Not only has corruption underdeveloped Nigeria, it has obviously, in more specific terms, contributed to the misallocation and mismanagement of scarce resources, increasing costs and deterring private investment. It also limits the growth potentials of the country and, more importantly, initiatives against poverty and inequality. Added to this is the negative impact it has on the administration of justice and enforcement of laws in the nation.[284]

Over the years, many practical steps (legal, institutional and administrative) have been taken to curtail this unwholesome behaviour, and to improve the image of Nigeria. Among the institutional bodies established to tackle the problem of corruption and economic and financial crimes are: War against Indiscipline (WAI), Independent Corrupt Practices and other related Offences Commission (ICPC) and Economic and Financial Crimes Commission (EFCC). The enormity of this problem seems however to be overwhelming for these established bodies, as they seem to have achieved only but insignificant results. Their low performance has been partly due to their inability to win the confidence and the much needed collaboration of international security agencies in tracing bank lodgements and investments abroad by corrupt Nigerians and also partly due to manipulations by political actors

3.1.2.2.6 Bad Patterns of Economic Development

The assessment of the structure and performance of Nigeria's economy and the patterns of economic development in the nation is definitely essential for understanding why poverty remains pervasive in the country, since they natural have strong implications for how much wealth a nation can produce and for the ability of the poor to participate in wealth generation and to have a fair share of available resources.

After more than 20 years of poor governance and weak economic growth, the civilian government of President Obasanjo installed in 1999 embarked on some reforms programmes aimed at ensuring political stability, strengthening democratic practices, and tackling corruption. The government adopted a comprehensive

283 Cf. Anthony Hodges, Children's and Women's Rights in Nigeria: A Wake-up Call, op. cit..

284 United Nations Development Programme (UNDP), Human Development Report Nigeria 2008 – 2009, op. cit., p. 105.

economic reform programme by which the nation vowed to commit itself to a "market-oriented, private sector-led economy with government serving as a catalyst and providing the enabling environment for the private sector to thrive".[285]

As a result of these reforms put in motion, the economy has recorded some appreciable improvement in recent years. The non-oil sector reportedly grew at a rate of 8.6 percent in 2005 and reached 9.6 percent in 2007. Average Inflation rate fell to 5.2 percent in 2007 as against 17.8 percent in 2005. The nation's international reserves reached about US$51 billion by the end of 2007. A federal Fiscal Responsibility Bill, a Public Procurement Bill passed into law, and a Bank consolidation programme implemented 2004/2005 boosted the financial sector and enhanced its ability to provide credit to the private sector. The gains of the reforms reflected also on the capital market, such that Nigeria is reckoned with today as a nation that has one of the most active stock markets in the world. All this has resulted in relative economic stability in the nation. While an average of about 6.0 per cent of the real gross domestic product (GDP) was recorded, per capita income rose steadily, crossing the $1,000 mark in 2006. Since then, growth performance has improved steadily until the recent global economic crises set in.[286] Progress was also made in the area of debt management and the budget preparation process. This has reportedly resulted in substantial decline of public debt from about 74.8 percent of GDP in 2003 to about 14.2 percent in 2006, mainly because of a successful debt relief agreement with the Paris Club.[287]

Despite these remarkable achievements made in recent time, the economy of the nation still faces significant challenges, particularly in translating the benefits of reforms into welfare improvements for citizens, and in extending reform policies to states and local governments.[288] There are also worries about the nation's pattern of economic development or growth, pattern of trade and employment generation.

Growth in GDP is yet to translate into overall improvement in the economy of Nigeria. Human development has remained unimpressive and employment situation critical.[289] Put differently, growth in the nation has not been pro-poor. This is partly due to deficiencies in the system of wealth distribution in the nation that favours only a few privileged people and partly due to the bad pattern of economic development adopted by Nigeria over the years.

Nigerian's economy has been dangerously dependent on the oil sector which ironically provides employment for only about 1 per cent of the total population. For this reason, Nigeria has been described as a nation that has a narrow

---

285 World trade Organization, Trade Policy Review: Report by Nigeria, op. cit., p. 12.

286 United Nations Development Programme (UNDP), Human Development Report Nigeria 2008 – 2009, op. cit., p. 30: See also: World Bank, Nigeria: Country Brief, at: http://web.worldbank.org/WBSITE/EXTERNAL/COUNTRIES/AFRICAEXT/NIGERIAEXTN/0,,menuPK:368906~pagePK:141132~piPK:141107~theSitePK:368896,00.html, @ 24.03.2011.

287 Ngozi Okonjo-Iweala and Philip Osafo-Kwaako, Nigeria's Economic Reforms: Progress and Challenges, op. cit., p. 10.

288 Ibid., p. 7.

289 World Bank, Nigeria: Country Brief, op. cit.

disarticulated, mono-cultural production base, characterized by a degraded environment and the predominance of subsistence and commercial activities.[290] Crude oil and gas account for about 95 per cent of the foreign earnings and over 80 per cent of the federal budget, the bulk of which is spent on civil service salaries.[291]

This over dependence on oil has been responsible for the failure of the Government to initiate appropriate policies, provide adequate funds and create the enabling environment that will ensure the exploration of the nation's rich minerals such as lignite, iron ore, gold, tack, bitumen, kaolin, barites, gypsum, tin, and coal.[292] Furthermore, over-reliance on oil has weakened interest and investment in other vibrant sectors of the economy especially the real economy, including agriculture which accounts for 70 percent of the entire employment in the nation. Consequently agriculture has become unattractive to Nigerian youths who now migrate to the cities in search of work in other sectors of the economy.[293] Manufacturing, which could gradually displace agriculture, has continued to lose its share of GDP instead. From 6 per cent in 1985, its share in overall GDP declined to a range of between 5 and 4 per cent during 1990-2007.[294] Also neglected over the year are the small and micro-enterprises (SMEs). These enterprises, it is however argued, are the main drivers of the economy and are believed to have the capacity to provide job opportunities that can meet the current demand in the labour market if given the necessary attention. In an interview granted to one of the leading national newspapers, Eric Idogun, a public administrator involved in the oil servicing sector, corroborated this view by arguing that the strength of any economy lies in the value of its small and medium scale industries as this guarantees national growth, thereby bringing down inflation. He therefore noted that one of the primary reasons for the high level of unemployment in Nigeria is the absence of viable small and medium scale enterprises.[295]

The pattern and trend of external trade also reflects Nigeria's over-dependence on oil which creates distortion in the economy and renders the economy highly vulnerable to external shocks as a result of which balance-of-payments have been very poor.[296] Facts on the composition of trade reveal that the non-oil exports are remarkably low.[297] This has a strong implication for poverty in a nation, where, as indicated above, the oil sector accounts for only one per cent of total employment.

---

290 Nigerian Democratic Health Survey 1999, as cited by: Sofo C.A. Ali-Akpajiak and Toni Pyke, Measuring Poverty in Nigeria, (Oxford: Oxfam GB, 2003), p. 27.

291 United Nations Development Programme (UNDP), Human Development Report Nigeria 2008 – 2009, op cit., p. 35.

292 Sofo C.A. Ali-Akpajiak and Toni Pyke, Measuring Poverty in Nigeria, op. cit., p. 28.

293 United Nations Development Programme (UNDP), Human Development Report Nigeria 2008 – 2009, op. cit., p. 37.

294 Ibid., p. 36.

295 Eric Idogun, Nigeria: 'Small Scale Enterprises Can Drive the Economy', an interview granted to "Vanguard" on 26 March 2011. The proceedings of the interview were put together by Gab Ejuwa.

296 Sofo C.A. Ali-Akpajiak and Toni Pyke, Measuring Poverty in Nigeria, op. cit., p. 29.

297 Cf. ibid., pp- 37-38.

In addition to this, Nigeria has for many years operated a complex, restrictive, and opaque trade regime. Ad hoc import prohibitions and tariff revisions often under domestic pressures in the nation has reduced the transparency and predictability of the tariff regime as, for instance, tariffs applied at ports could differ from published tariffs.[298]

Although Nigeria with its estimated population of 140 million and rich natural resources possesses great potential in the global market, the nation has unfortunately suffered serious setbacks in its effort at integrating its domestic economy into the world economy. This has been mainly due to its infrastructural weakness, inadequacy in technical manpower and again over-dependency of the economy on oil sector. Other factors responsible for the nation's poor integration and low competitiveness in global markets are the failure to inculcate financial prudence, the absence of favourable legal and policy environment for enterprise and investment, low technological development, and inadequate provision of physical infrastructure and financial and social services.[299] These shortcomings have had far-reaching consequences for both the economic and human development in the nation. Indeed Nigeria has been marginalized from full participation in global markets and thus its efforts to check high incidence and pervasiveness of poverty has been compromised.[300]

Furthermore, in implementing the trade liberalization that accompanied globalization, Nigeria has however continued to expose its local markets to external competition without first creating the enabling environment for a fair and just competition. This of course has had devastating consequences for local consumption and the development of local industry. For example, the excessive exposure of local manufacturers who depended mainly on traditional means of production to high technological capability of foreign competitor has eventually cost Nigeria her local industry.[301]

With regard to macroeconomic stability, the result has been rather disappointing. Nigeria has continued to witness high levels of macroeconomic instability that has in effect hampered both growth and socio-economic development in the nation, leading thereby to the deterioration of general wellbeing in the nation. No economy can flourish in the midst of macroeconomic instability. This is because large fluctuations in the price level, the exchange rate, the interest rate, or the tax burden serve as a major deterrent to private investment, the proximate driver of growth. In recognition of this, efforts were made to tackle the main source of macroeconomic instability in the economy through the oil price

298 Ngozi Okonjo-Iweala and Philip Osafo-Kwaako, Nigeria's Economic Reforms: Progress and Challenges, op. cit., p. 16.

299 Cf. United Nations Development Programme, UNDP Nigeria 2000/2001 Human Development Report Millennium Edition, (Lagos: UNDP, 2001), especially pp. 13, 14, and 21.

300 Sofo C.A. Ali-Akpajiak and Toni Pyke, Measuring Poverty in Nigeria, op. cit., p. 40.

301 World Trade Organization, Trade Policy Review, Nigeria: Report by the Secretariat, op. cit.

based fiscal rule. These were largely successful until recently when the effects of the global economic crisis became manifest in Nigeria.[302]

Another weakness in Nigeria's pattern of economic development is that of pursuing growth without corresponding expansion in employment. It has been argued that expansion in economic activity in the nation failed to strengthen both forward and backward linkages among the sectors, which is a more critical requirement for pro-poor growth and poverty reduction through increased employment and income generation.[303] The Nigerian labour market has been characterized by high rate of unemployment, underemployment, low wage and poor working conditions.[304] From 2000 to 2007 when Nigeria recorded high growth rates, the employment growth rate failed to keep pace with expansion in economic activity in the key sectors and overall economy. The most significant development in employment reportedly happened in 2001 when the policy shock caused by the introduction of General System for Mobil Communications (GSM) in the country created thousands of low-level jobs in the telecoms sector; and in 2005, when the consolidation in the banking sector created jobs rather than eliminate them, as many had feared.[305] Elsewhere in the manufacturing sector, employment growth rates were lower than the sector growth rates, except in 2001 and 2003. In agriculture, it was only in 2002 that employment recorded higher growth than the sector growth rate.[306]

The implication of this is that despite significant growth mainly however as result of increased foreign capital inflows from oil, employment generation has not been able to meet the demand in the nation. The oil industry and the gas sub-sector in Nigeria have, no doubt, attracted considerable foreign capital inflows and revenue spin-off from these sectors provides substantial capital that should have been used to jump-start other sectors of the economy, especially those that have the greatest socio-economic impact.[307] Doing this would have meant success in giving people better opportunity to participate and contribute more productively in the development of the economy. The result of it all would have been the generation of more wealth/revenue and more equitable distribution of responsibility and wealth in the nation. This unfortunately has not been the case as a result of bad governance and poor economic policies.

---

302 United Nations Development Programme (UNDP), Human Development Report Nigeria 2008 – 2009, op. cit., p. 122.

303 Ibid., p. 40.

304 Biodun Adedipe, The Impact of Oil on Nigeria's Economic Policy Formulation, a paper presented at the conference on Nigeria: Maximizing Pro-poor Growth: Regenerating the Socio-economic Database, organized by Overseas Development Institute in collaboration with the Nigerian Economic Summit Group, 16th / 17th June 2004.

305 United Nations Development Programme (UNDP), Human Development Report Nigeria 2008 – 2009, op. cit., p. 39.

306 Ibid., p. 13.

307 Biodun Adedipe, The Impact of Oil on Nigeria's Economic Policy Formulation, op. cit., p. 17.

What has turned out to be the actual state of affairs is that while the oil and gas industry especially the upstream sector remains well developed[308] and continues to provide better job opportunities and access to the wealth of the nation to a privileged few, other sectors of the economy especially those that have the greatest socio-economic impact continue to suffer neglect and have thus become providers of atypical jobs and poor remuneration for labour. As a result of this, the majority of the productive population have been denied the opportunity to participate meaningfully in the generation of wealth and to have a just share of the available wealth in the nation. Many Nigerians must therefore seek their livelihood in the subsistence economy where work conditions have been most unfavourable to the generation of wealth enough to stay out of poverty. It is therefore not surprising that labour returns for many Nigerian have remained generally poor. All of this has in no small measure contributed to the pervasiveness of poverty in nation. It also boils down to the fact that what households (both in rural and urban areas) lack mostly are adequate returns on their main asset, which is their labour, and what they need is greater and more rewarding employment. This in turn implies that raising the returns on the labour of the rural poor and the urban disadvantaged is therefore critical to promoting their opportunities for increased incomes and improved livelihood and ultimately for combating the menace of poverty.[309]

3.2 The Informal Economy in Nigeria

3.2.1 Emergence and Expansion of the Informal Economy in Nigeria

By tracing the historical and contemporary background of the informal economy, this work aims at giving a clear insight into the characteristic features of the informal economy in Nigeria and helps also to identify some major factors that shaped, still shape and reshape the informal economy in the nation.

The emergence and expansion of the informal economy in Nigeria cannot be attributed to any one particular factor but generally to the nation's weak socio-economic and political circumstances discussed above, namely, the political gap reflected in political instability, institutional fragility and fundamental weaknesses in the management of resources and governance; the social development gap reflected in the nation's wide infrastructural gap, low financial and social services, high incidence of social inequality and income gap, high incidence of corruption, and high unemployment and underdevelopment rates; the economic development gap reflected in low economic performance, poor patterns of trade and economic development, high levels of macroeconomic instability.

308 Ibid.

309 United Nations Development Programme (UNDP), Human Development Report Nigeria 2008 – 2009, op. cit., p. 127.

These factors have, in no small measure, limited the capacity of the public sector to create enough formal jobs and robbed the private sector enterprises the needed business environment that would have enabled them to step in as a supplement in the creation of good modern jobs. Consequently, while the number of jobs in the well established private and public sectors was falling, more and more young people were entering the labour market especially in the towns and cities. The emergence and expansion of an informal economy became therefore inevitable.[310]

Our survey above revealed how Nigeria has over the years adopted faulty patterns of economic growth that have until recently produced a mixture of slow and unstable growth particularly as a result of an over-concentration on oil that results in "jobless growth". The nation adopts policies that favour foreign investment in oil and allied companies and neglects the real economy, especially the agricultural sector and the micro and small enterprises on which most of its population largely depend.[311] It can be said therefore that Nigeria has pursued the "growth from above" and not the "growth from below" in which micro- and small enterprises are very dynamic and are able to create more formal jobs.

In the early years after Nigeria's independence, the economic activities that constituted what is known today as informal economy were considered neither as a separate sector nor as a negative phenomenon. They were classified variously as traditional crafts and petty trade in the subsistence sector, or as small-scale industries within the formal sector, and were treated as such. They were simply integrated into the system and were regarded as the real engine of economic growth. [312] The wage rates at that time were comparable to international standards and the average Nigerian worker could afford a decent living irrespective of whether he was a farmer or in any small firm.[313]

With the expansion of the oil industry in the 1970s, this situation changed. Although the "oil-economy" brought about an increase in urban-based opportunities in administration, construction, commerce, and services, it however led to the neglect of agriculture and the small and micro enterprises that were hitherto the back bone of the nation's economy. This situation prompted rural dwellers to migrate to the cities, thereby causing a rapid growth in the urban population. Certainly not all migrant could be absolved into the formal economy. The aftermath of this was the sudden emergence and expansion of the urban informal economy to meet the increased demand of low-income wage earners for

---

310 For more on how the inability of the formal public and privates sectors contributed to the emergence and explosion of the informal economy in Nigeria, see: E. Dike, Economic Development, Urban Labour Absorption and the Informal Sector in Nigeria, mimeograph, 1992.

311 Cf. Biodun Adedipe, The Impact of Oil on Nigeria's Economic Policy Formulation, op. cit.

312 Geoffrey I. Nwaka, The Urban Informal Sector in Nigeria: Towards Economic Development, Environmental Health and Social Harmony, Global Urban Development Volume 1 Issue 1 May 2005, PDF document, p. 4.

313 Cf. Biodun Adedipe, The Impact of Oil on Nigeria's Economic Policy Formulation, op. cit.

moderately priced consumer goods and services. While this was taking place, the link between the informal economy enterprises and the formal economy enterprises worsened.[314]

The ready availability of imported goods during this period of oil boom coupled with the low quality of production in the informal economy resulted to a sharp increase in the dependence of the informal economy on the low income consumer market, which made up 87 per cent of informal economy demand in the period leading up to the economic crises of the early 1980. In this way, the economic environment of the oil boom led to the emergence of an informal economy "which, though expanding, energetic and diversified, was also highly vulnerable on the supply side to formal and international market conditions, and, on the demand side, dependent on the buoyancy of working class incomes.[315]

Although some efforts[316] were made to upgrade productivity and earning in agriculture and the small scale industries, not much was done to protect the products from these economic activities from competition with imported and mass produced goods. This resulted in the swift drift mainly to trading, services, and transportation.[317] In designing employment policies, emphasis was place on shifting labour from the agricultural sector to the manufacturing sector. This however, did not yield much fruits, as "the Nigerian peculiarities of land tenure system, tenancy and the very rudimentary processes of farming made it extremely difficult to deploy substantially advanced technology in the sector."[318] A better policy option for reverting the trend would have required the development of a capacity for producing higher quality consumer and intermediate goods, as well as light capital goods. This however was not the option made at that point in time and as the economic crisis set in the 1980s, any possibility of making such a transition disappeared.

In the early 1980s policies targeting the informal economic activities were generally found to be very repressive. Misguided efforts were made especially by the General Buhari's regime to contain urban growth and to restrain the informal economy, as the informal economic activities were blamed for "all sorts of evil social influences – littering the streets, obstructing traffic, creating various forms of pollution and nuisance, crime, piracy, prostitution, foreign exchange malpractices,

---

314 Geoffrey I. Nwaka, The Urban Informal Sector in Nigeria: Towards Economic Development, Environmental Health and Social Harmony, op. cit., p. 4.

315 Kate Meagher, Mohammed-Bello Yunusa, Passing the Buck: Structural Adjustment and the Nigerian Informal Sector, UNRISD discussion paper, (United Nations Research Institute for Social Development, 1996), p. 3.

316 Some of the efforts made include, first the establishment of small Industrial Development Centres (IDC), and later the Small-Scale Industry Credit Scheme (SSICS), to provide technical advice and training, and to offer small loans. See: Geoffrey I. Nwaka, The Urban Informal Sector in Nigeria: Towards Economic Development, Environmental Health and Social Harmony, op. cit., p. 4.

317 Geoffrey I. Nwaka, The Urban Informal Sector in Nigeria: Towards Economic Development, Environmental Health and Social Harmony, op. cit., p. 4.

318 Cf. Biodun Adedipe, The Impact of Oil on Nigeria's Economic Policy Formulation, op. cit.

etc."[319] Kiosks, illegal structures, and shanty towns in cities, urban areas and state capitals were raided and demolished. Operators of informal economy enterprises such as hawking and other forms of street business were continuously harassed and forced to relocate to remote and inaccessible outskirts of the cities and towns.[320]

In the late 1980s, the oil boom finally gave way to a deep economic recession. This crisis exposed the extent of informal economy dependence:

> On the demand side, unemployment and falling real wages in the formal sector brought about a collapse of the traditional informal market. On the supply side, skyrocketing inflation in the formal sector pushed up informal production costs, while the collapsing conditions of formal sector employment intensified entry and competition within the informal sector, resulting in a dramatic squeeze on informal incomes.[321]

As a response to the crisis, the government of the time adopted some austerity measures that accompanied the Structural Adjustment policies imposed by the International Monetary Fund (IMF). The Economic reforms pursued by both the then military regime and later civilian administrations in a bid to cope with foreign debt and budget deficits were mainly measures designed to streamline public expenditure, cut government subsidies to public companies and privatize state-owned companies. These measure had untold adverse repercussions on the (informal) economy both on the demand and the supply sides, as markets contracted and input costs rose. The reductions in public spending, declining real wages, and dramatic cuts in the number of wage-earning jobs in both the public and private sectors swelled the ranks of the informal economy beyond its absorptive capacity. The borders between the formal and the informal economy enterprises became blurred, as formal enterprises began to establish new links, sometimes exploitative links with the informal economy enterprises in order to cope with the difficulties of the economic crisis. The resultant market pressure and the nature of the relationship with the formal economy began to undermine the ability of the informal economy to generate incomes and absorb labour. Government response to this situation was contradictory in some respects, on the one hand providing incentives to the informal enterprises by the establishment of training and credit facilities, and on the other hand, repressing the informal enterprises through overzealous prosecution in the so-called War Against Environmental Indiscipline.[322]

In the absence of serious state initiatives to revert the prevailing socio-economic trends, the expansion of the informal economy began to produce more market pressures within the narrow productive niche to which the informal economy itself was confined. The capital and skills necessary for entry into the

---

319 Geoffrey I. Nwaka, The Urban Informal Sector in Nigeria: Towards Economic Development, Environmental Health and Social Harmony, op. cit., p. 4.

320 Ibid., p. 7.

321 Kate Meagher, Mohammed-Bello Yunusa, Passing the Buck: Structural Adjustment and the Nigerian Informal Sector, op. cit., p. 4.

322 Geoffrey I. Nwaka, The Urban Informal Sector in Nigeria: Towards Economic Development, Environmental Health and Social Harmony, op. cit., p. 7.

more lucrative informal activities were often lacking. "The poor and unemployed became increasingly concentrated in low income activities, where incomes were barely adequate for survival, let alone accumulation."[323] Within this scenario, one sees clearly the close link between the high incidence of poverty and the emergence and expansion of the informality in Nigeria.

3.2.2 Magnitude and Size of Nigerian Informal Economy

The magnitude, size and rate of the growth of the informal economy in Nigeria have always proved difficult to establish mainly due to non-availability of statistical records. Most informal activities are neither reported nor recorded in official statistics. Further constraining the measurement of the size of the Nigerian informal economy is the fact that informal activities are never static but vary from time to time in accordance to the prevailing economic situations. Joseph Dada noted that during the early stages of economic development, the formal economy in Nigeria tends to be poorly developed and employment is usually in the informal economy.[324] Despite these constraints there exist some useful clues to the size and magnitude of Nigeria's informal economy.

From the Estimations made for the informal economy in the developing countries, Africa and sub-Saharan African, one can deduce that Nigeria has an informal economy that accounts for about 75 per cent of non-agricultural employment, 60 per cent of urban employment and 90 per cent of new jobs.[325] This estimation is not so much different from other available estimations. Way back in 1996 it was estimated that Nigeria has the largest and most dynamic informal economy in sub-Saharan Africa. The Informal economic activities in the nation were estimated to have increased from approximately 50 per cent of the urban workforce in the late 1970s to 65 per cent by the late 1980s. This trend did not change even during the oil boom of the 1970s. During that period, informal economy continued to grow, as rising urban wages encouraged migration from the rural areas to the cities.[326] In 2005, it was estimated that the informal economy

323 Kate Meagher, Mohammed-Bello Yunusa, Passing the Buck: Structural Adjustment and the Nigerian Informal Sector, op. cit., p. 3.

324 Joseph O. Dada, Harnessing the Potentials of the Informal Sector for Sustainable Development: Lessons from Nigeria, a PDF document available online, pp. 8-9.

325 It is generally believed that "Seventy-five per cent of poor people in developing countries live in rural areas and engage in activities which, for the most part, lie outside the bounds of the formal organized economy, whether in agriculture or in rural non-farm activities. It is also estimated that Informal work accounts for almost 80 per cent of non-agricultural employment, over 60 per cent of urban employment and over 90 per cent of new jobs in Africa. The estimation for sub-Saharan Africa is three-quarters of non-agricultural employment. Cf. ILO, A Global Agenda for Employment: Summary, Global Employment Forum, Geneva, 1-3 Nov. 2001, p. 6. See also: ILO, Decent work and the informal economy, Report VI, International Labour Conference, 90th Session, Geneva, 2002, (Geneva: International Labour Office, 2002), p. 16.

326 Kate Meagher, Mohammed-Bello Yunusa, Passing the Buck: Structural Adjustment and the Nigerian Informal Sector, op. cit., p. i.

accounts for between 45% and 60% of the urban labour force.[327] These estimates is officially confirmed in a statement credited to the Federal Ministry of Labour: "The informal sector, according to a new study, accounts for 80 per cent of non-agricultural employment, 60 per cent of urban employment and over 90 per cent of new jobs in Nigeria."[328]

3.2.3 Categorization of Informal Activities

The informal activities in Nigeria are often categorized into the Informal Productive Sector, Informal Service Sector, Informal Financial Sector and Informal Trade Sector.

3.2.3.1 The Informal Productive Sector

This sector encompasses all informal economic activities involving the production of tangible goods. They include agricultural production, mining and quarrying (excluding petroleum), small-scale manufacturing, building and construction. They operate basically in food production, woodwork, furniture making, garment making, welding and iron works, among others.[329]

3.2.3.2 The Informal Service Sector

The informal service sector includes repairs and maintenance, informal education services, health services, counselling services as well as labour for menial work. Repairs and maintenance services include tailoring, vehicle repairs and maintenance, tinkering, carpentry and servicing of various household and commercial tools. Informal health services, especially in the rural areas, include traditional birth attendants, herbalists and other traditional medical practitioners. The traditional spiritualists who offer counselling services are also included in this sector.[330]

3.2.3.3 Informal Financial Sector

The "susu" is the most predominant type of informal finance enterprise in Nigeria. Some 'susu' groups operate with written laws while others operate with unwritten laws but on oath of allegiance and mutual trust. The general mode of operation is the revolving loan system. Based on this, the members of the 'susu' associations contribute a fixed amount periodically and give all or part of the accumulated funds

---

327 Geoffrey I. Nwaka, The Urban Informal Sector in Nigeria: Towards Economic Development, Environmental Health, And Social Harmony, op. cit., p. 3

328 Vanguard, Informal Sector Accounts for 90 Percent of New Jobs in Country, a report put together by Victor Ahiuma-Young and Ashiat Adeniyi, 15 September 2008. Read more at: http://www.thenigeriabusiness.com/eco207.html.

329 A. H. Ekpo and O. J. Umoh, The Informal Sector, available at: http://www.onlinenigeria.com/economics/?blurb=495, accessed on 11.04.2011.

330 Ibid.

to one or more member(s) in rotation until all members have benefited from the pool.[331]

Other forms of informal financial activities are associated with informal money lenders, saving and credit associations and credit unions. Informal money lenders are however highly exploitative, imposing high rates of interest and demanding heavy collateral such as landed property cars and other valuable belongings. The saving and credit associations as well as credit unions are less informal than the 'susu' associations in the way they operate. They may or may not be registered under any legislation. However, savings and credit co-operatives must be registered under the Co-operative Association Act. Credit societies often come together to form larger units called credit unions. They can modify and expand their operations to include subscription of share capital, deposit-taking and lending.[332]

3.2.3.4 The Informal Trading Sector

The informal trading sector comprises mainly petty trading and retail trade in consumer products and household items and also hawking and peddling (vending) of minor articles on the streets. Cross-border trading is also very significant in Nigeria's informal economy. Some traders travel to some neighbouring countries to purchase goods which they bring back to Nigeria or transport to other countries for sale. Some traders, though just a hand full that has the capital, travel even as far as Dubai, Hong Kong and China, to purchase higher-quality goods at comparatively cheaper prices.[333]

3.2.4 Major Types of Labour Relationship in the Nigerian Informal Economy

In a typical African informal economy like that of Nigeria labour relationship tends to manifest some unique features. Taking a clue from a study conducted in Ghana,[334] a West African country that has an informal economy quite similar to that of Nigeria, seven distinctive types of informal labour relationship can be distinguished.

3.2.4.1 Family Labour

The family is engaged mainly in the family enterprises both in the urban and rural areas. It permeates all the sub-sectors within rural agriculture, but predominant in both food and cash crop farming, and in fishing and agro-processing. It has become

331 Ibid.

332 Ibid.

333 For the estimates of informal trading in Nigeria, see: Samson A. Adeyinka et al., An Evaluation of Informal Sector Activities and Urban Land Use Management in South West Nigeria, a pdf document vailable online at: www.fig.net/pub/fig2006/papers/ts35/ts35_02_adeyinka_etal_0641.pdf Accessed on 05.04.2009, accessed 11.04.211,

334 Cf. Kwasi Adu-Amankwah, Trade unions in the informal sector, in: "Trade union in the informal sector: Finding their bearings: Nine country papers," ILO, Labour Education, No. 116, pp. 1 – 14.

a kind of apprenticeship for the transfer of skills from one generation to the next. From a labour market and economic standpoint, family labour is considered crucial for the survival and viability of the enterprise.[335]

3.2.4.2 Casual Labour

This type of informal labour exists under different kinds of contract both in the rural areas and in the urban cities, and has a high level of mobility. In the rural area, it is found more in the food and cash crop sub-sector where it is needed to carry out different sorts of work like land clearing, preparation of mounds, planting, weeding, fertilizer and chemical application, and harvesting. Although some of the labourers are farmers who have farms of their own, they also hire themselves out to work for others who have bigger farmland that they cannot cultivate alone. Remuneration is based on how much energy one has and how much work one can do. Payment can also be made in cash or in kind.[336] Informal casual labour in the urban areas varies according to the different categories of informal activity and labour relationship. It is naturally attracted to areas where wages are high often due to good market conditions and high profits. Many of the casual workers are engaged by building and construction companies where they are paid only on daily basis.

3.2.4.3 Apprenticeship

Apprentices in the informal business units constitute another category of informal labour as they are usually required to do some form of work that eventually translates into economic gains. The apprentices have no claim to a fixed remuneration. They are only entitled to some kind of pocket money. They may also be rewarded with some of the crops they produce. Apprenticeship requires in most cases some form of written agreement which is usually formulated to protect the rights of the master. The masters reserve the right to assign the apprentices to work outside the areas of apprenticeship; sometimes to do some domestic chores in their (the masters) homes. The more successful and well-equipped enterprises attract more apprentices, since they have the technical capacity to train apprentices well, and sufficient business to provide them with practical experience and opportunities to earn a little on the side as they train. Conversely, enterprises with insufficient equipment or little business have experienced a scarcity of apprentices.[337] In the urban centres, apprenticeship exists in many informal fashion barbing saloons, in the plating of hair, in furniture works, etc.[338]

3.2.4.4 Permanent Labour

Permanence here should be understood better in terms of relative stability in employment relationship. Permanent informal labour constitutes a relatively small

335 Ibid., p.3

336 Ibid

337 Ibid.

338 Ibid., pp. 3 & 4.

proportion of the rural agricultural labour force and urban informal labour. It is usually employed in farms where perennial crops like oil palm, coconut, cocoa and rubber are cultivated. The size of the farm and the degree of permanence of the crop type determine, to a large extent, the permanence of labour. In the urban areas, permanent labour is engaged mainly in the higher income activities.[339]

3.2.4.5 Communal Labour

This category of informal labour is found more in the traditional agricultural setting. It is an arrangement by which farmers within a community pool their labour together to assist each other. It is done on a rotational basis. The person in whose farm work is done is only expected to show appreciation for the help received. The customary way to do this is by providing food and drinks for those who have worked.[340]

3.2.4.6 Child Labour

Child labour has become an integral part of the informal labour in Nigeria both in the rural areas and in cities and urban centres. It forms also a major part of family labour in which case they are not paid. Sometimes the children are hired out by their parents to work in other people's farms so that they can earn something to argument the family income. In the cities, child labour is seen more in the area of hawking, shoe shining, begging etc. Child labour is always very cheap although the children are sometimes made to work like adults or even more than adults.[341]

3.2.4.7 Commission Workers

Constitute yet another category of informal labour in Nigeria. This consists mainly of workers who possess the skills necessary for independent operation, but lack the capital. The commission workers are usually provided with inputs or essential equipment by an outside party, and are paid a proportion of the earnings from their work. This arrangement appears to be most common among low income activities with a particular concentration in hawking, hand-embroidery, express taxis and photocopying. The commission arrangements represent therefore the coming together of two sets of coping strategies: "the strategies of informal actors for coping with high capital costs, and strategies of the middle class to supplement their incomes by setting up informal businesses which are operated by others".[342] Outsourcing of work comes also under this category of labour.

These kinds of employment arrangements under which the various types of labour are engaged constitute their distinguishing feature. General practice reveals some differences in the conditions of employment of the different groups of

339 Ibid

340 Ibid

341 Ibid.: See also: International Confederation of Free Trade Union, International Recognised Core Labour Standard Review of the Trade Policies of Nigeria, Geneva, 11 and 13 May, 2005, P. 8.

342 Kate Meagher, Mohammed-Bello Yunusa, Passing the Buck: Structural Adjustment and the Nigerian Informal Sector, op. cit., p. 10.

informal workers. Factors that account for the differences included: nature of contract (written or verbal); employer responsibility to the work process in terms of provision of work tools; protective clothing and general health and safety; levels of skill of workers; levels of remuneration and other benefits.[343] In Nigeria, there is hardly any official regulatory system for these categories of labour. The absence of this regulation makes the system quite open to all forms of exploitation and marginalization of the informal workers. The labourers are at the mercy of those who employ their services. Indeed as victims of oppression, marginalization and exploitation, the majority of informal workers have continued to wallow in poverty.

3.2.5 Women and Gender Discrimination in Nigerian Informal Economy

The view that there are more women than men in the informal economy finds a consensus acceptance among researchers. Survey results show that women account for 56.0 per cent of the total work force in the Nigerian informal economy while men account for 44.0 per cent.[344] Opinion however differs significantly concerning which segments of the economy women are more represented than men because of regional differences. For instance it is believed that "women tend to dominate in informal trading activities which constitute the most common informal sector activity."[345] However, studies conducted in the predominantly Islamic province of Kaduna reveal that due to the practice of *purdah*[346], which discourages women to work outside the home, 72% of participants in informal retailing were men.[347]

Nigerian women in the informal economy are generally more disadvantaged than their male counterpart. They are found more in low-productivity and in low-income jobs in the informal economy. Women also tend to work more in the invisible sectors of the economy as casual workers, pieceworkers, seasonal workers, home-based workers. Many of them work either as self-employed or unpaid workers in family enterprises. These sectors of the economy are subject to various forms of exploitation. Women find it extremely difficult expanding their business due to lack of or limited access to credit and educational facilities.

Nigerian women are generally accorded inferior legal status which puts them in a more disadvantaged position and renders them highly vulnerable. For instance in

343 Cf. Kwasi Adu-Amankwah, Trade unions in the informal sector, op. cit., p. 4.

344 : Samson A. Adeyinka et al., An Evaluation of Informal Sector Activities and Urban Land Use Management in South West Nigeria, op. cit., p. 11.

345 C.E.E Okojie, Women Entrepreneurs: Opportunities and Challenged in Nigeria, in: Entrepreneurship Development: The Nigerian Experience, edited by F.O. McOliver et al. (Benin-City, Nigeria: Mareh Publishers, 2006), p. 103.

346 Purdah is an Islamic tradition of keeping married women in seclusion. It is commonly practised in the northern part of the Nigeria.

347 Jantjie Xaba et al., The informal Sector in Sub-Saharan Africa, (Geneva: International Labour Office, 2002), p. 15, PDF document available online; see also: I. Abumere et al, Informal sector in Nigeria's Development Process, (Ibadan, Nigeria: Development Policy Centre, 1998), p. 32.

many parts of Nigeria women do not have the right to acquire or own landed property. They are also not accorded any right of inheritance. They have a weak bargaining power, as they tend to be isolated and unorganized. The different forms of discrimination they experience account significantly for the disparity in income in favour of the men. Despite these, odds more and more women continue to enter into the informal economy. This, Okojie rightly observed, is mainly as a result of the following:

- Employment in the formal economy requires some minimum level of formal education which many women do not possess. They are therefore compelled into self employment in the informal sector.
- Employment in the informal economy can be easily combined with domestic responsibilities because working hours are flexible, and women can take their children to the workplace.
- Relatively little capital is required to establish a business in the informal sector.[348]

In a study,[349] Olushola Labeodan examines closely the status of Nigerian women in the informal economy. Concentrating on the informal house-building sector in Ibadan and Lagos (two major cities in Nigeria), the study reveals the precariousness of the conditions in which the women in the informal economy work. It shows that even fairly aged females are also involved in the informal house-building industry. Most of them are married, with an average of four children each. A greater percentage of them have very low academic qualifications. Some never went to school. They are generally relegated to secondary chores like fetching and carrying water, cement, blocks and sand. They provide the unskilled labour referred to as *Birisope* in the local language. Their income level is generally miserable, and the bulk of money earned is spent on the domestic needs of the family. Because of the time-demanding nature of their work, most of them hardly have the time for other part-time jobs. Some of them however manage to find time to perform petty trading or learn other trades.

These women cover, on a daily basis, long distances to reach the construction sites. The majority of female workers travel over 6 km daily, mostly on foot, to reach construction sites, while 83.3% of the female workers in Lagos travel between 3 and 4 km daily to the sites. Some are conveyed to the work sites in most undignified manner in trucks and trailers. The clients bring a vehicle to the recruiting centre as early as 5.30 a.m. to collect workers and transport them to the work sites.

The study further revealed higher dissatisfaction among the women in the house-building trade. 88.95% of respondents were utterly dissatisfied with the job, while 88.75% were dissatisfied with the money earned. The wages received were

348 E.E Okojie, Women Entrepreneurs: Opportunities and Challenged in Nigeria, op. cit.

349 Olushola Adebola Labeodan, Women in the Informal House-Building Industry in Nigeria, in: Habitat International, vol. 16, No. 1, (Great Britain by Pergamon Press Ltd, 1992), pp. 17-24.

not commensurate with the type of work done. If they had an option, about 93% would prefer trading and 3.3% would prefer to go back to school.

3.2.6 The Contributions of the Informal Economy to National Development

National development here includes economic growth, social development and poverty alleviation. As we have seen so far, the informal economic activities in Nigeria are not just what the poor do but those activities which supply the needs of the poor and improve their living standards; they are therefore businesses activities and social services that are vital to socio-economic development and creation of wealth in the nation. Of course one cannot expect that all will be bright and beautiful in any informal economy, bearing in mind that this is an economic field for nearly all comers. The problems poised by the informal economic activities are indeed multifaceted, ranging from environmental to social and of course to economic malaise. For instance, the majority of the informal firms are unregistered. They do not pay the taxes they are expected to pay. They fail to observe basic official labour and factory regulations and operate in many cases in residential areas not designated for commercial activities.[350] Some of them make use of adulterated and smuggled goods.[351] We however do not intend to dwell more on these negative contributions.[352] Our main concern is the relevance of the informal economy to socio-economic development and poverty alleviation.

The informal micro-enterprises are generally described as a major engine in industrial and commercial development. A number of studies[353] on the informal economy have shown that it is an important development phenomenon in less developed countries like Nigeria. Apart from laying the foundation and for promoting the development of large firms that ultimately dominate the formal economy, these informal economic enterprises also provide employment and income opportunities in both rural and urban settings.[354] On a wider note, they are

350 Kate Meagher, Manufacturing Disorder: Liberalization, Informal Enterprise and Economic 'Ungovernance' in African Small Firm Clusters, in: "Development and Change", volume 38, Issue 3, pages 473–503, May 2007, p. 479.

351 Ibid, p. 495.

352 For more insight into these negative aspects, see for instance: Emile Delvaux, The challenge of the informal economy. In: 'Unprotected Labour: What role for union in the informal economy', ILO: Labour Education 2002/2, No 127; United Nations, The Inequality Predicament, report on the world situation 2005. PDF document available at: http://www.sustainable-design.ie/sustain/un2005_ReportWorldSocialSystem.pdf.

353 Cf. Keith Hart, Informal Income Opportunities and Urban Employment in Ghana, The Journal of Modern African Studies, 1973, Vol.11, No.1: 61-89, F. Fluitman, eds. Training for Work in the Informal Sector, (Geneva, International Labour Office, 1989); C. Grey-Johnson, The African Informal Sector at the Crossroads: Emerging Policy Options, Africa Development, 1992, Vol. XVII: 65-92.

354 Cf. Kate Meagher, Identity Economics: Social Networks & the Informal Economy in Nigeria, (African Issues), (Woodbridge, Suffolk, UK: James Currey, 2010), p. 60.

"known to have contributed to job creation, apprenticeship training, income generation, asset accumulation, and the provision of credit facilities and social services. Furthermore, interaction in this domain and with the formal sector in terms of the supply of labour, goods and raw materials, equipment and the provision of financial and technical assistance is known to have contributed tremendously to economic development."[355] Let us now take a closer look at some of these points.

3.2.6.1 Supporting to Job Creation

Across Africa in general and particularly in Nigeria the informal economy has been celebrated for its ability to generate employment outside of the regulatory framework of the state. Much of the achievements in job creation, though of low quality, are evident in the rapid expansion of the informal economy as the state and formal economic enterprises fail to respond rapidly to changes in local and global economic conditions. As we earlier observed (cf. 3.2.2) the informal economy accounts for about 75 per cent of non-agricultural employment, 60 per cent of urban employment and 90 per cent of new jobs.[356]

But considering the poor quality of jobs that are created in the informal economy and the fragile nature of the economy of any nation that relies heavily on the contribution of the informal economy to its GDP, one cannot but view the said merits of the informal economy in job creation with caution. The deterioration of employment, if unchecked, will certainly weaken productivity and tragically increase the wage gap between the formal economy and informal economy.[357] This raises a series of urgent economic, social and political problems, in that the foreseeable rise in underemployment and low quality jobs poses a serious threat to the future economic stability of any country.[358] The prevalence in the informal economy of poor labour standards such as precarious employment, unfavourable working conditions, the lack of and ignorance of social welfare and health care measures, and the absence of any collective organization of labour, if not addressed, are no doubt capable of militating against economic growth, social development and political stability. They also provide a fertile ground that nurtures all forms of abuse and exploitation of informal workers and the formulation of unfavourable policies targeted toward workers in the informal economy. In order to fully harness the job creation potentials in the informal economy, there is an urgent need for policy interventions that will ensure that the jobs created in the informal economy are good jobs.

355 Gafar. T. Ijaiyi, Chika A. Umar, The Informal and Formal Sector Inter-linkage and the Incidence of Poverty in Nigeria: A Case Study of Ilorin Metropolis, African Development, Vol. XXXIX, No 3, 2004, p. 85

356 Read more: http://www.articlesbase.com/economics-articles/the-informal-economy-and-entrepreneurial-development-3015678.html#ixzz1JrLsdsRI.

357 Emile Delvaux, The challenge of the informal economy, in: 'Unprotected Labour: What role for union in the informal economy', ILO: Labour Education 2002/2, No 127, pp. 14 & 15.

358 Ibid

3.2.6.2 *Contributing to National Wealth*

Up-to-date information on the contribution of the informal economy to the Nigerian economy is extremely hard to come by. Available estimations that are reliable date back to the year 2000. The Gross National Product (GNP) at market prices (current US$, in billion) for that year 2000 was estimated at 367.3. Informal Economy's contribution in per cent of GNP 1999/2000 was 57.9. This translates to (current USD in billion) 212.6. The overall GNP per capita, Atlas method (current US$) in 2000 was estimated at 260 while the Informal Economy GNP per capita was estimated at 150.5 and private consumption per capita (current US$) was 147.[359] It is not surprising that the contribution of the informal economy to the Gross Domestic Product (GDP) is so minimal. One cannot of course expect anything higher than this, bearing in mind that about 95 per cent of the GDP is earned from the oil and gas industry that accounts for only 1 per cent of the nation's work force (cf. 3.1.2.2.6). However, for a developing nation like Nigeria that has a wide difference between the GNP and the GDP, the GNP is of more importance since it reflects the total market value of goods and services produced by Nigerians, as different from the GDP which includes the market values of the good and services produced by the citizens of other nationalities. The implication of this is that the GDP is not a true reflection of the wealth of a third world country like Nigeria.[360]

3.2.6.3 *Enhancing Innovation and Adaptation*

The flexible and manageable nature of the informal economic enterprises makes adaptability easier. Changes and innovation are crucial elements in business that eliminate the limitations that emanate from bureaucratic inertia. The informal economic enterprises are mostly owned and managed by a single person; major decisions can be made directly and promptly. Informal enterprises are therefore better positioned to respond to changes in the market. The operators of small business enterprises tend to establish a more intimate relationship with their customers and clients which results in greater accountability and responsiveness to their changing needs. They also have the highly desirable quality of being in virtually all cases home grown enterprises and as such do not carry with them the same risks encountered by foreign firms seeking to introduce operating methods that are inapplicable to local conditions.[361] Since they are found in virtually all corners throughout the country, they help the entrepreneurial base flourish among

---

359 Friedrich Schneider, Size and Measurement of the Informal Economy in 110 Countries around the World, a paper presented at a Workshop of Australian National Tax Centre, ANU, Canberra, Australia, July 17, 2002 also available as pdf document at: http://rru.worldbank.org/Documents/PapersLinks/informal_economy.pdf.

360 For more on this, see: Thomas Pogge, Wachtum is gut! Nur welches, in: Beatrice Weder di Mauro (ed.), "Chancen des Wachstums: Globalen Perspektiven für den Wohlstand von morgen", (Frankfurt: Campus Verlag, 2008).

361 D. Morgan, Micro Enterprises and their Role in the Development Process, Courier No. 115, 1989. As cited by Gafar. T. Ijaiyi, Chika A. Umar, op. cit. p. 91.

diverse ethnic groups and regions and among relatively low income people in rural areas.

3.2.6.4 *Helping in the Mobilisation of Resources*

Recycling of waste and discarded materials is an interesting feature of production in the informal economy. These waste materials (cigarette butts, metal pieces, waste paper, rags, glass, water sachets) ordinarily have little or no value in the environment in which they were formerly used and in most cases constitute environmental hazards. These waste materials are often gathered by informal operator who then converted them into useful economic products.

Some other typical examples would be the thriving trade in second-hand and discarded clothing and shoes etc. in and around the urban and semi-urban markets. Several workers in the informal markets buy used clothes which may be torn or have holes, repair them and sell them to low-income customers. Other informal workers collect old shoes, newspapers, plastic wraps, and empty bottles and resell them to shoe vendors, peanut sellers, restaurants etc. Similarly, used bottles are collected and supplied in bulk to glass works located in and around urban areas where they are converted into molten glass or sold to bottlers and packers.[362]

3.2.6.5 *Facilitating Distribution of Goods and Services*

The wide dispersal of small informal businesses positions them as veritable outlets for the distribution of good and services. They are easily accessible to consumers who would otherwise have to travel long distances to locations where big formal production firms are located. These informal businesses are therefore providers of important connecting points between the various sectors of the economy where flexibility of products and services supplied play a crucial role in the commercial network of the country.[363] In this way, enterprises in the informal economy are not only supportive of the enterprises in the formal economy they also function as worthy contributors to national economic development by facilitating the distribution of goods and services.

3.2.6.6 *Helping to Cushion the Effects of Unemployment and Economic Crisis*

In highlighting the importance of the informal economy in times of economic crisis, Joseph Dada cited the one time Head of State of Nigeria, Ibrahim Babangida in 1991, who at the peak of the Structural Adjustment Programme (SAP) crises, remarked: "...the Nigerian economy has defied all known economic prescriptions, yet it has not collapsed."[364] The reason for the non-collapse of the economy was

362 Joginda S. Uppal, Informal Sector in Third World Countries, Journal of Developing Societies, vol. V., 1989, p. 50.

363 D. Morgan, Micro Enterprises and their Role in the Development Process, op cit.

364 Joseph O. Dada, Harnessing the Potentials of the Informal Sector for Sustainable Development: Lessons from Nigeria, op. cit., p. 2.

attributed to the sustaining power and 'ability' of the then 'neglected' informal economy. With the virtual collapse of the formal economy in the country, it is the informal economy that kept the economy going. Indeed, "against the strong economic storm that pervaded the economic landscape of most African Countries, the informal sector stood its ground."[365] Many workers who were affected by the mass retrenchment exercises that accompanied the SAP found refuge in the informal economy which gave them relief and succour and provided them with employment opportunities. Thus, with little and diminishing employment opportunities in the formal economy, many graduates looked to the informal economy for jobs. It was estimated that during the time of SAP, that the informal economy in Nigeria provided at least the 80% of the workforce.[366]

The informal economy also provided an avenue for earning additional income for the vast majority who were not retrenched but could no longer cope with the high cost that resulted from the declining values or real income. During the SAP years, incomes earned by both public and organised private sector workers became so low that many of the workers, while keeping their jobs in the formal enterprises, took up additional jobs in the informal economy in order to survive. Many of them earned more in the informal economy than they did in the formal economy.[367]

During economic crises, the informal economy limits itself no longer to the supplementary role in the provision of employment and welfare, it transforms itself and becomes the primary medium for sustaining the livelihoods of millions of people who have been retrenched from their jobs, or whose incomes are no longer sufficient to support basic needs. Furthermore, the prices of goods and services produced in the informal economy are comparatively low and affordable by the vast majority of the poor whose meagre earnings leave nothing to be desired.[368] The informal economy can therefore be rightly described as the giver of hope to the poor, whom it helped to withstand starvation and abject poverty. Although it could be argued that the level of productivity and income in the informal economy is low, it is however higher than anything one can earn from full unemployment. At least the many people who would have become fully unemployed were able to subsist with some hope for a better future. This hope for a better future cannot be said to be a mirage as one often hears success stories of people in the informal economy who rose from rags to riches.

From the forgoing, it is evident that the informal economy in Nigeria is indeed an economic phenomenon that manifests great potentials and so merits special attention. Given the enormous potentials it has for employment creation and for promotion of economic growth and social development in the nation, its importance cannot be overlooked in public policy formulation for overall socio-economic development and poverty alleviation. In order to fully harness these

365 Ibid.

366 Ibid., p. 10

367 Ibid.

368 Ibid., p. 11.

potentials for the creation of more wealth and for sustainable alleviation of poverty in the nation and reposition the informal economy to boost the capacity of informal enterprises and workers, there is need to address the social-economic and political problems discussed above while at the same time taking adequate steps to improve the business environment and labour conditions in the informal economy.

3.2.7 Challenges of the Informal Economy in Nigeria

By the challenges of the informal economy in Nigeria, we mean here those factors that militate against the full development of the social and economic potentials in Nigeria's informal economy. Some of these challenges have already been discussed above: Firstly, in examining the connection between poverty and the socio-economic and political order in Nigeria (cf. 3.1.2.1 and 3.1.2.2) and secondly, in tracing the historical background of the emergence and expansion of the informal economy in Nigeria (cf. 3.2.1). These challenges, it was noted, have, in no small measure, hindered the creation of sufficient formal jobs in the public and private sectors and robbed the informal economy enterprises the needed business environment that would have enabled them to step in as a supplement to the public sector enterprises in the creation of decent job and thereby contribute to creation of more wealth in the nation. They constitute therefore the root causes of poverty and informality in Nigeria.

Another problem that has been repeatedly mentioned in this chapter is the absence of statistical records, especially on informal economic activities. This problem constitutes a big hindrance to meaningful planning and the formulation of policies. In what follows here, an effort will be made to identify other major challenges that confront both enterprises and workers in Nigeria's informal economy.

3.2.7.1 High Costs of Starting and Doing Business

We have already seen how Nigeria is rated poorly in terms Doing Business (cf. 3.1.2.2.5). Starting a business and doing business in a proper way means also becoming and staying formal. One major barrier for enterprises to operate in the formal economy has to do with registration and licensing. These are often very exorbitant and cumbersome processes. In addition to these problems, in their daily business transactions, informal economy operators are often subjection to illegal fees and extortion in the hands of the police officers and other government official.[369]

369 Kate Meagher, Identity Economics: Social Networks & the Informal Economy in Nigeria, (African Issues), (Woodbridge, Suffolk, UK: James Currey, 2010), p. 144.

3.2.7.2 *Exploitative Linkages between the Informal Economy and the Formal Economy*

Findings from various studies show that there are tremendous linkages between the informal economy and formal economy in Nigeria. These links manifest themselves in production, in chain of supply and distribution of goods and services and in labour relation. In terms of production and services, the formal economic firms rely to some extent on the informal economic firms. This however is restricted mainly to peripheral services, such as production of uniforms and canteen services. Some giant companies and multi-national firms, such as Nigerian Tobacco Company (NTC), Cadbury Nigeria Plc and oil companies engage the services of informal enterprises for the production and distributions of some of their goods and services.[370]

The link in the area of supply is an interesting one. Some local metal and wood informal industries supply rudimentary parts to formal economy industries for the production of mainly machines and equipment. Fast food companies such "Mr Bigs" and some big supermarkets get some of their supplies of local snacks from private suppliers who have found ways of packaging them in attractive and innovative ways. In a similar way, waste materials such as empty bottle, plastics, metals and aluminium material have continued to find their way back to the formal economy production industries where they are recycled into profitable economic products. In terms of distribution of goods and services, formal economy manufacturers of such goods as toiletries, beverages and common household items rely heavily on informal economy operators like owners of kiosks and hawkers in order to get their products to the end the users especially in the interiors. Distributors of toiletries also enter arrangements with informal hair dressing salons to showcase products for sales to their customer. The labour (employment) relation between the informal and formal economies occurs often through subcontracting and outsourcing by which some aspects of production are transferred to firms in the informal economy.[371] In recent times, this sub-contracting relationships with formal economy have become dominated by the opportunist relationships which are often executed through third parties who may get the contracts at a good deal and pass it on to other at the lower end of chain under unfavourable term of business.[372]

It is often argued that the linkages between the informal economy and the formal economy are important for the growth and survival of informal

370 Kate Meagher, Mohammed-Bello Yunusa, Passing the Buck: Structural Adjustment and the Nigerian Informal Sector, op. cit., p. 14.

371 S.I. Abumere et al, Informal sector in Nigeria's Development Process, (Ibadan, Nigeria: Development Policy Centre, 1998), p. 12: See also: Gafar. T. Ijaiyi, Chika A. Umar, The Informal and Formal Sector Inter-linkage and the Incidence of Poverty in Nigeria: A Case Study of Ilorin Metropolis, African Development, Vol. XXXIX, No 3, 2004; Ben C. Arimah, Nature and Determinant of the Linkages between Informal and Formal Enterprises in Nigeria, (Oxford: Blackwell Publishers, 2001).

372 Kate Meagher, Identity Economics: Social Networks & the Informal Economy in Nigeria, op. cit., p. 80.

enterprises.[373] But a closer look at them reveals that in most cases they are selective and exploitative against the informal enterprises.[374] For instance it has been observed that large formal companies prefer to do business only with firmly established informal enterprises with long year of experience, adequate equipment and sufficient labour force. The conditions for doing business with the informal economy enterprises which include speed, accuracy, quality and ability to make supplies on credit are obviously too high for many operators in the informal economy. Even in the case of scrap collection, only collectors who have the use of vehicles are able to collect scrap in sufficient quantity to secure direct contracts with formal economy industries. Informal enterprise operators with a low capital base, inferior equipment and a limited labour force are therefore discriminated against. They are often relegated to the lowest end of the continuum where they are further marginalised by sub-contractors. These victims are unfortunately the very poor ones who are in most need of these opportunities.[375]

Furthermore, the production of cheap consumer goods by firms in the informal economy leads to a low subsistence level for the poor. This in turn enables formal enterprises to pay low wages and to avoid the provision of costly social benefits. The excess labour reserve in the informal economy renders informal workers vulnerable to low wages and long working hours and affords operators of formal firms' undue advantage for the accumulation of capital and profit.[376] Policy interventions are therefore necessary to ensure equity and justice in the relationship.

3.2.7.3 Limited Access to Capital

As we have already pointed out (cf. 3.1.2.2.2), small business units in the informal economy are generally constrained in their ability to access credit in the formal financial institutions. Many banks are reluctant to grant credit facilities to them due to high business risks they present and their inability to meet the demands for collateral. The informal enterprises are usually unable to meet the demand for collateral due to lack of property rights. Under this constraint, most of them are left with no other option than to rely on personal savings or turn to family members or worst still to local money lenders who usually charge exorbitant interest rates that are capable of crippling the borrowers and keeping them in a cycle of debts. So many revolving credit groups, credit and savings associations, credit unions credit co-operatives and the traditional credit system ('susu') discussed above (cf. 3.2.3.3) have been springing up to fill the credit gap, but, given the level of need in the informal economy, the services they offer are woefully inadequate. In addition to

373 S. I. Abumere et al, Informal sector in Nigeria's Development Process, op. cit., p. 47.

374 Cf. Seibel, H.D., Coping with Scarcity: Microenterprise Strategies in Nigeria, (Saarbrücken, Verlag für Entwicklungspolitik, 1996), pp.1 – 10. Also available at: http://www.hf.uni-koeln.de/data/eso/File/seibel/ElFo70.pdf.

375 Kate Meagher, Mohammed-Bello Yunusa, Passing the Buck: Structural Adjustment and the Nigerian Informal Sector, op. cit., p. 14.

376 Cf. Seibel, H.D., Coping with Scarcity: Micro enterprise Strategies in Nigeria, op. cit.

this, these informal financial institutions also give loans with the interest rates that are too high for operators of informal businesses.[377] Efforts have been made to boost the access of informal business operators to financial services through microfinance institutions (MFIs). Funds offered by the MFIs are however very insignificant for meaningful investment.[378] There is therefore a clear need for policies to enhance the access of informal enterprises to credit so as enable them expand production.

3.2.7.4 Limited Access to Market

The low income market is on a general note targeted by the majority of informal enterprises because it is associated with low entry barriers. Enterprises in this market tend to compete for the same customers; a state of affairs which the majority of MSEs operators indicated as a major obstacle to the running of businesses.[379] This limitation exists more among operators of informal business units concentrated in clusters. By copying and imitating one another they end up producing similar products thereby limiting their market.[380]

3.2.7.5 Lack of Access to Modern Technology

Another challenge confronting informal businesses is that posed by lack of access to modern technology including information technology. The majority of the operators of informal businesses rely mainly on obsolete and antiquated equipment and tools. This is said to be particularly noticeable in low income activities. Some of them in a bid to remain in business resort to converting their household machines and equipment into commercial use.[381] It can easily be imagined how this retards productivity and earning thereby increasing the chance of falling into poverty and remaining in poverty.

---

377 Cf. S.I. Abumere et al, Informal sector in Nigeria's Development Process, op. cit., pp. 30 & 97: See also: Sher Verick, The Impact of Globalization on the Informal Sector in Africa, (Adis Ababa, Ethiopia: Economic and Social Policy Division, United Nations Economic Commission for Africa (ECA) and Institute for the Study of Labour (IZA)), p, 18.

378 Adam, Susanna, Competence Utilisation and Transfer in Informal Sector Production and Service Trades in Ibadan/Nigeria, (Munster, Hamburg: LIT Verlag, 1995), as cited by Esther K. Ishengoma and Robert Kappel, Economic Growth and Poverty: Does Formalisation of Informal Enterprises Matter? (Leibniz: German Institute of Global and Area Studies, 2006), p. 12.

379 Cf. Esther K. Ishengoma and Robert Kappel, Economic Growth and Poverty: Does Formalisation of Informal Enterprises Matter? (Leibniz: German Institute of Global and Area Studies, 2006), p. 12. See also: Helmut K. Anheier, Economic Environments and Differentiation: A Comparative Study of Informal Sector Economies in Nigeria, in: "World Development", Vol. 20. No. 11, pp. 1573-1585, (Great Britain: Pergamon Press Ltd, 1992), p. 1576.

380 Kate Meagher, Manufacturing Disorder: Liberalization, Informal Enterprise and Economic 'Ungovernance' in African Small Firm Clusters, op. cit., p. 22.

381 Kate Meagher, Mohammed-Bello Yunusa, Passing the Buck: Structural Adjustment and the Nigerian Informal Sector, op. cit., p. 17

3.2.7.6 Low Capacity Building to Promote Mobility and Diversification

The Nigerian informal economy has a relatively large population with low quality education.[382] In recent times however there has been increased entry of many school leavers and graduates into the informal economy as a result of declining opportunities in the formal labour market.[383] The higher educational level of new entrants does not however mean higher level of skill formation within the informal economy. Further enquiries reveal a high level of inefficiency and low level of technical and managerial skills among actors in the informal economy.[384] The reason for this is mainly because many of the informal operators venture into different informal economic endeavours without the prerequisite training. Some simply do not have the money to pay for the required training. Financial pressure leads other intending and new entrants to skip the requisite training. The pressure to get out and start earning money either for their own needs or to supplement household incomes also makes apprentices to either cut their apprenticeship short or abandon it half way or simply rush through their training. Some masters take advantage of the pressure to exploit the apprentices. They turn "their apprentices' haste into an income-generating strategy of their own by certifying apprentices to have completed the requisite training period well before that period has been completed, thereby shortening the turnover time for the same fee."[385] Adequate training is also hindered by lack of suitable tools, shortage of businesses from which to gain practical experience, and interference from other activities, including schoolwork, other jobs and household responsibilities.[386] The low capacity building in the informal economy certainly has negative impact on the ability to get integrated into the labour market. It also inhibits the ability of informal entrepreneurs to formalize their enterprises.

3.2.7.7 Violation of Labour Standards and Right

It was observed in the last chapter that right deficit and non-conformity to international labour standards are some of the main characteristic features of the informal economy in general. In the Nigerian informal economy, these deficits manifest themselves in various ways, but most importantly in the following:

Irregular Labour Relationships : Many labour relations are based on casual employment kinship or personal and social relations rather than contractual arrangements with formal guarantees. Most of them, especially in the micro-enterprises, lack a clear employer/employee relationship.[387]

---

382 S. I. Abumere et al, Informal sector in Nigeria's Development Process, op. cit., pp. 99.

383 Ibid., pp. 32 & 58.

384 Ibid., p. 47.

385 Kate Meagher, Mohammed-Bello Yunusa, Passing the Buck: Structural Adjustment and the Nigerian Informal Sector, op. cit., pp. 26-27.

386 Ibid., p. 27.

387 Valentina Forastieri, Implementation of Working Conditions and Environment in the Informal Sector through Safety and Health Measures, (Geneva: International Labour Office, 1999), p. 4.

Forced Labour and Child Labour: The Nigerian Constitution and the Labour Act prohibit forced labour and child labour. In spite of this, child labour and forced labour have continued to thrive in nation mainly due to a lack of effective inspectoral and implementation machinery in the nation. There are serious problems of child trafficking within Nigeria and from neighbouring countries. These children, boys and girls are usually forced to work as domestics, in prostitution, or other forms of forced labour, mainly in the informal economy.[388] The Ministry of Labour and Productivity's Inspections Department responsible for enforcing legal provisions relating to conditions of work and protection of workers has failed especially with regard to enforcing that aspect of the Nigerian Constitution and Labour Act relating to child labour and forced labour. The ministry has engaged only very few inspectors who conduct inspections often in the formal business sectors.[389]

Lack of Property Rights: Operators of informal business encounter many constraints in securing property rights. This contributes immensely to making the starting and expansion of business extremely difficult for them. It also restricts their chances of using theirs assets as formal collateral in order to raise capital from formal financial institutions, which can give more credit facilities and charge lower rates of interest than informal lenders. One area people encounter difficulties most with regard to property rights has to do with land acquisition, possession and transfer. The Nigerian Land Use Decree stipulates that land is owned by the government. Despite this, individuals and communities continue to sell land, thereby prolonging the process of attaining full ownership.[390] This is particularly because full ownership is not possible without the authorization of the competent government officials.

Furthermore, in some traditional settings, women are denied land ownership rights. All these factors make land not accessible not only to women but also to many male operators of informal businesses, who often are hardly able to pay the high costs or cope with the ambiguous processes that are involved.[391]

3.2.7.8 The Absence of Social protection

It is also clearly pointed out in chapter two that, on a general note, people in the informal economy have little or no social protection and receive little or no social security neither from their employers nor from the government. Beyond traditional social security coverage, workers in the informal economy are without social protection in such areas as education, skill-building, training, health care and

388 International Confederation of Free Trade Union, International Recognised Core Labour Standard Review of the Trade Policies of Nigeria, (Geneva, International Labour Office, 2005), P. 8.

389 Ibid.

390 Full ownership of land is conferred through the Statutory Right which is granted by the Governor and the Customary Right granted by a local government. The final stage of this process is the awarding of the certificate of occupancy with which land cannot be used as collateral. Securing a certificate of occupancy is an uphill task that last years especially for the poor.

391 S. I. Abumere et al, Informal sector in Nigeria's Development Process, op. cit., pp. 87 & 92.

childcare, which are particularly important for women workers (cf. 2.5.2). Majority of in the informal workers are therefore typically among the "have-nots" because they earn less and irregularly compared to those in the formal economy; they are often excluded from various legal protections and are prevented from accessing basic benefits.[392]

We have already observed that in Nigeria, not only that the income of the poor in the informal economy is low in relation to basic needs, the protection of the available meagre income is not even guaranteed and the pervasiveness of income inequality makes matters worse (cf. 3.1.2.2.4). In terms of income in the form of social security and other benefits, the truth of the matter is that the majority of the workers in the in formal economy in Nigeria are neither covered by any *formal* contribution-based social insurance scheme nor by tax-financed social assistance such as pension benefits, health care, child care, food security burial costs assistance etc.[393] The existing "Old Age, Disability and Survivors" security programme[394] which was signed into law in 2004 provides coverage only for employees in the public and private sector firms with five or more workers and strictly excludes self-employed persons. With these restrictions, a great majority of wage workers in the informal economy are automatically excluded from the scheme. Statutory social security coverage can therefore be said to be entirely out of the reach of informal workers and entrepreneurs.

There is however evidence that many informal workers are not able or willing to contribute a relatively high percentage of their incomes to finance social security benefits, as in most cases, they do not meet their priority needs. There are also indications that informal workers may not be familiar with, and/or distrust the way statutory social security schemes are managed.[395] As alternative to statutory social security some groups of informal workers tend to set up schemes that better meet with their priority needs and contributory capacity.[396]

---

392 United Nations, Report on the World Situation 2005, The Inequality Predicament, p. 29, PDF document, available online at: http://www.sustainable-design.ie/sustain/un2005_ReportWorldSocialSystem.pdf.

393 Olugboyega Oyeranti and Kolawole Olayiwola, Policies and Programmes for Poverty Reduction in Rural Nigeria, an Interim Research Report Submitted to the African Economic Research Consortium (AERC), Nairobi for the Second Phase Collaborative Poverty Research Project, 2005, p. 41.

394 For details see: Social Security Programmes throughout the World: Africa – Nigeria. http://www.ssa.gov/policy/docs/progdesc/ssptw/2006-2007/africa/nigeria.pdf.

395 Cf. Nick Silver, Emmanuel Acquaah, Oskari Juurikkala, Savings in the Absence of Functioning Property Rights, in: Institute of Economic Affairs 27(1), 71 – 75, March, 2007, (London: Institute of Economic Affairs, 2007). This article highlights two aspects of old-age security in Nigeria. It goes on to show why, despite several reforms of formal pension schemes, most Nigerian depend on informal structures. It further explains the causes of the failure of previous state-operated schemes and outlines the strengths and weaknesses of the recent reforms that move in the direction of the Chilean-style privatised pensions. It argues that the informal schemes posses several advantages over the formal arrangements especially in the socio-economic context of Nigeria and then concludes by insisting that the informal schemes should be supported and assisted to develop better.

396 Ibid.

3.2.7.9 Non-compliance with Occupational Safety and Health Standards

The work environment in Nigerian informal economy presents serious occupational safety and health standards concerns, ranging from inadequate premises and often very unsatisfactory welfare facilities to practically non-existent occupational health services. The most prevalent problems include exposure to hazardous chemicals and dusts, lack of protective equipment, inadequate work space and working tools, poor housekeeping, excessive heat, lack of ventilation, poor lighting and long hours of work.[397] The consequences of the poor work environment in the informal economy are indeed far reaching. They contribute enormously to large human and material losses, which burden the productivity of national economy, impair health and general well-being as well as the quality of life of informal workers and their families."[398]

3.2.7.10 Lack of Representation and Voice

In its web site, the Nigerian Labour Congress, which is the umbrella organization for labour unions in the nation, acknowledges that "Nigeria's massive and dynamic informal sector is also largely unorganised although the modalities for its unionisation are now the subject of internal debates in the movement".[399] However, informal workers and entrepreneurs, taking their destiny in their hand, have succeeded in forming their own unions in pursuance of their collective interests. Today, there are many informal associations and unions in the Nation. A few of these includes: National Automobile Technician Association, Black Smiths, Welders and Iron Benders Association of Nigeria, Association of Automobile Body Works and Panel Beating of Nigeria and, The National Association of Furniture and Carpentry Workers of Nigeria.[400]

These unions are however hardly able to realise their set goal due to the many limitations that confront them. A characteristic feature of most informal economy organizations is their fragility. As is the case in many developing nations, most the informal organizations in Nigeria "often disband even before achieving their objectives or as soon as these are reached, or pass periodically from activity to hibernation. Only rarely do they evolve into more settled, structured institutions pursuing long-term development and political objectives."[401] In addition to this, they are rarely officially registered or recognized and therefore have limited access to and influence over relationships with the institutions and enterprises of the

---

397 Valentina Forastieri, Implementation of Working Conditions and Environment in the Informal Sector through Safety and Health Measures, op. cit, p. 6.

398 Ibid

399 Nigerian Labour Congress, History of the Nigeria Labour Congress, http://www.nlcng.org/history.php, accesses on 26.04.2011.

400 Mustapha Oyewole Bello, Accessibility of Land as a Tool for Empowering the Low income Earner of the Informal Sector in Nigeria, p. 8, a PDF document available online at: www.fig.net/pub/fig2007/papers/ts_7a/ts07a_01_bello_1282.pdf.

401 World Labour Report, 1997-98, p. 199.

formal economy or with the public authorities. Only very few of them are affiliated to recognized national organizations of employers, chambers of commerce, trade unions or cooperatives.

The existing legal framework in the nation appears also to be hostile to freedom of association and right to collective bargaining among workers in general. It was reported that while in principle workers in Nigeria have the right to organise and the right to collective bargaining, in reality, these rights are constantly subject to restrictions. Collective agreements reached by labour unions, for instance, are often subjected to stringent scrutiny by the government. Workers in a number of sectors, especially those in export processing zones (EPZs), have extremely limited rights to freedom of association and collective bargaining. In addition strikers continually face serious police violence.[402]

3.3 Conclusion

Having taken an in-depth look in the first and second chapters at poverty and the informal economy in general, this chapter preoccupied itself with poverty and informal economy as they exist in Nigeria. The first task was a probe into the 'how' and the 'why' of poverty in Nigeria. We saw that although Nigeria is rich both in human and natural resources, poverty remains pervasive in the land. The poverty in the nation reflects itself in terms of both economic and social development indicators: low per capita income, poor social services, lack of opportunities and basic amenities of life, social exclusion, powerlessness and high incidence of working poverty (cf. 3.1.1).

An attempt at understanding why there is so much poverty in Nigeria in spite of the abundance of resources in the nation necessitated an enquiry into the nation's socio-economic and political heritage (cf. 3.1.2). The findings from this enquiry show that the poverty in the nation is indeed a social problem that has its root in the institutional and structural deficiencies in the political, social and economic life of the nation. In other words, poverty in Nigeria is an outcome of a social disorder and structural imbalances that emanate from weak and corrupt governmental institutions and systems, bad leadership, wrong patterns of social and economic development, limited access to opportunities (education, employment, land, capital, etc), inadequate investment in economic and human capital development, lack of markets for both agrarian and industrial products, etc.[403] Nigeria presents itself therefore as a nation in dire need of a profound institutional and structural reform for the restoration of the social, economy and political order that will ensure an environment conducive to sustainable economic growth and full human development.

402 International Confederation of Free Trade Union, International Recognised Core Labour Standard Review of the Trade Policies of Nigeria, (Geneva, 11 and 13 May, 2005), P. 5.

403 Sofo C.A. Ali-Akpajiak and Toni Pyke, Measuring Poverty in Nigeria, op. cit., p. 19.

The long periods of military dictatorship, corruption, political instability and poor governance have meant mismanagement and waste of resources, an unbalanced system of wealth distribution, insufficient investments in the country's physical infrastructure and basic services and a high incidence of inequality, unemployment and underemployment.

Since the return of democracy in 1999, Nigeria has embarked on series of micro and macro-economic reforms that have brought about tremendous improvement mainly in the gas and oil sector. This has resulted in stable Growth in GDP. This growth in GDP has however failed to keep pace with rapid growth in the population, increasing demand for employment and with the development of peer countries. It has also failed to translate into overall improvement in the economy and reduction of poverty. This has been partly due to enduring deficiencies in the system of wealth distribution in the nation that favours only a few privileged people and partly due to the bad pattern of economic development that the nation retains.

Nigeria has continued to depend on the oil and gas sub-sector for its revenue to the detriment of other sectors of the economy, especially those that have more relevance for poverty reduction – agriculture and the Small and Micro Enterprises (SMEs) – a situation that renders the economy highly vulnerable to external shocks and imbalance in terms of trade. The oil and gas sector continue to account for about 95 per cent of the foreign earnings and over 80 per cent of the federal budget. Surprisingly, this sector provides job opportunities for only 1 percent of the entire work force in the nation. Continued mismanagement through corruption and failure to reinvest the oil wealth into the development of the real economy has also hindered the creation of enough formal jobs in the public and private sectors. The implication of this is a non-inclusive system in which many of the citizens, especially the poor, are estranged from the wealth production processes in the nation and at the same time denied the opportunity of using their only asset, which is their labour, to participate meaningfully in the creation of wealth and in receiving a fair share of the wealth produce in the nation. Owing to this, many Nigerians must have to seek their means of livelihood in the subsistence economy – the informal economy – where labour conditions have been most unfavourable to the generation of enough wealth that can keep people out of poverty.

A further enquiry into the economy (cf. 3.2) revealed that the informal economic activities in the nation are not just what the poor do but those activities which supply the needs of the poor and improve their living standards; they are therefore business activities and social services that are vital to socio-economic development and creation of wealth in the nation. Simply put, Nigerian informal economy is crucial in terms of untapped revenue and, more importantly, as the driving force behind rapid social development for durable economic growth.

Despite the enormous potentials in the informal economy for socio-economic development and poverty alleviation, this segment of the economy has continued to record a high incidence of poverty as a result of the enormous constraints it encounters. While the enterprises continue to operate in an unfavourable business atmosphere, informal workers must reckon with high rate of decent work deficit: They lack skills, are not gainfully employed, enjoy little rights, have no access to social protection and are not formally organized. This condition has been mostly responsible for their low productivity and poor earnings and ultimately for the high incidence of poverty among them.

The presence of a large informal economy in Nigeria has major implications for poverty alleviation in the nation, given that 90 per cent of new jobs in the country are created in the informal economy and that most poor people work informally, and also considering its enormous potentials for boosting economic growth and social development.

From the foregoing, it is obvious that poverty will remain pervasive in Nigerians unless growth is sustained and also derived from sectors and economic units with high poverty-reducing impacts. Such economic activities, we have seen, are found mainly in the informal economy. Nigeria's long-term macroeconomic performance is therefore critically tied to its management of this segment of the economy that can eventually prove much more valuable than its rich oil reserve. This highlights the obvious need to seek better ways of harnessing the potential in the informal economy for sustainable growth and poverty reduction. The Nation must, above all, seek ways to transform the economic activities in the informal economy into formal economic ventures that can become a vehicle for genuine and broad-based economic progress.

CHAPTER FOUR
Impulses from the Catholic Social Teaching

Introduction

Having attempted in the previous chapters to understand the nature of poverty and the informal economy, how they exist in the world at large and in Nigeria in particular and the challenges they pose, the next task is the search for an ethical orientation for dealing with the problem of poverty. This task is taken up in this chapter. The outcome of this endeavour will provide a basis for assessing the past and current poverty alleviation efforts both at the international scene and in Nigeria.

In clear terms, this chapter attempts to articulate the impulses from Catholic social teaching (CST). It seeks to derive the needed ethical orientation from the catholic social teaching on poverty and its alleviation. We will start by presenting what we understand by Catholic social teaching. Next, we will take a look at the principles that form the basis of the CST, pointing out their relevance for poverty and its alleviation. We will then go on to examine the central Catholic social teaching on poverty and its alleviation. Our focus will be on what the Church teaches through her social doctrine and the guidelines offered for the alleviation of poverty. The different project and interventions of the Universal Church in favour of the poor through, for instance, charity work, is therefore outside the scope of this chapter.

4.1 Catholic Social Teaching: Conceptual Framework

Catholic social teaching, especially in its modern form, refers to the entire "doctrinal 'corpus' concerning issues relevant to the society which, from the Encyclical Letter *Rerum Novarum* of Pope Leo XIII, developed in the Church through the *Magisterium* of the Roman Pontiffs and the Bishops in communion with them."[404] It is the expression of the way the Church understands society and her position regarding social structures and changes.[405]

The object of the Catholic social doctrine is essentially "the human person called to salvation."[406] In other words, men and women, in the concrete circumstances of history, represent the heart and soul of Catholic social teaching.

404 Pontifical Council for Justice and Peace, Compendium of the Social Doctrine of the Church, (Vatican City: Libereria Edtrice Vaticana, 2005), no. 87, subsequently referred to as "Compendium of the Social Doctrine of the Church." See also Catechism of the Catholic Church, 2422.

405 Compendium of the Social Doctrine of the Church, 79.

406 Ibid., 81.

The whole of the social doctrine, in fact, develops from the principle that affirms the inviolable dignity of the human person.[407]

With her social teaching, the Church seeks to proclaim the Gospel and make it present in the complex network of relations. It is therefore a means by which the Church takes on the task of proclaiming what the Lord has entrusted to her and makes the message of freedom and redemption wrought by Christ, especially for the poor and the downtrodden, present in human history. And in proclaiming the Gospel, the Church "bears witness to man, in the name of Christ, to his dignity and his vocation to the communion of persons. She teaches him the demands of justice and peace in conformity with divine wisdom."[408] In affirming the inviolable dignity of the human person through her social teaching, "the Church has striven above all to defend human dignity in the face of every attempt to re-dimension or distort its image; moreover she has often denounced the many violations of human dignity."[409]

The Catholic social teaching does not proffer solutions to social problems nor is it in itself a solution. On the contrary, it proposes principles for reflection, provides criteria for judgement and gives guidelines for action.[410] Through her social teaching, "the Church does not assume responsibility for every aspect of life in the society."[411] She does not intervene in technical questions with her social doctrine. She does not purport to offer a 'blueprint' for an ideal society nor does she propose or establish systems or models of social organization.[412]

While acknowledging that the mission entrusted to her by Christ is more of a religious one, the Church insists however that she has the right and the duty "to develop social doctrine of her own and to influence society and societal structures with it by means of the responsibility and tasks to which it gives rise."[413] She backs this claim with the argument that religion must not be restricted "to the purely private sphere"[414] and that the Christian message must not be relegated to a purely otherworldly salvation incapable of shedding light on our earthly existence.[415] She further argues that because of the public relevance of the Gospel and faith, because of the corrupting effects of injustice, the Church cannot remain indifferent to social matters.[416] And so the Church has "the right always and everywhere to announce moral principles, including those pertaining to the social order, and to make

407 Ibid., 84.

408 The Catechism of the Catholic Church, Vatican City: Libreria Editrice Vaticana, 1993, 2419.

409 Compendium of the Social Doctrine of the Church, 107

410 The Catechism of the Catholic Church, 2423.

411 Compendium of the Social Doctrine of the Church, 68

412 Vatican Council II: The Conciliar and Post Conciliar Documents, Gaudium et Spes, Austin Flannery, ed., (Dublin: Dominican Publications, 1988), 42: This document will subsequently be referred to as Gaudium et Spes

413 The Catechism of the Catholic Church, 69

414 Cf. John Paul II, Message to the Secretary-General of the United Nation, on the occasion of the thirtieth anniversary of the Universal declaration of Human Rights, 2nd December, 1978.

415 Compendium of the Social Doctrine of the Church, 71.

416 Ibid.

judgements on any human affairs to the extent that they are required by the fundamental right of the human person or the salvation of souls."[417]

The Catholic social teaching which is of theological nature, specifically theological-moral,[418] has its root in the Sacred Scripture and tradition of the Church from which "it draws inspiration and light to understand, judge and guide human experience and history."[419] Of primary importance however is the universal *Magisterium* of the Pope and the Council which determines its direction and gives marks to its development.[420] The entire body of the social teaching of the Church is nonetheless enriched through contributions made by the bishops and the lay faithful in the various areas of their specialization.

While grounded in faith, the Church's social teaching, "insofar as it is knowledge applied to the circumstances and historical aspect of praxis, brings "*fides et ratio*"[421] (faith and reason) together and gives expression to that relationship. This interaction brings the Catholic social ethics into a friendly dialogue with all major branches of knowledge. In an interdisciplinary dialogue, the social teaching makes particular use of the significant contributions of philosophy as well as the descriptive contributions of the sciences. For this reason, it has been described as "knowledge enlightened by faith."[422] Philosophy, for instance, remains a suitable and indispensable instrument for arriving at a correct understanding of the basic concepts of the Church's social doctrine, concepts such as the person, society, freedom, conscience, ethics, law, justice, the common good, solidarity, subsidiarity, the state, etc.[423]

The Church's social teaching is not restricted to any particular section of the human family. It is addressed not to Catholics alone, nor to Christians alone but to all men and women of good will. Its first recipient is however the Church community in its entire membership.

It is a popular opinion that the Social teaching of the Church developed in the nineteenth century when the Gospel encountered modern industrial society with its new structures for the production of goods, its new concept of society, the state and authority, and its new form of Labour and ownership.[424] The encyclical letter *Rerum Novarum* of Pope Leo XIII is acclaimed as having "marked the beginning of a new path."[425] This new path is however not a complete departure from the old. While

---

417 The Code of Canon Law, (London: Collins Liturgical Publications, 1983), can. 747, § 2.

418 John Paul II, Encyclical, Centesimus Annus, (Vatican City: Libreria Editrice Vaticana, May 1, 1991), 55.

419 Compendium of the Social Doctrine of the Church, 74.

420 Cf. Ibid., 80.

421 Cf. John Paul II, Encyclical, Fides et Ratio, Vatican City: Libreria Editrice Vaticana September 15 1998.

422 Compendium of the Social Doctrine of the Church, 75.

423 Ibid., 77,

424 Cf. The Catechism of the Catholic Church, 2421.

425 Compendium of the Social Doctrine of the Church, 87. Although there seem to be a popular opinion among scholars that the Catholic social teaching began in 1891 with the encyclical letter of Pope Leo XIII, this has however remained a topic of controversy. For more on the history of Catholic Social Teaching, see: Michael J. Schuck, Modrn Catholic Social Thought, in: Judith A Dwyer ed., "The New

emphasizing this point, Pope John Paul II states: "The development of the doctrine of the Church on economic and social matters attests the permanent value of the church's teaching at the same time as it attests the true meaning of her Tradition, always living and active."[426]

4.2 Principles of the Catholic Social Teaching vis-à-vis Poverty

As earlier observed, Catholic social teaching has the major task of proposing principles aimed at creating 'right' social, economic and political relationships and the construction of social structures and institutions based on the cardinal moral principles – justice and human dignity and on some social principles such as the principles of common good, universal destination of goods, subsidiarity and solidarity. These principles which constitute the very heart of the CST provide orientation for policy formulation and structural reforms necessary for dealing with social questions and as such prove to be important in giving direction in the fight against poverty.

The Church teaches that these principles have "a profoundly moral significance because they refer to the ultimate and organizational foundations of life in society."[427] It is believed that these principles, if applied to the structures and institutions of the society, both nationally and globally, will promote human dignity, lead to social justice and contribute immensely to poverty alleviation.

What follows here is a brief presentation of these principles and their implications for poverty and its alleviation. We will concentrate on five principles in two categories: In the first category are justice and human dignity considered to be the cardinal ethical principles. In the second category are other principles considered to be the basic social principles: common good, universal destination of goods, subsidiarity and solidarity. While treating these principles, some other relevant social teachings of the Church would be looked into, for instance, the teaching pertaining to human rights, property/private ownership and option for the poor.

4.2.1 The Cardinal Ethical Principles

4.2.1.1 The Principle of the Human Dignity

This principle, together with justice, forms the foundation of all other principles and the content of the Church's social teaching. With the principle of human

---

Dictionary of Catholic Social Thought," (Collegeville, Minnesota: Liturgical Press, 1994). This work will as much as possible limit itself to this new path which the Church has taken. Reference would be made to the earlier path only when it is absolutely necessary.

426 John Paul II, Encyclical, Centesimus Annus, 24.

427 Compendium of the Social Doctrine of the Church, 163.

dignity, the Church upholds the sacredness and integrity of the human person and teaches that, created in the image of God and redeemed by Christ, every human person is worthy of respect, irrespective of his or her social status. This dignity of the human person is God-given and inalienable. People do not lose their dignity because of race, lack of success, age, poverty or disability. Similarly, what one owns or accomplishes does not give one a higher dignity over others.[428]

The Church also teaches that the dignity of the human person finds its fullest expression in social life, and so, the human person is not only an individual entity but also a social being made up of body and soul. The human being has therefore two major characteristics namely "Man is a material being linked to this world, and man is a spiritual being, open to transcendence and to the discovery of 'more penetrating truths' …."[429]

Asserting the equal dignity of man and woman, the Church teaches that "man and woman have the same dignity and are of equal value. In creating human beings 'male and female', "God gave man and woman an equal personal dignity. Man is a person, man and woman equally so, since both were created in the image and likeness of the personal God."[430] The CST also emphasises the superiority of people over things, 'being' over 'having', since God, after creation, gave man dominion over the created order.[431]

Closely connected to human dignity are some fundamental human rights[432] which are necessary for the preservation of human integrity. These rights include not only civil and political rights but also economic rights. Most fundamental is the right to the basic necessities of life: food, clothing, shelter, rest, medical care, and basic education. Other important human rights include: the right to security in the event of sickness, unemployment, and old age, the right to healthy working conditions, to wages, and other benefits sufficient to provide individuals and their families with a standard of living in keeping with human dignity, and to the possibility of property ownership.[433]

The principle of human dignity demands that all human beings should have ready access to all that is necessary for living a genuinely human life. Lack of access to these facilities plunges people into a condition that is inimical to their integrity. Human dignity can be protected and a healthy community can be

---

428 Cf. Edward P. DeBerri et al, Catholic Teaching: Our Best Kept Secret, fourth revised and expanded edition (Maryknoll, New York: Orbis Books, 2003), p. 20.

429 Catechism of the Catholic Church, 365; Compendium of the Social Doctrine of the Church, 129.

430 Catechism of the Catholic Church, 2334.

431 Cf. Genesis 1:28: For more on the dignity of the human person, see Compendium of the Social Doctrine of the Church, 105-159

432 A detailed outline and treatment of these rights are contained in the Encyclical Letter Pacem in Terris, in which John XXXIII echoes the United Nations Universal Declaration of Human Rights, implying that internationally accepted human rights standards are strongly supported by Catholic teaching.

433 U.S. Catholic Bishops, Economic Justice for All, Pastoral Letter on Catholic Social Teaching and the U.S. Economy, 1986, 80: This document will subsequently be referred to in this work as Economic Justice for All.

achieved only if human rights are protected and responsibilities are fulfilled. Corresponding to these rights are therefore duties and responsibilities to one another, to the family, and to the larger society.

In the light of this principle, it becomes clear how poverty constitute a big threat to human dignity, the unfolding and development of the human person and the actualization of the real goals of human existence. In the words of the Council Fathers:

> ... Whatever insults human dignity, such as subhuman living conditions ... as well as disgraceful working conditions, where men are treated as mere tools for profit, rather than as free and responsible persons; all these things and others of their like are infamies indeed. They poison human society, but they do more harm to those who practice them than those who suffer from the injury. Moreover, they are supreme dishonour to the Creator.[434]

It is primarily because poverty mars the image of God in human beings that its elimination represents a moral priority and a crucial first step in creating a world in which all people can live a fully human life. Every Government therefore has a moral obligation to eliminate poverty so that all citizens can live a life worthy of their dignity. Pope John Paul II adds that this task entails more than the mere elimination of poverty;

> ...it is not just a question of eliminating hunger and reducing poverty. It is not just a question of fighting wretched conditions, though this is an urgent and necessary task. It involves building a human community where men can live truly human lives, free from discrimination on account of race, religion or nationality, free from servitude to other men or to natural forces which they cannot yet control satisfactorily. It involves building a human community where liberty is not an idle word, where the needy Lazarus can sit down with the rich man at the same banquet table.[435]

4.2.1.2 Justice

In its classical formulation, justice "consists in the constant and firm will (of people) to give their due to God and neighbour."[436] Justice can be viewed from a subjective as well as from an objective point of view. From a subjective point of view, it translates into the behaviour that is based on the will to recognize the other as a person and from an objective point of view; it constitutes the decisive criteria of morality in the inter-subjective and social sphere.[437]

Of paramount importance to Catholic social teaching is however social justice. Social justice is that aspect of justice that "regulates social relationships...."[438] It concerns the way the larger social, economic, and political institutions and

---

434 Gaudium et Spes, 27.

435 Paul VI, Encyclical, Populorum progression, (Vatican City: Libreria Editrice Vaticana, Macrh 26, 1967), 47.

436 The Catechism of the Catholic Church, 1807; cf. St. Thomas Aquinas, Summa Theologiae, II-II, q. 58, a. I

437 Compendium of the Social Doctrine of the Church, 201.

438 Ibid.

structures of society are organized. Social justice implies that persons have an obligation to be active and productive participants in the life of the society and that society has a duty to enable them to participate in this way.[439] In light of this, social justice constitutes a major target of all the principles of Catholic social teaching: "A large part of the Church's social teaching is solicited and determined by important social questions, to which social justice is the proper answer."[440] It is through the lens of social justice that people will begin to take proper note of the problems and issues facing the human person in the community, the nation and finally the world, and begin to ask questions such as, "Why is there so much unemployment?" "Why are there so many poor people in our community?" "Why are the labour conditions poor in some areas of economic activities but good in others?" Social justice is particularly important in the present-day context, in which individual values of the person, dignity and rights are continuously threatened by exploitative institutions and individual who, propelled by greed, continue to bring untold misery on innumerable citizens.

Poverty is a dramatic problem of justice characterized by an unequal growth that does not recognize the "equal right of all people to take their seat at the table of the common banquet."[441] Its alleviation cannot afford to neglect the dictates of justice. "Love for others, and in the first place love for the poor…, is made concrete in the promotion of justice."[442] Justice is achieved when "each person – especially those persons in poverty or on the margin of society – has what she or he needs to survive, to develop and thrive, and to give back to the community. Social Justice demands that the right of each person to share in the goods of creation to that extent be recognised."[443]

4.2.2 The Basic Social Principles

4.2.2.1 The Principle of Common Good

This principle focuses on the human person as a social being. It underscores the fact that the human person is not only sacred but also social. As a social being, one realizes his or her dignity and rights in relationship with others in the community. It is only in the community and in relationship with the wider society that the human dignity can fully unfold and attains fulfilment. Throwing more light on this concept, the Vatican II Council Fathers clearly stipulate that the common Good indicates "the sum total of social conditions which allow people, either as groups or

439 Cf. Economic Justice for All, 71.

440 Compendium of the Social Doctrine of the Church, 81.

441 John Paul II, Encyclical, Sollicitudo Rei Socialis, (Vatican City: Libreria Editrice Vaticana, December 30, 1987), 33; Paul VI, Encyclical Populorum progressio, 6.

442 John Paul II, Encyclical, Centesimus Annus, 58.

443 Edward P. DeBerri et al, Catholic Teaching: Our Best Kept Secret, fourth revised and expanded edition, (Maryknoll, New York: Orbis Books, 2003), p. 30.

as individual, to reach their fulfilment more fully and more easily."[444] Every community has therefore the obligation to make these social conditions available not just to some but to all members of the community. This implies that "the distribution of created goods, which every discerning person knows, is labouring today under the gravest evil due to the huge disparity between the few exceedingly rich and the unnumbered propertyless, must be effectively called back to and brought into conformity with the norms of the common good, that is, social justice."[445]

In the same vein, everybody has duty to contribute to its attainment. Common good does not fall from heaven; it is worked for and attained in the human communities. The attainment of common good therefore makes some basic demands on the individuals, on the state at the national level and on the comity of nations at the international level. All individuals, groups and social institutions are to work together to ensure that all human persons "have ready access to all that is necessary for living a genuinely human life: for example, food, clothing, housing, the right to freely choose their state of life and set up a family, the right to education, work, to their good name, to respect, to proper knowledge, the right to act according to the dictates of conscience and to safeguard their privacy, and rightful freedom, including freedom of religion."[446] Put differently, Common Good Principle "implies that every individual, no matter how high or low, has a duty to share in promoting the welfare of the community as well as a right to benefit from that welfare."[447] Every individual therefore has a duty to contribute to the attainment of common good; no one is exempted.

Efforts at attaining the common good must however avoid restricting it to the historical und materialistic dimension which ends up transforming it into mere socio-economic well-being. These efforts must preserve the transcendental dimension which reaches its fullness by virtue of faith in Jesus' Passover and leads to the ultimate attainment of the ultimate goal of the person, which is God himself.[448]

The principle of Common Good has often been evoked in Catholic social doctrine in condemning poverty in all it ramifications but especially with regard to the aspect of exclusion from the social, economic and political life of the society. For this reason, it has been emphasized that "Common" implies "all-inclusive": the common good cannot exclude or exempt any section of the population. A situation in which any segment of the population is excluded from participation in the life of

444 Gaudium et Spes, 26.

445 Pius XI, Encyclical, Quadragesimo Anno, 197, as cited in: Compendium of the Social Doctrine of the Church, 167.

446 Gaudium et Spes, 26

447 Cf. Catholic Bishops' Conference of England and Wales, The Common Good and the Catholic Church's Social Teaching: A statement by the Catholic Bishops' Conference of England and Wales, 1996.

448 Compendium of the Social Doctrine of the Catholic Church, 170.

the community even at a minimal level is therefore a contradiction to the concept of the common good that calls for rectification.[449]

The principle of Common Good is also invoked in rejecting the trickle-down approach to poverty alleviation. To this end, the Catholic Bishops' Conference of England and Wales observes:

> There are some ideological thinkers who advocate this approach. We would question their proposition that the further enrichment of the already wealthy must, as the inevitable result of economic laws, eventually also improve the lot of the less well-off and the poor. This proposition is contrary to common sense as well as to actual experience. Some of those who employ it may merely be seeking justification for the pursuit of their own economic interests. Even from the point of view of the wealthy this is self-defeating.[450]

4.2.2.2 The Principle of the Universal Destination of Goods

The principle of the universal destination of goods fortifies the principle of common good. It stipulates that "God destined the earth and all it contains for all men and all peoples so that all created things would be shared fairly by all mankind under the guidance of justice tempered by charity."[451] The goods of the earth are created by God who destined them for the sustenance of human life. The ability of the human person to feed himself, grow, interact with others, and attain the highest purpose to which he is called is dependent on these goods.[452] Each human person must therefore have access to the basic level of well-being for his full development. This, Pius XII observes, is a natural right inscribed in human nature and not a merely positive right connected with changing historical circumstances.[453]

The Church emphasizes that wages, in other words, remuneration for work and social benefits "are still a practical means whereby the vast majority of people can have access to those goods which are intended for common use: both the goods of nature and manufactured goods."[454] For the working class, what is of paramount importance is the remuneration for the work they do. However, wages alone do not fulfil the dictates of justice. For this reason, the Church speaks of 'just remuneration' or 'just wage' which is more than the mere payment of what is agreed upon between the employer and the employer.

Because of the crucial importance of a just wage[455] to the well being of the human person, Pope Leo XIII insisted that the right to a just wage cannot be left to

---

449 Catholic Bishops' Conference of England and Wales, The Common Good and the Catholic Church's Social Teaching, op. cit, 70.

450 Ibid. 72.

451 Gaudium et Spes 69.

452 Pius XII, Radio Message on he fiftieth anniversary of Rerum Novarum, 1 June 1941.

453 Ibid.

454 John Paul II, Encyclical, Laborem Exeecens, (Vatican City: Libreria Editrice Vaticana, September 14, 1981), 19.

455 John Paul II went as far as saying that the "just wage" is the key means of verifying the justice of the whole socioeconomic system and, in any case, of checking that it is functioning justly. Cf. Laborem Exercens, 19.

the "free consent of the parties, so that the employer, having paid what was agreed upon, has done his part and seemingly is not called upon to do anything beyond."[456] Basing his argument on the two-fold nature of human work as a personal and necessary reality, the Pope insists that the fulfilment of justice in the negotiation and payment of wages should not be restricted to just what is agreed upon. "For if work as something personal belongs to the sphere of the individual's free use of his own abilities and energy, as something necessary it is governed by the grave obligation of every individual to ensure the preservation of life."[457] Against this backdrop, the Pope concludes that "every individual has a natural right to procure what is required to live; and the poor can procure that in no other way than by what they can earn through their work."[458]

Leo XIII consequently advocated for a family wage. A workman's wages, he said, should be sufficient to enable him to support himself, his wife and his children.[459] He added that: "If through necessity or fear of a worse evil the workman accepts harder conditions because an employer or contractor will afford no better, he is made the victim of force and injustice."[460] He called for the intervention of the State not just to ensure the fulfilment of what had been explicitly agreed upon, but also to ensure that justice is fully done through the payment of a just wage.[461] He however cautioned against undue interference on the part of the State and insisted for this reason that the State must collaborate with some relevant societies or boards or some other mode.[462]

Besides wages, various *social benefits* intended to secure the life and health of workers and their families are also crucial in ensuring that the poor have a fair share of the goods that people have in common. The social benefits are identified to include medical assistance/ health care, enough time for rest, including Sunday rest, a pension and insurance for old age and in case of accidents at work. In addition to these social benefits, provision should also be made for working environment and manufacturing processes which are not harmful to the workers' physical health or to their moral integrity. All of this, the Pope insists, should be treated not just as privileges but as "a whole system of particular rights which, together with remuneration for work, determine the correct relationship between worker and employer."[463]

---

456 Leo XIII, Rerum Novarum, (Vatican City: Libreria Editrice Vaticana, May 15, 1891), 43.

457 Centesimus Annus, 8.

458 Leo XIII, Encaclical, Rerum Novarum, 44.

459 Ibid., 46. See also John Paul II, Encyclical Laborem Exeecens, 19.

460 Leo XIII, Encaclical, Rerum Novarum, 45.

461 Ibid., 45.

462 Pope Leo enumerated the following bodies: the workman's union, societies for mutual help; various benevolent foundations established by private persons to provide for the workman, and for his widow or his orphans, in case of sudden calamity, in sickness, and in the event of death; and institutions for the welfare of boys and girls, young people, and those more advanced in years. Cf. Rerum Novarum, 48 & 49.

463 John Paul II, Encyclical Laborem Exeecens, 19.

In line with the principle of the universal destination of goods, the Church has also consistently defended the right to private ownership of property, insisting that "private property and other forms of private ownership of external goods contribute to self-expression and provide people with the opportunity of exercising a role in society and in the economy; they afford each person an indispensable zone for personal and family autonomy and the conditions for civil liberty."[464] Based on this, the Church condemns socialist communism as evil, "for it would injure those whom it is intended to benefit, it would be contrary to the natural right of mankind, and it would introduce confusion and disorder into the commonwealth."[465]

While defending the right to private ownership, the Church maintains that ownership of goods should equally be accessible to all,[466] but cautions however that this right should not be viewed to be absolute and untouchable but should rather be subordinated to the right to common use, since goods are meant for everyone.[467] For this reason, the Church's social teaching calls for the recognition of the social function of all forms of private ownerships. This social function entails that "man should regard the external things that he legitimately possesses not only as his own but also as common in the sense that they should be able to benefit not only him but also others"[468] In this way the right to private property becomes limited by the common purpose of goods.

Ownership of the means of production is judged just and legitimate when it serves useful work, but as unjust and illegitimate when it impedes, exploits or eliminates the work of others or breaks workers solidarity in pursuit of profit which is not the result of overall expansion of work and the wealth of the society.[469]

The Church, in her social teaching, is resolute in condemning any system that creates two classes of the "haves" and the "have-nots"; a situation in which very few people acquire a larger part of available wealth, having more than they need while many are left without the basic necessities of life.[470]

The principle of the universal destination of goods in general points to the fact that poverty (which also means the denial of access to the goods of the earth) is a great threat to the dignity of man. It also reveals the injustice inherent in any society that harbours poverty amidst affluence. It demands that the poor and the marginalized in the society should be the focus of particular concern. Such concern

464 Gaudium et Spes, 71.

465 Leo XIII, Encaclical, Rerum Novarum, 12.

466 John Paul II, Encyclical, Centesimus Annus, 6.

467 John Paul II, Encyclical Laborem Exeecens, 14.

468 Gaudium et Spes, 69.

469 John Paul II, Encyclical, Centesimus Annus, 43.

470 Benedict XVI, Encyclical, Caritas in Veritate, (Vatican City: Libreria Editrice Vaticana, June 29, 2009), 22.

should be directed towards empowering them to have their legitimate share of the goods of the earth.[471]

The Church further teaches that the principle of the universal destination of goods is "an invitation to develop an economic vision inspired by moral values that permit people not to lose sight of the origin or purpose of the good, so as to bring about a world of fairness and solidarity, in which the creation of wealth can take on a positive function."[472] Such a vision provides a means for promoting the well being of all peoples and for preventing the exclusion and exploitation of any human person.[473] In order to ensure that this right is exercised in an equitable and orderly fashion, regulated interventions are necessary - interventions that are the result of national and international agreement, and juridical order that adjudicates and specifies the exercise of this right.[474]

4.2.2.3 The Principle of Solidarity

This principle proves to be fundamental to the Christian view of social and political organization. Solidarity also gives depth to the concept of common good by insisting that it is essential to act in favour of the well-being of all, particularly those who are most poor and marginalized. It stresses the fact that the human person, though independent, is also dependent.

Solidarity was initially used by German social theorists such as H. Pesch, G. Gundlach, and Oswalld von Nell-Breuning to differentiate Catholic social theory from the modern theories of liberalism and communism, especially as expressed in liberal capitalism[475] and communist collectivism.[476] Catholic 'solidarism' was consequently developed and evoked to counteract the forces of liberal capitalism and communist collectivism of that time. It sort to transpose pre-modern understanding of human being as essentially social, and of society itself as organic and cooperative, into the modern context of industrialized societies with complex exchange economies.[477]

The principle of solidarity as developed by Jesuits H. Pesch, G. Gundlach, and Oswalld von Nell-Breuning has two dimensions. It highlights, on the one hand, the

---

471 For more on private ownership of property and universal destination of material goods, read for instance: Pius XI, Encyclical, Quadragesimo Anno, 45-52; John Paul II, Encyclical, Centesimus Annus, 30-43; Economic Justice for All, 114-115

472 Compendium of the Social Doctrine of the Church, 174

473 Ibid., 175.

474 Ibid., 173.

475 Liberal capitalism emphasizes individualism to the point of dehumanizing the individuals. It exalts individual choice and interest to the point of subjecting the common good to them, thereby derogating our common humanity and responsibility for one another.

476 Communist collectivism tends generally to depersonalize the individuals by totally subordinating them to the collective will. The theories of liberalism and collectivism view the state as an extrinsic aggregate constructed by the conventions of social contracts.

477 Mathew L. Lamb, "Solidarity" in: The New Dictionary of Catholic Social Thought, ed. Judith A Dwyer (Collegeville, Minnesota: Liturgical Press, 1994).

mutual ties between the individuals in the community (*Gemeinverstrickung*), and on the other hand, the ties between the individuals and the community (*Gemeinhaftung*). Oswald von Nell-Breuning, opined that in the bond of solidarity "all individuals are involved as members of the social totality in the common social destiny of this totality; similarly the totality (society or community) is inextricably involved in the destiny of the members."[478] Expressed in common language, 'we are all in the same boat.' Nell-Breuning further explains that from this "principle of common involvement there follows . . . the principle of common responsibility: every individual as a member of the community must 'respond', i.e., stand responsible for the welfare of each and every member."[479]

The principle of solidarity insists that the members of a society are all part of a network of relationships that tie them to others. Every individual person shares in a responsibility for the well being of others. Each and every individual person has also a responsibility to work towards the realisation of the common good. This duty must be understood as a moral obligation. It also obliges the stronger communities to render help to the weaker communities.[480]

This basic understanding of solidarity has been adopted and engraved into the Catholic social teaching. In the social encyclicals and in many other social documents of later years, solidarity is conceived mainly as "a question of interdependence, sensed as a system determining relationships in the contemporary world, in its economic, cultural, political and religious elements, and accepted as a moral category."[481] Viewing solidarity from this wider perspective, John Paul II argues: "(Solidarity) is not a feeling of vague compassion or shallow distress at the misfortunes of so many people, both near and far. On the contrary, it is a firm and persevering determination to commit oneself to the common good; that is to say to the good of all and of each individual, because we are all really responsible for all."[482] The Pontiff identifies the concept of solidarity with the poor and marginalized as a constitutive element of the Gospel and essential for lasting peace.

As a Christian virtue, Solidarity leads to a new vision of the unity of humankind, a reflection of God's triune intimate life. It promotes the respect for and guards against the exploitation of the human person. It helps one to see the "other" whether a person, people or nation not just as some kind of instrument, with a work capacity and physical strength to be exploited at low cost and then discarded when no longer useful, but as "neighbour", a "helper" to be made a sharer, on a par with ourselves, in the banquet of life to which all are equally invited by God.[483] This

478 Oswald von Nell-Breuning, "Solidarism," in: Sacramentum Mundi: An Encyclopedia of Theology, vol. 6, (New York: Herder and Herder, 1970), p. 113.

479 Ibid, pp. 113-114.

480 For details, see: Oswald von Nell-Breuning, Baugesetze der Gesellschaft: Solidarität und Subsidiarität, (Freiburg: Herder Verlag Gmbh, 1990), pp.16f

481 John Paul II, Encyclical, Sollicitudo Rei Socialis, 38

482 Ibid.

483 Ibid, 39 & 40.

reference to work is particularly useful in guarding against the deregulation and informalization of labour that have become, through sub-contracting and outsourcing, a characteristic feature of modern global economy. It encourages fair policies that protect the right of workers and encourage higher respect for the working person. In this way, solidarity proves to be a veritable instrument for guarding against working poverty.

The practice of solidarity is not restricted to the rich as it is often misconstrued. It is a moral responsibility of both the weak and the strong: It must manifest itself in the form of solidarity of the poor among themselves, between rich and poor, of workers among themselves, between employers and employees in a business and solidarity among nations and peoples.[484] People who are more influential because they have a greater share of goods and common services should feel responsible for the weaker ones and be ready to share whtat they possess with them. The weaker ones, for their part, in the same spirit of solidarity, should not adopt a purely passive attitude or one that is destructive of the social fabric. While claiming their legitimate rights, they should do what they can for the good of all. The intermediate groups, in their turn, should not selfishly insist on their particular interests, but respect the interests of others.[485]

Solidarity mandates the wealthy nations particularly to commit their resources and work assiduously to eliminate the hunger, misery and poverty of other nations whose citizens are unable to enjoy even elementary human rights. Interdependence in international relationships must be transformed into solidarity, based upon the principle that the goods of creation are meant for all. "That which human industry produces through the processing of raw materials, with the contribution of work, must serve equally for the good of all."[486]

The Church insists that solidarity is essential and indispensable in attempting to solve the numerous socio-economic problems responsible for human misery. It is therefore a key principle to be adhered to in order to wage a successful war against poverty. This principle is particularly proposed as a veritable instrument for overcoming the "Structures of sin" that dominate relationships between individuals and peoples. Through the creation of enabling laws, market regulations and appropriate policy reforms in judicial systems, the structures of sin that create human misery could be purified and transformed into structures of solidarity.[487]

Solidarity therefore must play its part in the realization of this plan, both on the individual level and on the level of national and international societies. "The "evil mechanisms" and "structures of sin"... can be overcome only through the practice of the human and Christian solidarity to which the Church calls us and which she

484 The Catechism of the Catholic Church, 1941

485 John Paul II, Encyclical, Sollicitudo Rei Socialis, 39.

486 Ibid.

487 Compendium of the Social Doctrine of the Church, 193.

tirelessly promotes. Only in this way can such positive energies be fully released for the benefit of development and peace."[488]

Another essential element of the principle of solidarity, especially with reference to poverty alleviation, is its insistence on the fundamental and preferential option for the poor. The fight against poverty receives a boost in the option for the poor or preferential love for the poor.[489] First and foremost, the Church maintains that in the spirit of solidarity, the poor should be seen "not as a problem, but as people who can become the principal builders of a new and more human future for everyone."[490] This implies that whatever is done to aid the poor and alleviate poverty should be seen as a rich investment in human persons who are carriers of great potentials of social reform and development. Justice will never be fully attained unless people see in the poor person, who is asking for help in order to survive, not an annoyance or a burden, but an opportunity for showing kindness and a chance for greater enrichment.[491]

The Church's preferential love for the poor is inspired by the Gospel of the Beatitudes,[492] by the poverty of Jesus and by his attention to the poor. This love for the poor is directed not only towards material poverty but also to the numerous other forms of poverty. Those who are oppressed by poverty are the object of a preferential love on the part of the Church because their misery elicited the compassion of its Head, Christ the saviour, who willingly took it upon himself and identifies himself with the least of his brethren.[493]

The principle of solidarity as expressed in the preferential option for the poor requires that the poor, the marginalized and in all cases those whose living conditions interfere with their proper growth should be the focus of particular concern especially in policy formulations and development plans. It urges individuals and governments "to share and employ their earthly goods, according to the ability of each, especially by supporting individuals or peoples with the aid by which they may be able to help and develop themselves."[494]

The option for the poor is also a demand for justice which makes imperative the integration of the poor into the social, economic and political life of the society. According to Pope John Paul II, "it is not merely a matter of giving from one's surplus, but of helping entire peoples which are presently excluded or marginalized to enter into the sphere of economic and human development."[495] For this to happen, he argues,

---

488 John Paul II, Encyclical, Sollicitudo Rei Socialis, 40.

489 This approach was taken up by the Latin American Bishops and given a strong pastoral formulation in 1976.

490 John Paul II, Message for the World Day of Peace 2000, 14.

491 John Paul II, Encyclical, Centesimus Annus, 58.

492 Cf. The Gospel of St. Mathew, 5:1-12.

493 The Catechism of the Catholic Church, 2448.

494 Gaudium et Spes, 69

495 John Paul II, Encyclical, Centesimus Annus, 58,

> ...it is not enough to draw on the surplus goods which in fact our world abundantly produces; it requires above all a change of life-styles, of models of production and consumption, and of the established structures of power which today govern societies. Nor is it a matter of eliminating instruments of social organization which have proved useful, but rather of orienting them according to an adequate notion of the common good in relation to the whole human family.[496]

Solidarity has also over the years provided a strong cohesion to worker's union in the struggles against authoritarian systems and injustices in labour relationships and for meaningful negotiations for, among other things, better wages, working conditions and social security. The historical movement that gave rise to workers' solidarity movements was acknowledged by John Paul II in his Encyclical Letter, *Laborem Exercens*. He noted that workers' solidarity movement came into being in the period of rapid industrialization as a reaction "against the degradation of man as the subject of work, and against the unheard-of accompanying exploitation in the field of wages, working conditions and social security for the worker."[497] By organizing themselves into appropriate associations, workers were indeed able to exercise influence over conditions of work and wages, and also over social legislations.

John Paul II further observed that in the contemporary world there are other forms of injustice much more extensive than those which in the industrial era stimulated unity between workers. He then emphasized the need for ever new movements of solidarity of the workers and with the workers. These movements should be formed to counter the social forces that encourage degrading of the subject of work, the exploitation of the workers and the prevalence of poverty and even hunger. The Church commits herself firmly to this cause, for she considers it one of the ways to become truly the "Church of the poor".[498]

In all, the principle of solidarity, "suggests that alleviating poverty will require fundamental changes in social and economic structures that perpetuate glaring inequalities and cut off millions of citizens from full participation in the economic and social life of a nation."[499] This participation which leads to the conviction that the most appropriate and fundamental solutions to poverty will be those that enable people to take control of their own lives. For this reason, efforts at overcoming the menace of poverty should target solutions that enable the poor to help themselves through such means as employment.[500]

4.2.2.4 The Principle of Subsidiarity

The principle of subsidiarity complements the principle of solidarity. Subsidiarity regulates social interactions in the hierarchy of the community. The principle

496 Ibid

497 John Paul II, Encyclical, Laborem Exeecens, 8.

498 Ibid.

499 Economic Justice for All, 187.

500 Ibid., 188.

stipulates that "a community of a higher order should not interfere in the internal life of a community of a lower order, depriving the latter of its functions, but rather should support it in case of need and help to co-ordinate its activity with the activities of the rest of society, always with a view to the common good."[501]

The first formal articulation of the subsidiarity principle occurs in the Encyclical Letter, *Qundragesimo Anno,* in which Pope Pius XI's describe it as a *fundamental* principle of social philosophy. In view of this, he postulates: "It is a fundamental principle of social philosophy, fixed and unchangeable, that one should not withdraw from individuals and commit to the community what they can accomplish by their own enterprise and industry."[502]

The principle of Subsidiarity focuses on functional interdependency in social life between the State, social groups and the individual citizens. It recognises that society is based on organizations or communities of people ranging from small groups or families right through to national and international institutions. It affirms the right of individuals and social groups to make their own decisions and accomplish what they can by their own initiative and industry.

This principle also affirms the duty of the State to provide all that is required to attain the common good. As Pope John Paul II puts it with particular reference to the economy:

> It is the task of the State to provide for the defence and preservation of common goods such as the natural and human environments, which cannot be safeguarded simply by market forces. Just as in the time of primitive capitalism the State had the duty of defending the basic rights of workers, so now, with the new capitalism, the State and all of society have the duty of defending those collective goods which, among others, constitute the essential framework for the legitimate pursuit of personal goals on the part of each individual.[503]

However, in any established human community, there is always the danger that the State while executing its statutory function would exceed its boundaries, infringe upon individuals and groups in society and begin to dominate rather than to serve them. This is where the principle of Subsidiarity should serve as an instrument of checks and balances. It limits government intervention to those necessary and indispensable functions that cannot be accomplished by individuals acting alone or even by smaller groups in society. Subsidiarity therefore guards against the situation in which the State robs individual citizens and smaller social groups of their legitimate functions, as this would amount to some form of injustice. Emphasizing this, Pope Pius XI writes: "Just as it is gravely wrong to take from individuals what they can accomplish by their own initiative and industry and give it to the community, so also it is an injustice and at the same time a grave

501 The Catechism of the Catholic Church, 1883.

502 Pius XI, Encyclical, Quadragesimo Anno, 79.

503 John Paul II, Encyclical, Centesimus Annus, 40.

evil and disturbance of right order to assign to a greater and higher association what lesser and subordinate organizations can do."[504]

Subsidiarity is "opposed to certain forms of collectivism, centralization, bureaucratization, and welfare assistance and to the unjustified and excessive presence of the State in public mechanisms. It guards in particular against the abuses in socialist and welfarist ideologies and systems that often assign too many functions to the state thereby increasing state expenses and stifling individual industry and enterprise. With regard to the excesses of a Welfare State, Pope John Paul II states: "By intervening directly and depriving society of its responsibility, the Social Assistance State leads to a loss of human energies and an inordinate increase of public agencies, which are dominated more by bureaucratic ways of thinking than by concern for serving their clients, and which are accompanied by an enormous increase in spending."[505]

One important implication of the principle of subsidiarity for poverty alleviation is participation. Subsidiarity does not only protect the weak from abuse in the hands of those in the higher levels of authority, it also obliges those in authority to support and empower all, especially the vulnerable citizens and groups to take their destiny in their own hands and so become active members of the society.

Since lack of participation is one major attribute of poverty, it follows logically that in the spirit of subsidiarity, efforts at alleviating poverty must, among others, seek to increase the chances of the poor to participate in the socio-economic and political life of the community. For the working poor in the informal economy this would invariably mean improving their labour conditions and developing, in particular, those aspects of the work that increases their chances of participating in decision-making processes both in the economic units in which they are engaged and in the community at large.

4.3 Analysis of Poverty in Catholic Social Teaching

Catholic Social Teaching approaches poverty from both theological and socio-economic points of view.

4.3.1 Theological Understanding of Poverty

From a theological point of view, the Church traces the deepest root of all the evils that afflict social relationships between people; of all the situations in economic and political life that attack the dignity of the person and assail justice to the estrangement of humanity from its creator. Based on this, the Church teaches that disobedience, through which the human person departed from God's loving

504 Pius XI, Encyclical, Quadragesimo Anno, 79.

505 John Paul II, Encyclical, Centesimus Annus, 48.

presence, and seeks to control his or her life and action in the world, has caused rapture in the internal unity of the human person, in the relations of communion between individuals and of the harmonious relations between mankind and other creatures.[506]

In the light of this theological understanding, the Church perceives the perpetration of human misery and material deprivation and the unjust oppression of the poor as the obvious sign of the inherited condition of frailty and need for salvation in which the human person finds him or herself as a consequence of original sin.[507] The conversion of the heart, on the part of the oppressors and a return to the source of grace become invariably a prerequisite for uprooting the afflictions of the human person. It is within this context that the call to conversion constitutes an important element in all the social documents, especially with reference to poverty and it alleviation.

4.3.2 Social Analysis of Poverty

The Analysis of poverty in social terms flows from the theological understanding presented above. In analysing poverty within socio-economic and political contexts, the Church in her social teaching approaches the phenomenon as a social question that has a direct relationship with social interactions in the society. The rebellion of human beings against God, Pope Benedict XVI argues, has deceived them into the conviction that they are self-sufficient and can successfully eliminate the evil present in history by their own action alone. It has also led them to confuse happiness and salvation with immanent forms of material prosperity and social action. This rebellion and confusion in the heart of man finds particular expression in his conviction that the economy must be autonomous, that it must be shielded from "influences" of a moral character. All these convictions, Benedict XVI further argues, have in the long term led to economic, social and political systems that trample upon personal and social freedom, and are therefore unable to deliver the justice they promise.[508]

Within the socio-religious framework, the Church attributes the causes of human misery not only to the obvious sign of the inherited condition of frailty but also to unjust structures or unwholesome socio-economic and political structures, which are sometimes referred to as "structures of sin."

4.4 Unjust Structures Responsible for Poverty

This concept, "unjust structures" or rather "structures of sin", has, in recent times, received a special consideration in the Encyclical letter of Pope John Paul II. In the

506 Cf. Compendium of the Social Doctrine of the Church, 27. See also: Gaudium et Spes, 13.

507 The Catechism of the Catholic Church, 2448.

508 Benedict XVI, Encyclical, Caritas in Veritate, 34.

fifth chapter of his encyclical *Sollicitudo Rei Socialis*, Pope John II gives a profound theological reflection of modern social questions. He analyzes the relationship between personal sin and "social sin that generates "structures of sin" and concludes that these structures of sin are created by numerous individual acts and decisions. According to him, "one can certainly speak of 'selfishness' and of 'short-sightedness,' of 'mistaken political calculations' and 'imprudent economic decisions'."[509]

Reflecting further on this, the Pope identifies two forces that are particularly responsible for the structures of sin: "on the one hand, the all-consuming desire for profit, and on the other, the thirst for power, with the intention of imposing one's will upon others."[510] He noted strongly that our world today is subjected to structures of sin owing to the fact that it is sustained by rigid ideologies in which different forms of imperialism hold sway instead of interdependence and solidarity.[511]

In the human society, these structures of sin that are responsible for poverty manifest themselves more concretely in the unequal distribution of the goods of the earth; in the exploitative manner in which human labour is valued and treated in the systems of production both at national and international levels and in economic injustice. Consequently, right from its earliest stage, the catholic social teaching on poverty and its alleviation has been closely tied to the struggles of the workingmen, who are often rendered vulnerable to unjust economic forces and denied a fair share of the goods of the earth.

4.4.1 Unjust Structures in the Distribution of Wealth

The Catholic social teaching recognises and gives elaborate attention to the link between poverty and lack of access to the goods of the earth or lack of access to property. It also recognizes the important role property rights can play in efforts to overcome poverty. The poor are conceived as those without access to property, wealth or the goods of the earth (these include both spiritual goods and material goods – economic, social and political goods). Hence Leo XIII refers to them as "those who do not posses the gift of fortune."[512]

The Church blames unjust socio-economic and political structures of sin for rendering the poor vulnerable and making it impossible for them to have a fair share of the goods of the earth. "As a result of this, many persons are quite aggressively demanding those benefits of which with vivid awareness they judge themselves to be deprived either through injustice or unequal distribution."[513] This is in the world today an "irony of growth", for as the world's wealth continues to

509 John Paul II, Encyclical, Sollicitudo Rei Socialis, 36.

510 Ibid, 37.

511 Ibid, 36.

512 Leo XIII, Encaclical, Rerum Novarum, 20.

513 Gaudium et Spes, 9.

grow in absolute terms, new forms of deprivation and poverty are also emerging in different parts of the rich countries and more and more people in the Third World are falling into absolute poverty – a clear sign of increasing inequalities in our world.[514]

4.4.2 Unjust Structures in the Organization of Human Labour

As noted above, one of the major ways that the structures of sin responsible for the poverty manifest themselves is in the exploitative manner with which human labour is valued and treated. They also manifest themselves in weak structure and labour policies that often create unemployment and deny people access to the means of production. In her social teaching, the Church maintains that poverty emerges and increases mostly as a result of neglect and violation of human work and the subject of work – the human person. Pope John Paul II confirmed this when he noted that the poor appear in many cases "as a *result of the violation of the dignity of human work:* either because the opportunities for human work are limited as a result of the scourge of unemployment, or because a low value is put on work and the rights that flow from it, especially the right to a just wage and to the personal security of the worker and his or her family."[515] "Labour question" has therefore remained a major characteristic of the Catholic social teaching on poverty.

During the period between *Rerum Novarum* and Pius XI's *Quadragesimo Anno* the Church's social teaching concentrated mainly on the just solution of the "labour question" associated mainly with industrial revolution within individual nations. At that time, *the "class" question* was especially highlighted as the centre of this issue. In the opening paragraph of his encyclical letter, *Rerum Novarum*, Pope Leo XIII alludes to the fact that failure in political institutions contribute in no small measure to the deterioration of the condition of the workingman which led to the escalation of poverty among workers. The deterioration of the workingman's condition, according to Leo XIII, began with the destruction of the workingmen's guild. "Hence by degrees it has come to pass that workingmen have been given over, isolated and defenceless, to the callousness of employers and the greed of unrestrained competition."[516]

The callousness of the privileged was heightened by rapacious usury and the custom of working by contract (seen today as an essential part of the liberalization or deregulation of labour forces) and the concentration of so many branches of trade in the hands of a few individuals, so that a small number of very rich people have been able to lay upon the masses of the poor a yoke little better than slavery itself.[517]

514 Benedict XVI, Encyclical, Caritas in Veritate, 22.

515 John Paul II, Encyclical Laborem Exeecens, 8: This view is also re-echoed by Pope Benedict XVI in Benedict XVI, Encyclical, Caritas in Veritate, 25.

516 Leo XIII, Encaclical, Rerum Novarum, 2.

517 Ibld.

In describing the economic circumstances that occasioned the writing of the *Rerum Novarum*, Pope Pius XI in his encyclical letter, *Quadragisimo Anno*, further highlights the structural injustice that was responsible for poverty among workers of that time:

> For toward the close of the nineteenth century, the new kind of economic life that had arisen and the new developments of industry had gone to the point in most countries that human society was clearly becoming divided more and more into two classes. One class, very small in number, was enjoying almost all the advantages which modern inventions so abundantly provided; the other, embracing the huge multitude of working people, oppressed by wretched poverty, was vainly seeking escape from the straits wherein it stood. Quite agreeable, of course, was this state of things to those who thought it in their abundant riches the result of inevitable economic laws and accordingly, as if it were for charity to veil the violation of justice which lawmakers not only tolerated but at times sanctioned, wanted the whole care of supporting the poor committed to charity alone.[518]

In the period following *Quadragesimo Anno*, emphasis shifted from the social question associated with industrial revolution within individual nations. The Church's social teaching in dealing with labour question widens its horizon to take in the whole world. The social ethical considerations in this epoch reveal with clarity how the structures of sin in socio-economic life manifest themselves not only in the relations between workers and managers but also in the relations between the various branches of the economy, between areas of varying productivity within the same political community, and between countries with a different degree of social and economic development.[519]

Pope John Paul II examines the structural injustice in socio-economic life with particular focus on the interaction between the worker and the tools and means of production which he observed has given rise to the development of various forms of capitalism and materialism, which in turn resulted in materialistic economism in which human work is treated merely as a special kind of "merchandise", or as an impersonal "force" needed for production. Within this process man is therefore treated merely as an instrument of production, whereas he ought to be treated as the effective subject of work and its true maker and creator.[520]

The Pope also sees a connection between the prevalence of poverty in many parts of the world and denial of accesses to the means and systems of production.[521] To this end he condemned the situation today in which "...many people, perhaps the majority today, do not have the means which would enable them to take their place in an effective and humanly dignified way within a productive system in which work is truly central."[522] According to him, people are exploited,

518 Pius XI, Encyclical, Quadragesimo Anno, 3 & 4.

519 The scope of this work will not allow a detailed treatment of these issues.

520 John Paul II, Encyclical Laborem Exeecens, 13.

521 John Paul II, Encyclical, Centesimus Annus, 6.

522 Ibid., 33.

marginalized and excluded from economic development, mainly because they do not have the "possibility of acquiring the basic knowledge which would enable them to express their creativity and develop their potential. They have no way of entering the network of knowledge and intercommunication which would enable them to see their qualities appreciated and utilized."[523] This, the Pope maintains, is the situation in which many people live in the Third World; a situation that has impacted negatively on their participation and gains in the global economy.

4.4.3 Economic Injustice

In the pastoral constitution on the Church in the Modern World, the second Vatican Council Fathers deeply lament the unjust socio-economic order in which "many people, especially in economically advanced areas, seem, as it were, to be ruled by economics, so that almost their entire personal and social life is permeated with a certain economic way of thinking that often results in a decline of the social status of the underprivileged and in contempt for the poor. Such a structure, they maintain, has created a socio-economic imbalance in which extravagancy and wretchedness exist side by side. While the majority of people lack the absolute necessities of life and are deprived of almost all possibility of acting on their own initiative and responsibility, and often subsist in living and working conditions unworthy of the human person, others continue to live in luxury, squandering wealth and enjoying very great power of choice.[524] Pope Paul VI describes this imbalance which grows with each passing day as the structural injustice that continues to give rise to more poverty.[525] This structural injustice in socio-economic life, the Pope observes, rears its ugly head more in unbridled liberalism which "presents profit as the chief spur to economic progress, free competition as the guiding norm of economics, and private ownership of the means of production as an absolute right, having no limits nor concomitant social obligations."[526] He further points out that free trade, as the norm for market dealings in a so liberalized economic order, though good in itself, has been rendered inadequate in governing international trade. In the world of today, the existing global economic order produces lopsidedly wealth and imbalance because while industrialized and developed countries export primarily manufactured goods, developing nations export mostly raw materials. And while the price of manufactured goods increases, that of raw materials remains vulnerable to wide fluctuations.[527]

Further analysis of the prevailing socio-economic and political realities is made by Pope Benedict XVI in his recent encyclical *Caritas in Veritate*. Benedict XVI examines the unjust structures of sin within the contemporary processes of

523 Ibid.

524 Gaudium et Spes, 63 ; also Paul VI, Encyclical Populorum progressio, 9.

525 Paul VI, Encyclical Populorum progressio, 8.

526 Ibid., 26.

527 Ibid., 57-58

globalization. Most of his observation confirms the observations made in the first chapter of this work (cf. 1.4.6). He observes that our world today is witnessing in alarming scale a complex global interrelations and an international economic order marked by grave deviations and failures. The technical forces in play he identifies include: "the damaging effects on the real economy of badly managed and largely speculative financial dealing, large-scale migration of peoples, often provoked by some particular circumstance and then given insufficient attention, the unregulated exploitation of the earth's resources."[528] Within the current global interrelations, "the State finds itself having to address the limitations to its sovereignty imposed by the new context of international trade and finance, which is characterized by increasing mobility both of financial capital and means of production, material and immaterial. This new context has gravely altered the political power of States."[529]

Benedict further observes that the global market has also prompted new forms of competition between States as they seek to attract foreign businesses to set up production centres, by means of a variety of instruments, including favourable fiscal regimes and deregulation of the labour market. There has been at the same time a desperate and intensified outsourcing of production at low cost, all in a bid to reduce the prices of many goods, increase purchasing power and thus increase the tempo of development in terms of greater availability of consumer goods for the domestic market.[530] Within this process, the organization of workers has become extremely difficult. Existing labour unions have encountered more constraints in playing their traditional roles "partly because Governments, for reasons of economic utility, often limit the freedom or the negotiating capacity of labour unions. Hence traditional networks of solidarity have more and more obstacles to overcome."[531]

From the social security point of view, Benedict XVI further observes that already existing systems of protection and welfare, are beginning to crumble, finding it hard and could find it even harder in the future to pursue their goals of true social justice in today's profoundly changed environment. In many countries citizens are becoming more and more powerless in the face of old and new risks mainly due to unfavourable budgetary policies and drastic cuts in social spending often made by the states under pressure from international financial institutions.[532]

528 Benedict XVI, Encyclical, Caritas in Veritate, 21.

529 Ibid., 24.

530 Ibid., 25.

531 Ibid

532 Ibid.

4.5 Guidelines for Poverty Alleviation

4.5.1 The Guidelines in General

What the Church offers as guidelines for effective and sustainable alleviation of poverty are socio-ethical proposals tailored towards a structural transformation that would create a favourable social order in which human dignity, the common good, social and economic justice would be guaranteed based on the principles of solidarity and subsidiarity. They are actions that are required to correct the structural failures responsible for poverty.

The transformation which the Church calls for, appeals to both spiritual and moral capacities of the individual, and the entire society. She maintains that a lively dedication and interior disposition to justice and kindness and to the common good are needed to establish a political, social, and economic life that is truly human.[533] Concern for the poor and alleviation of poverty should therefore incorporate efforts to achieve a more just social order, the practice of virtue, and the pursuit of justice in the social economic and political life of the society. "It requires action to confront structures of injustice that leave people poor."[534]

Acts of charity and personal commitment on the part of individuals could help to ameliorate the effects of poverty but what is more effective for poverty alleviation is the fulfilment of the basic moral responsibility to assist and empower the poor by working collectively through the government to establish just and effective public policies.[535]

Efforts at alleviating poverty must avoid some misgivings about the poor. They must also avoid punitive attitude towards the poor and attitudes that stigmatize them. Very common among them is the misconception that the poor are poor by choice or through laziness; that anyone can escape poverty through hard work alone, and that welfare programs make it easier for people to avoid work.[536]

The Church's social *Magisterium* also emphasizes that defeating poverty would require collaborative efforts from all segments of the society. This implies that the citizens, communities, the market, and government would need to work together in a more coordinated manner to overcome poverty and advance human dignity.[537] Adequate provisions must be made for changes both in the life of the individual persons and in societal structures and institutions.

Recognising the fact that there is a close link between poverty, property issues and labour questions, the Church proposes guidelines that are particularly

533 SECAM, Justice and Evangelization in Africa, Statement of Episcopal Conference of Africa and Madagascar 1981, 8.

534 U.S. Catholic Bishops, A Place at the Table: A Catholic Recommitment to Overcome Poverty and to Respect the Dignity of All God's Children, A Pastoral Reflection of the U.S. Catholic Bishops, 2002, p. 14. Online copy at: http://www.usccb.org/bishops/table.shtml.

535 Economic Justice for All, 189.

536 Ibid., 194.

537 U.S. Catholic Bishops, A Place at the Table, op. cit. p. 18.

formulated to ensure that the poor receive a fair share of the wealth of the earth through their own industry and not merely as fruits of charity.

4.5.2 Work: Key Instrument against Poverty

In the social teaching of the Catholic Church, work is conceived not only as an essential instrument against poverty but also as a 'key to all social questions.'[538] This key role is assigned to human labour in the fight against poverty based on the recognition of two basic facts. Firstly, that majority of the poor are in this condition either because they do not have access to work or because they are working under unfavourable conditions. Secondly, that human work constitutes the major and legitimate source of wealth, or at least of the conditions for a decent life. Non-precarious work guarantees a fair share of the goods of the earth.[539] According to Pope Leo XIII, "It is surely undeniable that, when a man engages in remunerative labour, the very reason and motive of this work is to obtain property (all that is necessary for food and living), and hold it as his own private possession."[540]

Human labour generates and increases wealth not only for the individual persons but also for the entire nation and so constitutes both for individual and a nation a major means for rising above poverty: "Every one knows, too, that no nation has ever risen out of want and poverty to a better and nobler condition save by the enormous and combined toil of all the people, both those who manage work and those who carry out directions."[541]

It is therefore an important element of the Catholic social doctrine that efforts at alleviating poverty should unfailingly include policy reforms and structural reforms that would guarantee not just the availability of job opportunities but the availability of jobs that befit the dignity of the human person. For this reason, the Church insists not only on the dignity of work but also advocates for the right to work, the right to organize and the right to decent and favourable conditions of work, which includes just remuneration for work so that people can acquire moderate ownership, and be able to support their families.[542] Based on this, the Church in her social teaching condemns all forms of alienation found in work, when it is organized so as to ensure maximum returns and profits with no concern whether the worker, through his own labour, grows or diminishes as a person, either through increased sharing in a genuinely supportive community or through increased isolation in a maze of relationships marked by destructive competitiveness and estrangement, in which he is considered only a means and not an end.[543] The Church insists that in organizing labour and distributing the fruit of

538 John Paul II, Encyclical Laborem Exeecens, 2.

539 Compendium of the Social Doctrine of the Church

540 Leo XIII, Encaclical, Rerum Novarum, 4

541 Pius XI, Encyclicyl, Quadragesimo Anno, 53.

542 Gaudium et Spes, 67.

543 John Paul II, Encyclical, Centesimus, 41.

labour, the human person must be seen as the "subject of work" and not as mere "object of work" and as such be accorded due precedence over capital, that is, by observing the 'priority of labour over capital' and 'primacy of people over things'.[544]

4.5.3 Improving Employment and Labour Conditions

In the encyclical letter *Laborem Exercens*, Pope John Paul II throws light on how full and suitable employment can be attained and how work should be organised so as to guarantee universal respect for the rights inherent in work in conformity with the dignity of man, the subject of work. The Pope argues that in order to ensure employment for all and achieve full respect for worker's rights, all agents responsible for this must make provisions for overall planning with regard to the different kinds of work by which not only the economic life but also the cultural life of a given society is shaped; they must also give attention to organizing that work in a correct and rational way.[545]

The responsibility of providing a just and rational coordination, within the framework of which the initiative of individuals, free groups and local work centres and complexes must be safeguarded, falls squarely on the shoulders of the State. The State acts in this regard as an indirect employer of labour. In this capacity the State assumes the responsibility of conducting just labour policies. While the direct employer (that is the person or institution with whom the worker enters directly into a work contract in accordance with definite conditions) determines in concrete terms the actual work contract and labour relations, the State as indirect employer substantially determines one or other facet of the labour relationship, thus conditioning the conduct of the direct employer.[546] Supporting this view the US Catholic Bishops add that the most urgent priority for domestic economic policy should be the creation of new jobs with adequate pay and decent working conditions."[547] The government must act to ensure that this goal is achieved by coordinating general economic policies and by other appropriate policy measures. The general or macroeconomic policies of the state are essential tools for encouraging the steady economic growth that produces more and better jobs in the economy. The fiscal and monetary policies of a nation such as federal spending, tax and interest rate policies should be coordinated so as to achieve the goal of full employment.[548]

Pope John Paul II insists however that in the field of planning and organizing labour, action must also be taken in the dimension of international collaboration by

---

544 John Paul II, Encyclical Laborem Exeecens, 11-12.

545 Ibid., 18.

546 Ibid., 17,

547 Economic Justice for All, 136.

548 Ibid., 156.

means of the necessary treaties and agreements. The International Organizations[549] have an enormous part to play in ensuring that the criterion for these pacts and agreements must more and more be the criterion of human work considered as a fundamental right of all human beings, work which gives similar rights to all those who work, in such a way that the living standard of the workers in the different societies will less and less show those disturbing differences which are unjust and are apt to provoke even violent reactions. They must also be more highly operative with regard to plans for action jointly decided on, that is to say, they must be more effective in carrying them out.[550]

The organization of human life in accordance with the many possibilities of labour should be matched by a suitable system of education and training, aimed first of all at developing mature human beings and secondly at preparing people specifically for assuming to good advantage an appropriate place in the vast and socially differentiated world of work.[551] It further emphasized that efforts at improving employment and empowering the poor should take into consideration the importance of education, noting that since poverty is fundamentally a problem of powerlessness and marginalization, the importance of education as a means of overcoming it cannot be overemphasized. To this end, it is recommended that any long-term solution to poverty should pay adequate attention to education, public and private, in school and out of school. This recommendation is further based on the fact that lack of suitable and adequate education condemns many to joblessness or chronically low wages and prevents many poor people from escaping poverty.[552] Particular efforts should therefore be made to improve the ability of educational institutions at all levels to provide the personal and technical skills that are necessary for participation not only in today's labour market but also in contemporary society.[553] New strategies also need to be explored in the area of education and training for the hard-to-employ, displaced workers, the handicapped, and others with special needs. By taking advantage of opportunities for education, employment, and training, and by working together for change, the poor can help themselves to be full participants in economic, social, and political life of a nation.

The guidelines for actions toward improving human labour for poverty alleviation also include recommendations and call for policies and programmes at all levels to support the strength and stability of families. There is need to guide against the negative effects of the economy on families. Society's institutions and policies should be structured so that mothers of young children are not forced by economic necessity to leave their children for jobs outside the home. In view of this it is necessary to enhance employment practices, health insurance policies, income

549 The Pope makes the particular mention of the United Nation and the International labour organization as the most important organs in this regard.

550 John Paul II, Encyclical Laborem Exeecens, 18.

551 Ibid.

552 Economic Justice for All, 203.

553 Ibid., 205.

security programmes, tax policy, and service programmes so that they do not undermine but rather enhance the abilities of families to fulfil their roles in nurturing children and caring for the infirm and dependent family members.[554]

Policy action should also be undertaken to remove barriers to full and equal employment for women and other disadvantaged groups who are often trapped in jobs with low pay, poor working conditions, and little opportunity for career advancement and so are continually counted among the working poor. Such barriers can be removed through appropriate job training, affirmative action, and other means that will enable them to skip the hurdles that prevented them from obtaining more lucrative jobs.[555] Particular attention is needed to achieve pay equity between men and women, as well as upgrading the pay scale and working conditions of traditionally low-paying jobs.

4.5.4 Social Security Programmes against Poverty

The recommendations for poverty alleviation also include calls for social programme that are capable of improving the quality of life of the poor and help them to cope with shocks. Social Security Programmes and social welfare programmes dramatically reduced poverty and improve the quality of life. They are also clear evidence of the commitment of a government to social justice and a decent life for everyone. These programmes should however be organized in such a way that they would be able to provide necessary assistance to the needy in a way that respects their dignity. What is crucial in this area are public policy decisions that would help create and sustain credible income transfer programmes in a nation - benefit programmes that can lift people out of poverty. They should be designed to assist recipients, wherever possible, to become self-sufficient through gainful employment.[556] They should equally provide recipients with adequate levels of support. This support should cover basic needs in food, clothing, shelter, health care, and other essentials.[557]

Based on the conviction that poverty can also be effectively attacked through programmes that are small in scale, locally based, and oriented toward empowering the poor to become self-sufficient, the need to foster self-help efforts among the poor through programmes and policies in both the private and public sectors are also recommended. Such assistance can be rendered by private organizations, and the public sectors in form of seed money, training and technical assistance, and organizational support for self-help projects in a wide variety of areas such as low-income housing, credit unions, worker cooperatives, legal assistance, and neighbourhood and community organizations. Efforts that enable the poor to

554 Ibid., 206. See also: John Paul II, Encyclical Laborem Exeecens, 19.

555 Economic Justice for All, 199.

556 Ibid., 211.

557 Ibid., 212.

participate in the ownership and control of economic resources are particularly recommended.[558]

The regular evaluation of the tax system in terms of its impact on the poor is another recommended line of action for achieving social equilibrium. The tax evaluation should aim at raising adequate revenues to pay for the public needs of society, especially to meet the basic needs of the poor. It should also aim at reducing inequalities of income and wealth in any particular nation and reduce or offset a disproportionate burden on those with lower incomes.[559]

4.5.5 Just Economic Order: An Essential Requirement for Poverty Alleviation

The guideline offered by the Church's social *Magisterium* for an economic life that leads to improved employment and labour conditions and consequently to successful alleviation of poverty contains also proposals that will help "to achieve in social justice a national and international juridical order, with its network of public and private institutions, in which all economic activities can be conducted not merely for private gain but also in the interest of the common good."[560] Insisting that full employment which guarantees the rights of workers and gives them access to a fair share of the goods of the earth is the foundation of a just economy and that unless a just social economic system is established, equitable distribution of resources, creation of full employment and respect of workers' right can never be attained, the Church recommends reasonable regulation of the market-place and economic initiatives, in keeping with a just hierarchy of values and a view to the common good.[561]

The economic and moral orders should not be viewed as distinct from and alien to each other; that the former depends in no way on the latter. In the area of the economy, one must be open to the demands of morality. Economic justice demands, among other things, that in the conduct of economic affairs, "the dignity and complete vocation of the human person and the welfare of society as a whole are to be respected and promoted for the human person is the source, the centre, and the purpose of all economic and social life."[562]

There are two aspects of economic justice that must be emphasized: equal participation and just distribution. Equal participation requires that appropriate policies and institutions be established to ensure that everybody is given the opportunity to participate in the economic life of the community through his or her labour or/and productive capital. The just distribution requires the establishment of objective and democratic means for determining just wages, just prices and just

558 Ibid., 200.

559 Ibid., 202. See also: John Paul II, Encyclical Laborem Exeecens, 20.

560 John XXIII, Encyclical, Mater et Magistra, (Vatican City: Libreria Editrice Vaticana, May 15, 1961), 40.

561 The Cathechism of the Catholic Church, 2425-2436.

562 Gaudium et Spes, 63:

profits so that all participants in economic life will be guaranteed a fair reward for their labour and capital.

The establishment of a just economic order is not an exclusive responsibility of the State. Other agent of and participant in economic life such as the intermediate social bodies and the market (here understood as all profit oriented individuals and enterprises) also have their respective roles to play. In other word, the attainment of economic justice requires the responsibility and capacity of the various agents concerned, such as the markets, the State and intermediate social bodies.

4.5.5.1 The Role of Markets towards a Just Economic Order

The Church's social teaching appreciates the secure advantages that the mechanisms of the markets offer, making it possible as they do to utilize resources better and facilitating the exchange of products.[563] It also acknowledges that a truly competitive market is an effective instrument for attaining important objectives of economic justice. Markets moderate the excessive profits of individual businesses, respond to consumers' demands, bring about a more efficient use and conservation of resources, reward entrepreneurship and innovation and make information available so that it is really possible to compare and purchase products in an atmosphere of healthy competition. While recognizing the market-system as an irreplaceable instrument for regulating the inner workings of the economic system, the Church in her social teaching points out however the need for it to be firmly rooted in its ethical objectives, which ensure and at the same time suitably circumscribe the space within which it can operate autonomously. The freedom which markets guarantee in the economic sector must also be regulated by appropriate legal norms so that it will be placed at the service of integral human freedom.[564]

Care should be taken to avoid the so-called civilization of 'consumption' or 'consumerism'[565] To this end, the Church's social *Magisterium* condemns the treachery inherent in an economic development that is only quantitative, for the "excessive availability of every kind of material goods for the benefit of certain social groups, easily makes people slaves of 'possession' and of immediate gratification. The Church insists that a system in which social relationships are determined entirely by economic factors is contrary to the nature of the human person and his or her acts.[566] In line with this view all collectivist and statist economic approaches are totally rejected. The notion that a free market automatically produces justice is however not welcome. Distributive justice, for example, cannot be achieved by relying entirely on market forces.

Competition and markets are essential elements of economic systems. The markets must however be checked and kept within their limits. An idolatry of the

563 John Paul II, Encyclical, Centesimus Annus, 34.

564 Compendium of the Social Doctrine of the Church, 347-350

565 John Paul II, Encyclical, Sollicitudo Rei Socialis, 28

566 The Cathechism of the Catholic Church, 2423. See also John Paul II, Encyclical, Centesimus Annus, 24.

market alone cannot do all that should be done. "There are collective and qualitative needs which cannot be satisfied by market mechanisms. There are important human needs which escape its logic. There are goods which by their very nature cannot and must not be bought or sold."[567] The state has the duty to intervene in order to ensure that these needs are met.

4.5.5.2 The Contributions of the State towards Economic Justice

The Church's social doctrine recommends that in contributing to the just ordering of the socio-economy system, the action of the state and other public authorities must be consistent with the principles of subsidiarity and solidarity. This will help to create situations favourable to the free exercise of economic activity and establish limits for the autonomy of the parties in order to defend those who are weaker.[568] In summary, the principle task of the state would therefore include: Providing a regulatory framework, guaranteeing economic security, overseeing and directing the exercise of human rights in the economy, creating conditions which will ensure job opportunities, regulating monopolies, substituting for or protecting weak systems that are just emerging, responding to social needs according to the principle of subsidiarity. Pope John Paul II puts it in this way: "The State has a duty to sustain business activities by creating conditions which will ensure job opportunities, by stimulating those activities where they are lacking or by supporting them in moments of crisis. The State has the further right to intervene when particular monopolies create delays or obstacles to development. In addition to the tasks of harmonizing and guiding development, in exceptional circumstances the State can also exercise a substitute function."[569]

4.5.5.3 The Role of International Community towards Economic Justice

The role of the international community proposed in the Church's social *Magisterium* is better understood within the context of the modern processes of globalization. A major outcome of the current process of globalization consists in the gradual loss of effectiveness of nation-states in directing the dynamics of national economic-financial systems. The Church points out that in the face of this challenge, there is a greater need today more than ever for more commitment on the part of the international community (especially the national governments of developed nations and transition nations and the respective international organizations they dominate) to exercise a strongly guided role in directing these processes towards the goal of attaining the common good of the human family. In facing this challenge, the international community should support the states with suitable and more effective political and juridical instruments. It should also help to guard against the emergence of a dramatic situation detrimental to the weakest and

567 John Paul II, Encyclical, Centesimus Annus, 40.

568 Ibid.,15

569 Ibid., 48.

defenceless classes and nations and communities of the world.[570] In the formulation of the required political and juridical instruments, sufficient considerations should be given "to peoples and countries which have little weight in the international market, but which are burdened by the most acute and desperate needs, and are thus more dependent on support for their development."[571]

It is also a position taken in the Catholic social teaching that there is need for political policy interventions at the international level so that current globalization processes would not be directed "only according to economic parameters but also according to moral criteria."[572] True economic justice and sustainable economic development will undeniably become attainable and lasting only if it takes place within a clear and defined normative context within a broad plan for moral, civil and cultural growth of the entire human family. This would require using all available tools, organs and institutions to guide economic process in order to ensure that the dignity of man and his complete development as a person are respected, in the context of the common good.[573] In order to properly execute this task, there is clear a need to accelerate the consolidation of existing institutions and to create new organs better positioned to take up the responsibility.[574]

4.5.5.4 The Role of Business Owners and Management towards Economic Justice

In the first place, it must be borne in mind that in order to build an economy that is truly at the service of mankind and to create programmes of real cooperation among the different partners in labour, all those involved in a business venture must be mindful that the business community in which they work represents a good for everyone and not a structure that permits the satisfaction of someone's merely personal interests. This applies more to business owners and managers. To this end, the United States Catholic Bishops observe that property owners, managers, and investors of financial capital can contribute immensely to creating a more just society because the way resources and wealth are managed has a lot to contribute to the ability of the economy to fulfil the demands of justice.[575] This is in line with the observation earlier made by Pope John Paul II: "The degree of well-being which society today enjoys would be unthinkable without the dynamic figure of the business person, whose function consists of organizing human labour and the means of production so as to give rise to the goods and services necessary for the prosperity and progress of the community."[576]

570 Compendium of the Social Doctrine of the Church, 370-371.

571 John Paul II, Encyclical, Centesimus Annus, 58.

572 Cf. Compendium of the Social Doctrine of the Church, 372.

573 Cf. Paul VI, Apostolic Letter Octogesima Adveniens, 43-44.

574 Cf. The Catechism of the Catholic Church, 2440; Paul VI, Encyclical Populorum progressio, 78; John Paul II, Encyclical, Sollicitudo Rei Socialis, 43.

575 Economic Justice for All, 110.

576 Pope John Paul II, Address to Business Men and Economic Managers (Milan, May 22, 1983), in: L'Osservatore Romano, weekly edition in English (June 20, 1983). 9.1

In her social doctrine, the Church insists that in relating with workers, owners and managers of business have the moral obligation not to treat them as slaves. They must also uphold the dignity of workers and let workers attend to their religious and family obligations. They must not impose more work than a person's strength can endure and not tamper with a worker's savings. And finally, they must pay a just wage and give to the poor after needs have been met.[577] Care must also be taken to ensure that work is structured in such a way that family life would be promoted and mothers enabled to fulfil their duties in the family.[578]

In exercising their business responsibilities, they must constantly reflect on the moral motivation that should guide the personal choices they make. They should not allow themselves to be guided only by personal profit in term of the decisions they make, for instance, what to produce and where to invest their capital. Adequate considerations should be given to the wellbeing of their workers, the consumers and the entire society.[579]

4.6 Appraisal and Conclusion

This chapter is a search for an ethical orientation for a sustainable alleviation of poverty. It focused on the impulses from the Catholic social teaching. The social teaching of the Church drawn from the deposits of faith – Sacred Scripture, tradition and *Magisterium* – is contained basically in Papal Documents and the Pastoral Letter of National Episcopal Conferences and enriched through the contributions made by experts in various disciplines (cf. 4.1).

In her social teaching, the Church conceives poverty as a social problem that has its root in the rebellion in the heart of human beings; a rebellion that sets them against their creator and against one another. This rebellion manifests itself in social life (social, economic and political) in the structures of sin that have generated various forms of human misery, especially poverty (cf. 4.3 – 4.4).

Within this socio-religious framework, the Church offers some guidelines for dealing with the menace of poverty. These guidelines are founded on justice, human dignity and the principles of common good, universal destination of goods, subsidiarity and solidarity. Central to these guidelines is 'human work'. In these guidelines, the Catholic social teaching calls for the conversion of heart and structural reform in social economic and political life. This reform should ensure that human persons will be able to develop their God-given potentials and through their work acquire what they need to live the life that befits human dignity and be able to attain their final destiny which is the beatific vision. To this end, economic justice should be desired and pursued to ensure that people are given the

577 Cf. Leo XIII, Encaclical, Rerum Novarum, 20.

578 John Paul II, Encyclical Laborem Exeecens, 19.

579 Cf. The Cathechism of the Catholic Church, 2432; John Paul II, Encyclical, Centesimus Annus, 35.

opportunity to participate in the processes of wealth creation and so be able to have a fair share of the goods of the earth (cf. 4.5).

These guidelines, no doubt, provide some ethical basis that proves to be useful in the search for a lasting solution to the problem of poverty. The visions and proposals contained in them provide indeed a wellspring from which policy makers and executors can draw in their search for enduring solutions to the nagging problem of poverty. These guidelines have however some noticeable limitations. It is an established fact that the modern CST emerged within a European context. It has unfortunately remained ever since then more conversant with the Western terrain and focuses more on the events taking place in the Western world, giving only but a limited attention to concrete social problems in the less developed nations of the world. One obvious setback one would encounter in any attempt to apply the guidelines provided by the CST to the Nigerian situation or to any other Third Word economy is this western flavour that dominates the general orientation. In dealing with labour issues for instance, the CST concentrate more on the problems faced by paid labour and so has little to offer with regard to the many problems faced by self employed workers. In a nation like Nigeria in which 90% of new job creation is in the informal economy dominated by self employed workers, the local labour question goes certainly beyond the scope of paid labour. It inevitably includes the many problems encountered by the many self-employed workers in the informal economy.

In order to be relevant to the socio-economic realities that prevail in Nigeria, the ethical ideals of the CST must be given proper adaptation. This takes us to the next level of our search for a plausible ethical orientation for an effective and sustainable alleviation of poverty in Nigeria. What we need now in concrete terms is a suitable framework or strategy for adapting the labour-based guidelines offered by the Church through her social teaching. This will form the major pre-occupation of the next chapter.

CHAPTER FIVE

Poverty Alleviation Strategies in International Discussions

Introduction

Through out the history of human development, many programmes have been embarked upon in the fight against poverty. Each programme has sought to reduce the level of poverty either in the entire world or in a country or in a community or amongst a group of people. Just as the design of programmes varied from one another, so also are the focus and the strategies adopted. While some of them aimed at removing social and legal barriers, others focused on economic poverty or facilitating income growth among the poor. Spiritual purification, inculcation of moral uprightness, forced labour, quality social services (education, health etc), and income redistribution are however some other methods adopted over the years in combating the menace of poverty. How the phenomenon of poverty and its causes are understood in any giving epoch in history and in any part in the world have played a crucial role in the formulation of these anti-poverty programmes and in choosing any particular strategy or approach.

In the search for a suitable framework or strategy for adapting the work-based guidelines for poverty alleviation offered by the Church through her social teaching, this chapter embarks on a chronological and systematic examination of various efforts that have been made at the international scene towards alleviating poverty. We have chosen a more or less historical approach stretching from the ancient times to the contemporary times.

The examination of the various programmes and strategies will be done in three phases: the pre-industrialization era, the industrialization era, and the post industrialization era. It is important to note at this initial stage that what we will be dealing with are poverty alleviation programmes and strategies that have historically overlapped and sometimes coexisted in mutuality and contradiction. This means that in some cases a clear-cut demarcation may not be possible.

5.1 Previous Efforts

5.1.1 Pre-industrialization Era

Poverty has been a concern in societies since the beginning of recorded history. Sociologists and anthropologists have observed that, social stratification – the division of a society into a hierarchy of wealth, power and status was a defining characteristic of the earliest civilizations, including those of ancient Greece,

Babylon and Egypt and Sumer in the Middle East and the Indus Valley of what is now India.[580] Under traditional (i.e., non-industrialized, basically agrarian) modes of economic production, poverty was widespread but was accepted as inevitable part of community life.[581] This was the prevailing attitude from the early times, through the middle age into the early stage of the modern era. Resignation was adopted as one of the methods of dealing with poverty. The poor were encouraged to resign to fate and accept their condition as their destiny. In line with this, Babylonian, Talmudic, and early Christian writings from later times entreated people that had resources and good fortune to relate to the poor with compassion.

As the powerful nations of Western civilization became established, they codified relationships between the poor and non-poor into law, as was done in Babylonia[582] through the Code of Hammurabi.[583] The eradication of poverty however did not constitute a major priority at this time. Efforts were rather channelled toward the care of the poor. This meant giving them what was considered then to be due to them - charity. Justice in this case meant giving to the poor in charity what was said to be due to them. It is therefore not surprising that the favoured response to poverty at this time was purely charity at the personal level. This, according to Carter Lindberg, was particularly the church's preferred relationship to the poor from the 1st to the 16th century.[584] This approach and method proved however to be futile with regard to alleviating poverty. It only contributed to cushioning the effects of poverty without encouraging efforts at eliminating the causes of the problem itself.

In the era of powerful landlords, the poor became frequently victimized by the rulers and other powerful and wealthy people in the society. The political system of the middle age agrarian society in Europe was basically a feudal system centred on land lordship. The ownership of land was controlled by the landlords. Land was leased to farmer who remained dependent on the landlords. The poor farmers were maltreated and sometimes subjected to hard labour and enslavement. Throughout Europe, land changed hands between lenders and borrowers. Foreclosure and forfeit became an enduring aspect of a type of primitive capitalism that dominated trade and manufacturing at that time. Society, even in long-settled areas, revealed a constant flux. In the typical village of western Europe, gradations emerged between the well-to-do farmer, for whom others worked and whose strips would grow if he continued to be thrifty, and the day labourer, who lived on casual labour, hedging, ditching, thatching, repairing terraces, pruning vines, or making roads. Heavy

580 Thomas J. Corbett, "Poverty," in: Microsoft Student 2006 [DVD]. Redmond, WA: Microsoft Corporation, 2005.

581 Carter H. Lindberg, Property, poverty and the Poor, in: Encyclopaedia Britannica 2005, Deluxe Edition CD-Rom.

582 Thomas J. Corbett, "Poverty" op. cit.

583 For a cursory description of this code, see: "Code of Hammurabi." Microsoft Student 2006 [DVD]. Redmond, WA: Microsoft Corporation, 2005.

584 Carter H. Lindberg, Property, poverty and the Poor, op.cit.

taxes, rents and dues, forced people to drift from sufficiency to destitution.[585] Many of the farmers at that time lived at the edge of minimal existence. Efforts at bringing poverty under control were however limited to those charity practices that emerged through Christian initiatives that were approved and supported by the feudal system.

5.1.2 The Era of Industrial Revolution

The second half of the 18th century witnessed an accelerated technical and economic development especially in Britain. Within the 19th and 20th century, the Industrial Revolution spread throughout Europe and the USA, and to Japan and the various colonial empires. The traditional agricultural economy became gradually replaced by one dominated by machinery and manufacturing. Following this development, power was no longer concentrated in the hands of landowners but rather in the hands of industrial capitalists who were owners and operators of factories and industries. This new socio-economic order created an urban working class.

The economic fluctuations and instability of the time and above all the liberalization of labour led inevitably to mass poverty. The rate of unemployment increased and the majority of the employed proletarians were so poorly paid that it was almost impossible for them to sustain their lives and those of their family members. Further compounding the problem of poverty were the problems associated with rural-urban migration, the dependence of the cities on industrialization and emergent capitalist economic tendencies. Poverty became an 'urban-menace' or 'city problem'.[586]

In seeking ways to check the spread of poverty at that time, some measures were taken to address the problem of unemployment. Most of the anti-poverty programmes and anti-unemployment programmes embarked upon at that time were unfortunately beclouded by political agenda and motifs. The initial public attempts made in most part of the central Europe in response to the high unemployment rate recorded towards the end of the 19th century manifested the political ambition that sought to mainly shield the government from all forms of endangerment.[587] Public labour interventions at the time joined forces with other programmes geared towards integrating the poor and job seekers into the society so as to prevent coup d'état or any other political unrest. This led to the emergence of a kind of politics

585 Cf. Richard J. Mayne, Europe, history of: The human condition, in: Encyclopaedia Britannica 2005, Deluxe Edition CD-Rom

586 Michael Schäfers, Prophetische Kraft der kirchlichen Soziallehre? Armut, Arbeit, Eigentum und Wirtschaftskritik, (Münster – Hamburg – London: Lit Verlag, 1998), p. 332.

587 Cf. Florian Tennstedt, Sozialgeschichte der Sozialpolitik vom 18. Jahrhundert bis zum Ersten Weltkrieg, (Göttingen: Vandenhoeck & Ruprecht 1981), p. 203.

that preoccupied itself with the task of protecting property owners from any form of invasion.[588]

Other intentions behind the programmes were the monitoring and moral discipline of the poor. These programmes were instituted because poverty was mainly viewed as a moral problem that has no social character. It was claimed that people were unemployed and poor because they were lazy and did not want to work. Work institute and Work centres (places were people were forced to work, mostly under inhuman conditions) were therefore established for the purpose of monitoring, deterring, rehabilitating and integrating the poor people who could work into the work-life of the community. To those who were mentally retarded and bodily disabled and so could not work, medication and segregation were applied in order to keep them away from the society. Strict legislations were also formulated to serve this purpose. The 19th century witnessed the intensification of such legislations applicable to poor people who were unemployed. For instance, under the Prussian criminal code of April 1851 tramping and begging were classified under punishable offences. If tried and found guilty, the offender was handed a jail-sentence, stipulating how long he or she would stay in a Workhouse (*Arbeithaus*). This was instituted with the view to restate the work-moral of the offender and to rescue him or her from ethical and moral dilapidation. The criminal code of the Northern German Federation which came into force in 1870 contains similar specifications.[589]

In due course, it became also obvious that another hidden interest in the so-called anti-poverty and anti-unemployment programmes was the recruitment of cheap labour for public duties such as work on the construction of canals and

588 Michael Schäfers, Prophetische Kraft der kirchlichen Soziallehre? Armut, Arbeit, Eigentum und Wirtschaftskritik, op. Cit., p. 335.

589 Cf. Ibid., p. 333: „Die gesetzliche Grundlage für die Einweisung in ein Arbeitshaus bildeten (...) die §§ 361 und 362 des Strafgesetzbuches. § 361 Nr. 3 bis 8 beschrieb den Personenkreis bzw. die Delikte, die Haft bis zu sechs Wochen und gegebenenfalls korrektionelle Nachhaft (Arbeitshaus) nach sich ziehen konnten: `3) wer als Landstreicher umherzieht, 4) wer bettelt oder Kinder zum Betteln anleitet oder ausschickt... 5) wer sich dem Spiel, Trunk oder Müßiggang dergestalt hingibt, dass er in einen Zustand gerät, in welchem zu seinem Unterhalte und zum Unterhalte derjenigen, zu deren Ernährung der verpflichtet ist, durch Vermittlung der Behörde fremde Hilfe in Anspruch genommen werden muss, 6) eine Weibsperson, welche wegen gewerbsmäßiger Unzucht einer polizeilichen Aufsicht unterstellt ist, wenn sie den in dieser Hinsicht zur Sicherung der Gesundheit, der öffentlichen Ordnung und des Öffentlichen Anstandes erlassenen polizeilichen Vorschriften zuwiderhandelt, oder welche, ohne einer solchen Aufsicht unterstellt zu sein, gewerbsmäßige Unzucht treiben, 7) wer, wenn er aus öffentlichen Armenmitteln eine Unterstützung empfängt, sich aus Arbeitsscheu weigert, die ihm von der Behörde angewiesene, seinen Kräften angemessene Arbeit zu verrichten, 8) wer nach Verlust seines bisherigen Unterkommens binnen der ihm von der zuständigen Behörde bestimmten Frist sich kein anderweitiges Unterkommen verschafft hat...' Der Kommentar definiert zu § 361(3; denjenigen als Landstreicher, der `habituell zweck-, geschäfts- und arbeitslos vor einem Ort zum anderen umherzieht, ohne die Mittel zu seinem Unterhalte zu besitzen und ohne eine Gelegenheit zum Erwerbe derselben aufzusuchen'. Diese Bestimmungen galten bis zum Ende der Weimarer Republik."

roads.[590] State social security was accordingly re-organized only in such a way that would increase the supply of labour to the industries and factories. They served also the interest of the labour market in favour of the owners of factories and industries. No serious attention was paid to the conditions of labour.[591]

Paternalistic welfare programmes were put together mainly in pursuance of ethical refinement. They were also used to coerce the poor into the world of employed labour. In executing these programmes, labour was gradually reorganised and was tied to the various forms social securities. A proof of a recognised labour relationship or work engagement (employment) became the prerequisite for a minimum social security. This structure led to the exclusion of the unemployed from all forms of security services. For instance, anyone receiving aid or any welfare services meant for the poor and unemployed would automatically loose his or her right to vote. To avoid being disenfranchised, job seeker had no choice rather than to forego whatever aid or support that was available.[592]

From the foregoing it is clear that industrialization with its economic and technological breakthrough did not bring much improvement to the condition of the poor. On the contrary, in the times of economic difficulties, the unemployed became identical with the poor. The identification and elimination of the real causes of poverty was never given the deserved attention. The measures adopted by the state for the alleviation of poverty were rigid and served more of the interest of the state to prevent social and political unrest and to suppress the danger of revolution which was perceive as a threat to political power holders. The measures also favoured the work ethos of the bourgeoisie and property owners in the society, used to prevent abuse, thrift, and to guarantee the protection of property.[593]

5.1.3 Post-Industrialization Era

Since the second half of the last century the conceptualization of and approach to poverty have drastically evolved. Poverty has come to be conceptualized more as an integral aspect of the issues affecting human development. Accordingly new approaches to reducing poverty have been adopted within this period in response to deepening understanding of the complexity of development.[594]

590 Ibid., p. 335

591 Ibid.

592 Cf. Florian Tennstedt, Sozialgeschichte der Sozialpolitik vom 18. Jahrhundert bis zum Ersten Weltkrieg, op. Cit., p. 205.

593 Michael Schäfers, Prophetis Kraft der kirchlichnen Soziallehre? Armut, Arbeit, Eigentum und Wirtschaftskritik, op. Cit., p. 336

594 Cf. World Bank, The World development Report 2000/2001: "Attacking Poverty, (New York: Oxford University Press, 2001).

5.1.3.1 *Economic Growth and Trickle-down Approach*

A new phase was opened after the World War II. This phase ran from 1945 to approximately 1955 and could be described as "growth does it all"[595] In the 1950s and 1960s many viewed large investments in physical capital and infrastructure as the primary means of development. The 'trickle-down'[596] view and the 'big-bush' theory found at this time wide prevalence, as it was argued that growth[597] leads to development and ultimately to poverty reduction. This view which was also mixed with the flavour of protectionism was backed up with arguments based on the presupposition that growth would spread or "trickle down" and that there existed a trade-off between growth and distribution.[598] In his 'big-push' or 'Nurkse's balanced growth' theory, Rosenstein-Rodan, for instance, argued that large-scale investment planning of industry and infrastructure were the prerequisites for growth.[599] It was suggested that inequality is necessary to generate the surplus required for the accumulation of capital.

Another proponent of the view, Simon Kuznets, argues based on his empirical findings that there is an inverse U-shape relationship between growth and poverty.[600]

> In the early stages, growth would not just require, but lead to, a worsening of income distribution, but then there would come a stage in which income inequality would begin to fall again: the idea is that primary agricultural economies start out with an initially equitable distribution with a low average, but that as they develop, portions of the population migrate to other sectors with greater inequality. But, as countries continue to

---

595 Ravi kanbur and David Vine, The World Bank and Poverty Reduction: past, present and future, in: Christopher L. Gilbert and David Vines (eds), The World Bank: Structure and Policies, (Cambridge: Cambridge University Press, 2000), p. 88.

596 Trickle down was the dominant development thinking in the 1950s and 1960s. It implies a vertical flow from the rich to the poor that happens of its own accord. The benefits of economic growth go to the rich first, and then in the second round the poor begin to benefit when the rich start spending their gains. Thus, the poor benefit from economic growth only indirectly through a vertical flow from the rich. It implies that the proportional benefits of growth going to the poor will always be less. The incidence of poverty can diminish with growth even if the poor receive only a small fraction of total benefits. See: Nanak Kakwani and Ernesto M. Pernia, What is Pro-Poor Growth?" in: Asian Development Review 18(1): 1–16, 2000. A study at the World Bank by Dollar and Kraay seems to suggest that growth is good for the poor irrespective of the nature of growth and that governments should attain stable development and poverty reduction by simply maximizing economic growth provided they avoid high inflation and maintain fiscal discipline.596 See: David Dollar and Aart Kraay, Growth is Good for the Poor, in: Journal of Economic Growth, vol. 7, no. 3, September 2002, pp. 195-225.

597 This is defined as an increase in a country's national income or per capita national income.

598 Devesh Kapur, John P. Lewis and Richard Webb, The World Bank: Its First Half Century, vol. I, (Washington D.C.: Brooking Institution Press, 1997), p. 89.

599 For more on this, see, James M. Cypher and James L. Dietz, The Process of Economic Development, (London, New York: Routledge, 1997).

600 Cf. Simon Kuznets, Economic Growth and Income Inequality, in: American Economic Review, 45 (1): 1 – 28.

progress, more of the rural sectors move out of agriculture and inequality eventually decreases.[601]

The result of all this is that efforts began to be channelled towards "physical output rather than human betterment, economic opportunity rather than social justice."[602]

The period from the mid-1950s until the end of the 1970s witnessed the questioning and rethinking of the trickle down approach. The idea of a necessary trade-off between growth and inequality became highly controversial, as there arose within this period a debate centred on the implication of the initial rise in inequality for the objective of poverty reduction. The ensuing discussions focused on the kind of intervention that would be required to prevent this undermining factor. Interventions that were put into consideration included: food subsidies, welfare, state support, highly progressive taxes, etc.[603]

5.1.3.2 Basic Human Needs Approach

By the 1970s, as persistent pessimism led to further enquiries into the viability of the trickle-down view and as the inequality that accompanied it continued to grow, there emerged a loss of confidence in national economic growth as adequate means of combating poverty and many scholars and economic experts began to express disbelief in the claim that market-based economic growth would really trickle down to the poor masses. A series of studies and academic debates at that time began to expose the limitations of the trickle-down agenda. This development, led to a shift of emphasis in favour of more labour-intensive methods of production as a clear path way to poverty reduction. In view of this, the basic human needs approach first formulated by the International Labour Organization (ILO) began to receive more attention. This approach regarded the development of human capital and the fulfilment of basic needs of the individual as the overriding objective of a poverty reduction strategy. Developing countries were also supported to put in place some incentive structures and complementary investments to ensure that quality education and improved health services were made available to the poor.[604] There was also a large increase in projects targeted directly at the poor - called poverty lending - mainly towards agricultural and rural development. The result of this was the emergence of a development strategy deliberately directed towards reducing poverty. This made a positive impact on wages and productivity more in favour of the poor than in favour of the non poor. Issues concerning security and political stability also received increased attention.

---

601 Simon Kuznet, as presented by Ravi kanbur and David Vine, The World Bank and Poverty Reduction: past, present and Future, op. cit.

602 Devesh Kapur, John P. Lewis and Richard Webb, The World Bank: Its First Half Century, op. cit., p. 95.

603 Ravi kanbur and David Vine, The World Bank and Poverty Reduction: past, present and Future, op. cit., p. 88.

604 Ibid., p. 90.

Although the understanding of poverty was substantially broadened throughout this period, the level of success recorded was painfully disappointing. The failure was attributed to failures of projects regarding poverty relief and difficulties in designing adequate policies. Obviously several important policy areas were not given due attention, for example participation and empowerment, discrimination, environment and major health issues.[605]

5.1.3.3 Neo-liberal Approach

The period from the late 1970s to the early 1990s witnessed a major upsurge in neo-liberal ideas concerning the development process and poverty reduction strategies. The neo-liberal position placed much credence on individualism and market liberalism and tended to restrict the role of the state to merely maintenance of law and order, provision of physical infrastructure and safeguarding of macroeconomic stability, i.e., providing a predictable environment for economic actors to make economic decisions.[606] The basic agitation was that state interventions amounted to distortions and rigidity in the market mechanism. It was argued that removing state intervention and ensuring free international trade and free play of market forces would guarantee fast growth and sustainable poverty reduction.[607] In viewing the state as an obstacle to economic growth and sustainable development, neo-liberalists consequently pursued programmes for "decreasing state involvement in the economy through trade liberalism, privatization and reduced public spending; freeing key relative prices such as interest rates and exchange rates and lifting exchange controls."[608]

The trickle- down theory was once exhumed to support the neo-liberal tendency of that time. This signalled a return of the view which stressed economic efficiency and growth as the main driving force for reducing poverty. This mode of thought exerted much influence on the Bretton Woods Institutions (the International Monetary Fund, the World Bank, and the U.S. Treasury Department) in formulating and implementing the Structural Adjustment Programme in the 1980s and the Washington Consensus in the 1990s.

5.1.3.4 Structural Adjustment Era

The 1980s are known as the period of Structural Adjustment. In the early years of the decade, the World Bank and International Monetary Fund (IMF) introduced the Structural Adjustment Programmes (SAPs) as economic policies for developing

---

605 See Devesh Kapur, John P. Lewis and Richard Webb, The World Bank: Its First Half Century, op. cit., p. 321 – 329.

606 Cf. Christopher Colclough and James Manor, (eds), States or Markets? Neo-liberalism and the Development Policy Debate, (Oxford: Clarendon Press, 1991); see also Peter Wallace Preston, Development Theory: An Introduction, (Oxford: Blackwell, 1996).

607 Ravi kanbur and David Vine, op. cit., p. 91

608 Cf. Ziya Öniş and Fikret Şenses, Rethinking the Emerging Post-Washington Consensus: A critical Appraisal, ERC Working Papers 03/09 ERC – Economic Research Centre, Middle East Technical University, Novermber, 2003.

countries. Under this programme, nations with poor economies received loans, made available by the World Bank. The Structural Adjustment Loans were designed to encourage the structural adjustment of an economy by, for example, removing "excess" government controls and promoting market competition as part of and in accordance with the neo-liberal agenda adopted by the Bank. The IMF on its part introduced the Enhanced Structural Adjustment Facility as a financing mechanism to support macroeconomic policies and SAPs in low-income countries through loans or low interest subsidies.

SAP policies embodied the neo-liberal ideology that eventually became the driving force for globalization. They were aimed at achieving long-term or accelerated economic growth in poorer countries by restructuring the economy and reducing government intervention. SAP policies include currency devaluation, reduction of government services, including cuts in social spending in order to reduce public deficits, reducing tax on high earners, reducing inflation, wage suppression, privatization, lower tariffs on imports and tighter monetary policy, increased free trade, and business deregulation. Governments were particularly encouraged or forced to reduce their role in the economy by privatizing state-owned industries and opening up their economies to foreign competition.

At the heart of SAP policies, were stabilization measures that were introduced to reduce the national rate of inflation. They usually include cutting the budget deficit and improving the balance of payments. Such measures later became a condition for Heavily Indebted Poor Countries (HIPC) to obtain fresh loans or further assistance and were therefore a part of the conditionality clause.[609]

Shortly after SAP has been fully implemented in many developing countries, its shortcomings began to manifest. The economic stagnation and a series of macroeconomic shocks – debt crisis, energy crisis and global recession – that were witnessed at the middle of the 1980s signalled the need for wider changes in economic policy and approach to poverty alleviation. In the face of all this, the course and the impact of structural adjustment became a subject of public debates and came under strong scrutiny and condemnation: at the end of the 1980s the issue of social costs of structural adjustment was raised and the discussion about the poverty agenda renewed.[610]

5.1.3.5 Washington Consensus

At the dawn of the 1990s, there emerged what was termed a consensus for development and was implemented to initiate the reforms that were considered urgent in the developing and transformation countries. This consensus came to be known as the Washington Consensus. The phrase was originally coined in 1990 by John Williamson, an economist of international repute, "to refer to the lowest common denominator of policy advice being addressed by the Washington-based

609 See: http://www.who.int/trade/glossary/story084/en/index.html, accesses on 03.03.2011.

610 For elaborate discussion on this, see: Devesh Kapur, John P. Lewis and Richard Webb, The World Bank: Its First Half Century, op. cit., p. 349 – 357.

institutions to Latin American countries as of 1989."[611] At its heart is an emphasis on the importance of macroeconomic stability and integration into the international economy - in other words a neo-liberal view of globalization based on liberalization, privatization and deregulation.

Its basic elements include macro policies incorporating fiscal discipline, interest rate liberalization and competitive exchange rates. They also include structural policies such as redirection of public expenditure priorities toward fields offering both high economic returns and the potential to improve income distribution, such as primary health care, primary education, and infrastructure; tax reform (to lower marginal rates and broaden the tax base): trade liberalization, liberalization of inflows of foreign direct investment; privatization; deregulation (to abolish barriers to entry and exit); secure property rights[612]

The Washington Consensus was indeed used as a development strategy based on market fundamentalism emphasizing privatization, liberalization and macroeconomic/price stability, downscaling and minimizing the role of government. These ideas proved however very controversial, both inside and outside the Bretton Woods Institutions.

Within the passage of time, the phrase "Washington Consensus" lost is original meaning in debates about trade and development. Today, it is widely viewed by its opponents as being synonymous with "neo-liberalism" and "globalization." This was confirmed by the originator of the concept, John Williamson when he remarked in one of his presentations: "Audiences the world over seem to believe that this (Washington Consensus) signifies a set of neo-liberal policies that have been imposed on helpless countries by the Washington-based international financial institutions and have led them to crisis and misery. There are people who cannot utter the term without foaming at the mouth."[613]

The Washington Consensus has been particularly criticized for putting too much faith in markets and constituting a threat to social justice. It is often argued that its excessive emphasis on market led it to ignore some developmental policy areas such as, land reform, industrial policies, strengthening the financial sector, improving education, competition policy, governance issues in both the public and private sector. It is also criticized for ignoring key role of finance in growth such as: Making credit available at affordable terms. Also believed to have been ignored, is the role the government can play in ensuring stability and preventing market failure. Critics believe that all of these were not given due consideration mainly as a result of the neo-liberal tendencies inherent in the agenda of the Washington Consensus.

---

611 John Williamson, What Should the World Bank Think About the Washington Consensus? World Bank Research Observer, Washington, DC: The International Bank for Reconstruction and Development, Vol. 15, No. 2 (August 2000), pp. 251-264.

612 Ibid

613 Cf. John Williamson, Did the Washington Consensus Fail? Outline of Remarks at CSIS, (Washington DC: Institute for International Economics, 2000).

The neo-liberal political economy has always been built on the basic assumption that interventionist strategies necessarily work against long-term public interest and that growth is accelerated by developing market and eliminating state intervention. Based on this, the proponents of Washington Consensus argued for instance that the Newly Industrialized Countries (NIC) in East Asia were successful in the 1980s because they were less protectionist, more outward-oriented and closer to norms of the free market than other developing countries.[614] On the contrary, some later empirical evidences revealed that the superior economic performance of the Asian NICs during the said period was rather as a result of interventionist strategies and an active industrial policy, dictated by considerations relating to longer-term competitiveness and dynamic comparative advantage.[615] Effective state interventionism and appropriate mix of state and market and import-substitution and export-promotion are therefore believed to be the key ingredients of their superior economic performance.

It was pointed out that South Korea and Taiwan, for instance, had managed to combine outstanding rates of economic growth with striking performance in the domain of employment expansion, poverty reduction and income distribution. This kind of empirical evidence further weakens the basic assumption of neo-liberal political economy that interventionist strategies necessarily work against long-term public interest. According to Ziya Öniş and Fikret Şenses, the strategy adopted by the NIC in East Asia suggests that under certain specific conditions, state interventionism can act in public interest and play a constructive role in the developmental process. Empirical facts were used to prove that during the era of neo-liberal restructuring, not only was overall growth lower, the degree of inequality in the global economy also appeared to have increased.[616] Based on these facts, the structural reforms which IMF and World Bank implemented in pursuance of the goals of the Washington Consensus have continued to attract wider criticisms. Doubts have continued to mount particularly concerning its effects on poverty und income distribution.[617]

The inadequacies and limitations of the Washington Consensus were further made manifest in its inability to achieve its set goal – growth that will reduce poverty in developing countries of the world. Contrary to expectations, rise in poverty has been recorded in many developing countries especially in Sub-Saharan

---

614 For more on this, see: I.M.D. Little, Economic Development: Theory, Polity and International Relations, (New York: Basic Books, 1992).

615 See for instance, Joseph Stiglitz, The World Bank Research Observer; Aug 1996; 11, 2; ABI/INFORM Global pg. 151-177.

616 For more on this debate see: Ziya Öniş and Fikret Şenses, Rethinking the Emerging Post-Washington Consensus: A critical Appraisal, op. cit., pp. 4-5.

617 For empirical evidence of rising inequality during the neo-liberal era, see, Robert Hunter Wade, Winners and losers: the global distribution of income is becoming more unequal: that should be a matter of greater concern than it is, in: The economist, 359 (8219), 2001. pp. 93-97. See also, UNCTAD, Trade and Development Report, 1997. New York, 1997.

Africa. All these joined forces in discrediting this neo-liberal policy agenda and political economy.

As a result of these weaknesses, limitations and failures of the Washington Consensus, some questions have been raised concerning how the global economic architecture should be reformed to promote stability, efficiency and equity among countries, and concerning the ability of developing countries to pursue their objectives in confronting the problem of poverty. The limitations also raise questions concerning how the Global Financial system should be reformed to make it more stable and perhaps reduce the risks facing the developing countries by reforming the global reserve system and developing better mechanisms for shifting risk.[618] All of these, point to the need for a new strategy and approach to development issues.

5.1.4 Appraisal of Previous Poverty Alleviation Efforts

We have seen that in the pre-industrial era poverty was conceived as an inevitable part of community life. In other words, some people are destined to be poor. This attitude invoked total resignation as the best means of dealing with poverty. Efforts were channelled toward the care of the poor. The only obligations assigned to the non-poor and their entire community was charity or alms-giving to enable the poor cope with the state in life.

In the industrial era, poverty was viewed basically as a moral problem that has no social character. The poor were blamed for their poverty. It was argued that poverty was a consequence of laziness. Consequently, punitive measures were adopted and channelled towards moral purification and inculcation of work discipline into the poor. Not much effort was made to correct the social-economic problems, especially poor labour conditions that force people into poverty.

The predominant feature of poverty alleviation efforts in the pre-industrial era and industrial era is therefore the determinist and individualistic conception of poverty, through which poverty was viewed not as a social problem but a problem of the individuals. Based on this understanding, the need for social change or structural reform was not considered a priority. Charity and moral purification were instead adopted as the best instruments against poverty.

This deterministic understanding and individualistic approach to poverty deviate significantly from the ethical orientation established in the fourth chapter of this work based on the impulses from the Catholic social teaching. Within this ethical framework, poverty is conceived not as the problem of the poor but rather as a social problem that emanate from structural failures in the social, economic and political life of the society. Actions that are required to deal with poverty are therefore not actions that concentrate on charity and moral uprightness of the

618 Joseph E. Stiglitz, The Post Washington Consensus, a power Point presentation, August, 2005, available at: http://www.policyinnovations.org/ideas/policy_library/data/01232.

individuals but actions that will bring about the structural transformation that would create a favourable social order in which human dignity, common good, social and economic justice would be guaranteed based on the principles of solidarity and subsidiarity so that every individual will be given the opportunity to develop his potentials and be able to earn a decent living.

Although in the post-industrial era poverty came to be conceptualized more as an integral aspect of the issues affecting human development, the too much faith in markets and over-concentration on economic efficiency and growth as the main driving force for reducing poverty that dominated the period however narrowed down development and poverty alleviation efforts to large investments in physical capital and infrastructure, while human development received little or no attention. Such an approach will definitely be ineffective for advancing the work-centred guidelines for poverty alleviation proposed in the Catholic social teaching. It also lacks the capacity for producing the favourable social order that offers the human person enough opportunities to develop his potentials and be able to earn a decent living.

5.2 Current Efforts at Alleviating Poverty

In recent times there has been a shift away from the purely economic approach that emphasizes economic growth to a pro-poor growth that emphasizes the growth that leads to poverty alleviation. Before examining these approaches, let us briefly but closely examine this concept.

5.2.1 Pro-Poor Growth Concept

Pro-poor growth is broadly defined by a number of international organizations as growth that leads to significant reductions in poverty.[619] Attempts to provide analytical and operational content to the concept have however given rise to two broad definitions of the concept.

The relative definition of pro-poor growth compares changes in the incomes of the poor with changes in the incomes of people who are not poor. Growth is 'pro-poor' if the incomes of poor people grow faster than those of the population as a whole. In other words, for growth to be pro-poor, income inequality must fall.[620] In this way, pro-poor growth would amount to inequality-reducing growth This understanding of pro-poor growth favours interventions that reduce inequality

619 See: Organization for Economic Cooperation and Development, Rising to the Global Challenge: Partnership for Reducing World Poverty, Statement by the DAC High Level Meeting in Paris. April 25–26 2001. See also: United Nations, A Better World for All, (New York: United Nations 2000).

620 Cf. DFID, What is Pro-Poor and Why Do We Need to Know? Pro-Poor Growth Briefing Note, February 2004; Howard White and Edward Anderson, Growth vs. Redistribution: Does the Pattern of Growth Matter? Development Policy Review 19(3): 167–289, 2001.

regardless of their impact on growth.[621] The strategy that is required for promoting pro-poor growth in this sense is one that "is deliberately biased in favour of the poor so that the poor benefit proportionally more than the rich. This is with the belief that such an outcome would rapidly reduce the inequality that exists between the poor and the none-poor.

The absolute definition of pro-poor growth is closely related to the speed at which absolute poverty is reduced: if the rate of pro-poor growth accelerates, then all standard measures of income poverty fall faster. In other words, if the incomes of poor people were to grow faster, this would lead to a more rapid reduction both of the extent of poverty (as measured, for example, by the proportion of people living on less than $1 a day) and of the depth of poverty (how far most poor people are below the poverty line).[622] This definition focuses mainly on the link between poverty and growth: growth is pro-poor if it reduces poverty. It pays less or no attention to developments on the inequality front.[623] It reflects pro-poor growth "as one that enables the poor to actively participate in and significantly benefit from economic activity. It is a major departure from the trickle-down development concept. It has been described as *inclusive* economic growth. Its outcome should be that no person in society is deprived of the minimum basic capabilities."[624] This understanding of pro-poor growth stresses the need to accelerate the rate of income growth of the poor through faster growth and by expanding the opportunities of poor households to participate in growth.[625] This is with the belief that such an outcome would rapidly reduce the incidence of poverty so that those at the bottom end of the distribution curve of consumption would have the resources to meet their minimum basic needs.

In general, pro-poor growth strategy entails "... the removal of institutional and policy induced biases against the poor, as well as the adoption of direct pro-poor policies.[626] Pro-poor policies put the poor at the centre of development policy. They require accurate information on the living conditions and livelihood strategies of different kinds of poor people: rural, urban, female, jobless. Such information can help to ensure that social sector spending reflects the nature of poverty in a particular country.[627]

In its absolute sense (promotion of both growth and poverty reduction), the pro-poor growth proves to be consistent with present day understanding of poverty

---

621 See: World Bank, Pro-Poor Growth in the 1990s: Lessons and Insights from 14 Countries, (Washington D.C.: International Bank for Reconstruction and Development, 2005).

622 DFID, What is Pro-Poor and Why Do We Need to Know? Op. cit.

623 Cf. Martin Ravallion and Shaohua Chen, China's (Uneven) Progress Against Poverty, The World Bank, Policy Research Working Paper No. 3408, 2004.

624 Nanak Kakwani and Ernesto M. Pernia, What is Pro-Poor Growth? op. cit., p. 3.

625 World Bank, Pro-Poor Growth in the 1990s: Lessons and Insights from 14 Countries, op. cit., p. 17. See also: Martin Ravallion and Shaohua Chen, What Can New Survey Data Tell Us about Recent Changes in Distribution and Poverty? The World Bank Economic Review 11(2): 357–82, 1997.

626 Nanak Kakwani and Ernesto M. Pernia, op. cit., p. 4.

627 http://www.who.int/trade/glossary/story019/en/, accessed on 03.o4.2011

and the current commitment of the international community to drastically reduce it. We will, on our part, keep a pace with this understanding of pro-poor growth since we are concerned with a country with a high rate of absolute poverty. We are however of the view that a harmonious bled of these two understandings (reducing inequality and reducing absolute poverty) would prove more beneficial for a developing country like Nigeria in which both the level of absolute poverty and the level of inequality are high. The outcome of this for poor people will however always depend both on the overall rate of growth and on changes in inequality. Inequality, if neglected, can slow down growth rate – both by reducing the ability of the poor to contribute to production and by causing social and political tensions, which discourage investment. In most developing countries, there is therefore the need for policies that can achieve this optimal combination. There is more scope for reducing inequality where its level is high. In this case, pro-poor growth would entail promoting both growth and poverty reduction by supporting policies and actions that promote growth and at the same time reduce inequality.

5.2.2 Post-Washington Consensus

By the second half of the 1990s, the time was already rife and the stage set for the introduction of a new strategy to global development that will usher in a new approach to poverty reduction. In the face of rising poverty in many developing countries and the financial crisis that hit the South-East Asia in the late 1990s, the leadership of the World Bank embarked on a project of interaction and consultations with bilateral and multilateral donors, NGOs, notable academic institutions governments and other protagonists of development. This was carried out basically within the circle of 'Partnerships for Development'. Through these consultations by which new insight were gained and new decisions and declarations made, the need for a development strategy that goes beyond the economic level became more pressing. The new pro-poor paradigm that was consequently developed formed the basis for the formulation of the Post-Washington Consensus.

The Post-Washington Consensus (PWC) that eventually emerged became a model for current efforts being made by the World Bank, IMF and allied institutions to respond to the major criticisms levelled against the global neo-liberalism and so develop a better strategy for tackling poverty.

The concept, Post-Washington Consensus was proposed by the then World Bank Chief Economist Joseph Stiglitz in a speech given in 1998 at the World Institute for Development Economics Research (WIDER) in Helsinki, titled "More Instruments and Broader Goals: Moving towards the Post-Washington Consensus". Stiglitz introduced three new dimensions of development:

i) Sustainable development, which includes preserving natural resources;
ii) Equitable development, which ensures that all groups in society enjoy the fruits of development; and lastly

iii) Democratic development, in which citizens participate in making the decisions which affect their lives[628]

The Post Washington Consensus eventually became adopted as a global attempt to proffer answers to the questions raised at the collapse of the Washington Consensus. Its main elements include:

a) Importance of equity
b) Importance of employment, which has been missing in earlier concepts.
c) Balanced role of government and market in
   - Promoting and regulating markets
   - Providing institutional and physical infrastructure
   - Promoting education, innovation and technology[629]

Some of the areas that are considered crucial for state intervention include regulation of the financial system to minimize risk and increase confidence, improving the quality of education, providing basic infrastructure, developing and transmitting technology (such as agricultural extension services) and alleviating poverty by reducing inequality.[630]

The Post-Washington Consensus also focuses on the question of how to improve the performance of the state and avoid government failure. Stigtlizt's contribution in this respect has gained popularity: The effectiveness of the state, he argues, can be improved by using market-like mechanism. Based on this, an important balance has been established by noting that states are important for the effective function of the market but also market or market-like mechanisms are important for the effectiveness of the states themselves. This can be promoted by stimulating competition within and between public and private sectors. Privatization at all cost that fails to pay sufficient attention to competition and ignores the role of a proper regulatory infrastructure is therefore inconsistent with logic of the Post-Washington Consensus.[631]

The Post-Washington consensus could be interpreted as a departure from the neo-liberal, market-friendly approach of the original consensus. While the Washington consensus took a neo-liberal approach and place economic growth at the centre of development and poverty alleviation, the Post-Washington Consensus appears to incorporate a more poverty-focused approach that protects and supports the poor and prioritizes social spending on education and other social amenities. Its proponents believe that it places sustainable, egalitarian and democratic

---

628 Joseph Stiglitz, More Instruments and Broader Goals: Moving Toward the Post-Washington Consensus, a paper presented at the second annual Lecture of the World Institute for Development Economics Research (WIDER), (Helsinki: U.N. University Press 1998).

629 Joseph E. Stiglitz, The Post Washington Consensus, op. cit.

630 Ziya Öniş and Fikret Şenses, Rethinking the Emerging Post-Washington Consensus: A critical Appraisal, op. cit., p. 15.

631 Joseph Stiglitz, More Instruments and Broader Goals: Moving Toward the Post-Washington Consensus, op. cit., pp. 29 & 30.

development at the heart of its agenda. This however is not the whole truth. At a closer look, it seems more likely that the Post-Washington Consensus is only but an improvement on the earlier consensus and not a complete departure from it. The neo-liberal agenda of the original consensus, no doubt, still underpins this new consensus. What appears to be incorporated is the cautious tolerance of state intervention. In their critical appraisal of the Post-Washington Consensus, Ziya Önis and Fikret Senses further confirm this link between the old consensus and the new consensus.

> Perhaps a key element of the PWC is the recognition that states have an important role to play in the development process. In the simple-minded version of neo-liberal orthodoxy, expanding the domain of the market had necessarily meant reducing the domain of the state in the economy. While, the PWC also favours liberalization of the economy and greater reliance on the market, states and market are conceived of as complements rather than substitutes.[632]

5.2.3 Poverty Reduction Strategies Papers

The Poverty Reduction Strategy (PRS) has proved to be a major instrument for implementing the Post-Washington Consensus. Poverty Reduction Strategy Papers (PRSPs) were meant to replace the Structural Adjustment Programs (SAPs) which proved to be ineffective. The Boards of the World Bank and the International Monetary Fund introduced the PRSP in December 1999 as a new approach to their relations with low-income countries. The introduction of PRSPs was based on the importance the IMF and the World Bank have come to attach to national ownership as well as the need for a greater focus on poverty reduction. This new approach made the preparation and presentation of a nationally owned Poverty Reduction Strategy Papers (PRSP) a precondition for obtaining debt relief and concessional financing from both institutions.[633] Thus all countries that qualify for assistance under the World Bank/IMF programmes have the obligation to prepare and tender a PRSP.

The PRSP is therefore a national cross-sectoral development framework, designed and implemented by the national Government, specifically to tackle the causes and impact of poverty in a country. A PRSP must be prepared by the national government involved and should describe a country's policies and programs to promote growth and reduce poverty.

Five core principles underline the PRSP approach. The Poverty reduction strategies should be:

- **country-driven**, promoting national ownership of strategies through broad-based participation of civil society;

---

632 Ziya Öniş and Fikret Şenses, Rethinking the Emerging Post-Washington Consensus: A critical Appraisal, op. cit., p. 15.

633 The World Bank and the International Monetary Fund, Review of the Poverty Reduction Strategy Approach: Balancing Accountabilities and Scaling Up Results prepared by the Staffs of the World Bank and International Monetary Fund September 2005

- **result-oriented** and focused on outcomes that will benefit the poor;
- **comprehensive** in recognizing the multidimensional nature of poverty;
- **partnership-oriented**, involving coordinated participation of development partners (government, domestic stakeholders, and external donors); and
- **long-term perspective** for poverty reduction.[634]

The PRSPs were also expected to serve as a framework for better coordination of development assistance among other development partners. It targets specifically the provision of crucial link between national public actions, donor support, and the development outcomes needed to meet the United Nations' Millennium Development Goals (MDGs). PRSPs help guide World Bank and IMF concessional lending as well as debt relief under the Heavily Indebted Poor Countries (HIPC) Initiative.[635] It therefore seeks to empower governments to set their development priorities and persuade donors to align their assistance around a country's priorities rather than their own.

Having applied the PRSP approach in a substantial number of low-income countries, the World Bank and the IMF believe that it has led to notable progress and success in country ownership, making poverty reduction more prominent in policy debates, and facilitating more open dialogue. By the end of June 2009, over 90 full PRSPs have been circulated to the Fund Executive Board, as well as more than 50 preliminary, or "interim", PRSPs.[636] The latest in-depth assessment conducted jointly by IMF and World Bank staff further emphasized the role PRSPs can play in balancing the different tensions inherent in the formulation of national development strategies, notably between realism and ambition, and between domestic accountability—closely related to ownership—and external accountability vis-à-vis donors and other development partners.[637] There is however no explicit emphasis on employment as an essential component of Poverty Reduction Strategy Papers.

5.2.4 The United Nations Millennium Declaration

In September 2000 the world leaders under the aegis on the United Nations signed "The United Nations Millennium Declaration". This commitment was initiated with a view to committing the member-nations to strengthening global efforts for peace, human rights, democracy, strong governance, environmental sustainability and poverty eradication, and to promote the principles of human dignity, equality, and equity. To this end, eight development goals were classified and documented a year later. They include the following:

634 See: International Monetary Fund. Fact Book as up-dated as at August 2009.

635 Ibid

636 The World Bank and the International Monetary Fund, Review of the Poverty Reduction Strategy Approach: Balancing Accountabilities and Scaling Up Results. Op. cit.

637 Ibid.

Goal 1: Eradicate extreme poverty and hunger
Goal 2: Achieve universal primary education
Goal 3: Promote gender equality and empower women
Goal 4: Reduce child mortality and empower women
Goal 5: Improve maternal health
Goal 6: Combat HIV/AIDS, malaria and other diseases
Goal 7: Ensure environmental sustainability
Goal 8: Develop a Global Partnership for Development.

These eight Millennium Development Goals (MDGs) are broken down into 21 quantifiable targets that are measured by 60 indicators. They highlight the causes and dimensions of poverty. The eradication of extreme poverty and hunger ranks the first among the goals. It has three targets. The first and third targets aim to halve, between 1990 and 2015, the proportion of people whose income is less than $1 a day and the proportion of people who suffer from hunger. The second target is to achieve full and productive employment and decent work for all including women and young people. [638] This acknowledges the crucial role labour play in the eradication of poverty.

The "UN Millennium Declaration" brought forward the importance of eradicating poverty and promoting development to achieve sustainable and broad-based economic growth.[639] It synthesises, in a single package, many of the most important commitments made separately at the international conferences and summits of the 1990s; it recognises explicitly the interdependence between growth, poverty reduction and sustainable development; it acknowledges that development rests on the foundations of democratic governance, the rule of law, respect for human rights and peace and security; it is based on time-bound and measurable targets accompanied by indicators for monitoring progress; and it brings together the responsibilities of developing countries with those of developed countries, founded on a global partnership endorsed at the International Conference on Financing for Development in Monterrey, Mexico in March 2002, and again at the Johannesburg World Summit on Sustainable Development in August 2002.[640]

In furtherance of the global commitment to eradicate poverty, the World Development Report (WDR) "Attacking Poverty: Opportunity, Empowerment, and Security" *(World Bank,* 2000) proposes what seem be the current global strategy for attacking poverty. This strategy, which pays insignificant attention to employment issues, is built on three key principles:

638 For more on these goals and what has been achieved so far, see: United Nations, The Millennium Development Goals Report 2009, (New York: United Nations 2009)

639 See the Report of the UN Secretary-General: Road map towards the Implementation of the United Nations Millennium Declaration, (New York: United Nations, 2001).available on the following web pages: www.un.org/millenniumgoals/ and www.developmentgoals.org.

640 UNDP, About the MDGs: Basics (What are the Millennium Development Goals?), retrieved from: http://www.undp.org/mdg/basics.shtml.

i) *Promoting opportunity:* This requires stimulating economic growth through well functioning and internationally open markets, and investments in infrastructure and education. This will translate into making markets work better for poor people, and building up their assets.

ii) *Facilitating empowerment* by making state and social institutions more responsive to them. Facilitating empowerment amounts to including people in the decision-making process. This requires government accountability, a strong media, local organizational capacity, and mechanisms for participation in making decisions.

iii) *Enhancing security* by reducing vulnerability and risks. This calls for insurance programmes, disaster relief procedures and a solid health infrastructure.[641]

5.2.5 Appraisal of Current Growth-approach to Poverty Alleviation

The global efforts at reducing poverty in the post-industrialization era, and especially in contemporary time have been concentrated around the United Nations and its agents. We have taken a look so far at the efforts made mainly through the Bretton Wood Institutions (BWI) and the United Nation Development Programme.

II is obvious that in the history of their dealing with poverty reduction and development issues, the BWI and their allies seem to have made growth the main policy objective, be it in the neo-liberal trickle-down approach or the pro-poor growth approach, Employment and labour questions, although often mentioned, are however not at the heart of their development strategies. The structural adjustment programmes implemented in the later part of the 1980s and the early part of the 1990s were accordingly dominated by the objectives of macroeconomic rebalancing and microeconomic transformations in order to create an environment favourable to the market forces which were at that time believed to be the drivers of growth and a 'rational' development path. Since the 1990s, the ideology of growth within the context of globalisation expanded to include the poverty reduction agenda – pro-poor growth. However, liberalization and economic growth continue to play a central role with less attention given to employment and labour development.

The seemingly change in the universal policy prescription by the Bretton Woods Institutions in the PWC cannot yet be described as a complete departure from the neo-liberal approach to development. It is obvious that in the new approach, there is still a persistent presumption that liberalization leads to integration; integration leads to economic growth; economic growth leads to poverty reduction. Every other policy prescription seems to revolve around this basic presumption including the promotion of opportunity, facilitation of empowerment and enhancement of security that prove to be their most current strategy for attaining sustainable development and poverty reduction. Within this

641 Cf. UNDP, The World development Report 2000/2001: Attacking Poverty, op. cit.

framework, the only assured way of achieving growth and reducing poverty is to become integrated into the global economy. Growth, as it were, would no longer pose a problem and poverty would be drastically reduced in any poor nation once all measures are taken to get the nation integrated into the global economy. All resources should therefore be channelled to the core high performance activities. This ascribes to national governments only limited obligation of creating the favourable, enabling and conducive (economic, social and political) environment base on democracy and good governance.

The core elements of the new development strategies promoted by the IMF, the World Bank, and the World Trade Organization (WTO) and supported by the European Commission amount to: Growth helps the poor and liberalisation helps growth. If you want to reduce poverty, pursue economic growth by liberalising and getting integrated into the global market/economy. How each country wants to achieve this must be articulated in the national Poverty Reduction Strategy Paper (PRSP) which must reflect how the country intends to promote opportunity, facilitate empowerment and enhance security for this purpose.

Although the BWI and their allies seem not to be oblivious of the dangers posed by the intensification of poverty, inequalities and exclusion at global level as could be seen in most of their documents, their policies and strategies are however clearly deficient in giving orientation and perspectives with regard to reverting the trend in favour of sustainable development and poverty reduction. It is incontrovertible that liberalization, global integration and economic growth, as important as they are, do not inevitably and automatically translate into sustainable development and poverty reduction. Growth is good and necessary for poverty reduction, but growth can also be counter-productive if the fruits of the attained growth are not equitably distributed. The increase in inequalities, the informalisation of economies, increasingly precarious conditions of labour, the rise in poverty and the deterioration of the social cohesion witnessed in many developing nations especially in Sub-Saharan African call for an improved strategy that goes beyond liberalization, integration and economic growth; a strategy that incorporate growth and the equitable distribution of the gains of economic growth.

From the foregoing it is obvious that the growth-approach we have seen so far falls short of being a suitable socio-political concept or strategy for adapting and implementing the labour-centred guideline offered by the Catholic social teaching for poverty alleviation. At the base of the growth-centred approach to poverty alleviation is the emphasis on economic efficiency and growth as the main driving force for reducing poverty. Moreover, the improvement of labour is clearly not considered to be a priority. Consequently, the growth-centred poverty alleviation approach promotes physical output rather than human development, economic opportunity rather than social justice. This sets it at variance with the core ethical values upheld in the human development and work-centred guideline for poverty alleviation proposed in the Catholic social teaching in which human dignity, common good, social and economic justice would be guaranteed based on the principles of solidarity and subsidiarity.

The searchlight will now be turned to an institution that has over the years made positive contributions to poverty alleviation by promoting not only economic growth but also the development of human resources in an atmosphere of social justice – the ILO.

5.3 The ILO Pro-Poor Approach: Labour Intensive Growth

The ILO approach to development and poverty reduction is characterized by a multidimensional policy framework, in which economic issues are not isolated from the social sphere, but are part of an integrated strategy to improve the living and working conditions of the working poor in particular and of course the entire population. Within this paradigm, poverty is viewed no longer as a problem of the poor but rather as a challenge for all who are interested in social justice and for all who endeavour to achieve sustainable growth and human development.

The ILO visions are clearly articulated in its constitution, Declarations, conventions, and recommendations. In the Preamble to its Constitution, the ILO lays much emphasis on social justice and project the vision for justice and peace: "Whereas universal and lasting peace can be established only if it is based on social justice."[642] This vision of social justice opens the way to an innovative approach to issues pertaining to human development and poverty eradication in which economic growth is giving only a complementary position. In line with this approach, the 'social factor' must therefore take precedence over the 'economic factor'; it must regulate and guide it in the highest cause of justice.

Against this background, the ILO has consistently put employment at the heart of development strategies and maintains the strong conviction that employment – or more precisely, decent work – is the partway to poverty reduction. And for economic growth to be effective in reducing poverty, policies relating to employment, including human resource development must play an important role.[643] Particular emphasis should be laid on promoting pro-poor employment-centred growth strategies and integrating of employment and decent work objectives in National Development Frameworks (NDF).

The importance the ILO attaches to labour in the context of poverty reduction stems from the fact that poor people rely mainly on the use of their labour power – whether as wage-labour or in self-employment – to earn their livelihood. The ILO therefore believes that, employment creation policies and improved labour

---

642 ILO Constitution, available at: http://www.ilo.org/ilolex/english/constq.htm.

643 For an empirical analyses of the inter-connectivity between labour market, economic growth and poverty reduction, see: Rizwanul Islam, The Nexus of Economic Growth, Employment and Poverty Reduction: An Empirical Analyses. (Geneva: ILO – Recovery and Reconstruction Department, 2004).

standards are the essential instrument for raising living standards and widening access to incomes. Some elements that form the foundation of ILO approach includes:

i) *Dignity of human Labour*: The ILO elevates human labour over and above capital and insists that "labour is not a commodity or article of commerce."[644] The ILO Director-General, Juan Somavia, once observed: "The ILO clearly affirms its conviction that work, personal dignity, family stability and peace are more important than capital."[645]
ii) *Tripartism*: Acknowledging the need for co-operation between governments employers and workers, the ILO adopts tripartism, accords the representatives of governments, employers and workers equal status in dialogue and recommends that all should join in "free discussion and democratic decision with a view to promote the common welfare."[646]
iii) *Equality of Opportunity*: The ILO also treats the issues of gender equality in a wider perspective covering education, social attitudes and design creation of jobs, training, and workplaces, measures for ensuring equal remuneration, maternity, living and working conditions, social infrastructure and social security.[647]
iv) *Collective Bargaining*: Right from the early years of it existence, the ILO has always rejected the total faith in the benevolent operation of economic law and markets self-regulating mechanisms. It supports instead a systematic collective action. Holding firm to this position, it proposes the following: planning and deliberate interference by government with the economic structure in order to achieve certain social objectives; unemployment insurance and other social insurances providing against sickness and old age; provision of public work through large scale public investment and; the regulation of hours of work.[648]

5.3.1 ILO's Decent Work Agenda: Key to Social Justice and Poverty Reduction

The ILO mandate of social justice is expressed today as decent work for all. "Decent work" is central to ILO's efforts to reduce poverty, and is a means for achieving equitable, inclusive and sustainable development. The ILO works to develop Decent Work-oriented approaches to economic and social policy in

644 See: The appendix of the Final Texts of the Labour Section of the 1919 Treaty of Versailles which contains a set of "General Principles" (Art. 427) also called "the Labour Charter".

645 Juan Somavia, Perspectives on decent work, (Geneva: International Labour Office, 2000), p. 7.

646 ILO, Declaration of Philadelphia, para. I (d).

647 These provisions are contained in the 1975 Declaration but also enshrined in earlier Conventions, especially the Discrimination (Employment and Occupation) Convention, 1958 (No. 111), the Equal Remuneration Convention, 1951 (No. 100), or their corresponding Recommendations.

648 ILO, Report of the Director, (Geneva: International Labour Office, 1935), p. 7.

partnership with the principal institutions and actors of the multilateral system and the global economy.[649] "Decent work" calls for greater policy collaboration between institutions – from the international to the local level.[650] It engages all stakeholders and targets all sectors and individuals. According to the Director-General of ILO, the goal of "Decent Work for All" helps to focus research and policy action on practical measures that can both have an immediate impact on poverty and build the infrastructure for longer-term progress. It is also a means of mobilizing broad support for policies that require the commitment of the non-poor and the poor themselves in order to succeed.[651] It has therefore a wide spectrum that goes beyond economic issues. "Increasing opportunities for decent work is about incomes, but it is also about the social and political empowerment that flows from acting to overcome vulnerability and exclusion."[652] It underscored the concern for all workers, not limited to employees who receive wages or salaries but applies equally to all working people: women and men, young and older workers, nationals and migrants, and though often harder to realize, self-employed, farmers, home-workers and entrepreneurs:[653] 'All those who work have rights at work,' the ILO maintains and adds that it strives for decent work in the sense of opportunities for men and women to obtain decent and productive work in conditions of freedom, equity, security and human dignity`.[654] More precisely,

> ... decent work involves opportunities for the kinds of work that are productive and that deliver fair income, security in the workplace and social protection for the family, better prospect for personal development and social integration, freedom for people to express the concerns, organize and participate in decisions that affect their lives and equality of opportunity and or treatment for all women and men.[655]

This concept which was developed in 1999 encompasses four key dimensions or pillars or 'strategic objectives', which are considered to be interdependent:

- *Employment*: the availability of an adequate number of productive, quality jobs, which provide incomes to cover at least basic needs.
- *Social security*: protection from work-related injury and from lack of income due to unemployment, illness or old age.

---

649 Cf. http://www.ilo.org/global/About_the_ILO/Mainpillars/WhatisDecentWork/lang--en/index.htm, accessed on 04.04.2011.

650 Anne Trebilcock, Decent Work and the Informal Economy, Discussion Paper No. 2005/04, (Helsinki: EGDI and UNU-WIDER 2005), p. 1.

651 ILO, Working out of Poverty, Report of the Director-General, International Labour Conference, 91st Session, (Geneva, International Labour Office, 2003), p. 22

652 Ibid.

653 Cf. Swiss Agency for Development and Cooperation, Decent Work: a target to achieve the MDGs Fact sheet, (Berne: Employment and Income Division, 2008).

654 ILO, Report of the Director-General: Decent work, (Geneva: International Labour Conference, 1999).

655 United Nation – Department of Economic and Social Affairs, The Employment Imperative: Report on the World Social Situation 2007, (New York: United Nations Publications, 2007), pp. 2-3.

- *Rights in the workplace*: in particular fundamental rights such as the freedom of choice and equality of treatment, freedom of association, protection from forced labour and child labour, and opportunity at work.
- *Social dialogue*: the ability to participate in making decisions about working conditions and to represent their interests collectively in all types of negotiations between or among representatives of government, employers and workers.[656]

The Decent Work Agenda (DWA) promotes the ILO Declaration on Fundamental Principles and Rights at Work (1998) which identified four principles as essential to enabling people to enjoy a fair share of the wealth they have helped to generate. These are referred to as Core Labour Standards (CLS) that all labour markets must strive to meet. They include:

- Freedom of association and effective recognition of collective bargaining:
- The elimination of all forms of forced or compulsory labour
- The effective abolition of exploitative child labour
- The elimination of discrimination in respect of employment and occupation.[657]

The ILO Declaration on Fundamental Rights at Work is based on the fundamental principles contained in the ILO Constitution: Labour is not a commodity; freedom of expression and of association is essential to sustained progress; poverty anywhere constitutes a danger to prosperity everywhere.

Beyond the four Core Labour Standards, however, are other "*basic minimum standards* on substantive matters such as conditions of work, safety and health and income security, as well as basic rules for fair treatment, for example with regard to job security and vulnerable groups"[658] which the ILO believes are particularly importance for effectively addressing the decent work deficit in the informal economy. Theses *basic minimum standards* on substantive matters are set in status law and are not universal rights. They are however standards that directly affect labour conditions.

Gender equality is an integral cross-cutting theme in the decent work agenda with particular focus on the process of creating equal opportunities for women, enhancing their social protection, ensuring that the human rights of women are addressed and in enabling them to participate in social dialogue.[659]

---

656 Swiss Agency for Development and Cooperation, Decent Work: a target to achieve the MDGs Fact sheet, op. cit.

657 ILO: ILO Declaration on Fundamental Principles and Rights at Work and its Follow-Up, op. cit., para. 2.

658 ILO: Decent work and the informal economy, Report VI, International Labour Conference, 90th Session, (Geneva, international Labour Office, 2002, p.44.

659 ILO, The Decent Work Agenda and Poverty Reduction: ILO Contribution to IMF/World Bank Comprehensive Review of Poverty Reduction Strategy Process Washington 14-17 January 2002, available at: http://training.itcilo.it/decentwork/staffconf2002/presentations/ref-ILODecentWorkAgendaandPovertyReduction.pdf.

With regard to the processes of globalization, Decent Work Agenda recognises that the global economy has to deliver increased employment but that this has also to involve improvement of working conditions, social protection and representation based on respect for fundamental principles and rights at work.[660]

5.3.2 Decent Work: A Global Goal

The Decent Work Agenda has developed from being an internal agenda of the ILO to a global one, following its acceptance and adoption at the level of various intergovernmental organizations and at the regional and international levels. "Today, the Decent Work agenda is no longer only an ILO-strategy. Bilateral and multilateral donors, the European Union and other international organizations are now making it an integral part of their policies."[661] Thus the ILO Director-General, Juan Somavia, could assert that, "The ILO's Decent Work Agenda is now globally endorsed as key to the international community's effort to reduce poverty and sustain development and central to a process of globalization that is equitable and inclusive."[662]

The Decent Work Agenda received perhaps its most important international endorsement when world leaders agreed in 2005 to amend the MDGs to explicitly include reference to decent work (cf. 5.2.4). MDG 1, which aims to eradicate extreme poverty and hunger, now includes a target to 'achieve full and productive employment and decent work for all, including women and young people' by 2015.[663]

At the regional level, the UN Economic and Social Council (ECOSOC) Ministerial Declarations adopted in 2006 and 2007 recognized Decent Work explicitly as essential for achieving a fair globalization and reduction of poverty. The summits of heads of state of Africa and of the America have also on their part adopted Decent Work as the goal for their national development and the best route out of poverty. Decent Work for all has therefore been accepted as a key element of the international development agenda, a priority objective of international cooperation as well as of national and international development policies.[664]

---

660 Ibid.

661 Swiss Agency for Development and Cooperation, Decent Work: a target to achieve the MDGs Fact sheet, op. cit.

662 ILO, Strengthening the ILO's Capacity to Assist its Members' Efforts to Reach its Objectives in the Context of Globalization, (Geneva, International Labour Office, 2007), p. vi.

663 Stuart Bell and Kirsten Newitt, Decent Work and Poverty Eradication: literature Review and Two Country Study, a study for the Decent Work and Labour Standards Forum, (London: Ergon Associates Limited, 2010).

664 Swiss Agency for Development and Cooperation, Decent Work: a target to achieve the MDGs Fact sheet, op. cit: For more on the adoption of Decent Work Agenda as global strategy for development and poverty reduction, see the following: World Commission on the Social Dimension of Globalization. A fair globalization: creating opportunities for all, (Geneva: International Labour Office, 2004), p. 145; United Nations General Assembly, World Summit Outcome, A/60/L.1, 20 Sept. 2005, para. 47; United Nations

5.3.3 The Informal Economy – The Priority of the Decent Work Agenda

In promoting the Decent Work Agenda as the way out of poverty, the ILO gives priority attention to the informal economy. This is in recognition of the fact that "the bulk of new employment in recent years, particularly in developing and transition countries, has been in the informal economy."[665] But work in the informal economy cannot be termed "decent" compared to recognized, protected, secure, formal employment. The ILO therefore argues that since the informal economy is characterized by poor-quality, unproductive and poor remunerative jobs that are not recognized or protected by law, and by the absence of rights at work, inadequate social protection, and the lack of representation and voice, especially at the bottom end among women and young workers, the most meaningful way of looking at the situation of those in the informal economy is in terms of *decent work deficits*.

The goal is to promote decent work along the entire continuum from the informal to the formal end of the economy, and in development- oriented, poverty reduction-focused and gender-equitable ways.[666] This is practically the way the ILO intends to achieve a pro-poor growth: Against this background, the ILO argues: When increases in output are concentrated in economic sectors in which most of the poor work and this generates more income for people living in poverty, growth is pro-poor. Put differently, pro-poor growth leads to an improvement in the conditions of the poor proportionately greater than that for the population as a whole.[667]

The ILO intends to achieve this goal through a progressive approach that would imply starting with the informal end, where most new job creation in recent years has been taking place, and promoting the transition upwards along the continuum toward the formal, decent and protected end. Therefore, an integrated and comprehensive strategy to achieve decent work along the entire continuum would proceed in this order:

- *In the immediate term,* give priority to *reducing decent work deficits in the informal economy*, importantly through ensuring that those who are currently in the informal economy are recognized in the law and have rights, legal and social protection and representation and voice;

Economic and Social Council, Ministerial Declaration, Official Records of the General Assembly, 61st Session, Supplement No. 3 (A/61/3/Rev.1), chap. III. See also Resolution 2007/2 of 17 July 2007 and Resolution 2008/18, Promoting full employment and decent work for all; International Labour Conference, 97th Session (Geneva, 2008), Provisional Record, No. 13, (committee report) and 13A (proposed text of the Declaration).

665 ILO, Decent work and the informal economy, op. cit., p. 1.

666 Ibid, p. 4.

667 ILO: Working out of Poverty, op. cit., p.33.

- *In the short and medium term, enable those currently in the informal economy to move upwards along the continuum and at the same time ensure that new jobseekers and potential entrepreneurs are able to enter the more formal, protected and decent parts of the continuum.* Priority would be given to ensuring that workers and entrepreneurs have the capacity, flexibility and the conducive legal and policy frameworks to do so. Special attention would need to be given to those who are especially disadvantaged or discriminated against in the labour market, such as women, young jobseekers and migrant workers;
- *In the longer term, create enough employment opportunities that are formal, protected and decent for all workers and employers.*[668]

The implication of this is that the informal economy should not be developed or promoted as a low-cost way of creating employment, since decent work is not about a job at any price or under any circumstances.

5.3.4 Decent Work, Informal Economy and Poverty Reduction Strategy Process

In furtherance of its social justice agenda and in accordance with its pro-poor approach to development, the ILO has, since mid 2001, sought to engage in the PRS process at country level. In contributing to the PRS process, the ILO intends particularly "to address the multitude of workers and enterprises who are often not recognized and protected under legal and regulatory frameworks and who are characterized by a high degree of vulnerability and poverty, and to redress these decent work deficits."[669] This objective acknowledges the fact that "the promotion of decent work for all workers, women and men, irrespective of where they work, requires a broad strategy: realizing fundamental principles and rights at work; creating greater and better employment and income opportunities; extending social protection; and promoting social dialogue. To this end, The General Conference of the International Labour Organization, meeting in its 90th Session, 2002, having undertaken a general discussion on the basis of Reports on *Decent work and the informal economy*, concluded that "Poverty reduction strategies, in particular the Poverty Reduction Strategy Papers (PRSPs), should specifically address the problems in the informal economy. The creation of decent jobs should be a measure of success for these strategies."[670]

Through its Decent Work Agenda, the ILO aims at placing employment at the heart of economic and social policies. This provides a useful conceptual foundation for engaging in PRSs at country level. What has been identified as the starting point is "the fact that work is the main, often the only, way for poor people to get and

---

668 ILO, Decent work and the informal economy, op. cit., p. 5.

669 ILO, Conclusions concerning decent work and the informal economy ILC90-PR25-292-En.Doc. No. 1

670 Ibid., no. 26.

stay out of poverty."[671] The overarching vision for the ILO's support to PRSs is therefore to develop and promote coherent and integrated policy frameworks for connecting the poverty reduction and decent work agenda at the national level. This vision draws on all four strategic objectives of decent work, employment, rights, social protection and social dialogue. The strategy involves four interconnected elements:

- Empowering the constituents (ministries of labour, employers' and workers' organizations) by strengthening their capacity to influence the drafting, implementation and monitoring of national PRSs;
- Incorporating employment and other relevant dimensions of the decent work agenda into PRSs by identifying appropriate entry points and country-specific priorities and by articulating a visible and marketable platform for action;
- Influencing and developing partnerships through strategic communication at the country level: seeking to influence other government ministries and departments (especially ministries of finance/planning) in driving the design and implementation of PRSs, and development organizations (including multilaterals, bilaterals and civil society organizations) to embrace the decent work route out of poverty;
- Maintaining critical dialogue at the global and regional levels with the international financial institutions, regional commissions, regional development banks and UNDP on the overall assessment of the content and process of PRSs.[672]

Also in engaging in the PRS process, the ILO has sought specifically to give more attention to equity in addition to growth, arguing that PRSs need to give more coverage to the policy implications related to redistribution. Trade unions, employers' organizations and labour ministries need to be more regularly engaged in the consultative process underpinning the design and implementation of PRSs.[673] In all, the ILO advocates for Poverty reduction strategies that include "an employment-centred development strategy, a comprehensive perspective of social safety nets and social transfers, changes in institutions, laws, regulations and practices that are part of the process that creates and perpetuates poverty."[674]

671 ILO, Decent Work and Poverty Reduction Strategies A reference manual for ILO staff and constituents, (Geneva: International labour Office, 2005), p. 1:1

672 ILO, Decent Work and Poverty Reduction Strategies, (Geneva: International Labour Office, 2007), p. 3.

673 ILO, Decent Work and Poverty Reduction Strategies A reference manual for ILO staff and constituents, (Geneva: International labour Office, 2005), p. 1:1

674 ILO, Decent Work and Poverty Reduction Strategies, op. cit., p. 1.

5.3.5 Appraisal of ILO Approach and Possible Consequences for the CST

We have seen in 3.5 the position the ILO takes concerning what should be the best approach to poverty alleviation. In striving to achieve the goal of poverty reduction and social justice, the ILO argues that high growth is a necessary but not a sufficient condition. This means, according to the ILO framework, that sustainable pro-poor growth cannot be based on the "trickle-down" paradigm – not even when it is backed with development measures targeted at improving the opportunities of the poor to participate in growth and its benefits. For growth to be pro-poor it must be associated with redistributive, labour-intensive and basic needs oriented policies. The ILO therefore stresses that the economic growth goal should be incorporated into an integrated development strategy, in which growth is considered to be an important aspect but should be given no more importance than the creation of productive jobs, the improvement of working and living conditions, the development of workers rights, the provision of reliable security, the fairer distribution of income and the meeting of basic human needs.

The ILO has a lot in common with the Catholic social teaching with regard to poverty and its alleviation. Although a secular institution with a purely secular mandate, the ILO promotes social justice and the respect for human dignity which forms the cardinal ethical principles of Catholic social teaching. The ILO elevates human labour over and above capital and insists that labour is not a commodity or article of commerce (cf. 5.3). In other words, both the ILO and Catholic social teaching view poverty as a social problem that infringes on justice and dignity of the human person.

Furthermore, the ILO and Catholic social teaching put 'work' at the heart of development strategies and maintain the strong conviction that human labour is surer partway to poverty reduction. Within this framework, the ILO as well as the Catholic social teaching supports a policy framework, in which economic issues are not isolated from the social sphere, but are part of an integrated strategy to improve the living and working conditions of the working poor in particular. They also rejected the total faith in the benevolent operation of economic law and markets self-regulating mechanisms and insist on the right of governments to intervene where necessary.

The ILO also shows a strong backing for other basic principle of the Catholic social teaching. For instance, through its advocacy for the tripartism and social dialogue the ILO identifies itself with the principle of subsidiarity and solidarity and promotes solidarity among the working poor and between the poor and other social groups.

In addition to the fact that both the ILO and the Catholic social teaching put 'work' at the heart of development strategies and maintain the strong conviction that human labour is surer partway to poverty reduction, the ILO-DWA supplies for the deficiency in the guideline proposed by the Church in her social teaching by providing more concrete answers to the problems the poor encounter in their living and working conditions.

However, the ILO framework lacks a solid ethical foundation for regulating the social interactions both within smaller communities and at the global level. This is an aspect in which the Catholic social teaching can act as a boost to the ILO-DWA, for 'it provides a firm ethical basis that proves to be useful in the search for a lasting solution to the problems'

Another limitation common to both the ILO and the Catholic social teaching is the lack of a cohesive force. Both the ILO-DWA and Catholic social teaching possess only a power of persuasion and lack the capacity to formulate policies that are binding on individual nations. The member-nations of the ILO enjoy, for instance, the freedom to ratify or not to ratify any of its instruments. They are not bound to abide by any non-ratified instrument.

5.4 Conclusion

This chapter has shown how efforts at alleviating poverty have moved from uncoordinated personal efforts to improved national and regional efforts culminating today in well organised and sophisticated global network. It is clear that the strategy adopted at any given period is enormously influenced and determined by the prevailing understanding of poverty. There are basically two outstanding approaches in recent times.

The first approach is the growth-centred approach which is founded on the presumption that liberalization leads to integration; integration leads to economic growth; economic growth leads to poverty reduction. Based on the presumption, the growth-centred approach focuses more on economic growth at the expense of labour development. This is the approach the Bretton Wood Institutions and their allied institutions adopted over the years (cf. esp. 5.2.2.).

The ILO takes the second approach which is a broader approach to poverty, incorporating both growth element and the human development element. The ILO approach addresses, in a concrete manner, the major problems the poor encounter in their struggles to use their most valuable asset – their labour – to stay out of poverty. It also concentrates on the segment of the economy where the poor work and earn their living – the informal economy. In that way, it promotes solidarity with the poor (cf. 5.3.). The ILO approach proves therefore to be a suitable strategy for enriching, adapting and applying the work-oriented guidelines for poverty alleviation proposed in the Catholic social teaching to the Nigerian context in which majority of the poor have engaged themselves in precarious work in the informal economy in a bid to stay out of poverty.

Informal workers, as we have seen in earlier chapters, are less productive and earn little from their work due to the harsh, unfavourable and inhuman labour conditions in the informal economy. Improving the labour conditions in the informal economy, would increase their productivity and earning. This invariable will put them and their dependants on the right path out of poverty. The overall result would mean drastic reduction of poverty in the nation.

CHAPTER SIX

Previous and Current Poverty Alleviation Efforts in Nigeria

Introduction

In the third chapter of this work, we saw that the high incidence of poverty in Nigeria has been as a result of structural failures in the political, social and economic life of the nation which permits only a few to have access to available means of production and to the wealth of the nation. We also saw that the pervasiveness of poverty in the nation is worsened by the high incidence of the informality or rather the existence of a large informal economy and t he failure of the government to improve the labour conditions in this segment of the economy and so be able to tap the huge economic potential in it. Based on these findings, it became obvious that Nigeria is a nation in dire need of a socio-economic reform that will enable its citizens to participate more productively in the creation of more wealth in the nation and by so doing be able, through their labour, to have a fair share of the wealth produced. It was also obvious that what poor households (both in rural and urban areas) lack mostly are adequate returns on their main asset, which is their labour, and what they need is greater and more rewarding employment. The huge decent work deficit in the informal economy where the majority of the people in the nation's workforce work and earn their living poses also a big challenge to poverty alleviation efforts.

This chapter evaluate the past and current strategies, programmes and efforts made in Nigeria towards poverty alleviation with a view to ascertaining how suitable they are for dealing with the concrete problems pertaining to human misery and impoverishment. This evaluation will be done in the light of the ethical orientation and guideline from the Catholic social teaching and also based on the conclusions drawn from the last chapter.

In Nigeria, several efforts have indeed been made towards stemming the scourge of poverty. Alleviation of poverty has never been considered an exclusive reserve of the states. Various actors have always been involved in initiating, executing, co-ordinating, monitoring and reviewing anti-poverty programmes. These actors include Community Based Organizations (CBOs), Non-Governmental Organizations (NGOs) which include religious organizations, local communities, government at the local, state and federal levels, the private sector group (corporate bodies and individuals) and international organizations. In evaluating these contributions, emphasis will however be on the efforts made by the government and the Church in Nigeria. Other actors and agencies would, where necessary, be briefly discussed. The approach adopted here is a chronological presentation followed by appraisal.

6.1 Previous Efforts

The previous efforts made at alleviating poverty in Nigeria will be evaluated in three chronological eras, namely: the pre-colonial era, the colonial era and the post-colonial era, that is after independence. The post colonial era will be further phased into the pre-SAP era, the SAP era and the post-SAP era.

6.1.1 Poverty Alleviation in Pre-colonial Nigeria

During the pre-colonial period, poverty was conceived mainly in terms of deprivation of the basic necessities of life and in terms of being disabled: sick, deaf, blind, leprous, physically incapacitated and so on. Poverty alleviation was at that time embarked upon collectively by the communities.[675] Food security, for instance was the responsibility of the entire community. The laws and customs of the people made some exceptional provisions for the weak; those who could not fend for themselves. In most communities, going into a neighbour's farm to harvest certain food crops when one is hungry and has nothing to eat, was therefore not considered to be an act of stealing. Nyerere was therefore right when he stated, although hyperbolically, that in African traditional setup, "nobody starved, either for food or human dignity, because he lacked personal wealth; he could depend on the wealth possessed by the community of which he was a member"[676]

U.K. Kalu further highlights the crucial roles played by extended and nuclear family system, age grades and associations as agencies of poverty alleviation. According to him, "neighbourhood associations, village community development agencies, and other types of civil societies - whether based on ethnicity or beyond boundaries -could serve as poverty alleviation agencies because they possessed organic roots and bonds that ensured viability."[677] In times of crises, affected members of the community were never abandoned as they were often rallied around and assisted by the community, family and social solidarity groups.

6.1.2 Poverty Alleviation in Colonial Nigeria

The impact of colonial rule not only reshaped the socio-economic, political, moral and even religious foundation of the nation, it impoverished the nation and brought untold hardship on the citizens. Colonial economy raised the problems of unemployment and created a new class of working poor who emerged to earn meagre wages. In addition to creating a new face of poverty, colonialism

675 A "community" in the pre-colonial Nigeria could be likened to the "state" in the modern society.

676 Julius Nyerere, as cited by U.K. Kalu, Poverty and its Alleviation in Colonial Nigeria. In: A. Oyebade, (ed), The Foundations of Nigeria, (Trenton and Asmara: African World Press, 2003), p. 424.

677 U.K. Kalu, Poverty and its Alleviation in Colonial Nigeria, in: A. Oyebade, (ed.), "The Foundations of Nigeria," (Trenton and Asmara: African World Press, 2003), p. 436.

transformed the geography of the nation by creating urban centres, leading to rural-urban migration and population shifts.[678]

When colonial tax was introduced in the first decade of the 20th century, reliance on land was replaced by dependence on wages for sustainability and the payment of the new taxes. Poverty at that time ceased to be a phenomenon peculiar to life in the rural areas, as it spread rapidly to the urban areas. The urban poor and fixed-income groups suffered terribly due to price fluctuations. The heavy burden of the colonial taxes was evidently excruciating. Traditional anti-poverty measures at that time proved inadequate and crumble under the weight of the new forms of poverty.[679] This situation was reportedly described as follows by one who witnessed it in the northern part of the nation:

> ...throughout the district, I am convinced of absolute poverty; they have nothing but few fouls, a handful of old ragged clothes and just enough corn to keep them going until the next harvest. For the majority people, I should say 90 percent, there is no other way of obtaining the currency needed for their tax this year (1934) than selling of their corn, and to do that will mean selling a large amount of it.... It will short ration for most and in most cases hunger.[680]

Also in the colonial era, a series of natural catastrophe befell Nigeria: draught, flood, locust invasion, food shortage and attendant famine etc. Following these events, poverty kept growing in the land. The World Wars and the 1930 depression joined forces to make matters worse. During these turbulent times, however, the interest and welfare of the common citizens especially the poor did not constitute the priority of the colonial masters. Poverty alleviation was left almost entirely to the indigenous communities and missionaries. Several attempts made by the local residents and authorities to establishment local granaries at each district headquarters in order to attain self reliance through the conversion of tax to grain were however imprudently resisted by the British who were obsessed with financial parsimony and afraid of the threat to welfarism. They were obviously more concerned with cementing their authority than with social issues. Measures were hardly put in place to diffuse the hardship of the time. New and harsh methods of central government controlled marketing monopolies were instead introduced. These control measures and other war time policies impacted negatively on the lives of peasant farmers, producers and the poor in general. In order to justify their non-committal attitude to poverty alleviation, "the British claimed that the sufferings of the people during these terrible times were not as a result of governments' neglect,

678 Mohammed Sanni Abdulkadir, Poverty Alleviation in Northern Nigeria: C. 1900 – 1960, in: Mustapha C. Duze et al. (eds), Poverty in Nigeria: Causes Manifestations and Alleviation Strategies, (London: Adonis & Abbey Publishers Ltd, 2008), p, 25.

679 Ibid, pp. 25-26.

680 Richard Wheeler Crocker, Nigeria: A Critique of British Colonial Administration, (London: George Allen and Unwin, 1936), p.115. As cited by Mohammed Sanni Abdulkadir, Poverty Alleviation in Northern Nigeria: C. 1900 – 1960, op. cit., p, 29.

but due essentially to their laziness, backwardness, incompetence and lack of planning."[681]

It was precisely in the 1950s that the colonial system readjusted itself and began to give attention to the misery in the nation. The outcry against the colonial structure at the time had become very loud. This compelled the colonialists to introduce changes in the economy. From the 1950s through the 1960 some risky and contradictory reforms were reportedly initiated to bring about improvement in the level of well being. The central and regional governments announced various incentives in order to promote business activities and provide social services - with intervention at those levels.[682] Issues of development and welfare were reportedly linked to production because it was believed that increased agricultural production would lead to improved living conditions. Consequently efforts and resources were channelled to increasing agricultural production through loan schemes. The loans were unfortunately misdirected to non-agricultural sectors.[683]

Other major efforts made in pre-independence days were in the area of farm settlement schemes. The schemes aimed at bringing scattered small communities together so that they could take advantage of economies of scale in farm inputs, agro services, marketing, etc. Reportedly, these schemes recorded little or no achievement, mainly because of the exclusion of the target groups at the planning stages.[684]

However, in what became known as the first development plan spanning from 1945 to 1955, resources were allocated to social services, education and other projects that could create jobs. The execution of this plan was however not backed up with good will from the colonial masters, and so poverty continued to rare its ugly head in the land. [685]

6.1.3 Poverty Alleviation since Independence

Since independence, successive governments, both military and civilian, have initiated various anti-poverty programmes. While some of them are merely related to poverty alleviation, others have been designed to directly impact on the lives of the poor and so alleviate poverty. Various nomenclatures have been applied, as

---

681 Mohammed Sanni Abdulkadir, Poverty Alleviation in Northern Nigeria: C. 1900 – 1960, op. cit., p, 31.

682 Ibid, p. 26.

683 Toyin Falola, Economic Reforms and Modernization in Nigeria: 1945-1965, (Kent, Ohio: The Kent State University Press, 2004), p.89. As cited by Mohammed Sanni Abdulkadir, Poverty Alleviation in Northern Nigeria: C. 1900 – 1960: In: Mustapha C. Duze et al. (eds), Poverty in Nigeria: Causes Manifestations and Alleviation Strategies, (London: Adonis & Abbey Publishers Ltd, 2008), p, 31.

684 I. Omale and S. Molem, A Survey of Approaches to Poverty Alleviation and an Assessment of Previous Programmes": In: M. Obadan, A.A. Fajingbesi, and E.O. Uga, eds. 'Integrating Poverty Alleviation Strategies into Plans and Programmes in Nigeria', (Ibadan: NCEMA, 2003), pp. 107-121.

685 For more insight, see: Mohammed Sanni Abdulkadir, Poverty Alleviation in Northern Nigeria: C. 1900 – 1960, op. cit., pp. 23-35.

deemed suitable by the various governments, for example, poverty reduction, poverty eradication, poverty alleviation, etc. But all of them have the same goal, namely, to help the poor come out of poverty and ride the nation of poverty.

The Poverty alleviation efforts since independence will be examined in three phases: Poverty Alleviation in the Pre-SAP Era, Poverty Alleviation in the SAP Era and Poverty Alleviation in the Post-SAP Era. These poverty alleviation programmes have focused in various degrees on the basic needs approach, rural development approach and the growth approach.[686]

a) *Basic Needs Approach* calls for the provision of basic needs such as food, shelter, water, sanitation, health care, basic education, transportation etc (cf. 5.1.3.2). This approach has proved to be highly limited and has often failed to impact directly on the poor because of their inherent disadvantage in terms of political power and the ability to influence the choice and location of government programmes and projects. It also targets both rural and urban dwellers.[687]
b) *Rural Development Approach*: This approach, which could be view as an aspect of the basic needs approach, focuses on integrated rural development and considers the rural area as a unique area of concentration in terms of poverty reduction. This emphasis is based on the recognition of the fact that majority of the poor live in the rural areas. Most of them are engaged in the agricultural sectors. The approach aims therefore at providing basic necessities of life such as food, shelter, safe drinking water, education, health care, employment and income generating opportunities to the rural dwellers in general and the poor in particular. It also includes such programmes as Social Safety Nets and Micro Credits.[688]
c) *Economic Growth Approach*: This approach encourages broad based economic growth. By adopting the economic growth strategy, the government takes an indirect approach to poverty alleviation. This method involves an untargeted general increase in incomes in which it is hoped that the average poor people would be lifted above the poverty line. In the short run income distribution may be positively skewed but the belief is that in the long-run, through trickle down effects, poverty will be reduced both in the absolute and the relative sense (cf. 5.1.3.1).[689] This is more or less the

686 Fidelis O. Ogwumike, An Appraisal of Poverty Reduction Strategies in Nigeria, CBN Economic & Financial Review. Vol. 39 No. 4, p. 7.

687 Mustapha Muktar, Poverty Alleviation as a Machinery for Economic Reconstruction in Nigeria: In: Mustapha C. Duze et al. (eds.), Poverty in Nigeria: Causes Manifestations and Alleviation Strategies, (London: Adonis & Abbey Publishers Ltd, 2008), p, 190.

688 Ibid.

689 Cf. S. I. Oladeji and A. G. Abiola, Poverty alleviation with economic growth strategy: prospects and challenges in contemporary Nigeria: In: Journal of social development in Africa, vol. 15, No. 2. July, 2000.

approach adopted in Nigeria during the SAP era[690] and since then has continued to dominate government development and poverty alleviation programmes.

d) *Human Capital development*: Programmes that focus on human capital formation have to do basically with education, health, nutrition and housing needs of labour. They were linked with efforts aimed at accelerating growth. As it was believed that investment in these sources of human capital improves the quality of labour and thus its productivity and hence "to ensure growth that takes care of poverty, the share of human capital as a source of growth in output has to be accorded the rightful place."[691] This could be said to be closer to the ILO labour-centred pro-poor approach (c.f. 5.3).

6.1.3.1 Poverty Alleviation in the Pre-SAP Era

Most of the developmental programmes in the pre-SAP era were neither explicitly targeted at the poor people, nor exclusively designed to alleviate poverty. They however targeted objectives that, if achieved, could improve the lives of the poor. Some of them were designed, for instance, to bring about general development of opportunities in health, employment and education as well as improve access and opportunities in these areas. Others were meant to enhance agricultural output and income, and curtail the tide of rural-urban migration. Still others emphasized increase in real income of the average citizen but were not meant explicitly to reduce income inequality.[692] The programmes designed for pursuing objectives such as employment generation, enhancement of agricultural output and income and stemming the tide of rural – urban migration include, for instance, the River Basin Development Authorities (RBDA), the Agricultural Development Programmes (ADP), the Agricultural Credit Guarantee Scheme (ACGS), the Rural Electrification Scheme (RES), and the Rural Banking Programme (RBP).[693] While the Operation Feed the Nation (OFN) established in 1977 and Green Revolution established in 1980 aimed particularly at boosting agricultural production, Free and Compulsory primary Education (FCPE) set up also in 1977, targeted access to knowledge and the Low Cost Housing Scheme sought to make decent housing affordable to people especially in the urban centres.[694]

---

690 Fidelis O. Ogwumike, An Appraisal of Poverty Reduction Strategies in Nigeria, op. cit., p. 6.

691 Mustapha Muktar, Poverty Alleviation as a Machinery for Economic Reconstruction in Nigeria, op. cit., p. 190.

692 For more on this, see: F. O. Ogwumike, Poverty and Basic Needs: An Approach to Development in Nigeria, unpublished Ph.D. Thesis, Department of Economics, University of Ibadan, 1987; F. O. Ogwumike, Poverty Alleviation Strategies in Nigeria., in: Measuring and Monitoring Poverty in Nigeria, Proceedings of the Seventh Annual Conference of the Zonal Research Units of CBN, 1998; F. O. Ogwumike, The Effects of Macro-level Government Policies on Rural Development and Poverty Alleviation in Nigeria, Ibadan Journal of the Social Sciences, Vol. 1, NO. 1, 1995, pp. 85 – 101.

693 Fidelis O. Ogwumike, An Appraisal of Poverty Reduction Strategies in Nigeria, op. cit., p. 7.

694 Ibid.

Although not directly aimed at poverty alleviation, these programmes certainly made some impacts on the lives of the poor and enhanced the quality of life of many Nigerians. They could unfortunately not be sustained due to lack of political will and commitment, policy instability and insufficient involvement of the beneficiaries in these programmes, etc,[695] consequently the incidence of poverty failed to abate at the said period.

6.1.3.2 Poverty Alleviation in the SAP Era

There is a consensus among scholars that it was during the structural adjustment era that the Nigerian government began to take concrete steps towards poverty alleviation. This was in response to the economic crisis in of the early 1980s that resulted in the drastic deterioration of the quality of life in the nation.[696] The government of the time sought to bring the crisis under control by adopting and implementing the Structural Adjustment Programme (SAP). It is believed however that "while structural adjustment had its salutary effects on economic growth, it lacked emphasis on development and also accentuated socio-economic problems of income inequality, unequal access to food, shelter, education, health and other necessities of life. It indeed, aggravated the incidence of poverty among many vulnerable groups in the society."[697] As a result of the continuous deterioration of living conditions in the late 1980s other poverty alleviation programmes were brought into existence, particularly between 1986 and 1993.[698] Below is a summary of the major anti-poverty programmes packaged and implemented by the government during the SAP era.

Directorate of Food, roads and Rural Infrastructure (DFRRI) was embarked upon in 1986 aimed at impacting directly on the lives of rural dwellers through the provision of basic needs such as food, shelter, potable water, etc. It was also designed to provide for the necessary basic infrastructures that can stimulate the growth of agro-allied small-scale enterprises in rural areas. The programme became however defunct in 1994, following its inability to yield the expected results.[699]

The National Directorate of Employment (NDE) was charged with the task of creating employment, enhancing productivity, increasing income earning potentials and combating mass unemployment and underemployment especially among young school leavers and graduates. This task included the articulation of policies aimed at developing work programmes with labour intensive potentials. This programme itself exhibited great potentials for alleviating poverty from the labour

695 Central Bank of Nigeria, Enugu Zone, A Profile of Regional/Zonal Poverty in Nigeria: The Case of Enugu Zone: In: Measuring and Monitoring Poverty in Nigeria, Proceedings of the Seventh Annual Conference of the Zonal Research Units, 1998.

696 Mustapha Muktar, Poverty Alleviation as a Machinery for Economic Reconstruction in Nigeria, op. cit., p. 92.

697 697 Mike I. Obadan, Poverty Reduction in Nigeria: The Way Forward, CBN, Economic and Financial Review, vol. 39, No. 4, p. 6.

698 Ibid., p. 5.

699 Fidelis O. Ogwumike, An Appraisal of Poverty Reduction Strategies in Nigeria, op. cit., p. 9.

point of view, given that poverty manifests itself among the working class in the form of unemployment and underemployment and unfavourable labour conditions. The NDE has four main programmes, namely: The Vocational Skills Development Programme (VSD), the Special Public Works Programme (SPWP), the Small Scale Enterprises Programme (SSE) and the Agricultural Employment Programme (AEP)[700]

Through these programmes, many youths including disabled persons were trained in the National Open Apprenticeship Scheme between 1987 and 1996. Some of them benefited from the Resettlement scheme at the end of 1996. Others have also been offered various forms of employment.[701] There are however doubts about the quality of jobs created through the NDE.

The Better Life Programme (BLP): was introduced in 1987 and transformed into the Family Support Programme (FSP) 1994 aimed at enhancing the quality of life in the rural areas but with emphasis on the life of rural women.[702] It addressed itself to fighting gender inequality by harnessing the potentials of rural women and thereby impacting positively on their economic activities and incomes. Among other things, women were assisted to gain access to micro-credits and various educational/enlightenment/training programmes. To further empower them, they were formed into women cooperatives. The Family Support Programme (FSP) concentrated more on the provision of health care delivery, child welfare, youth development, and improved nutritional status to families in rural areas. Both programmes were however short-lived, as they were particularly marred by diversion of funds and other corrupt practices.[703]

The People's Bank of Nigeria (PBN) was established in 1989 with a view of making credit facilities available to both rural and urban poor who were usually denied such services by the conventional banks. The bank was directly funded by the government and so was over-dependent on the government.[704].

Community Banks (CBs) came into existence in 1990 and replaced the People's Bank. They were specifically established to provide banking facilities for rural dwellers as well as to support micro-enterprises in urban areas. To better achieve this aim, they were constituted around the informal mutual savings and loan associations operating in rural areas. Unlike the People's Bank, the Community Banks were meant to be self-sustaining. Since their inception, these Community Banks have attained some degree of success in providing financial services to those

700 I. J. Okpe and G.A. Abu, Foreign Private Investment and Poverty Reduction in Nigeria (1975 to 2003), in: Journal of social Sciences: Interdisciplinary Reflection of Contemporary Society, vol. 19, No. 3, May, 2009, p. 207.

701 For more on the achievements of the NDE see: Central Bank of Nigeria's annual reports 1992-1996.

702 I. J. Okpe and G.A. Abu, Foreign Private Investment and Poverty Reduction in Nigeria (1975 to 2003), op. cit., p. 207.

703 Fidelis O. Ogwumike, An Appraisal of Poverty Reduction Strategies in Nigeria, op. cit., p. 10.

704 Ibid.

people most likely to be left out of the financial mainstream. Their operational system drew heavily from the strong local networks existing in many rural areas.[705]

Family Economic Advancement Programme (FEAP) was designed to create employment opportunities at ward levels. It was charged with the task of encouraging the designing and manufacturing of local plants, machinery and equipments, and providing opportunities for the training of local-based business operators. It also supported the establishment of cottage industries in both rural and urban areas by providing credit facilities.[706]

6.1.3.3 Poverty Alleviation in the Post-SAP Era

The notable programme embarked upon within this period is the Poverty Alleviation Programme (PAP), which aimed to create jobs and curb social crimes among youths. This programme was launched in 2000. Although it had wide range of features, emphasis was however placed on the creation of jobs through public work system.[707] PAP's main thrust was to reduce the problem of unemployment and hence raise effective demand in the economy; increase the productiveness of the economy and drastically reduce the embarrassing crime in the society.[708] It sought to achieve these objectives by creating a credit delivery system from which farmers will have access to credit facilities, by increasing the adult literacy rate, improving health care delivery system, increasing rural water supply and rural electrification and by developing simple processes and small industries[709] It is important to note that PAP was only an interim programmes that has since been subsumed into the current national poverty alleviation programmes.

6.1.4 Appraisal of Previous Efforts at Reducing Poverty

From the foregoing in this section, we have seen how efforts have been made in the past from different angles to combat at least absolute poverty in Nigeria. Efforts have been made through the various poverty alleviation programmes in the areas of food crop production in the agricultural sector, also in the area of industrial extension services, education enrolment, primary health care, mass transit programme and financial sector services, infrastructure and housing facilities and employment creation.[710] The continued existence of high incidence of poverty in

---

705 I. J. Okpe and G.A. Abu, Foreign Private Investment and Poverty Reduction in Nigeria (1975 to 2003), op. cit., p. 207.

706 Fidelis O. Ogwumike, An Appraisal of Poverty Reduction Strategies in Nigeria, op. cit., pp. 10-11

707 Mike I. Obadan, Poverty Reduction in Nigeria: The Way Forward, op. cit., p. 13

708 Mustapha Muktar, Poverty Alleviation as a Machinery for Economic Reconstruction in Nigeria, op. cit., pp. 194 & 195.

709 Ibid.

710 Mike I. Obadan, Poverty Reduction in Nigeria: The Way Forward, op. cit., pp. 6 & 7. See also: Fidelis O. Ogwumike, Poverty Alleviation Strategies in Nigeria, in Measuring and Monitoring Poverty in Nigeria, Proceedings of the Seventh Annual Conference of the Zonal Research Units of CBN, 1998.

Nigeria is however a clear pointer to the colossal failure of these Anti-poverty programmes.[711]

The failure of the previous poverty alleviation programmes have been blamed on a number of factors. Prominent among them are poor implementation, corruption of government officials and public servants, poor targeting mechanisms and failure to identify and focus directly on the poor.[712] It has also been observed that within the framework of the previous National Development Plans, the implicit thinking was that a positive relationship existed between growth in the GDP and increased welfare for the general citizenry. "And so, the approach to poverty alleviation as expressed in the fundamental objectives of the Development Plans did not involve policies and programmes which directly targeted the poor. The poor were implicitly expected to benefit from the "trickle -down efforts" of the overall process of development. But this has not been the case. And so growth must be accompanied by a deliberate policy of targeted interventions."[713]

6.2 Current Efforts at Alleviating Poverty

The National Poverty Eradication Programme (NAPEP) and the National Economic and Empowerment Development Strategy (NEEDS) represent the efforts currently made by the Nigerian government to combat poverty in the nation.

6.2.1 The National Poverty Eradication Programme

NAPEP was created in 2001 as the primary agency of the government charged with the responsibility of coordinating and monitoring all poverty eradication activities in the country.[714] It therefore assumed the function of providing policy programmes meant to give focus to activities aimed at alleviating poverty. Its major focus has been the provision of "strategies for the eradication of absolute poverty in Nigeria."[715] Its primary objective as stated in the official website is "to make sure that strong winning partnerships are forged in the country so that well synergised and sustainable programmes are implemented for the benefit of the people."[716]

Its major activities has been to help generate mass participation in the economic reform process, through catalytic partnerships and intervention, to assist state and local governments develop direct anti-poverty programs that include Micro-Credit and Micro-Finance, to build strategic public and private sector

711 Mike I. Obadan, Poverty Reduction in Nigeria: The Way Forward, op. cit., p. 8.

712 Ibid., pp. 8 & 9.

713 Ibid., p. 6.

714 National Poverty Eradication Programme (NAPEP), http://www.napep.gov.ng/whatwedo.php, accessed on 23.05.2011.

715 Cf. Federal Republic of Nigeria, National Poverty Eradication Programme (NAPEP): A Blueprint for the Schemes, NAPEP Secretariat, Abuja, 2001.

716 National Poverty Eradication Programme (NAPEP), op. cit..

partnerships that provide Information to the disadvantaged and to stimulate political action against poverty to centre on providing confidence and Stable Markets for the goods & services of poor people.[717] These activities centre on youth empowerment, rural infrastructure development, provision of social welfare services and natural resource development and conservation.

In striving to fulfil its mandate, NAPEP adopted a participatory, bottom-up approach in the implementation and monitoring of its programmes. Other features of the programme reflected in its four areas of activities include:

- Making provisions for rational framework which lays emphasis on appropriate and sustainable institutional arrangement;
- Making provisions for pro-active and affirmative actions deliberately targeted at women, youths, farmers and the disabled;
- Creating opportunity for inter-ministerial and inter-agency cooperation;
- Promoting participation of all registered political parties, traditional rulers, and the communities;
- Creating opportunities for technology acquisition and development particularly for agriculture and industry;
- Making provisions for capacity building for existing skills acquisition and training centres;
- Expansion of agricultural and industrial extension services to rural areas;
- Promotion of institutional development for marketing of agricultural and industrial products;
- Making provision for integrated schemes for youth empowerment, development of infrastructure, provision of social welfare services and exploitation of natural resources.[718]

6.2.2 National Economic Empowerment and Development Strategy

The NEEDS[719] was conceived in April 2003 but launched officially in 2004. It is a set of strategies for achieving the objectives set by NAPEP. Being an off-shoot of NAPEP, its objectives are basically not different from those of NAPEP. It is considered to be an instrument or strategy for government's direct involvement in poverty alleviation and has since received international approval and support "for

717 Ibid.

718 Cf, A. Aliu, National Poverty Eradication Programme (NAPEP): Completion, Implementation, Coordination and Monitoring, (Abuja: NAPEP Secretariat, 2001), pp. 12 & 13, as cited by Mike I. Obadan, Poverty Reduction in Nigeria: The Way Forward, op. cit.

719 What is present here is condensed. For details on NEEDS, See the original document: International Monetary Fund, Poverty Reduction Strategy Paper—National Economic Empowerment and Development Strategy, IMF Country Report No. 05/433Nigeria: (Washington, D.C. International Monetary Fund Publication Services, 2005).

being, at least in theory, Nigeria's home-grown programme."[720] This NEEDS which was intended to be a medium term agenda (spanning from 2003 to 2007) takes a multi-dimensional approach to poverty. It aims basically at reducing unemployment, stimulating growth, improving governance, increasing access to basic health and education and transforming values to overcome corruption and inefficiency. It also aims at improving agriculture, protecting the environment, promoting gender equality, security and rule of law, infrastructure development and Small and Medium-size Enterprises (SME) development. Its ultimate goals therefore are poverty reduction, employment generation and wealth creation.[721]

The NEEDS is said to be fashioned in such a way that it would be able to promote nation-wide participatory process in which all Nigerians and stakeholders are given a chance to contribute to a plan that affects their lives. "Such a participatory approach facilitates people's active involvement at all phases of the programme cycle from design and implementation to monitoring and evaluation. It also has the potential to ensure people's ownership of development programmes, crucial for sustainable development."[722]

To further highlight the need for the effective stakeholders' participation and to ensure that the NEEDS get to the grass-root, the state governments and local governments were mandated to pursue an adaptation of the NEED strategy. The adaptation of the NEEDS by States and Local Governments would mean formulating their strategies in line with the national strategy. This adaptation has led to the emergence of State Economic Empowerment and Development Strategies (SEEDS) and the Local Government Economic Empowerment and Development Strategies (LEEDS). Both LEEDS and SEEDS are intended to be time bound (mostly medium term) policy frameworks designed to promote macroeconomic stability, improve the performance of the agricultural, manufacturing, solid minerals and oil and gas sectors, improve delivery of basic services, create an enabling environment for the private sector and invest in human capital towards reducing the poverty of the people.

The NEEDS has been fully implemented and a follow-up strategy—NEEDS 2 which is supposed to run from 2008–11 is still being awaited. Meanwhile, the third democratically elected government has committed itself to reforms in line with the '7-Point Agenda' focusing on the development of human capital; critical infrastructure; food security; land tenure changes and home ownership; national security; wealth creation; and the Niger Delta.

---

720 Sadiq Isah Radda, The Millennium Development Goals (MDGS) and Poverty in Nigeria: An Appraisal, in: Mustapha C. Duze et al. (eds), Poverty in Nigeria: Causes Manifestations and Alleviation Strategies. (London: Adonis & Abbey Publishers Ltd, 2008), p. 182.

721 UNDP, Methodology for the Participatory Formulation of Local Government Economic Empowerment & Development Strategy (LEEDS) in Local Government Areas (LGAs) in Nigeria, a pdf document available at: http://www.ng.undp.org/publications/poverty/LEEDS_Methodology.pdf, accesses on 06.60.2011.

722 Ibid.

An assessment of the full implementation of the NEEDS highlights its accomplishments and shortcomings as well as outstanding issues. It is claimed that having been fully implemented, the NEEDS has achieved macroeconomic stability and sustained a broad-based high growth underpinned by a range of deep structural reforms in most sectors of the economy.[723] It is also claimed that significant progress has been made in terms of increasing the transparency of the government budgets and accounts, reforming the civil service and ministries, and reducing inefficiencies in government expenditure.[724]

6.2.3 Some Recent Economic Reforms

The realisation of the objectives the NEEDS is predicated on a number of reforms including public sector reform. These reforms involved privatization and commercialization, adoption of due process and transparency in procurement, budget and planning process, service delivery and expenditure reforms. Reforms were also carried out in financing strategies and tax/revenue administration. These reforms were implemented in three main areas: macroeconomic reform, structural reform, public sector reform and institutional and governance reform.

6.2.3.1 Macroeconomic Reforms

A central objective of the macroeconomic reform measure was to stabilize the Nigerian economy, to improve budgetary planning and execution, and to provide a platform for sustained economic diversification and non-oil growth. A major challenge in this regard was to de-link public expenditures from oil revenue earnings by introducing an appropriate fiscal rule. It was believed that the adoption of such a rule could boost the accumulation of government savings, which would be valuable, whether for precautionary reasons, for smoothening public expenditures or for ensuring intergenerational equity.[725]

As part of the major efforts to address this challenge, an oil price-based fiscal rule was introduced in which government expenditure was based on a prudent oil price benchmark. Accumulated revenues above the reference prices were saved in a special excess crude account.[726] The economy reportedly responded with strong growth between 2003 and 2009, averaging 7.4 percent. Part of the oil savings was used by the government to conclude the debt relief agreement with the Paris

723 International Monetary Fund, Joint Staff Advisory Note on the Progress Report for the National Economic Empowerment and Development Strategy (NEEDS), (Washington D.C.: IMF Publication Service, 2007), p. 1, paragraph 1.

724 Ibid, p, 3, paragraph 10.

725 Ngozi Okonjo-Iweala and Philip Osafo-Kwaako, Nigeria's Economic Reforms: Progress and Challenges, a working paper, op. cit., p. 9.

726 Ibid., p. 10.

Club.[727] Attempts were also made to instil discipline into the implementation of monetary policy, with the central bank adhering to various monetary targets and reducing inflation. The Wholesale Dutch Auction System was adopted to facilitate the convergence of foreign exchange markets and to eliminate a previous black market premium.[728]

6.2.3.2 Structural Reforms

Major structural reforms were mainly embarked upon in the area of privatization, civil service, bank consolidation and trade policy to improve the domestic business climate and enhance competitiveness, to deregulate and reduce government activity in various economic sectors, and to address various structural constraints to growth.

6.2.3.2.1 Privatization

In a bid to promote efficiency, to curb corruption and also to reduce the financial costs to the federal government the government embarked on the privatization of some state-owned enterprises, as well as deregulation of government activities in some sectors. The privatization process was accompanied by deregulation of some economic sectors with a view to encouraging private sector participation, notably in telecommunications, power, and downstream petroleum sectors. As the privatization and deregulation process progresses, doubts have however been expressed as to whether the processes have been fair and transparent and whether private business monopolies are being established in the processes.[729]

6.2.3.2.2 Civil Service Reform

The Civil service reform embarked upon was basically to eliminate redundancy and promote efficiency among civil servants. This resulted in the expunging of ghost worker, retrenchment of redundant workers and recruitment of new workers. Government pay scales were also reviewed in the process while various public sector benefits such as housing and cars were also monetized and consolidated with basic salaries. [730]

6.2.3.2.3 Banking Sector Reform

A bank consolidation exercise was launched in 2004 with the aim to boost the financial sector and improve availability of domestic credit to the private sector. The exercise, it was claimed, helped deposit banks to build stronger capital base, as they were mandated to raise their minimum capital base from about US$15 million to US$192 million by the end of 2005. A similar exercise carried out in the

---

727 World Bank, Nigeria: Country Brief, retrieved from: http://web.worldbank.org/WBSITE/EXTERNAL/COUNTRIES/AFRICAEXT/NIGERIAEXTN/0,,menuPK:368906~pagePK:141132~piPK:141107~theSitePK:368896,00.html, accessed on 24.03.2011

728 Ngozi Okonjo-Iweala and Philip Osafo-Kwaako, Nigeria's Economic Reforms: Progress and Challenges, op. cit., p. 10.

729 Ibid, pp. 13-14.

730 Ibid, p. 14.

insurance sector targeted the consolidation and reduction of 103 insurance businesses to about 30 with a capitalization of about $1.6 billion by February 2007. Three important legal instruments were promulgated to ensure smooth and effective capitalization and subsequent supervision of the banking sector. These include, the CBN/BOFI Act Amendment Bill, which was intended to improve autonomy of the central bank in its monetary policy decisions; the Nigeria Deposit Insurance Corporation (NDIC) Act which provides a comprehensive framework for addressing the case of private depositors who may be affected by the liquidation process; a new Microfinance Act which aims at developing a reliable microfinance industry in the nation.[731]

6.2.3.2.4 Trade Policy Reform

The trade reforms that have been implemented aimed at simplifying the tariff structure and improving the transparency and predictability of the nation's trade policies that have, over the year been complex, restrictive, and opaque. And with a view to liberalizing import tariff regime, the Common External Tariff (CET) of the Economic Community of West African States (ECOWAS), was adopted[732]

6.2.3.3 Institutional and Governance Reforms

Some major institutional and governance reforms were in the areas of accountability and transparency. Having reviewed the public procurement system in Nigeria to determine the costs of corruption especially in government contracts, the government introduced a Value for Money audit, or Due Process mechanism, in public contracts. This, it was believed, would create the possibility for an open tender process with competitive bidding for government contracts. The Due Process mechanism requires that the government publishes a public tender journal periodically as a means of reducing patronage in the award of contracts and that certification of completed government projects is fully done before final payments are made. In line with this, strengthening *Public expenditure management* was deemed necessary in order to improve transparency and the quality of government capital projects. To this end a monthly publication of federal, state, and local government shares of revenue from the country's federation account was introduced in January 2004.[733]

In the oil and gas sector, the Nigeria Extractive Industries Transparency Initiative (NEITI) was adopted to help improve governance of the oil sector. In order to achieve this objective, an independent audit of the oil and gas sector was commissioned. Two institutions were established to tackle corruption at the home front especially in the domestic business environment. These are the Economic and

731 Ibid, 15-16.

732 Ibid, 16.

733 Ibid, 18.

Financial Crimes Commission (EFCC) and the Independent Corrupt Practices and other Related Offences Commission (ICPC).[734]

6.2.4 Appraisal of Current National Efforts

Not withstanding the accomplishments in the current efforts at alleviating poverty in Nigeria, there are still serious issues that need to be addressed in order to combat the menace of poverty in an efficient and sustainable manner. It is claimed that "the primary goal of economic planning in Nigeria is the attainment of rapid increase in the nation's productive capacity with a view to improving the living standards of the people"[735] but a closer examination of the current development and poverty alleviation programmes reveal however that more emphasis has been placed on economic growth. It has indeed been observed that "the development debate in Nigeria over the past few years seems to have focused too narrowly on growth for its own sake rather than as a means of improved human development."[736] This narrow focus, it is further observed, has reduced the nation's prospect of tapping "the potential of countless millions of Nigerians who are poor today but can be highly productive in the future with the right combination of public and private policies and investments"[737] There is obviously a lack of clear vision and appropriate framework for job creation and labour development, especially where it matters most – in the informal economy in the nation.

The current poverty alleviation strategy and programmes (NEPAP and NEEDS), though an improvement on the previous ones, have however failed to properly recognise and address poor labour conditions in the informal economy which, as we saw in chapter three, harbours more than 60% of the nation's labour force and generates almost 95% of new job opportunities. This failure to properly identify, recognise and deal with the factors responsible for the poor labour conditions in the informal segment of the economy has been the bane of the inability of the nation to defeat poverty. There is certainly no way Nigeria will overcome absolute poverty, if more than 60% of its labour force continues to toil in poor labour conditions; a condition bedevilled by unhealthy working environment, poor remuneration, absence of rights, discrimination against women, weak dialogue and negotiation, low productivity, etc.

In the same vain, empowerment, opportunity and security which have become today the international acclaimed goals of human development will continue to be a mirage in Nigeria as long as the majority of the workers (the working poor) are not given enough access to basic training and decent employment. Exclusion from decent employment is a basic problem of the poor, in particular the less educated

734 Ibid, pp. 18-19.

735 Mike I. Obadan, Poverty Reduction in Nigeria: The Way Forward, op. cit., p. 3.

736 United Nations Development Programme (UNDP), Human Development Report Nigeria 2008 – 2009 Achieving growth with equity, (Abuja, Nigeria: Development Programme, Nigeria, 2009), p. 3.

737 Ibid

and those without schooling. It is evident in Nigeria, for instance, "that these groups are not only displaced by the more educated people in formal sector employment, they also stand increasingly the risk of being relocated into informal sector activities"[738]

Although Nigeria strives to attain the economic growth that will enable the nation overcome poverty, creation of 'decent work' is evidently neither a priority nor an indicator of the nation's Poverty Reduction Strategy. It is quite obvious that the minimum conditions required for poverty alleviation with growth to be successful are a growth process that favours labour-intensive activities and an improved access of the populace to the social services that enhance human capital. As we sew in the previous chapter, the ILO through the Decent Work Agenda (DWA) has provided a workable framework for attaining this gaol. The ILO strategy we noted is in accord with the ethical orientation and guideline offered by the Catholic social teaching which insists on the socio-economic development that promotes social justice and respect for the dignity of the human person based on the principles of common good, subsidiarity and solidarity. But the question is: Does Nigeria as a Nation and a member of the ILO take this serious?

There is enough evidence that Nigeria is yet to take the Decent Work Agenda serious. The government has consistently shown dogged commitment and dedication to employment generation. This was confirmed by the one time Minister of Labour, Adetokunbo Kayode, who, while speaking with particular reference to the National Employment policy approved in 2001 but abandoned on the shelf without implementation, observed: "We cannot say the government had been serious about employment because in 2001 it approved the National Employment Policy, but that policy remained on the shelf. It was never implemented."[739]

The Nigerian government has also failed to commit itself fully to the implementation of the Decent Work Country Programme which was lunched in the year 2005. Calling for the revalidation and strengthening of the processes of implementing Nigeria's Decent Work Country Programme (DWCP), the one time Permanent Secretary in the Ministry of Labour and Productivity Ambassador Alex Anigbo confirmed that not much progress has been made since the ministry and the International Labour Organization (ILO) as well as other social partners formulated the DWCP for Nigeria in November 2005. The disheartening reason he adduced for this is: "mainly because of the time needed to revisit and revalidate the agreed priority areas."[740]

In order to wage a successful war against poverty, Nigeria needs a poverty alleviation strategy that will promote growth with equity for poverty reduction; a

---

738 S. I. Oladeji and A. G. Abiola, Poverty alleviation with economic growth strategy: prospects and challenges in contemporary Nigeria, op. cit., p. 48.

739 Cf. Agence de Presse Africaine: http://www.apanews.net/public/spip.php?article117596.

740 Daily Trust, Nigeria: Permanent Secretary Calls for Strengthening of Decent Work Country Programme, a report put together by Francis Okeke, accessed from http://allafrica.com/stories/201003250669.html, on 23.05.2011.

strategy that will direct more attention to that segment of the economy where the e majority of the poor citizens work and earn their living.

6.3 Contributions of the Nigerian Church to Poverty Alleviation

The Nigeria Church has committed herself to the course of the poor basically through the official pronouncements of the Church's hierarchy, through works of charity, through some social action in form of providing material succour and social services and through her prayers. In this way she endeavours to portray herself as the Church of the poor.

6.3.1 Official Pronouncements: Communiqués

Through the voice of her bishops, the Catholic Church in Nigeria has endeavoured to proclaim moral principles in respect of the social order. In this ways she aims at influencing and stimulating socio-economic and political reforms that would help to create a just society and bring succour to the suffering masses, especially the poorest of the poor. The commitment and dedication of the Church in Nigeria to the course of the poor are clearly articulated in many of the pastoral letters and communiqués of the Catholic Bishops Conference of Nigeria (CBCN). In reaffirming this commitment, the Nigerian Church declares that "she is not afraid of raising her voice and committing herself to the poor wherever she sees the powerful, the power-conscious and the privileged pressure groups browbeating the weak."[741] She strives to be on the side of the poor, following the example of Christ.

The communiqués of the Nigerian Catholic Bishops touches various facets of the socio-economic life in the nation; calling attention to the structural malaise that has been responsible for the degeneration of the economy and impoverishment of the masses, while at the same time making recommendations for social reforms that would ensure improvement in the general wellbeing of all in the nation.

Agriculture and Rural Dwellers: The church, as far back as 1972, condemned the deplorable state of farmers in Nigeria, the negative attitude to farming and the government's nonchalant attitude to the development of agriculture. She stressed the urgent need for improvement in the status of farming and for actions that would bring respite to farmers who were condemned, as it were, to work under harsh and inhuman conditions and with primitive techniques and implements: "Every effort must be made to improve the status of farming by introducing new methods and techniques to prove that farming is an occupation of dignity and honour, that is worthwhile and lucrative."[742]

---

741 Catholic Bishops' Conference of Nigeria, The Church and Nigerian Social Problems: Memorandum of the Catholic Bishops' of Nigeria, February, 1972.

742 Ibid.

This clarion call for action was followed up in February, 1975 when the Nigerian bishops issued another communiqué on the current unrest in the nation, occasioned by the wide spread hunger, frustration and abject poverty among the masses especially those in the agrarian rural areas. Noting that the population of Nigeria is mainly rural and that agriculture remains a major occupation of the rural dwellers, the Church solicited improved access to better life for the rural dwellers through improved social services, through decentralization of amenities and industries and through rural electrification and water schemes.[743] This appeal was re-echoed in other documents of the Nigerian Bishop's Conference issued in February 1978; February, 1983; February, 1985; and September, 1998.

Social and Economic Justice: The Nigerian Church has contributed reasonable to questions of social and economic justice as a means of promoting the well-being of the masses. In their memorandum of 1972, the Nigerian Bishops observed that "the problem of (social and economic) injustice in Nigeria may well become one of the gravest and most urgent problems of our immediate future. Unfair competition, bribery, corruption, rising costs, brigandage, embezzlement are now recurrent themes in our daily press.... There is spreading a cancer of injustice suffered by the 'little ones' of the land, from the hands of some public officials interested too frequently in their personal promotion rather than in their community service."[744] In concrete terms, the bishops expressed their support for the arguments for the privatization of some of the state enterprises and condemned 'expanding state-control and government take-overs' and the eagerness of the State to 'put its hand in every pie' which has resulted in relative scarcity of private enterprises and capital and also to private initiatives being dulled. It was noted that "political freedom and independence are important, but unless they are accompanied by economic and social justice, they are meaningless."[745] Based on this observation, a clarion call was made for a full-scale war against all forms of economic exploitation in all facets of the society and for judicious management and equitable distribution of the resources available in the nation. There was also a demand for economic policies that are at the services of the people, stressing that economic policies that negate the dignity of the human person, should be denounced as deprivations.[746]

Apart from the efforts made by Catholic bishops of Nigeria through established Church organs, numerous lay organizations also contribute to bringing about fairness, justice and equity on behalf of the weak groups. They also contribute to new understanding of the cultural, economic and human development of man. The scope of this work, however, would not permit elaborate deliberations on the contribution of the lay faithful individually or in the various groups.

743 Catholic Bishops' Conference of Nigeria, Current Unrest, Lagos, February 13, 1975.

744 Catholic Bishops' Conference of Nigeria, The Church and Nigerian Social Problems, op. cit.

745 Catholic Bishops' Conference of Nigeria, Peace through Justice and Love, Lagos, February, 1989.

746 Catholic Bishops' Conference of Nigeria, The Jubilee and National Reconciliation, Lagos March, 2000.

Corruption: Consistent with the commitment to social and economic justice, the Nigerian Church has raised her voice in condemning all forms of corruption that have brought untold hardships to a greater portion of the population. In February, 2002, the Nigerian Bishops attributed the deplorable state of the nation and the high rate of poverty in the country to the sins of corruption and lack of love and concern for one another.

> Our seemingly incurable wounds are symptoms of a deeper and more chronic sickness, namely sin of corruption. This is manifested in our lack of love, lack of concern, and selfishness at individual and group levels. The pervasive presence of greed, selfishness, corruption, the culture of impunity, the politics of power rather than development all attribute to a nation of wounded people. These vices prevent us from putting in place structures that heal and unify. While some have more responsibility than others for our wounds, no one is totally without blame.[747]

Having made this observation, the Church called on the government to rid itself of corrupt practices and empower the existing anti-graft institutions to wage an effective war against corruption at all levels of government and business.[748]

Just Wage and Good Conditions for Worker: The Nigerian Church insists on just wages, social security and adequate or good labour conditions for workers, and denounces all forms of exploitation of workers. This was given a strong ascent in the Memorandum of the Catholic Bishops of Nigeria in February, 1972. This issue was revisited in 1982 when the bishops again insisted on the right of worker to just wages adding that the delay of salaries is inimical to the morals of workers, to their personal dignity and that of their families, to the moral authority of the employers and to the entire nation.[749]

Workers Union and Right to Strike: The Church acknowledged the important role played by trade unions in establishing fair wages, in improving working conditions and in advancing the general interest of workers. Way back in 1960, the Nigerian Church deplored unjust means of strike breaking and insisted that labour unions should be accorded their proper position in modern industrial society. The Church also condemned the weaknesses inherent in the labour unions themselves, noting that they cover but only a fraction of the country's workers; they are sadly disunited; they are short of educated and capable leaders; they have too often had recourse to extreme methods; they have been in constant trouble about funds.[750] In their 1972 communiqué, the Nigerian bishops re-echoed their support for labour

747 Catholic Bishops' Conference of Nigeria, Healing the Wounds of the Nation, Abuja: February, 2002.

748 For more on the reactions of the Nigerian Church to corruption and crime, see the following communiqués of the Nigerian Bishops: For Peace and Progress, Lagos, June 30, 1982; Year of Destiny, of Election and of Holy Redeemer, February, 1983; The Wind of Change in Nigeria, Lagos, March, 1990; The trust Shall make us Free, Jos, September, 1992.

749 Catholic Bishops' Conference of Nigeria, For Peace and Progress, a communiqué issued at the end of the meeting on June 13, 1982.

750 Catholic Bishops' Conference of Nigeria, The Catholic Church in an Independent Nigeria: Joint Pastoral Letter of the Nigerian Hierarchy. October 1st, 1960.

union rights and emphasized once more the importance of the role of labour unions in representing the various categories of workers and in collaborating in economic advancement and the realization of the common good.[751]

6.3.2 Prayer

The Nigerian Church views prayer as one of the veritable instruments at her disposal in the fight against the negative forces and unjust structures that have trapped many Nigerians in poverty. Two popular prayers (Prayer against Bribery and Corruption and Prayer for Nigeria in Distress) composed at the instance of the CBCN have been fervently prayed at community worships and in families. One of the prayers is directed against bribery and corruption in the nation[752] and the other is for Nigeria in distress[753]. It is the belief of the faithful that, in answer to these prayers, God has, through his intervention, saved the nation from the calamities that would have befallen it as a result of the grave acts of social injustice committed by its citizens.

6.3.3 Concrete Actions for Social Justice and Poverty alleviation

The contributions of the Nigerian Church to the improvement of the quality of life in the nation are not restricted to prayers and pronouncements made by the bishops. The Church has also embarked on various projects that render varied services that impact directly on the life of the poor and ultimately contribute meaningfully to nation building. Such contributions of the Church to poverty alleviation and nation

---

751 Catholic Bishops' Conference of Nigeria, The Church and Nigerian Social Problems, op. cit.

752 PRAYER AGAINST BRIBERY AND CORRUPTION IN NIGERIA: Father in heaven! You always provide for all your creatures, so that all may live as you have willed. You have blessed our country Nigeria with rich human and natural recourses to be used in honour and glory and for the well being of every Nigerian. We are deeply sorry for the wrong use of these your gifts and blessings through acts of injustice, bribery and corruption, as a result of which many of our people are hungry, sick, ignorant and defenceless. Father, you alone can heal us and our nation of this sickness. We beg you, touch our lives and the lives of our leaders and people so that we may all realise the evil of bribery and corruption and work hard to eliminate it. Raise up for us God-fearing people and leaders who care for us and who will lead us in the path of peace, prosperity and progress. We ask this through Jesus Christ our Lord. Amen. Most Sacred Heart of Jesus, Have mercy on us.

753 PRAYER FOR NIGERIA IN DISTRESS: All powerful and merciful Father! You are the God of Justice, Love and peace, you rule over all the nations of the earth. Power and might are in your hands and no one can withstand you. We present our country Nigeria before you, we praise and thank you for you are the source of all we have and are. We are sorry for all the sins we have committed and the good deeds we have failed to do. In your loving forgiveness, keep us safe from the punishments we deserved. Lord, we are weighed down not only by uncertainties but also by moral, economic and political problems. Listen to the cries of your people who confidently turn to you. God of infinite goodness! our strength in adversity, our health in weakness, our comfort in sorrow. Be merciful, to us your people; spare this nation Nigeria from chaos, anarchy and doom. Bless us with your kingdom of Justice, Love and Peace. We ask this through Jesus Christ our Lord. Amen.

building have been mainly in the areas of charity and social services such as education and health. Financial services are also provided but on low scale.

Education: In the area of education, the Church has played a leading role in creating a vast educational network in answer to the social needs of the masses. Numerous religious-oriented primary schools, teacher training colleges, secondary grammar schools, secondary modern schools, and universities and other higher institutions have been built by different institutions of the Church. Involving herself in providing educational services, the Church intends to provide quality education, sound religious and moral instructions and co-operate effectively with the government and other agencies in fostering moral uprightness in the society and eradicating ignorance and illiteracy at all levels and empowering "people to free themselves from misery and degradation as well as work for their own well-being".[754] The Church strives to extend her educational institutions to both the poor and the non-poor. There is however concern about the fees charged in some Catholic mission schools. The feeling is that these high fees keep the mission schools beyond the reach of the poor. The Church must therefore endeavour to ensure that while efforts are made to maintain good standards in the schools, care should at the same time be taken to also ensure that the schools are not run purely as money-making ventures.

Health: In the area of health care and hospital treatment, many hospitals, maternity homes, clinics, leprosaria managed by Catholic institutions have been built to serve the health needs of the people in different communities. In their 1995 communiqué on the distress in the nation, the Nigerian bishops declare: "Health is a fundamental right and integral part of the Church's mission. The Church is already intensely committed to health-care through the providing of Hospitals, Clinics and Primary Health Care Programmes, reaching out to individuals, families and communities."[755] In order to reach the poor, these health services are often taken to the rural areas where State health-care delivery services are not available.

Economic Empowerment: In recent time the Church has co-operated with many international agencies in providing economic support to the poor in the form of soft loans. She provides also some other micro-financial services. The Nigerian Church conceives that as part of the efforts towards making people self-reliant and providing self-employment for the poor. The Church makes available not only credit facilities but also other support materials the poor people need to start their own business; things such as sawing machines, motor cycles, mobile kiosks etc. In this way people, especially young people are being provided with job opportunities and also helped to use their talents to work and earn a decent living and so be able to stay out of poverty. This is done mainly through the Justice, Peace and Development Commission (JDPC) and some few micro-finance and credit institutions of the Church.

754 Catholic Bishops' Conference of Nigeria, The Church in the Face of our Nation in Distress, Lagos, March, 1995.

755 Ibid.

Charity Works: The Catholic Church in Nigerian also involves herself in works of charity, through which she seeks to relieve the suffering of the poor. There are so many projects such orphanages, homes for destitute and rehabilitation centres. Through these projects, the poor and needy are assisted irrespective of their creed.

6.3.4 Appraisal of the Church's Contribution

The Nigerian Church has obviously identified herself with the poor in the society. From the foregoing, it is clear that the Nigerian Church strives to live up to her role as the guard-fly of the nation and a political watchdog by identifying and condemning social ills and various forms of injustice in the system that have trapped a great portion of the citizenry to poverty. From time to time, the Church speaks out against the alarming rate of poverty growth in the nation and the marginalization of the poor.

The contributions of the Church in terms of bringing spiritual and material succour to the poor and in the area of providing financial assistance, economic empowerment and social services, especially education are also commendable. It is a known fact today that mission schools rank among the best educational institutions in Nigeria.

It is however necessary to note that enough is yet to be achieved. While the Church strives to fulfil her social mission by providing social services and spiritual and material succour to the poor and by making her voice heard in condemnation of the structural injustice responsible for the inhuman conditions in which the poor live and work in the nation, she must also reposition herself and get more actively involved in addressing the plight of the sufferings masses especially the working poor. This is where the Nigerian Church faces a number of challenges. Stressing the need for the Nigerian Church to do more, George Ehusani writes:

> When it comes to prophetic confrontation with unjust social structures; when it comes to challenging the evil status-quo, the social teaching of the Church does not seem to have "taken flesh" in the Nigerian context. The majority of Nigerians, even Catholics, are not aware of the powerful pronouncements of the Church on issues of justice and human development, perhaps because the public statement of the hierarchy have remained largely on the level of pious exhortations, passionate appeal, and benign denunciations, but lacking any practical gesture of solidarity with the oppressed and distraught with the oppressor.[756]

In the concluding phase of the work, detailed suggestions will be made about some concrete actions the Nigerian Church would need to embark on in order to be more relevant in the fight against poverty in the contemporary society.

756 George Omaku Ehusani, A Prophetic Church, (Ede: Provincial Pastoral Institute Publication, 1996), pp. 100-101

6.4 Conclusion

The major task undertaken in this chapter has been a critical evaluation of the past and current development and poverty alleviation initiatives in Nigeria. This evaluation highlights two striking points. The first point is that for a long time Nigeria pursued a development plan that anchored on the ideology that sees a positive and direct link between growth in the GDP and increased welfare for the general citizenry. Within this framework of development, the approach to poverty alleviation did not involve policies and programmes which directly targeted the poor especially those in the informal economy. The poor were implicitly expected to benefit from the trickle-down efforts of the overall process of development. The second point is that the development debates in Nigeria over the past few years have focused too narrowly on growth for its own sake rather than as a means of improved human development.

Although some programmes were designed to pursue some pro-poor objectives such as employment generation, enhancement of agricultural output and income, these programme unfortunately had little or no impact on poverty alleviation in the nation, as its incidence remained pervasive. Not only that these programme were not designed to target the poor directly, they also could not be sustained, particularly due to lack of political will and commitment, policy instability and insufficient involvement of the beneficiaries in these programmes and also due to diversion of funds and other corrupt practices.

As we saw in the fifth chapter of this work, a development and poverty alleviation strategy that concentrates on trickle-down and growth ideology and pays less attention to human development does not accord with the labour-intensive pro-poor approach to poverty alleviation that has been adjudged most suitable for attaining higher growth and alleviating poverty in an effective and sustainable manner. Narrowed emphasis on growth seems to have reduced Nigeria's prospect of harnessing the potential of countless millions of its citizens who are poor today but can be highly productive in the future with the right combination of public and private policies and investments The current development and poverty alleviation strategy lacks indeed a clear vision and appropriate framework for job creation and labour development, especially where it matters most – in the informal economy in the nation. Employment is not consistently integrated as the *raison d'être* of the NEEDS. It is rather regarded as a by-product of sectoral policies which cannot address the challenge of employment by themselves. Above all and more importantly, the NEEDS failed to adequately analyse the dynamics of the informal economy or present a well-orchestrated approach to poverty reduction for working people in informal employment. Meanwhile, informal employment both in subsistence rural agricultural activities and in urban employment continues to account for the majority of the employed in Nigeria.

It is doubtful whether Nigeria understands that resolving the numerous challenges posed by the high incidence of poverty and informality in the nation requires an effective coordination across numerous policy areas and cannot be addressed within the provisions of the current framework and strategy for economic development and poverty alleviation. Clearly, the nation lacks a development strategy that can adequately employ the nation's human resources and raise the returns to labour; a development strategy that does not relegate employment to the margins of policy formulation. Nigeria certainly needs a broad economic development plan and a poverty alleviation strategy that accommodate the different elements of growth and human development.

CHAPTER SEVEN

Recommendations for an Integrated Poverty Alleviation Framework in Nigeria

Introduction

Having examined the nature and causes of poverty in Nigeria and having seen in the last chapter how deficient the past and current poverty alleviation efforts in Nigeria are in dealing with the social problems that are responsible for the human misery in the nation, this chapter sets out to make some concrete recommendations for the development of a an integrated framework for a sustainable alleviation of poverty in the nation. The recommendations are based on the ethical orientation gained from the Catholic social teaching in chapter four and the political perspective derived from chapter five that provides a basis for adapting and applying the Catholic social guidelines for poverty alleviation to the Nigerian context. This ethical orientation revolves around "work" as the essential key to poverty alleviation and insists on a structural reform in social, economic and political life founded on justice, human dignity and on the social principles of common good, universal destination of goods, subsidiarity and solidarity. This reform should ensure that every human person will be able to develop his God-given potentials and through his work acquire what he needs to live the life that befits his dignity.

This Chapter presents, therefore, some elements of employment framework that will broaden and enrich future debates on poverty alleviation in Nigeria. It makes concrete recommendations for strengthening the employment content of the current framework for fostering economic growth and fighting poverty in Nigeria.

The NEEDS in which Nigeria's current framework for fostering economic growth and alleviating poverty is articulated recognises employment as a core objective of the policy framework. It goes therefore to say that in formulating the NEEDS, the Nigerian Government has already established a foundation of employment-targeted programmes. However, despite this recognition, the employment content of the NEEDS must be strengthened across a number of dimensions if sustainable poverty alleviation is to be achieved in the nation.

In view of the critical importance of employment for attaining high growth and sustained poverty alleviation, there is a need to review the content of the NEEDS with specific attention to the issue of employment. This need is predicated also on the conviction reached in chapter five of this work that the improvement of the quality and quantity of employment opportunities directly links economic growth to poverty alleviation. An integrated employment framework for poverty alleviation should be developed as part of the revision process for the NEEDS-2 or any other development and poverty alleviation strategy Nigeria may opt for in the future. In the process, employment must be placed at the centre of Nigeria's human development and poverty reduction efforts. What Nigeria needs therefore is a strategy with three elements that must be pursued simultaneously: (1) sustaining economic growth, (2) increasing the employment intensity of production, and (3) targeting poverty reduction.

This chapter presents a range of recommendations that, if adopted and implemented, would increase the rate of growth, promote employment opportunities and increase labour productivity that distribute the benefits of growth more effectively. It would, in other words, facilitate an employment-intensive growth path to sustainable poverty alleviation and push forward the frontiers of human development in Nigeria. It outlines the elements of such an employment framework and provides concrete recommendations for moving towards a growth path that will generate decent employment and reduces poverty in Nigeria. It adopts a tripartite integrated framework of employment-growth-poverty alleviation.

The first section of this chapter elaborates the nature and components of the employment-intensive growth framework that would lead to sustainable alleviation in Nigeria as a whole. It also highlights the essential policy reforms for achieving this objective. The second section concentrates on policy interventions that are essential for improving the labour conditions in the informal economy where the majority of people work to earn their living.

7.1 Employment-Intensive Growth for Poverty Alleviation

Employment, especially decent employment has been judged important for poverty alleviation. Decent employment links economic growth to poverty reduction. It is a potent tool for meeting almost all the requirements in the guidelines for poverty alleviation set in the Catholic social teaching. Decent employment is, for instance, the surest way of attaining social and economic justice, in the sense that it guarantees equal participation in economic processes and a fair distribution of wealth. In addition to this, it guards against the exploitation and 'instrumentalization' of the human person – the subject of work – in economic life. It actualizes subsidiarity and solidarity, for it empowers the individual to contribute to the common good and achieve what they can on their own while the state concentrates on other things that the individuals cannot achieve on their own. The Emphasis on employment is therefore a direct recognition of the centrality of human work in addressing social questions (cf. 4.5.2). Above all decent employment guarantees the rights of the "working-man" and ensures due respect for the dignity of the human person at work.

Evidence abounds that the greater the employment focus, the more pro-poor economic growth becomes attained in the fight against poverty.[757] When economic growth generates new and decent employment opportunities, especially for the working poor in the informal economy, household incomes rise across the board. Employment creation also provides a direct channel for distributing and redistributing the benefits of economic growth broadly throughout the population; it is a means of attaining social justice and equity.

It must be noted however that employment is not the only tool of translating growth into poverty reduction. For this reason, the additional resources that growth generates should be utilised to increase poor peoples' access to basic services such as education, health, and child maintenance grants. In this way, the creation of decent employment and economic growth becomes a veritable instrument for achieving the common objective of human development.

The impact of employment, especially decent employment, reflects itself in other aspects of human development. For instance, in improving the access of the poor to new opportunities; their income improves, the distribution of resources within the household becomes more equitable and child health and developmental outcomes also improve. The overall outcome is clear: absolute poverty begins to diminish in the families and in the entire nation.

7.1.1 Components of the Employment-Intensive Growth Framework

Since Nigeria faces the formidable challenge of achieving faster growth, more equitable distribution of income and poverty reduction,[758] toeing the path of an employment-intensive growth for poverty reduction in Nigeria, would require putting three interrelated components into consideration: A *Growth Component* - generating higher rates of economic growth; an *Employment Component* - insuring that economic growth produces a significant number of new employment opportunities and improves existing ones; a *Poverty Focus* - linking poor individuals and households to new and improved employment opportunities.[759] The connections between these three elements highlight the important presupposition in chapter five of this work, namely: Economic growth is necessary, but not sufficient for sustainable poverty alleviation. Growth must be employment-intensive. "Moreover, the generation of new employment is not enough to guarantee poverty-alleviation. Policies must be designed such that the poor can take advantage of the

757 See for instances: Azizur Rahman Khan, Growth, employment and poverty: An analysis of the vital nexus based on some recent UNDP and ILO/SIDA studies, DESA Working Paper No. 49 ST/ESA/2007/DWP/49 (New York: United Nations Department of Economic and Social Affairs, 2007); Rizwanul Islam, The nexus of growth, employment, and poverty reduction: an empirical analysis, (Geneva: International Labour Office, 2004).

758 United Nations Development Programme (UNDP), Human Development Report Nigeria 2008 – 200: Achieving growth with equity, (Abuja, Nigeria: Development Programme, Nigeria, 2009), 119.

759 Cf. ILO/UNDP, Elements of an Employment Framework for Poverty Reduction in Ghana, a report of a joint ILO/UNDP mission prepared by James Heintz.

new opportunities."[760] In developing a conceptual framework for an employment strategy, it is important to examine each of these three components in details.

7.1.1.1 A Growth Component

Attaining higher rates of economic growth requires improvements on three areas: (1) expanding investment in productive capacity, (2) raising productivity, and (3) securing adequate demand. What this means is that when the productive capacity is expanded through new investments, this will result generally in increased labour demand, owing to the fact that increased production requires additional labour as well as capital. In addition, productivity improvements lay the foundation for sustained improvements in living standards and wages. In order to ensure that demand for domestically-produced goods and services is matched with productivity improvements and investments in productive capacity, there is need to improve access to markets – the expansion of the domestic demand and the ability to export to foreign markets.[761] It is important to note that these elements of an effective growth strategy for employment creation, (that is, increased investment, productivity improvements, and access to an expanding market) will flourish only when appropriate macroeconomic policies are put in place.

7.1.1.2 An Employment Component

Policy interventions both in agricultural and industrial sectors are needed to insure that growth is employment intensive. In this regard more investment should be directed not to the capital-intensive sectors like the oil and gas sector but to the labour-intensive sectors, enterprises and activities in order to bring about an adjustment in the composition of economic activity that will generate more employment. Investment in these sectors and economic activities will definitely generate a larger number of employment opportunities compared to investment in other capital-intensive sectors, such as in oil exploration. Appropriate policy adjustments, especially with regard to resource allocation, should however be made to leverage downstream and upstream linkages and to take advantage of larger employment multipliers.[762]

7.1.1.3 A Poverty Focus

Employment-intensive growth is not sufficient for poverty alleviation in Nigeria. This means that the process required to alleviate poverty through employment-intensive growth in the nation will not be complete and considered successful until the poor are able to benefit from the employment strategy. Targeted employment policies directed at the segment of the economy where the poor are concentrated are therefore essential for the realization of this objective.[763]

760 Ibid, p. 13.

761 Ibid, pp. 14-15.

762 Ibid,

763 Ibid, p. 16.

We saw in the third chapter of this work that in Nigeria, the largest number of the poor is located in the nation's informal economy, both in the rural areas and in the urban centres; in agriculture and in other sectors. Policy interventions targeting employment opportunities for poverty alleviation must therefore focus on harnessing the abundant economic potential in the informal economy of the nation. Improving returns to the labour of the working poor in the informal economy is indeed a moral imperative in this regard. The poor must be equipped to take advantage of new opportunities.

Care must be taken to ensure that the employment framework for reducing poverty in Nigeria identifies and addresses the specific needs of the working poor engaged in informal activities. Creating an "enabling environment" for the private sector in general is not a guarantee that the specific needs of small-scale, informal, or labour-intensive enterprises will be addressed. A targeted approach to meeting these challenges is therefore needed, with the ultimate objective of improving the quality and quantity of employment opportunities for the working poor.[764]

People involved in marginal and subsistence activities in the informal economy should be assisted in such a way that their incomes rise, that their working conditions improve and that they move out of poverty. Some policy interventions for achieving this include the provision of credit, education and skills training, improved access to physical infrastructure, the extension of social protection, assistance in the formation of self-help groups and business and workers associations, and the strengthening of linkages with the formal economy. In addition to this, the aspects of the informal economy that is modern and dynamic and has the potential for growth and economic viability should be supported in such a way that they can graduate to the formal economy. Policy interventions in this regard include the removal of excessive barriers to entry into the formal economy in terms of registration costs, regulations and bureaucratic requirements.[765] These and other strategic areas will be discussed in the second part of this chapter within the context of the ILO Decent Work Agenda.

In what follows in this section, concrete recommendations will be made for improving and enhancing the employment-intensive growth framework for reducing poverty in Nigeria and, thereby, address the core elements of an integrated employment framework.

7.1.2 Economic Policies to Support Employment-Intensive Growth

Eliminating the constraints that impede employment-intensive growth requires a conducive economic environment. Creating such a conducive environment would require broad economic policies in four important areas that directly impact on employment creation. These areas include the macroeconomic environment and

764 Ibid., p. 23.

765 Cf. United Nations Economic and Social Council, Poverty and the Informal Sector: Role of the Informal Sector in Poverty Reduction, E/ESCAP/CPR(3)/12 October 2006.

price stability, the financial sector, budgetary policy and public investment and trade policy.

7.1.2.1 The Macroeconomic Environment and Price Stability

Macroeconomic stability is one of the targets of Nigeria's current poverty alleviation framework articulated in the NEEDS.[766] Macroeconomic stability is indeed essential to employment-intensive growth strategy for poverty alleviation. It guarantees a predictable environment for investors, employers, the self-employed, and the poor to make economic decisions. An unstable environment on the contrary increases business risks and uncertainties that impact negatively on economic growth and hinder the creation of new employment opportunities.

Fiscal management, controlling inflation and maintaining a predictable level of price stability are important tools for attaining economic stability. Lower inflation leads to improvement in macroeconomic environment in terms of price stability. Although Nigeria has made some progress in recent times to keep the rate of inflation low,[767] there is need however to ensure that the tempo is sustained over a long period of time. To this end, adequate measure must be taken to mob up excess liquidity in good time. On-going reductions in inflation using monetary policy require also tighter control on the money supply and levels of credit.

It must also be borne in mind that high interest rates lead to rise in inflation and constrains employment-intensive economic activities. Efforts to attain macroeconomic stability must therefore include measures for keeping the interest rate low. Care must however be taken to ensure that tight control on money supply and levels of credit does not lead to weak investments, as this will undermine the creation of new employment opportunities.

Since a large number of Nigerians rely on the income from informal employment, the costs of lowering inflation must also take into account its possible effect on informal workers and enterprises. There is no doubt that informal employment depends on domestic demand in local markets and that the availability of credit has a significant influence on the enterprise's efficiency and, therefore, its income-generating potential. Overly tight monetary policy that makes funds less accessible or slows domestic spending will impact negatively on output and earnings in the informal economy.

Although controlling inflation and maintaining a predictable level of price stability are important tools for attaining economic stability in the country and creating an enabling environment that minimises constraints for employment-intensive growth, they do not however by themselves constitute an effective employment framework for poverty reduction. Against this backdrop, it is highly

---

766 Cf:. K.S. Adeyemi, Economic Policy Reforms in Nigeria: Achievements and Challenges, a pdf document available at: http://www.valuefronteira.com/vf/images/UnionBank/economic%20policy%20reforms%20in%20nigeria.pdf, accessed on 30.04.2011.

767 Ngozi Okonjo-Iweala and Philip Osafo-Kwaako, Nigeria's Economic Reforms: Progress and Challenges, a working paper, (Washington, DC: The Brookings Institution, 2007), p. 10.

recommended that they be supplemented by other targets, if the macroeconomic environment is to support poverty reduction. One important target is the lowering of real exchange rate. There is no doubt that rising real exchange rate will reduce access to global markets by raising the price of exports and increasing import penetration into the domestic market. Such a condition will be a barrier to employment-intensive growth. The challenge here is to ensure that falling inflation rate does not lead to higher exchange rate. In all, both monetary and exchange rate policies are viewed as crude tools for affecting economic outcomes. They could be implemented only as measures for jump-staring a process of stabilization. They however do not constitute an effective employment framework for poverty reduction.[768]

7.1.2.2 The Financial Sector

Apart from making the right monetary policy choices, there is always the need to ensure that the structure of the financial system supports the movement of credit towards poverty-reducing development. For a long time, the banking sector in Nigeria was weak and fragmented, often financing short-term arbitrage opportunities rather than productive private investments. The root to this weakness has been traced to the nation's poorly managed liberalization during the structural adjustment programme. Many banks maintained bad balance sheets and conducted only limited lending to the private sector while engaging predominantly in more lucrative short-term arbitrage foreign exchange "round-tripping" activities.[769] The recent reform and consolidation of the banking sector implemented by the Central Bank of Nigeria (cf. 6.2.3.2.3) were all but a step in the right direction. The consolidation must however be sustained and propelled to support the employment framework in the nation. A major challenge in this regard is the funding of the labour-intensive economic activities in the real sector. Efforts must be made to restore the confidence and the capability of formal financial institution in Nigeria to take risks in granting credit to labour intensive enterprises, especially in the informal economy.

Some major policy areas that should be looked into in strengthening the financial sector include: Developing land property registries to enable banks to offer secured lending products and mortgage finance; formalizing property rights with supporting legal institutions to facilitate local investment and entrepreneurial activity, including the scaling-up of successful businesses; determining the extent to which the country's microfinance policy objectives have been achieved and the attendant constraints; enhancing the quality of regulation of the Nigerian capital market to guarantee its safe operation, providing greater access to credit and information to the poor. Credit facilities, no doubt, opens markets to the poor and can make small farmers and artisans more economically viable by allowing them to enlarge their

768 Cf. ILO/UNDP, Elements of an Employment Framework for Poverty Reduction in Ghana, op. cit., p. 30.

769 Ngozi Okonjo-Iweala and Philip Osafo-Kwaako, Nigeria's Economic Reforms: Progress and Challenges, op. cit., p. 15.

scale of production, to take more risks and take a longer-term view on their productive activities.[770]

Here are some measures that could be taken to transform the financial sector into one that supports broad-based employment creation.

1) Incentives should be established to encourage banks to hold assets that channel resources towards employment-targeted investments. In other words, asset-based reserve requirements for employment-targeted projects should be introduced. This will help to channel financial resources to strategic projects that reduce the impediments to employment creation. In recognition of this need, legislation was passed in 2006 mandating commercial banks to set aside 10% of pre-tax profits for equity investment in micro, small and medium enterprises (MSMEs). This should however be supported with a strong system of implementation.
2) Loans for strategic development projects could be underwritten by the government, with a view to lowering the cost of credit. What this requires of the government is simply to guarantee a portion of the loans that are directed to employment-targeted development projects. This will encourage financial institutions to extend credit facilities to medium and long-term productive investments, which banks do not consider attractive because of high risks associated with them. This measure should however be implemented with adequate safeguards to prevent abuse.
3) Coordination among banks, government, and businesses could be increased to achieve employment outcomes. Banks, project managers, and entrepreneurs could be brought together in order to coordinate financing for employment-oriented projects. In this case, government agencies could act as intermediaries and help also to improve information about prospective borrowers and the nature of their projects. Where the need arises, the government could also take an active part in providing infrastructure, training programmes, or extension services to help insure the success of the projects.[771]
4) Linkages could be forged between informal credit markets and the banking sector to mobilise resources for the generation of new employment opportunities and for the development of informal employment opportunities. This is in recognition of the fact that informal and formal credit institutions have distinct advantages in relation to one another. Informal financial institutions enjoy better understanding of and access to labour intensive enterprises. They also incur lower transactions costs when extending credit to underserved communities and regions. The formal financial institutions on their part enjoy economies of scale and can mobilise

770 Development Programme (UNDP), Human Development Report Nigeria 2008 – 2009, op. cit, p. 124.

771 Cf. ILO/UNDP, Elements of an Employment Framework for Poverty Reduction in Ghana, op. cit., p. 32-33.

large amounts of deposits for credit extension. By forging linkages between formal and informal credit institutions, more financial resources could be made available to support the expansion and improvement of informal activities. This has large potentials that could make positive impacts on employment outcomes.[772]

7.1.2.3 Budgetary Policy and Public Investment

Budgetary policy is considered the most important tool for supporting employment-intensive Growth. In order to ensure the success of an employment-intensive development framework, budget priorities must be made to reflect the needs of the framework. A critical budgetary intervention for employment creation is to ensure that adequate resources are made available for public investment and infrastructure provision. In order to ensure a robust budgetary allocation, appropriate measures should be taken to generate more revenues and manage them properly. Revenue collection could be strengthened and improved by altering the tax structure, blocking leakages, and widening the tax base where appropriate. Nigeria has recently made some commendable efforts to bring in accountability and discipline in the management of revenues that accrue to it. This has resulted in the establishment of the Excess Crude Account (ECA), the Nigeria Extractive Industries Transparency Initiative (NEITI)[773] and the Sovereign Wealth Funds (SWFs)[774] recently signed into law. Proper governance of the sovereign wealth fund with clear rules to guide investment and withdrawal must however be ensured.

---

772 Ibid., p. 33: For details on how these linkages could be developed, see: Ernest Aryeetey, Informal finance for private sector development in Africa, Background paper prepared for the African Development Report 1998; Ernest Aryeetey, Recent Developments in African Financial Markets: Agenda for Further Research, Journal of African Economies, 12(supp 2): ii111-ii152, 2003; Joe Amoako-Tuffour, Forging links between formal and informal financial sectors: emerging practices in Ghana, The African Finance Journal, 4(1): 1-31, 2002.

773 Nigeria Extractive Industries Transparency Initiative (NEITI) is the national version of Industries Transparency Initiative (EITI); a global movement aimed at ensuring that revenues from oil, gas and mining sectors aid economic growth and reduce poverty. That global movement is called the Extractive.

774 The Sovereign Wealth which replaces the Excess crude Account was established by the Nigeria government to enable the nation build a strong revenue reserve that could be used to finance growth and social development. It comprises comprised of three separate funds. Future Generations Fund, Nigerian Infrastructure Fund and Stabilization Fund. The Future Generations Fund reflects the desire to ensure that the resources of today are not all consumed – rather, that part will be saved, increased financially and shared as a legacy for unborn Nigerians and the development of the economy over the decades to come. The Nigeria Infrastructure Fund will make investments specifically related to and with the objective of assisting the development of critical infrastructure in Nigeria and the diversification of the economy. The Stabilization Fund would also allow the nation to more effectively conduct a sound and responsible fiscal policy, while reducing the effects of the "boom and bust" commodity cycle of oil on Nigeria. For this and a detailed analysis of the Sovereign Wealth Funds, see: Ben Eguzozie, How Sovereign Wealth Fund Can Drive Nigeria's Growth, Infrastructure Development, a newspaper article in "Businessday", 16 May, 2011.

Budgetary allocation that targets employment growth and poverty alleviation must also give priority to investment in economic infrastructure such as roads and transportation, storage facilities, and basic utilities, such as water, telecommunications and electricity, if the constraints to employment-targeted investment are to be reduced.[775]

7.1.2.4 Trade Policy

Appropriate trade policy is central to gaining access to both domestic and foreign markets. Trade is also a central component of the balance of payments. A deteriorating trade balance can upset macroeconomic stability with the rest of the world, leading to burgeoning external debts or undermining human development goals. Policies targeting market access, competitiveness, and product quality will definitely increase Nigeria's chances of success in generating employment by exporting to world markets. Increased access to market can be secured through trade agreements, often requiring the reciprocal removal of tariffs and trade liberalisation. For the purpose of an employment-oriented development strategy, the benefits that accrue from market access must be weighed against the potential negative impact of greater import penetration and job losses. Other measures that fundamentally influence market access are efficient production, best-practice management systems and guarantees of product quality.[776]

7.1.3 Strengthening Institutions and Governance

As already observed, increasing the rate of growth and employment opportunities and reducing poverty in Nigeria require a reform in governance. An employment-intensive growth framework for poverty alleviation in Nigeria must therefore include measures for introducing legislation to reinforce policy changes; promoting broad-based institutional ownership of reforms. It must also introduce suitable measures for cutting administrative costs and improving administrative efficiency. Related to this is the need to deepen the reform of the public finance system by enhancing the Budget Office of the Federation's supervision of budget preparation and implementation procedures and also to institutionalize effective monitoring and evaluation of development programmes. Procedures for strengthening institutions should embody popular participation and interagency coordination for enhanced results.[777] An integrated framework will be needed to manage the interactions and cooperation between the government, market agents and civil society organizations.

Poverty alleviation agenda cover pro-poor interventions across a wide range of areas: education, health, agriculture, social assistance and social insurance. This broad spectrum of efforts at alleviating poverty raises the enormous challenge of

775 Cf. ILO/UNDP, Elements of an Employment Framework for Poverty Reduction in Ghana, op. cit., pp. 34-37

776 Ibid., pp. 37-40.

777 Cf.: Development Programme (UNDP), Human Development Report Nigeria 2008 – 2009, op. cit, p. 123.

institutional coordination across different agencies that are responsible for their implementation. It has been observed that in Nigeria, lack of effective coordination limits the overall effectiveness of poverty reduction initiatives. In the past, coordination among government agencies has proved difficult because each agency has its own priorities and is reluctant to relinquish control over resources.[778] This presents a challenged that must be given adequate attention in the employment-intensive growth framework, if Nigeria will win the fight against poverty. There is therefore the need to seek better ways of improving inter-agency coordination.

Greater access to appropriate channels through which the poor can express their opinions would promote their participation in public affairs. Similarly, stimulating the participation of the media and civil society, for instance, could promote reforms of the budget system and ensure effective budget monitoring and implementation.[779] The Freedom of Information (FoI)[780] signed recently into law will definitely prove to be a useful tool in this regard. Signing a bill into law is however only an initial step that must be backed with a reliable system of enforcement, if it must produce a good result.

7.1.4 Improving the Rule of Law and Transparency

We have already seen the enormous damage that corruption does to social and economic development in Nigeria (cf. 3.1.2.2.5). Waging a successful war against it is therefore a necessary condition for accelerating growth and employment development for the purpose of alleviating poverty in Nigeria. By embedding anti-corruption programs in the reform agenda presented above, the battle against corruption will become an integral part of a broader exercise of economic reform needed to stimulate growth, generate more employment opportunities and address poverty in Nigeria. In order to attain this objective, it will be necessary to properly identify areas of major corruption so as to enable the administration to focus reform measures on high impact areas.[781]

The most effective way to tackle corruption under the employment-intensive growth framework is by improving the rule of law and transparency. To achieve this goal, it is crucial to strengthen and actively follow through on existing anti-corruption laws, mechanisms and institutions; create a more favourable legal environment through appropriate legislation and amendment of existing laws; strengthen law enforcement; increase transparency in the conduct of government

778 Ibid., p. 124.

779 Ibid., p. 123.

780 The Freedom of Information Law is a legal instrument that gives Nigeria citizen access to public records. The new law mandates government bodies to produce requested information within seven days. It also makes it a criminal offence to destroy official records. With the new law, Nigerians now have a vital instrument to uncover facts, fight corruption and hold officials and institutions accountable.

781 Cf. Ngozi Okonjo-Iweala and Philip Osafo-Kwaako, Nigeria's Economic Reforms: Progress and Challenges, op. cit., p. 17.

business – transparency of government operations and sanctioning of corrupt officials and private individuals.[782]

The fight against corruption should be intensified through the establishment of a special anti-graft court that will guarantee speedy prosecution of cases of corruption. This would assist in sending the right signals to corrupt government officials.[783] The repeated calls made since 2008 by Nigerian anti-graft agency EFCC for special courts that will grant speedy hearing to cases of corruption is yet to receive a favourable response. Until this is done, anti-graft agencies in the nation will continue to record slow pace of trials in corruption cases. This, no doubt is a setback on the fight against corruption in the country.

Moreover, recent steps to increase transparency and accountability in government, and thus combat allegations of fraud and corruption, must be pursued if international confidence in Nigeria's economy is to be regained. A rapid implementation of important WTO Agreements, full compliance with multilateral principles and increased transparency and accountability would signal Nigeria's commitment to a rules-based market economy and attract investment into the nation.[784]

7.1.5 Eliminating Inequality

Building a fairer and more equitable society is no doubt an essential requirement for reducing poverty in a sustainable manner, particularly with a target to promoting social justice. In view of the high incidence of inequality in Nigeria (cf. 3.1.2.2.4), especially with regard to income and assess to opportunity, the principles of equality should be accorded prominence in social and economic policy-making to ensure that economic growth is conducive to social development, stability, fair competition and ethical conduct. This is in accordance with the recommendations made at world summit for social development in Copenhagen.[785]

Overcoming inequalities requires in particular an investment in people, with priority given to the enhancement of educational attainment, skill development and overall well-being. Priority attention should also be given to the expansion and improvement of opportunities for quality employment. Serious commitment should equally be made to ensure that discrimination is eliminated and that a better balance is achieved in the distribution of resources. People should also be empowered to

782 Development Programme (UNDP), Human Development Report Nigeria 2008 – 2009, op. cit., p. 124.

783 Cf. K.S. Adeyemi, Economic Policy reform in Nigeria: Achievements and Challenges, op. cit

784 World Trade Organization, Trade Policy Review Body Trade Policy Review, Nigeria: Report by the Secretariat. WT/TPR/S/39 27 May 1998.

785 Cf.: United Nations, Report of the World Summit for Social Development, Copenhagen, 6-12 March 1995, A/CONF.166/9 19 April 1995.

express their concerns and participate more actively in decision-making processes.[786]

Ensuring equal access for all to public services, particularly education and acquisition of skills, which are needed for the expansion of opportunities and capabilities, is of paramount importance to the reduction of intergenerational transmission of poverty and inequality. For this reason, the principles of universality, solidarity and social inclusion should be made to guide the delivery of social services.[787]

7.2 Improving Labour Conditions in the Informal Economy

As noted above in 7.1.1, one of the three components of an Employment-Intensive Growth Framework required for alleviating poverty in Nigeria is the "poverty focus". This poverty focus points to the need to ensure that the poor are empowered to benefit from the employment strategy. Targeted employment policies directed at the segment of the economy where the poor are concentrated are therefore essential for the realization of this objective. Employment framework for reducing poverty in Nigeria must therefore identify and address the specific needs of the working poor engaged in informal activities.

As noted in previous chapters (especially in 2.5.2 and 5.3.1-5.3.5), the most consistent way of analysing and dealing with problems of the enterprises and workers in the informal economy is by considering them in terms of decent work deficit. This particularly highlights the urgent need to prioritise policies that raise levels of work security, income security and social security and improve working conditions and income opportunities. This would help to ensure that human labour retains its true dignity and thus provides opportunity for the expression of personal ability, creativity and taking initiatives. For it is through work that man achieves fulfilment as a human being. The ILO Decent Work Agenda (DWA) has proved to be the surest mean of attaining this goal.

The DWA recognizes that in order to wage a successful war against poverty, the economy has to deliver increased employment, but this must also involve the improvement of working conditions, social protection and representation based on respect for fundamental principles and rights at work. With its four strategic objectives, covering *employment, rights at work, social protection and social dialogue*, the DWA presents a comprehensive set of policy perspectives and interventions geared towards lifting people out of poverty, and providing them with

786 United Nations, Report on the World Situation 2005, The Inequality Predicament, p. 27, a PDF document, available online at: http://www.sustainable-design.ie/sustain/un2005_ReportWorldSocialSystem.pdf, accessed on 08.06.2011.

787 Ibid.

sustainable livelihoods.[788] Integrating the DWA into Nigeria's plan for poverty alleviation would therefore help to focus research and policy action on practical measures that can both have an immediate impact on poverty and build the infrastructure for longer-term progress. It also provides a viable means for mobilizing broad support for policies that will commit both the non-poor and the poor themselves.

In what follows in this section, the areas of need in the informal economy will be treated within the four pillars of the DWA, namely: employment creation and enterprise development, standards and rights at work, social protection and social dialogue. We will however start with some recommendations for improving statistics on informal activities and workers.

7.2.1 Improving Statistics on Informal Economic Activities

The findings in chapter three (cf. 3.2.2) about statistical records on the activities in Nigeria's informal economy highlight the need for improved statistics that will help develop a reliable data base on which specific policies could be designed and implemented. The first step in this direction is to recognize the informal economy as an important catalyst in the nation's development process rather than a nuisance. This will require a change of attitude towards the informal economy. As rightly observed, addressing the labour problems in the informal economy "requires more than just policy directives; it calls for an emphatic mind-shift in official and popular perception on the validity and inherent economic worth of activities that have colloquially been docketed, not for lack of better idiom, as 'black market' enterprises."[789]

Without the right attitude and adequate information on the informal economy, predictions for the impact of policy changes are likely to be imprecise. There is therefore a particular need to undertake a deliberate study of the phenomenon. Such a study of the phenomenon is crucial for gathering useful information that can promote awareness and better understanding that will possibly lead to a change of attitude toward the informal economy. The knowledge gained from the study will also be particularly of immense help to policy makers and programme designers taking decisions on how to focus interventions, channel resources and set priorities aright in order to get better results. It will also help to avoid targeting wrong groups or only a part of the informal economy.

The study and clear delineation of the informal economy should be followed up with an enumeration of activities and actors in the informal economy. In

---

788 International Trade Union Confederation, Decent Work for All: A Key Objective for Economic and Social Development, Statement to the 46th Session of the UN Commission for Social Development, New York, 6-15 February, 2008.

789 Peter Osalor, The Informal Economy and Entrepreneurial Development, an internet article available at: http://www.articlesbase.com/economics-articles/the-informal-economy-and-entrepreneurial-development-3015678.html#ixzz1JrLsdsRI.

view of the heterogeneous nature of the informal economy, appropriate measures and more elaborate programmes should be designed to ensure that the difference in status and needs of the informal workers and enterprises are given proper recognition and corresponding attention. Specific issues that need to be tackled include: the contribution of women to home-based and often unpaid activities and other workers such as street vendors that are missed by labour force surveys and population censuses. This will indeed require the collection of data at the household and individual-level. The focus of the analysis must however go beyond mere development of an aggregate statistic representing the informal economy. The database should contain aggregate and micro-data on the informal economy in the nation so as to provide a good guide for making appropriate decisions regarding economic growth, job creation and welfare.[790] A major challenge in this regard is to improve the capacity of national statistical offices.

In improving statistics on the informal economy, Nigeria can draw some inspiration from the useful guidelines and information provided by the studies sponsored by the ILO.[791] The ILO acknowledges that Labour statistics play an essential role in the efforts of member States to achieve decent work for all. The *Conclusions on Decent Work and the Informal Economy*, adopted by the International Labour Conference at its 90th Session in June 2002 called upon the organization to "assist member States to collect, analyse and disseminate consistent, disaggregated statistics on the size, composition and contribution of the informal economy."[792] The Department of Statistics is saddled with the task of developing international standards on labour statistics and helping member States develop and improve their labour statistics. Through this department, the ILO organizes training programmes in the application of standards and use of its manuals.[793]

---

790 cf.: Sher Verick, The Impact of Globalization on the Informal Sector in Africa, a pdf document available at: http://tradeinservices.mofcom.gov.cn/upload/2008/08/14/1218702966828_170237.pdf, accessed on 03.06.2011.

791 See for instance: Jacques Charmes, "Women working in the informal sector in Africa: new methods and new data," Paper prepared for the United Nations Statistics Division, the Gender and Development Programme of the United Nations Development Programme (UNDP) and the project "Women in Informal Employment: Globalizing and Organizing" (WIEGO). 1998; Martha Chen et al., Counting the Invisible Workforce: The Case of Home-based Workers, "World Development", Vol.27, No.3, 1999, pp.603-610; ILO (2002c) "Women and Men in the Informal Economy: A Statistical Picture", (Geneva: International Labour Conference, 2002).

792 The General Conference of the International Labour Organization, meeting in its 90th Session, 2002: Conclusions concerning decent work and the informal economy, paragraph 37(n).

793 Detailed information is made available on the web site of the Department.

7.2.2 Creating Decent Employment Opportunities for People in the Informal Economy

In seeking to develop an integrated and coherent strategy that aims principally to place employment at the heart of economic and social policies, it is necessary to keep in view the two sides of the problem: the problem of unemployment on the one hand, and on the other hand, the problem of underemployment and poor employment or low quality of employment in the informal economy. The implication of this is that while necessary measures are to be taken to create new employment opportunities, it should not be forgotten that the informal workers and operators of informal enterprises are already engaged in different forms of economic activities that are however beset with enormous degrees of poor working conditions and labour relationships.

Nigeria has consistently witnessed the situation in which the creation of new employment opportunities was so prioritized that policies were formulated and programmes designed merely to create new employment opportunities without adequate considerations for the quality of jobs being created. This has only contributed to worsening the already precarious state of employment and incidence of poverty in the nation. There is indeed no doubt that the nation has a serious challenge to create more job opportunities, but this should not be just any job, if the nation must wage a successful war against poverty. "In the twenty-first century, the employment challenge is about much more than a job at any price or under any circumstances."[794]

Full, productive and freely chosen employment is the primary means of reducing and eventually eliminating absolute poverty (cf. 4.5.2). Nigeria has therefore a moral obligation to channel efforts towards creating decent employment opportunities that are productive and befitting to the dignity of the human person; jobs that will enable people to develop their God-given potentials; and jobs that will offer them what they need to pursue and attain their destiny. Moving towards this objective requires a steady and brisk pace of growth that is sustainable in environmental, social and economic terms.

It must however be acknowledged in all honesty that creating enough decent jobs that will satisfy the current demand in the nation is indeed an arduous task that no government can fulfil in a short term. In formulating policies for addressing the problem of employment in the nation, it is therefore necessary to consider keeping and improving the already existing job opportunities in the informal economy while at the same time making frantic efforts to create new decent jobs and forestall further entry of job seekers into the informal economy.

Keeping the job opportunities in the informal economy or improving the informal economy must however not be misconstrued and applied as a convenient low-cost way of creating employment. While stressing this point in one of his reports, the director general of the ILO noted: "there can be no question … of

794 ILO: A global agenda for employment: Summary, Global Employment Forum, Geneva, 1-3 Nov. 2001.

helping to 'promote' or 'develop' an informal sector as a convenient, low-cost way of creating employment unless there is at the same time an equal determination to eliminate progressively the worst aspects of exploitation and inhuman working conditions in the sector".[795] The ultimate goal should therefore be to promote decent work along the entire continuum from the informal to the formal end of the economy, and in development-oriented, poverty reduction-focused and gender-equitable ways.[796]

In order to achieve the goal of creating decent employment towards reducing poverty in Nigeria, it is recommended that policy makers and programme designers adopt the progressive approach proposed by the ILO. This approach requires "starting with the informal end, where most new job creation in recent years has been taking place, and promoting the transition upwards along the continuum towards the formal, decent and protected end."[797] This should be made an integral part and parcel of a decent work agenda in the nation and should be given priority attention in the nation's Poverty Reduction Strategy Paper (PRSP).

The most effective strategy for creating decent work along the entire continuum is that which lays emphasis on quality jobs in the upper rather than lower end of the continuum and insists on the creation of new jobs not in the informal but rather in the formal economy. Adopting this strategy in Nigeria would mean pursuing the employment development process in three phases: In the immediate term, priority should be given to reducing decent work deficits in the informal economy, importantly through ensuring that those who are currently in the informal economy are recognized in the law and have rights, legal and social protection and representation and voice. In the short and medium term, efforts should be channelled to enabling those currently in the informal economy to move upwards along the continuum and at the same time ensure that new jobseekers and potential entrepreneurs are able to enter the more formal, protected and decent parts of the continuum. In doing this, priority should be given to ensuring that workers and entrepreneurs have the capacity, flexibility and the conducive legal and policy frameworks to do so. Special consideration should be given to the vulnerable groups and those discriminated against in the labour market, such as women, young jobseekers and migrant workers. In the longer term, emphasis should be shifted to creating enough decent employment opportunities for all workers and employers.[798]

In addressing the pivotal medium- and longer-term issue of how to move workers and entrepreneurs currently in the informal economy upwards along the continuum into formal decent jobs and how to ensure that new jobs are created in the formal and not in the informal economy, appropriate measures must be taken to

---

795 ILO: The dilemma of the informal sector, Report of the Director-General, (part 1), (Geneva: International Labour Office, 1991).

796 ILO, Decent work and the informal economy, Report VI, International Labour Conference, 90th Session, Geneva, 2002, (Geneva: International Labour Office, 2002), p. 4.

797 Ibid.

798 Cf. ILO: Decent work and the informal economy, op. cit., p. 5.

invest in the nation's workforce (with special attention to the most vulnerable and disadvantaged) so as to promote their employability,[799] productivity and ability to move upwards along the continuum. In addition to this, adequate policy measures should be taken to make it easier for micro- and small enterprises to start up and grow in the formal economy and to adopt high-road strategies that enhance productivity and provide quality jobs for workers. Simply put: "A successful approach to promotion of productive employment is founded on investing in people and encouraging their entrepreneurial initiative."[800]

7.2.2.1 Investing in the Workforce: Improving Knowledge and Skills

An essential ingredient for improving the quality of employment and access to decent employment is education and skill development. Especially in today's knowledge-based economy, the illiterate have little or no other choice but to enter into precarious work relationships. Certainly, education and training play a pivotal role for attaining both economic and social goals. Nigeria must pursue a well-functioning system of education and training which enhances both economic and social integration, (i.e. full participation in social and economic life of the society) by offering opportunities to many groups who would otherwise be excluded from the labour market. A system that ensures equal access to education, training and skills development is also important for promoting gender equality and overcoming many forms of discrimination against women and other disadvantaged groups in the informal economy in the labour market.

Nigeria's employment promotion strategy and efforts at reducing poverty will hardly succeed if the nation does not take the proper measure to provide literacy, basic education and skills especially for the underprivileged workers and entrepreneurs in the informal economy. Skills, knowledge and competencies are indeed the basic social amenities that informal workers need most to enhance their ability to secure and retain decent jobs, progress at work and cope with change, secure new jobs if they so wish or have been laid off, and enter more easily into the

---

799 ILO: Conclusions concerning human resources training and development, (Geneva: International Labour Office, 2000): The 9th paragraph of the conclusion throws more light on the concept of employability and why employability is critical if workers are to be able to move up the continuum from the informal to the formal end and to decent work: Employability ... is a key outcome of education and training of high quality, as well as a range of other policies. It encompasses the skills, knowledge and competencies that enhance a worker's ability to secure and retain a job, progress at work and cope with change, secure another job if she/he so wishes or has been laid off, and enter more easily into the labour market at different periods of the life cycle. Individuals are most employable when they have broad-based education and training, basic and portable high-level skills, including teamwork, problem-solving, information and communications technology (ICT) and communication and language skills, learning to learn skills, and competencies to protect themselves and their colleagues against occupational hazards and diseases ... Workers' employability can only be sustained in an economic environment that promotes job growth and rewards individual and collective investments in human resources training and development.

800 ILO: A Global Agenda for Employment: Discussion paper, (Geneva, International Labour Office, 2001). See also ibid: A Global Agenda for Employment: Summary, Global Employment Forum, para. 10.

labour market at different periods of the life cycle.[801] Good knowledge and quality education also play a vital role in ensuring mobility and higher incomes.[802]

> Individuals are most employable when they have broad-based education and training, basic and portable high-level skills, including teamwork, problem-solving, information and communications technology (ICT) and communication and language skills, learning to learn skills, and competencies to protect themselves and their colleagues against occupational hazards and diseases.[803]

To properly address the important issue of education as both a basic right and the foundation of an individual's employability in a decent job, it is hereby recommended that appropriate measures be taken to provide expanded programmes for literacy, basic education and training where it will make higher difference, that is, in the informal economy. Nigeria as a nation therefore enjoined to take serious, the targets set at United Nations Education, Scientific and Cultural Organization UNESCO's Education for All Forum in Dakar in 2000, namely: a 50 per cent improvement in adult literacy by 2015, especially for women, and equitable access to basic and continuing education for all adults; universal access to primary education for all children by 2015. It is also important to improve rapport and strengthen collaboration with UNESCO and its International Centre for Technical and Vocational Education and Training in promoting access of adults and youth to employment through the creation of opportunities for skills and knowledge development.

The education and training to be provided must, among other things, aim to enhance the performance and the employability of informal workers in order to transform their often marginal, survival activities into decent work fully integrated into mainstream social and economic life.[804]

Owing to the heterogeneous nature of the informal economy, a wide range of training programmes would definitely be required to cover the various areas of need and impart the different kinds of skills needed, which of course are not limited to technical and entrepreneurial skills. In addition to this, care should be taken not to destroy but to build on existing knowledge and skills. It is therefore important to determine carefully what sort of skills are currently being used in the informal enterprises, how people working there have acquired these skills and what, if anything, might be wrong with either the skills or the way in which they were acquired. It is important to be aware of the often quite remarkable ingenuity and capacity to innovate and improvise that exists in the informal economy. Such ingenuity, it is believed, is the result of years of learning how to survive in a hostile

801 Cf., ILO: Conclusions concerning human resources training and development, op. cit., para. 9.

802 Cf., ILO: World Employment Report 1998-99: Employability in the global economy – How training matters (Geneva, International Labor Office, 1998), p. 173.

803 ILO: Conclusions concerning human resources training and development, op. cit., para. 9.

804 Ibid., para. 7.

environment. Such skills should therefore not just be discarded, but rather transformed for higher economic pursuits.[805]

In designing training programmes, attention must be paid to the affordability and attractiveness of the programmes for the target groups who, often than not, show a poor disposition due to financial constraints and other contingencies of life. Well packaged enlightenment programmes should be used to bring to their awareness the benefits that can be derived from the training programmes being offered to them. Linking training with production, micro-credit and other support services, establishing micro-enterprise extension facilities or small business advisory services which address training needs in an integrated manner, and providing information on new technologies are some effective means of promoting improved skill acquisition and making them attractive among the actors in the informal economy.

In its efforts at investing in the workforce and improving knowledge and skills, the Nigerian government must endeavour to work more closely with the private sector and NGOs to create more effective training interventions and to boost the already existing ones. Local stakeholders (local government, enterprises, the social partners and training institutions) have indeed a vital role to fulfill. They can also pull their resources together to finance training programmes. They can contribute useful ideas in the formulation of education and training schemes.[806]

7.2.2.2 Investing in Enterprise Development

Entrepreneurship development and enterprise creation, innovation and expansion are other essential measures for the successful development of decent employment for poverty alleviation. In formulating and implementing employment development policies, it is necessary to properly evaluate the incentives and disincentives they are likely to create for micro- and small enterprises especially in the informal economy. This will help to identify the constraints on the development and growth of efficient and competitive enterprises.

Some important requirements for entrepreneurial development that deserve further consideration in this sub-section include: Creating Enabling Legal and Regulatory Framework for Enterprise Development (→ 7.2.2.2.1), Good Governance and the Role of National and Local Governments (→ 7.2.2.2), Creating an Enterprise Culture for Formal Decent Jobs (→ 7.2.2.2.3), Securing Property Rights (→ 7.2.2.2.4), Access to Finance (→ 7.2.2.2.5), Improving Linkages with the Formal Economy(→ 7.2.2.2.6)

7.2.2.2.1 Creating Enabling Environment Framework for Enterprise Development

Creating a favourable environment for enterprise development would mean to upturn the current Nigerian business environment that mainly favours large capital-

805 ILO: Decent work and the informal economy, op. cit., pp. 101&102.

806 ILO: Conclusions concerning human resources training and development, op. cit., paragraph. 19.

intensive enterprises to the detriment of micro-enterprises that are more labour-intensive (cf. 3.2.4). To this end, Nigeria must as a matter of necessity endeavour to create the business regulatory framework that seeks to lower the costs of establishing and operating a small business (easier registration procedures, reasonable and fair taxation) and increase the potential benefits of legal registration (access to commercial buyers in the formal economy, more favourable credit markets, legal protection, obtaining foreign exchange). This encourages business start-ups and helps lever micro- and small enterprises to move easily into the formal economy.[807]

7.2.2.2.2 Good Governance and the Role of National and Local Governments

The relevance of good governance for attaining an employment-intensive growth that facilitates poverty alleviation has been addressed above in 7.1.3. The emphasis here is that good governance is also a crucial requirement for an entrepreneurship development geared towards achieving decent employment, especially in the informal economy. Good Governance is needed at both at national and local levels to effectively deal with and eliminate the harassment, indirect cost, endemic extortion, bribery, and other acts of corruption that operators of informal enterprises encounter daily in the hands of public officials. It is important to improve transparency and consistent application of rules and regulations. Curbing corrupt practices help also to increase municipal revenue, thereby enhancing the ability of local government to provide the infrastructure and services needed by those in the informal economy.

Ensuring good governance entails also formulating the right economic and social policies and the provision of support services conducive for entrepreneurship and business growth. What the informal enterprises need most in this regard is the creation of a level playing field in regard to access to credit and working capital. They also need other services that a properly functioning market economy should provide, and the creation or reform of the institutions needed to support an entrepreneurial economy.[808] Effective legal systems is also required to properly apply fair labour practices set out in international labour standards in order to ensure an efficient and stable labour market for workers and employers alike. It must however be kept in mind that mere legislation is no solution to the problems of either entrepreneurs or workers in the informal economy. Adequate efforts must also be made to ensure that laws are properly enforced. This will be possible when good governance is properly put is place in the nation; a government that respects the will of the citizens and pursues the welfare of all.

807 ILO: Decent work and the informal economy, op. cit., p. 106.

808 S. de Silva: The informal economy: Issues and challenges, unpublished paper cited in: ILO: Decent Work and Informal Economy, p. 108

7.2.2.2.3 Creating an Enterprise Culture for Formal Decent Jobs

In order to develop a healthy enterprise culture among micro- and small operators in the informal economy, particular attention should be given to awareness campaigns. Such campaign programmes should be directed towards helping micro- and small entrepreneurs to recognize that job quality and quality products mean better business. They should also be encouraged to develop a more positive attitude towards appropriate risk-taking and to recognize business failure as a learning process and be schooled in techniques for resilience.

Efforts to improve the existing enterprise culture in Nigeria should also give attention to the gender dimension of it. Particular efforts should be made to upturn the current enterprise cultural context that is clearly hostile to women entrepreneurs. To achieve this aim, the principle of equal chance for all should be promoted. The prevailing cultural context also encourages non-conformity to regulations that are necessary for the effective functioning of enterprises. There is therefore additional need to establish a cultural system that "reinforces basic acceptance of, respect for and adherence to the law and the rule of law"[809]

7.2.2.2.4 Securing Property Rights

Securing property rights here concerns particularly the legal provisions that guarantee legal property rights, including intellectual property that enable potential entrepreneurs to use, build, recombine or exchange their assets in the most productive way in order to generate additional value. Such rights, for instance, make it possible for informal operators, especially women to hold title to their land, and be able not only to build on the land but also to use it as collateral. To adequately secure property right, enabling legal and policy framework must be created and the laws must be impartially, consistently and speedily enforced. Of paramount importance for women informal operators in Nigeria is the reform or revocation of legislations and customs that forbid women to legally acquire and possess landed property. This is particularly important for those in the agriculture sector. The issue of rights will be discussed later in details.

7.2.2.2.5 Access to Finance

Adequate financing is generally a major contributive factor to the establishment and development of business enterprise. Conversely, lack of access to it constitutes a major constrain to the development of enterprises, especially in the informal economy.

As we saw earlier in chapter three that the poor and low income segments of the population are underserved with financial services. They often lack access to credit, which makes it hard for them to start a business or expand one (cf. 3.1.2.2.2). This makes the need to improve financing and access to credit one of the top priorities for the operators of informal enterprises. The problem in most cases is not the non-availability of credit facilities but the terms for obtaining the credit

809 ILO: Decent work and the informal economy, op. cit., p. 108.

which are often beyond the capacity of micro-entrepreneurs and potential entrepreneurs (cf. 3.2.7.3). Joining to make matters worse, is the corrupt practices associated with obtaining the available credit. Informal finance organization and microfinance institutions which are supposed to provide succour to the informal economy unfortunately do not have the capacity to meet the needs of informal entrepreneurs (cf. 7.1.2.2). Appropriate policy and regulatory framework must therefore be put in place to facilitate and ensure better outreach and performance of financial mechanisms in the informal economy, encourage the emergence of more functional microfinance institutions, financial cooperatives and other service providers and ensure the stability of the financial system.

7.2.2.2.6 Improving Linkages with the Formal Economy

Need for improving linkages between the formal and the informal enterprises in Nigeria was established in chapter three (cf. 3.2.7.2). The important policy issue for improving the linkages is not whether the informal business units have direct ties with the formal economy – certainly, they do – but whether these ties are benign, exploitative or mutually beneficial. The policy concern is to enhance the linkages that are positive.[810] The formal economy enterprises should be encouraged to support the informal economy enterprises by providing them with inputs, marketing their products, supplying them with work, and providing credit and technical assistance in order to improve the quality of their goods and overall productivity. The informal economy enterprises also need technical assistance to enable them integrate gainfully with the formal economy enterprises.

In all, appropriate measures should be taken to avoid situations in which the formal economy enterprises use their dominant positions in the market to exploit those in the informal economy. This is often the case when the formal economy enterprises unilaterally sets the prices of the inputs and outputs and, in the process, appropriates a substantial part of the surplus generated in informal units. One way of dealing effectively with the problem of exploitation is to provide informal units with information on market conditions and prices. Another useful way is to organize informal producers into business associations in order to strengthen their bargaining power.[811] The government and policy makers should also take into consideration measures such as capacity building, the reconciling and the converging of both informal and formal economy enterprises, most especially in the aspect of finance and macroeconomic stability.[812]

---

810 Ibid., p. 38.

811 United Nations Economic and Social Council, Poverty and the Informal Sector: Role of the Informal Sector in Poverty Reduction, op. cit., p. 12.

812 Gafar.T. Ijaiya and Chika A. Umar, The Informal and Formal Sector Inter-linkages and the Incidence of Poverty in Nigeria: A Case Study of Ilorin Metropolis, in: Africa Development, Vol. XXIX, No. 3, 2004, pp. 84–102.

7.2.2.2.7 Clustering

Clustering is an important strategy that can also be adopted to boost efforts at developing informal enterprises. Clustering aims at bringing together small firms in the same or related industries in a specific physical location and providing them with the necessary infrastructure and services. It improves the efficiency of individual enterprise and leads to cooperation among them, bringing about an increase in the collective efficiency of all the firms in the cluster. By pooling their inputs together, and working together, informal enterprises are able to increase their chances of achieving economies of scale. Such a collaborative approach also paves the way "for easier access to new technologies, skills sharing, greater in-house innovative capacity and new product design capabilities; all of these lead to higher value-added activities."[813] These economic gains are clearly visible in some Nigerian cities like Aba, Nnewi and Ilorin where clusters already exist. The Government has a responsibility to support the already existing cluster and help new ones to spring up. This can be effectively done by putting the necessary infrastructure in place and providing necessary services and incentives.

7.2.3 Enhancing Labour standards and Workers' Rights in the Informal Economy

As earlier observed in the third chapter, the informal economy is where most jobs have been created in recent years in Nigeria (cf. 3.2.2), but it is also where the greatest problem with regard to labour standards and workers' rights are found (cf. 3.2.7.7.3). The cause of this problem was traced to how rights are expressed and enforced through national and local law and practice, and to how workers are empowered to claim their rights. Addressing this problem squarely must therefore be an essential part of the efforts to attain the decent work agenda for poverty alleviation in the nation.

In order to enforce standards and extend labour rights to workers in the informal economy, Policy makers in Nigeria must pay proper attention to the provision of appropriate and effective labour legislation and administration and legal literacy. It is equally important to ensure that enabling legal framework for informal enterprises is developed, including removing the barriers to legal registration and enforcing property rights and contracts. It is also important to look into the activities of the formal firms that hire workers under informal employment relationships.[814] Simply put, the nation must take the necessary steps to improve labour legislation (→ 7.2.3.1), Improving Commercial and Business Regulation (→7.2.3.2), promoting legal literacy (→ 7.2.3.3).

---

813 United Nations Economic and Social Council, Role of the Informal Sector in Poverty Reduction, op. cit., pp. 12-13.

814 ILO: Decent work and the informal economy, op. cit., p. 48.

7.2.3.1 Improving Legislation and Enforcement

In order to effectively extend labour rights to workers and entrepreneurs in the informal economy, it is important to ensure that an enabling legal framework is put in place and to ensure that informal workers are fully covered by existing labour legislation. For this reason, existing scope of rights and labour legislations, which in many areas excludes those not in a formal employment relationship and so do not adequately cover the informal workers, need to be reviewed and updated.

Labour legislation in Nigeria often does not, for instance, take into account the deficiencies of modern organization of work. This is particularly the case with specific reference to flexible specialization on a global scale in commodity or supply chains in which firms embark on the decentralization of production and the organization of work along the lines of non-permanent or irregular labour relationships. This of course is an area that needs improvement. The governments must take necessary measures to review labour legislation for informal workers operating within such labour relationships. A special commission may be set up to study and analyze these labour relationships that emerge in the process of economic liberalization and recommend some credible policy actions.

Another problematic area is that, although the existing national labour legislation is designed to protect 'employees', there are however no clear legal criteria for defining employment relationships. This has in many cases blurred the distinction between self-employment and wage-employed, putting the many self-employed workers in the informal economy in a legal dilemma. Same is applicable to those in outsourcing and subcontracting arrangements, who should be regarded as "disguised wage workers" rather than self-employed. A typical example of this category of informal workers are the many women home-workers who in the real sense are employees, traceable sometimes to employers in far away countries, but are often treated by the real employers as self-employed workers, all in a bid to shelve some responsibilities such as contributing to their social protection. Cases like this further underscore the need to review the existing legal framework in the nation.

With regard to wage-labour, labour legislation should be reformed in accordance with "ILO Recommendation on the Employment Relationship 2006". This will make it easier to establish whether or not an employment relationship exists in situations where the respective rights and obligations of the parties concerned are not clear, where there has been an attempt to disguise the employment relationship, or where inadequacies or limitations exist in the legal framework, or in its interpretation or application

In order to adequately protect self-employed workers, there is a strong need to adopt the use of the term "worker" rather than "employee" so as to develop a new conceptual framework for legal definition that will give more consideration to economic dependency with actors other than employers.

There is of course need to look into other areas of rights that call for improved legislations such as enhancing national legislation to guarantee and defend the freedom of all workers, irrespective of where and how they work, to form and join organizations of their own choosing without fear of reprisal or intimidation; need to prioritise policies that raise levels of work security, income security and social security and improve working conditions and income opportunities; need for improving legislation to protect women in the informal who continually face social discrimination and are often trapped in survivalist activities and to eliminate all forms of forced labour and child labour.

While embarking on the reforms, it is desirable to carry out consultations with the social partners to determine, first, how rights provided for in existing labour legislation in the nation can be practically and effectively applied to the informal economy; and, second, where it may be necessary and possible to extend the existing legal scope of rights to cover informal workers.

In order to achieve good results, there is still need to take further steps towards strengthening the administration and enforcement of the labour legislation. This calls for the creation of institutions and mechanisms which can enforce labour standards and workers' rights in the informal economy. Labour administration and enforcement of labour right in the nation has, no doubt, witnessed some setbacks owing mainly to the fact that labour inspection services are not adequately staffed or equipped to effectively enforce standards in the informal economy, especially in terms of covering the myriads of micro- and small enterprises or the growing numbers of home-workers.

One of the ways to cope with this challenge is to complement existing labour services with some innovative schemes that would involve labour inspection auxiliaries, trade unions and informal workers themselves. Through trade unions, for instance, informal workers can be effectively shielded from corrupt juridical personnel and systems. The provision of free or heavily subsidized legal aid services by the government can also be adopted to boost efforts at enforcing labour rights. Developing good procedures and institutions for resolving labour disputes is also required in dealing with differences that erupt between local authorities and informal economy operators.

7.2.3.2 Improving Commercial and Business Regulation

Improving commercial and business regulation is all about creating a regulatory and legal system that will bring about a favourable environment in which the informal enterprises in Nigeria will be able to operate in a more formal and robust manner. This will further make it easier to enforce labour legislation in the informal economy and ensure that the rights of informal workers are respected.

In order to effectively promote standards and enhance rights in the informal economy, it will be necessary to observe strictly the provision of the ILO *Job Creation in Small and Medium-Sized Enterprises Recommendation, 1998 (No. 189).*[815] Concrete measure should be taken, first and foremost, to remove existing

815 Particularly emphasized in the recommendation is the importance of removing constraints on enterprises, including "inappropriate, inadequate or overly burdensome registration, licensing, reporting and other

barriers, reduce the transaction costs and enhance the benefits of registration and legalization. While doing this, it is always important to remember that there are two types of regulation. First, there are regulations related to becoming legal: notably registration and licensing. Then, there are regulations related to remaining legal, notably: taxation, observance of the labour code and health and safety regulations. None of these should be ignored or neglected in dealing with right deficits in the informal economy.

7.2.3.3 Promoting Legal Literacy

As earlier observed, one of the main reasons why the entrepreneurs do not observe the requirements of labour laws and international labour standards is the so-called cost and complexity of legality.[816] The biggest constraint on the part of informal workers, especially with regard to claiming their rights, is the ignorance of the existence laws, the relevance of and the benefits derived from labour legislation. In reviewing and improving the application of labour legislation to informal workers and enterprises, it should be consider whether legal requirements should therefore be simplified in order to make it easier for employers and third parties, including intermediaries to comply with them and for workers to understand their rights. But in the process of simplifying the legal requirements, care should however be taken to avoid compromising the core labour standards.

7.2.4 Strengthening Social Protection in the Informal Economy

Improving social protection in the informal would require basically three practical measures. The first is to expand the scope of the statutory social protection schemes. The second is to encourage micro-insurance schemes. And the third is improving occupational safety and health in the informal economy.

7.2.4.1 Extending the Statutory Social Protection Scheme to the Informal Economy

The following recommended measures could be helpful in extending the statutory social protection scheme in Nigeria to the informal economy:

- Revising the statutory schemes to facilitate membership by the self-employed, domestic workers, agricultural workers and those with a regular income from informal activities;
- Strengthening the administrative capacity of the social security schemes, particularly in compliance, record-keeping and financial management;

---

administrative requirements, including those which are disincentives to the hiring of personnel, without prejudicing the level of conditions of employment, the effectiveness of labour inspection or the system of supervision of working conditions and related issues". It may also be considered necessary to review the activities of formal firms that hire workers under non-standard or informal employment relationships.

816 Cf. Corinne Vargha: Case Study on international labour standards and micro-enterprises promoted by the project URT/88/007 – Employment promotion in the informal sector, (Geneva, International Labor Office, 1992), p. 18.

- Undertaking education and public awareness programmes to improve the image of the social security system;
- Extending coverage within a prescribed timetable to all persons working as employees,
- Opening up new "windows" and offering benefits that suit the needs and contributory capacity of currently non-covered groups.[817]

It should be emphasized that it is not always necessary or feasible to have the same range of social security provisions for all categories of people. The successful extension of social security requires taking into consideration the different needs and status of workers. Certain groups have special needs and some have very low contributory capacity. Since everybody does not earn enough to contribute adequately to the existing official scheme, support for the vulnerable groups in the informal economy should therefore be financed by society as a whole in order to ensure the welfare of every citizen.[818] An effective expansion of the social security would however require social dialogue. Policies and initiatives on the extension of coverage should be taken within the context of an integrated national social security strategy.

7.2.4.2 Developing and Strengthening Micro-insurance for Informal Workers

In addition to the efforts at extending the statutory social security, some other measures should be taken to encourage micro-insurance schemes (i.e. arrangements whereby people pool their resources together, mostly in a contributory manner, to protect themselves from basic risks) for informal workers. To this end, attempts should be made to explore the potentials for micro-insurance (in areas where it does exist) and possibly use them as the basis for a comprehensive social security system. These micro-insurance schemes have proved to be a useful and effective first step, particularly in responding to the poor people's urgent needs. One policy challenge is to assist people in the informal economy to form organizations among themselves, which will enable them to achieve various objectives, including stronger negotiating power with regard to the government as well as public and private health providers, sharing of knowledge and greater financial stabilization through reinsurance.

Another measure is to channel efforts towards publicizing and marketing the micro-insurance schemes, since a large percentage of the target population may still not be well informed of the benefits of being insured. The support of the government is critical for the successful upgrading of these schemes; Government subsidies are of particular importance in facilitating them.

---

817 W. van Ginneken: Social protection for workers in the informal economy: New challenges for Asia and the Pacific, report to the Twelfth ISSA Regional Conference for Asia and Pacific, Bangkok, 20-23 Nov. 2000, p. 13.

818 Cf.: ILO: Conclusions concerning social security, International Labour Conference, 89th Session, Geneva, 2001, paras. 5-6.

Local governments can play an important role in setting up area-based micro-insurance schemes in partnership with local groups of civil society. Area-based schemes contribute immensely in ensuring that administration is kept low and that local participation and control are included in the design of the scheme.[819] It is however necessary to point out that using the micro-insurance to address the needs of informal workers must be seen only as a temporary measure. It is crucial to ensure that employers in the formal economy do not abuse the schemes as a cheap substitute for social security and thus as an encouragement to further informalize their activities".[820]

7.2.4.3 Improving Occupational Safety and Health in the Informal Economy

In addressing the safety and health problems of workers, especially the poor in the informal economy, there is a serious need to look into the role of labour inspectors, health inspectors and sanitation officers whose duty it is in Nigeria to ensure compliance with occupational safety and health standards in places of work. It is sad that Labour and health inspection in the nation has been grossly misused as an exercise for monitoring whether standards are being met and penalizing those who contravene them. For this reason, the exercise has come to be perceived purely as a punitive measure.

Correcting this harmful notion would mean: instead of simply monitoring and issuing penalties, as is often the case in many parts of the nation, labour and health inspectors should be trained to assist the workers with some techniques that would enable them to improve their health and safety by themselves and thereby improve their working conditions and increase their productivity and earnings. By so doing, labour and health inspectors would not only be enforcing standards but would at the same succeed in playing a facilitative role. What official labour inspectors and health-care personal need most is the knowledge and the ability to pass on to informal workers and entrepreneurs low-cost measures for preventing accidents and protecting health through the introduction of ergonomic improvements, better workplace conditions and practices, improved use of tools and machinery and replacement of toxic or potentially toxic substances. Furthermore, inspectors involved in ensuring improved working and living environment for poor workers should seek the help and cooperation of people who are familiar with life and work in the informal economy. To this end, labour inspection auxiliaries could be recruited from among active informal workers and operators and retired craftspeople and from among business development service providers. Training, for the informal workers is also a crucial tool to raise awareness and improve work practices in the informal economy. At the same time, efforts should be made to

819 Cf.: ILO: Decent work and the informal economy, op. cit., p. 64.

820 ILO: Trade unions and the informal sector: Towards a comprehensive strategy, background paper for the International Symposium on Trade Unions and the Informal Sector, (Geneva, International Labour Office, 1999), p. 37.

convince owners of micro- and small enterprises that good environment of work is good for business.[821]

Business development service providers, when properly engaged, can play a vital role in raising awareness among business owners. Mass media and social marketing are also effective means for changing people's attitudes and behaviours regarding how occupational safety and health, human rights at work, production and environmental protection are related and inter-connected.

Occupational safety and health in the informal economy could also be promoted by organizing cluster programmes for informal workers and entrepreneurs. It will be necessary to first identify the clusters within which activities will be organized. Special consideration should be given to clusters where large numbers of informal workers are active and where health and safety problems exist more. A practical step in executing the programmes would include a walk-through survey and interviews of the workers by trained health and safety officers whose primary task would be to identify the problems and then propose some immediate corrective actions to be taken.

In order to achieve better results in this area, cluster programmes could be linked to wider municipal or district programmes that might include environmental health, environmental management and primary health-care programmes. Establishing links and involving workers' and employers' organizations would go a long way in making the task lighter for health and safety officers. For this purpose,

---

821 Fr more on this, see: ILO: Job quality: It's just good business, (Turin: International Training Centre of the ILO, 2001). This document originally prepared by SEED, a special organ of ILO for Promoting more and better jobs in micro-and small enterprises, is a kit for business development, shows, among other things, how safe and healthy workplace affects both the speed and quality of production. It argues convincingly that poor working conditions result in high overheads, waste of materials and energy and dissatisfaction of workers and customers and shows clearly how safe and healthy workplace and good conditions of employment improve both the speed and quality of production. The ILO has developed other helpful training packages with different objective of social protection. For example, a modular training package, "Participatory Action Training for Informal Sector Operators (PATRIS)"821, was produced to demonstrate the link between productivity and improvement of working conditions. This practical and simple training method, which was also tested in Nigeria among other nations, emphasizes voluntary participation in the implementation of concrete improvements in the participants' workplace. It deals with such issues as the physical environment, the premises, ergonomics, welfare facilities, work organization and health promotion. The "Improve your Work Environment and Business (IWEB)" is another modular package offered by the ILO for combining training to improve occupational safety and health in the informal economy with small business management training. The IWEB programmes normally organised for micro-manufacturers combines small business management training (based on the Start and Improve Your Business (SIYB)821 training package) with the promotion of job quality, in particular improved working conditions and good management of workers and their environment. The IWEB package which is based on the argument that better job quality will result in a more competitive and successful business, links better working conditions with other management goals, such as higher productivity. In this way, it attempts to deal with the fears of informal operators who often tend to ignore their working conditions and those of their employees in order to maximize profit. The approach adopted in this programme is quite simple and attractive. It builds on local practices, uses a learning-by-doing method, encourages the exchange of experience and promotes workers' achievements.

capacity building of workers' and employers' organizations should be embarked upon. First-aid training could be given to a selection of volunteers within the clusters.[822]

Improving the legal framework for proper enforcement of the laws related to social protection requires also that out-dated laws be reviewed. Labour inspection officers, for instance, will continue to face a number of challenges in the enforcement of the provisions of the Factories Act, 1990 CAP 126, laws of the Federation which regulates Occupational Safety and Health Standard, in workplaces in Nigeria if urgent steps are not taken to update the legal provision. This act has long been adjudged inadequate in scope and content to address the myriads of occupational hazards and exposures especially in the nation's informal economy.

It is necessary to point out that the issue of occupational safety and health at work is a collective affair and responsibilities of the government, cooperate stakeholders, employers, and worker. The government must however take the lead by providing the necessary funding, enabling policies and logistics. Adequate staffing of the Labour Inspection directorate of the Ministry of Labour and Productivity is also a direct responsibility of the government. On their own part, employers must endeavour to provide the necessary safety tools/kits and instructions for their safe usage. The employees have the obligation to comply with the instructions (for usage) to guard against workplace accidents and general health hazards. Trade unions should lobby government and employers' organizations to undertake new initiatives for social protection and establish workers co-operatives and self help groups. They should also lobby and pressurize the government to formulate separate legislation for informal workers.

7.2.5 Strengthening Representation in the Informal Economy

The most effective way of dealing with the representational gap and lack of voice in the informal economy is to assist informal workers and business operators to form self-help groups and business and workers associations and link the existing groups and association with mainstream organizations. Supporting self-help groups is a useful way of promoting solidarity among workers and between workers and other social groups as discussed in the fourth chapter of this work (cf. 4.2.2.4 and 4.5.4). By organizing informal workers and business operators into self-help groups, their capacity will be enhanced not only to be represented but also to assist one another and to contribute meaningfully to the common good of the entire society. Self-help groups and business and workers associations in the informal economy can also arrange training for informal economy workers, and assist in introducing modern technologies and in dealing with harassment from regulatory authorities. In addition to this, they can exert collective pressure on the Government to eliminate unnecessary regulations and to formulate favourable

822 ILO, Decent work and the informal economy, op. cit., p. 68.

policies that would be of benefit to the informal economy.[823] The self-help organizations are indeed a vibrant economic force for poverty alleviation, wealth creation, job creation, rural development and economic empowerment of the poor in the informal economy.

Through self-help groups, people in the informal economy can, in a participatory way, contribute in providing basic infrastructure and in maintaining existing ones. A reported success in this regard is the Orangi Pilot Project, a community-based non-governmental organization (NGO) in Karachi, Pakistan. This NGO organized the rural dwellers of the squatter settlement of Orangi, in Karachi, and with little outside financial support, it was able to make arrangements for garbage disposal, paved streets, sewage facilities and a secure drinking water supply. It was also able to secure legal property rights for its members and made arrangements for the provision of social services, such as basic health facilities and primary education.[824] A replication of this in Nigeria would go a long way in enhancing capacity and in improving living and working conditions in the nation's informal economy.

Self-help organizations can facilitate credit for informal enterprises. What exists in Nigeria as self-help organizations is more in this area of facilitating credit. An example of this is the Self-Help Group Linkage programme which was launched under the Agricultural Credit Guarantee Scheme (ACGS) in 1991 and became operational in 1992. Under the programme, farmers are mobilized and encouraged to form themselves into small groups of between 5 and 15 members. These groups are encouraged to undertake regular savings with a partner bank of their choice. After operating such savings for at least six months, they could then apply to the partner bank for loan. The amount deposited with the bank provides part cash security for loans to the saving groups.[825] Many of such groups exist today in the nation, backed by private initiatives.

Some organizations of the informal worker in Nigeria have been mentioned in chapter three of the work (cf. 3.2.7.10). Cooperatives are also formed by informal workers in Nigeria in dealing with welfare issues, space allocation, local taxes, permits, and so on. These cooperatives are found in various forms: producers' cooperatives, consumer cooperatives, service or marketing cooperatives, etc. While some are formally registered, others remain informal.

Responding effectively to the organizational and representational gap and voice deficit in the informal economy, especially in terms of assisting the informal workers to form their own organization and recognising the existing informal organizations, requires a strong and cohesive tripartism – the government, workers' and employers' organizations. The various civil society groups, movements and

823 United Nations Economic and Social Council, Poverty and the Informal Sector: Role of the Informal Sector in Poverty Reduction, op. cit., p. 12.

824 Ibid., p. 10.

825 Cf.: Central Bank of Nigeria, Agricultural Credit Guarantee Scheme Fund (ACGSF) Self Help Group Linkage Banking, accessed from: http://www.cenbank.org/devfin/selfhelp.asp, on 06.06.2011.

NGOs have also important contributions to make. Though it is possible for each party to work separately and still make achievements, it is however necessary to bear in mind that many benefits are derived from working collectively through social dialogue.

We wish to dwell more here on the roles that the government, the labour organizations and the employers' organizations can play in enhancing the right of informal workers and entrepreneurs to organize and be represented for the purpose of achieving the decent work goal for poverty alleviation in the nation

7.2.5.1 The Role of National and Local Governments

The representational gap in the informal economy cannot be effectively addressed without a supportive legal framework and governance. The government has a key role to play in creating appropriate policies and legislation for ensuring an enabling environment for the organization and representation of those in the informal economy. Of paramount importance in this regard is to formulate policies and create the legal framework that guarantee the freedom of all workers and employers, irrespective of where and how they work, to form and join organizations of their choosing without fear of reprisal or intimidation.

It is however not enough to secure the right for informal workers to join or create organizations of their choosing. Democratic, independent, membership-based organizations of wage workers, self-employed persons or employers in the informal economy should be allowed to operate under local or national legislation. To this end, the State must take appropriate steps to ensure that the organs of representation formed by the informal workers and entrepreneurs are accorded legitimacy and due recognition as interlocutors and/or partners in policy-making or programme implementation at national and local levels. Official recognition by government authorities certainly gives informal organizations a stronger voice in public policy debates and better access to the services and infrastructure they need to operate effectively and efficiently. It also makes them less vulnerable to harassment or eviction by the authorities. All of these help to reduce informality and facilitate their move towards formal activities within the economic and social mainstream and regulatory frameworks.

The local governments have a crucial role to play in achieving this goal, since they operate at the grass-root level and deal directly with informal organizations in most of the issues vital to their cooperate existence and functioning. The national government must however ensure that there is consistency of policies and effective implementation at local level, so that the organizations in the informal economy can smoothly develop and become strong and stable.

The government should also play an intermediary role by creating mechanisms and opportunities for regular dialogue involving organizations of informal workers and established trade unions and employers' organizations, as well as for collective bargaining and other forms of civil dialogue. This could be effectively done, for instance, by widening the scope of existing national tripartite bodies or collective bargaining processes, or facilitating innovative mechanisms specifically tailored to a particular segment of the informal economy.[826]

It must however be kept in mind that informal economy workers cannot be effectively organised and integrated into the existing mainstream union without some necessary adjustments and changes in the way the unions are constituted and the way they operate. For instance, the current Trade Union Act, the Employment Act and the Labour Act in Nigeria do not make any explicit reference to the informal economy. The direct implication of this is that informal workers are technically excluded from the coverage of this legal instrument. This type of legal environment constitutes a major obstacle to efforts at organizing and integrating informal workers into mainstream unions. It also retards progress in efforts made by unions representing informal economy workers.

7.2.5.2 The Role of Trade Unions

The informal economy has always posed an enormous challenge to statutory trade unions in term of organizing and integrating them into the mainstream organizations. On its official website, the Nigerian Labour Congress (NLC) acknowledges that "Nigeria's massive and dynamic informal sector is also largely unorganised"[827] and points out that "the modalities for its unionisation are now the subject of internal debates in the movement."[828] The national labour body is indeed in a fix concerning how to facilitate the organization of the unorganised groups in the informal economy. There is particularly confusion regarding the most appropriate measures to be implemented.

The major constraints generally encountered in organizing informal workers and incorporating the existing informal organizations are already discussed in chapter two (cf. 2.5.2). Overcoming these challenges will require a varied and flexible approach incorporating a range of differing relationships between unions, informal worker associations and cooperatives, networks and alliances. It requires most importantly a strong political will on the part of union leadership to prioritize organizing workers in the informal economy and to make available the human and financial resources to do so. It requires new conceptual thinking and new mind sets on the part of the (mainly male) union leadership, especially with regard to gender issues. It requires an openness and flexibility with regard to different organizational models, strategies and activities, the disposition to seize new openings and opportunities, and the building of alliances with informal workers' organizations and their collaborator within and outside the union movement. Finally, it will require on the part of unionists the readiness to learn in some cases from informal

826 ILO: Decent work and the informal economy, op. cit., p. 75.

827 Nigeria Labour Congress, History of the Nigeria Labour Congress, http://www.nlcng.org/history.php, accessed 09.06.2011.

828 Ibid.

workers and members of NGOs who have more experience in organizing informal workers.[829]

There are two major ways of effectively addressing the organizational needs in the informal economy in the nation. The first requires that the traditional unions extend their fields of activity to include informal economy workers. Incorporating the informal economic workers into the mainstream organization would indeed boost their negotiation capacity and bring them into wider circles of social and economic interaction. The second is to establish separate unions to specifically organize workers in the informal economy.[830] These approaches have been tested with success in different parts of the world.[831] Both of them can conveniently be adopted in Nigeria, as they are of course neither conflicting nor opposed to one another.

Some important and helpful commitments have already been made at the international level towards organizing the informal workers.[832] These commitments provide a good platform and a point of departure for Nigeria in seeking to organize informal workers both at the national level and at the local level. The NLC which acts as the umbrella organization for the trade unions in the nation should rise to its responsibility in catering for the welfare of all workers by, at least, diffusing some of these commitments made at the international level and letting them reflect in its activities, structures and institutions.

Unions also have a task to accomplish in creating awareness and sensitising informal workers to their rights as workers to organize and of the benefits of unionization. Such awareness-raising campaigns, which could also be utilized to create awareness on union services and policies that benefit workers in the informal economy, should be directed more to areas where informal workers remain

829 Christine Bonner and Dave Spooner, Organizing in the Informal Economy: A Challenge for Trade Unions, p. 103, a pdf document available at: http://library.fes.de/pdf-files/ipg/2011-2/08_a_bonner.pdf, accessed on 09.06.2011.

830 Global Labour Institute: Informal Work: Notes on Trade Unions and the Informal Sector (1999). Available at: http://www.globallabour.info/en/2007/09/notes_on_trade_unions_and_the_1.html.

831 For examples see: ibid.

832 For instance, in 1999, the ILO Bureau for Workers' Activities organised an "International Symposium on Trade Unions and the Informal Sector" which brought together trade union representatives from developing and industrialized countries to discuss ways to effectively organize and represent the interests of workers in the informal economy. Responding in a similar way, the International Confederation of Free Trade Unions (ICFTU) and the World Confederation of Labour (WCL), acting separately before their dissolution and subsequent merger in 2006, took some bold steps by first recognising the positive contributions of the informal economy and then setting up some machinery for effective organization of informal workers. In 2000, the 17th World Congress of the International Confederation of Free Trade Unions (ICFTU) gave a mandate for the establishment of a Task Force on Informal or Unprotected Work to develop more effective strategies to assist vulnerable workers to help themselves and to respond to the growing pace of informalization and the deterioration of conditions of the economy in the face of globalization. The WCL, adopting the informal economy as one of its action priorities for the years 1998-2002, made an active commitment to collaborate with its affiliates to organize the workers in informal economy, bearing in mind their specific needs and with a view to protecting collectively their interests.

unaware or suspicious of the aims of unions. Innovative strategies for reaching wider audience among informal workers should be developed. Experience has shown that important pieces of information are better transmitted in the rural areas through town leaders and in the urban centres, through radio or television programmes and street theatres. Such enlightenment campaigns should give special attention to women and youth in the informal economy.

In addition to this, unions, both collectively at the national level and separately at the local level, would have to review and, where necessary, revise their internal regulations and statutes to remove limitations to their ability to organize informal workers. Some important areas that would require amendments include: membership dues, the right to membership, participation in negotiation teams, inclusion in collective agreements and gender equality. Different strategies may be necessary to organize women and men.[833] To achieve this goal, gender focal point should be given priority. Unions may also have to consider creating special structures, including specific departments or units to organize and represent informal workers more effectively. It also may be necessary to create an apex national body/organization that would effectively represent the informal economy. The close cooperation between national union centres and informal workers' organizations will significantly enhance informal workers' effectiveness in representation, defence of workers' rights, and international visibility and support.[834]

7.2.5.3 The Role of Employers' Organizations

The role of the employers' organizations is similar to those of the trade union: namely extending their membership and services to the entrepreneurs in the informal economy and helping them to form their own organizations. The method and measure to be adopted to achieve this is also not so different from those of the trade unions, because, in many ways, the problems of organizing informal workers are similar to the problems employers' organizations encounter while organizing small enterprises in the formal economy.

The employers' organizations must take serious, the task of organizing informal entrepreneurs, since it is in the interest of both parties. Effective organization in the informal economy certainly leads to increase in productivity and purchasing power and so helps to transform the informal economy into "a more important market for the goods produced by the formal economy and at the same time a more efficient source of a broader range of high-quality inputs required by formal enterprises."[835]

In seeking to incorporate the informal enterprises, it is better to encourage the various business units to form their own associations, which could later become

---

833 ILO: Decent work and the informal economy, op. cit., p. 79.

834 Christine Bonner and Dave Spooner, Organizing in the Informal Economy:A Challenge for Trade Unions, op. cit., p. 100.

835 ILO: Decent work and the informal economy, op. cit., p. 87.

members of established employers' organizations, since targeting single enterprises may turn out to be very difficult and expensive. In some cases, micro- and small entrepreneurs have long organizing themselves for the purpose of carrying out various joint actions: collective bargaining, securing reliable, up-to-date and complete information on market performance strategies, accessing technical and financial assistance, advocacy with local authorities, etc. Employers' organizations can further assist these associations of informal entrepreneurs in a number of ways: developing a lobbying agenda specially geared to the needs of micro- and small enterprises; providing business support (developing business plans, project formulation, access to credit) and other relevant services (personnel management, productivity improvement, basic management skills, accounting and entrepreneurship training programmes); helping to link micro-enterprises with the formal economy; providing a range of information which micro- and small enterprises may find difficult to obtain, for instance on laws and regulations, market opportunities and facilitating access to markets.

Providing these services directly to the informal operators will definitely mean much expenses and inconveniencies that the employer organizations may not be able to cope with on their own. In order to avoid these constrains, employers' organizations should do more to lobby for the creation of institutes, such as entrepreneurship development institutes, that can serve as the conduit for service delivery to the informal economy.[836]

Above all and most importantly, the employers' organizations have an important role in assisting small producers to make a transition to formality and sustainable competitiveness in the global economy. This could be done by adopting the social market system which has become today a high-profile system for linking informal enterprises with buyers and consumers in advanced countries so as to create an alternative way of doing business that is beneficial and fair. Notable for this system worldwide are the Alternative trading organizations (ATOs)[837] and the Fair Trade Federation (FTF).[838]

---

836 ILO: Resolution concerning decent work and the informal economy, para. 33.

837 The Alternative Trading Organizations (ATOs) are mission-driven business organizations aligned with the Fair Trade movement which aims to contribute to the alleviation of poverty in developing regions of the world by establishing a system of trade that allows marginalized producers, especially single women heads of households, displaced people, seasonal agricultural workers and slum dwellers, in developing regions of the world to gain access to developed markets. ATOs seek to bypass exploitative intermediaries and work directly with producers, so as to be able to cut costs and return a greater percentage of the retail price to the producers. The ATOs are coordinated at the international level by the International Federation for Alternative Trade (IFAT)

838 The Fair Trade Federation (FTF) is part of the global fair trade movement, building equitable and sustainable trading partnerships and creating opportunities to alleviate poverty. It is particularly an association of fair trade wholesalers, retailers and producers that directly links low-income producers with consumer markets and educates consumers about the importance of purchasing fairly traded products which support living wages and safe and healthy conditions for workers in the developing world. For

more information please go to: http://www.fairtradefederation.com/ or http://www.fairtradefederation.org/.

GENERAL CONCLUSION AND CHALLENGES FOR THE NIGERIAN CHURCH

Résumé

As stated in the general introduction, this work aims at broadening the framework for poverty alleviation in Nigeria by probing into some of the dimensions that have received insufficient attention so as to make some recommendations for a coherent strategy for sustainable poverty alleviation in the nation. In view of this, an attempt was made to understand the concept of poverty and how it exists in the contemporary world – its conceptualization, types, scope, measurement and causes. Poverty was defined broadly as deprivation and lack of basic capacity to participate effectively in society. It means not having enough to feed and cloth a family, not having the opportunity to acquire knowledge and skills; not having the land on which to grow one's food or a job to earn one's living, not having access to credit. It means insecurity, powerlessness and exclusion of individuals, households and communities from economic and social life. It means not being protected. It means lack of voice and denial of rights. It means susceptibility to harassment, and it often implies living on marginal or fragile environments, without access to clean water or sanitation. It is a violation of human dignity.

Special attention was given to the concept of working poverty, since the reality for most poor people is that they must work often in bad conditions and at works that are not productive enough to enable them lift themselves and their families out of poverty. The working poor are therefore working people living in poverty; individuals engaged in either paid or self employment. They are involved in works that not only provide an insufficient level of income but also lack social security, good working conditions, voice and representation and other basic rights at work.

In examining the causes of poverty in the world today, it was discovered that poverty is a direct consequence of social and economic processes that interact and frequently reinforce each other in a way that exacerbate the state of deprivation in which people live and work. At the very heart of the problem is the issue of governance or rather bad governance at the national level that generates unjust structures, systems and institutions. Some major aspects of bad governance identified include, the absence of strong institutions governed by the rule of law, a lack of physical structures and essential services, labour market deficiencies and bad economic policies. These structural failures prevent people, especially the working poor, from taking advantage of new economic opportunities or engaging in activities outside their immediate area of security. They particularly produce an unfavourable business atmosphere and generate unemployment, underemployment and precarious labour conditions. But above all, they prevent the poor from utilizing their labour – the most valuable if not the only resource they have – to earn enough income that can keep them out of poverty.

It was also discovered that as a result of poor governance of the processes of global integration in the last decades, there has been a rise in poverty in many parts of the Third World, especially in Sub-Saharan Africa. While on the one hand, unstable and weak national economic and political systems of many poor nations of the world continue to hinder internal economic and human development and full integration into the global market, global governance, on the other hand, marred by unfair rules and policies, fails to ensure the equal participation and equitable distribution of the gains accruing from the integration of the global economy. Within this global socio-economic order, increased competition and an unbridled quest for profit thrive unhindered and steadily give rise to the deregulation of labour through off-shoring, outsourcing and downsizing. All of these have given rise to a high rate of unemployment, the informalization of labour and production and the high incidence of poverty among low and unskilled workers, especially in Sub-Saharan African countries.

The second chapter studied the informal economy – the economic field where most of the poor people work to earn their living. This is with a view to determining why people are poor despite the fact that they work. The informal economy by definition refers to all economic activities by workers and economic units that are – in law or in practice – not covered by formal arrangements. Their activities are not fully covered by the law, which means that either they are operating outside the formal reach of the law; or they are not covered in practice, which means that, although they are operating within the formal reach of the law, the law is not applied or not enforced or the law discourages compliance because it is inappropriate, burdensome, or imposes excessive costs.[839]

The size and economic potential of the informal economy is quite enormous. Going by available estimations, in Sub-Saharan Africa, for instance, it accounts for 72 per cent of non-agricultural employment and 93% of new jobs and contributes significantly to the economy. Despite this economic importance of the informal economy, the conditions of work in it remain predominantly precarious. It is highly characterized by decent work deficits which include: employment deficit, rights deficit, social protection deficit and representational deficit. These poor labour conditions in the informal economy were traced to weak legal and institutional frameworks; poor economic performance and non-pro-poor economic growth; and flexible specialization and global chains in production and labour.

It was established that the informal economy has a significant co-relation to poverty in the sense that the vast majority of the poor work, but only few are able to work their way out of poverty because most of them are engaged in the informal economy, where they are likely to face lower incomes, greater financial risks, lower standards of human development and greater social exclusion due to the decent work deficits in that segment of economy.

The third chapter examined how and why poverty exists in Nigeria as a whole and among the working population in particular. In view of this, the political,

839 ILO, Resolution concerning decent work and the informal economy ILC90-PR25-292-En.Doc. para. 3.

economic and social circumstances in the nation were examined with a view to understanding how they have impacted on human development and on the overall wellbeing of the nation. Thereafter, an in-depth consideration was given to the informal economy where most of the poor people in Nigeria work and earn their living. This was also done with a view to ascertaining how the prevailing socio-economic and political circumstances which determine the condition in which the poor live and work affect their ability to use their labour (the most valuable if not the only asset they have) to contribute meaningfully to wealth creation, to have a fair share of the increased availability of public and private resources and to participate fully in the life of the society.

We observed that although Nigeria is rich both in human and natural resources, poverty remains pervasive in the land, with a high incidence of working poverty. The poverty in the nation manifests itself both in terms of economic and social development indicators: low per capita income, poor social services, lack of opportunities and basic amenities of life, social exclusion, and powerlessness.

Poverty in Nigeria also manifests itself as a social problem that has its root in the institutional and structural deficiencies in the political, social and economic life of the nation. In other words, poverty in Nigeria is an outcome of a social disorder and structural imbalances that emanate from weak and corrupt governmental institutions and systems, bad leadership, wrong patterns of social and economic development, limited access to opportunities (education, employment, land, capital, etc), inadequate investment in economic and human capital development, lack of market for both agrarian and industrial product, etc.

Although the nation has in recent years attained a stable growth in GDP, this growth has however failed to keep pace with the rapid growth in the population, increasing demand for employment and with the development of peer countries. It has also failed to translate into overall improvement in the economy and reduction of poverty. This is attributed partly to enduring deficiencies in the system of wealth distribution in the nation that favours only a few privileged people and partly due to the bad pattern of economic development that the nation retains. Nigeria has continued to depend on the oil and gas sub-sector for its revenue to the detriment of other sectors of the economy, especially those that have more relevance for employment generation and poverty reduction – agriculture and the Small and Micro Enterprises (SMEs). This has resulted in a non-inclusive system in which many of the citizens, especially the poor, are estranged from the wealth production processes in the nation and by that same token denied the opportunity of using their only asset, which is their labour, to participate meaningfully in the creation of wealth and in receiving a fair share of the wealth produced in the nation. Many Nigerians must therefore seek their livelihood in the subsistence economy – the informal economy – where labour conditions have been most unfavourable to the generation of sufficient wealth to keep people out of poverty.

An examination of the informal economy in Nigeria reveals that the informal economic activities in the nation are not just what the poor do but those activities which supply the needs of the poor and improve their living standards; they are business activities and social services that are vital to the socio-economic development and creation of wealth in the nation. Nigeria's informal economy is therefore crucial in terms of untapped revenue and, more importantly, as a driving force for rapid social development for durable economic growth.

Despite the enormous potentials in the informal economy for socio-economic development and poverty alleviation, the segment of the economy has continued to record a high incidence of poverty as a result of the enormous constraints it encounters. While the enterprises continue to operate in an unfavourable business atmosphere, informal workers must reckon with a high incidence of decent work deficit: They lack skills, are not gainfully employed, enjoy little rights, have no access to formal social protection and are not formally organized. As a result of these constraints, productivity and earnings have been very low in the informal economy, explaining why the high incidence of poverty has been higher among informal workers than it is among workers in the formal economy.

The major factors that shape and reshape the informal economy in Nigeria were identified to include the political gap, social development gap and economic development gap. The political gap in the nation is reflected in political instability, institutional fragility and fundamental weaknesses in the management of resources and governance; the social development gap is reflected in the nation's wide infrastructural gap, low financial and social services, high incidence of social inequality and income gap, high incidence of corruption, and high unemployment and underdevelopment rates; the economic development gap is reflected in low economic performance, poor patterns of trade and economic development, high levels of macroeconomic instability and lack of competitiveness in the global market. These factors limit, in no small measure, the capacity of the public sector to create enough formal jobs and robbed the private sector enterprises mostly in informal economy of the opportunity to step in as a supplement to the public sector enterprises in the creation of quality jobs.

The presence of a large informal economy in Nigeria has major implications for poverty alleviation in the nation, given that 90 per cent of new jobs in the country are created in the informal economy and that most poor people work informally, and also considering its enormous potentials for boosting economic growth and social development. Based on this and other observations made in the third chapter, we came to the conclusion that poverty will remain pervasive in Nigerians unless growth is sustained and also derived from sectors and economic units with high poverty-reducing impacts. Such economic activities, we observed, are found mainly in the informal economy. It is therefore strongly believed that Nigeria's long-term macroeconomic performance is critically tied to its management of this segment of the economy that can eventually prove much more valuable than its rich reserves of oil. This highlights the obvious need to prioritise measures for improving labour conditions and for harnessing the potentials in the informal economy for sustainable growth and poverty reduction. Nigeria presents itself therefore as a nation in need of structural reforms that would transform the economic activities in the informal economy into formal economic ventures that can become a vehicle for genuine and broad-based economic progress. This implies that Nigeria needs an integrated and coherent development strategy that aims principally to place employment at the heart of economic and social policies.

Having attempted to understand the nature of poverty its causes and its link to the informal economy, the next task was taken up, namely, the search for an ethical orientation and political concepts for dealing with the problem of poverty. The fourth chapter of this work constitutes the first step in this direction. It is an attempt to articulate the impulses from the Catholic social teaching (CST). The chapter reveals that poverty is conceived in the social teaching of the Church basically as a social problem that infringes on the core principles of social life – the principles of justice and the principle of human dignity and also on other social principles, namely, the principles of the universal destination of goods, the principle of solidarity and the principle of subsidiarity.

In her social teaching, the Church insists that poverty emanates as a consequence of the structures of sin in the society. These structures of sin are traced to the inner rebellion in human heart. This rebellion sets human beings against their creator and against one another. In social life, this inner rebellion transforms itself into unjust structures that are made visible in the unequal distribution of the goods of the earth; in the exploitative manner in which human labour is valued and treated in the systems of production and in economic injustice. It is based on this understanding that the Church offers some basic guidelines for the alleviation of poverty.

The guidelines the Church proposes in her social teaching are tailored towards a structural transformation that would create a favourable social order in which human dignity, common good and social and economic justice would be guaranteed based on the principles of solidarity and subsidiarity. They are actions that are required to correct the structural failures responsible for poverty. The transformation which the Church advocates, appeals to both spiritual and moral capacities of the individual, and the entire society. She maintains that lively dedication and interior disposition to justice and kindness and to the common good are needed to establish a political, social, and economic life that is truly human. For this reason, the concern for the poor and alleviation of poverty must incorporate efforts to achieve a more just social order, the practice of virtue, and the pursuit of justice in the social, economic and political life of the society. This requires actions to confront the structures of injustice that make people poor.

Arguing that 'work' is the key to social problems, the Church insists that special considerations for human work should be at the heart of the proposed reform. This implies that the reform should be carried out in such a way that all who are capable of working would be given the opportunity to do so in a way that is befitting to human dignity, so that through the sweat of their brow they will be able to meet at least their basic needs and those of their family members. The reform should above all aim at enabling human persons to have a fair share of the good of the earth, develop their potentials and attain their true destiny.

We acknowledged indeed that the CST, although not a solution in itself, offers however a sound ethical orientation and basis for evaluating development plans and poverty alleviation concepts. It also provides a wellspring from which policy makers and executors can draw on in their search for enduring solutions to the nagging problem of poverty. The CST manifests however some shortcomings. Being more conversant with Western socio-economic terrain, the CST, while dealing with "work" as the key to social problems, concentrates more on the problems encountered by paid labour and offers very little with regard to the many problems faced by self employed workers. In a nation like Nigeria where 80 per cent of non-agricultural employment, 60 per cent of urban employment and over 90 per cent of new job creation is in the informal economy, the local labour question goes certainly beyond the scope of paid labour to include the many problems faced by workers in the informal economy, majority of whom are self employed. The guidelines for a work-oriented poverty reduction approach proposed by the CST prove therefore to be inadequate in providing direct answers to the labour questions in Nigeria's informal economy. This not withstanding, the ethical orientation and perspective gained from the CST in chapter four still form a good basis for evaluating the poverty alleviation concepts and strategies adopted over the years both at international and national levels. This is the task taken up in the fifth chapter.

Two approaches to poverty alleviation were found to be outstanding in international discussions in the past few decades: the economic growth-centred approach of the Bretton Woods Institutions and the labour-intensive growth approach of the ILO: The growth-centred approach is founded on the presumption that liberalization leads to integration; integration leads to economic growth; economic growth leads to poverty reduction. Based on this presumption, the growth-centred approach focuses more on economic growth at the expense of labour development. This approach may prove effective for achieving rapid economic growth which, nevertheless, is an important requirement for poverty alleviation. It however proves inadequate for pursuing other targets of development necessary for poverty alleviation, namely human capacity development and employment generation, for it places a premium on economic development, giving little attention to the development of the human person. As a result of this, economic principles take precedence over the social principles (especially social justice and solidarity) accorded priority in the CST.

Furthermore, this approach makes provision for growth but lacks a functional mechanism for equitable distribution of the wealth that is derived from growth. Market forces are believed to be the drivers of growth and a 'rational' development path. The growth-centred approach to development is no doubt established on the economic ideology that has been blamed in many social encyclicals for the socio-economic imbalances in which extravagance and wretchedness exist side by side.

While the majority of people lack the absolute necessities of life and are deprived of almost all possibility of acting on their own initiative and responsibility, and often subsist in living and working conditions unworthy of the human person, others continue to live in luxury, squandering wealth and enjoying very great power of choice.[840] The economic-growth approach to development and poverty alleviation is indeed believed to have impacted negatively on labour, resulting in the expansion of the informal economy and poverty in many developing nations.

The ILO labour-intensive growth approach to poverty alleviation proves to be more compatible with the CST. It builds on the core principles of social life, especially social justice, and promotes human dignity. While upholding the importance of growth in the fight against poverty, the ILO believes that due consideration for labour conditions is crucial, not only for attaining growth but also for the equitable distribution of wealth and for the full integration of all citizens into the life of the society. It however insists strongly that more efforts should be channelled to improving the labour conditions in the informal economy where most of the poor are working to earn their living.

The ILO labour-intensive poverty alleviation strategy is considered to be a better and more coherent approach and is therefore adopted in this work as a plausible and effective strategy for dealing with poverty in a nation like Nigeria where a huge number of the productive workers have engaged themselves in the informal economy in a bid to stay out of poverty. It is strongly believed that improving the labour conditions in the nation's informal economy would increase the productivity, earnings and general welfare of the working poor. This invariable will put them and their dependants on the right path out of poverty.

The ILO's tool for achieving this goal is the Decent Work Agenda (DWA). The DWA recognizes that the economy has to deliver increased employment, but that this has also to involve the improvement of working conditions, social protection and representation based on respect for fundamental principles and rights at work. It helps to focus research and policy actions on practical measures that can both have an immediate impact on poverty and build the infrastructure for longer-term progress. It also provides a viable means for mobilizing broad support for policies that will commit both the non-poor and the poor themselves.

The sixth chapter takes a look at the past and current efforts made especially by the Nigerian government and the Church towards alleviating poverty. The findings are clear: The Nigerian government has pursued predominantly a development and poverty alleviation plan that is judged inadequate for sustainable poverty alleviation, going by the work-centred guideline of the Catholic social teaching and the ILO labour-intensive growth approach. For a long time, Nigeria's development and poverty alleviation strategy lacked a clear vision and appropriate framework for job creation and labour development, especially where it matters most – in the informal economy of the nation. This development plan promoted policies and programmes that do not directly target the poor, especially those in the informal

840 Gaudium et Spes, 63 ; also Paul VI, Encyclical Populorum progressio, 9.

economy. The poor were implicitly expected to benefit from the trickle-down efforts of the overall process of development. Furthermore, the development debates in Nigeria over the past few years have focused too narrowly on growth for its own sake rather than as a means of improved human development. Employment and the development of the human person are not consistently integrated as the *raison d'être* of the NEEDS – Nigeria's current Poverty Reduction Strategy Paper (PRSP).

Although Nigeria has striven in recent times to attain economic growth in order to alleviate poverty, the creation of sufficient 'decent work' is evidently neither a priority nor an indicator of the nation's Poverty Reduction Strategy. Nigeria consistently shows dogged commitment and dedication to the full implementation of the Decent Work Agenda. The failure to properly identify, recognise and deal with the factors responsible for the poor labour conditions in that segment of the nation's economy where the poor live and work has been the bane of the failure to defeat poverty. It is therefore clear that Nigeria needs a broader framework for sustainable alleviation of poverty.

On her part, the Nigerian Church has contributed to poverty alleviation, by making pronouncements and issuing communiqués through which she appeals for social actions that will put an end to the sufferings of the poor. The Church also embarks on social actions on the side of the poor. These are basically in the areas of education, health care delivery and charity services. She believes also in the power of prayer as an instrument of changes and so continually prays particularly for an end to corruption and distress in the land. The Church is however faced with the challenge of making her voice heard in condemning the structural injustice responsible for the inhuman conditions in which the poor live and work in the nation. She is also faced with the challenge of repositioning herself and getting more actively involved in addressing the plight of the suffering masses especially the working poor.

Based on the foregoing, the seventh chapter of this work makes some concrete recommendations for the development of a broad and integrated framework for sustainable alleviation of poverty in the nation. The chapter basically highlights some important areas of policy intervention that should be given priority attention. It is not aimed at producing another Poverty Reduction Strategy Paper for Nigeria.

The recommendations that are made flow from the ethical orientation derived from the catholic social teaching which identifies "work" as the essential key to poverty alleviation and insists on a structural reform in social economic and political life founded on justice, human dignity and the principles of common good and universal destination of goods, solidarity and subsidiarity; a reform that would ensure that every human person will be able to develop his or her God-given potentials and through his or her work acquire what is needed to live the life that befits the human dignity. The recommendations also manifest a direct bearing to the labour-intensive growth framework of the ILO. What is presented in chapter seven is therefore a range of recommendations that would facilitate an employment-intensive growth path to sustainable poverty alleviation and push forward the frontier of human development in Nigeria. It outlines the elements of such an employment framework and provides concrete recommendations for moving towards a growth path that will generate decent employment and reduces poverty in Nigeria.

The employment-intensive growth framework recommended for poverty alleviation in Nigeria has three components: A Growth Component - generating higher rates of economic growth; an Employment Component - insuring that economic growth produces a significant number of new quality employment opportunities and improves existing ones; a Poverty Focus - linking poor individuals and households to new and improved employment opportunities.

Some economic policy interventions that would support the employment-intensive growth include: Ensuring macroeconomic and price stability: enhancing financial services; enhancing budgetary Policy and public investment; formulating appropriate trade policy. Other areas for policy interventions include: Strengthening institutions and governance; improving the rule of law and transparency, eliminating inequality.

In order to ensure that the poor are able to benefit from the employment-intensive growth strategy, employment policies must be directed at the informal economy where the poor are concentrated. This should be done with a view to identifying and addressing the specific needs of the working poor engaged in informal activities. These areas of need are treated within the four pillars of the ILO Decent Work Agenda, namely: employment creation and enterprise development, standards and rights at work, social protection and social dialogue. Addressing these needs would require policy interventions for creating decent employment opportunities for people in the informal economy by investing in knowledge and skills acquisition and in enterprise development

Some policy interventions for addressing the needs of informal workers and business units include the provision of education and skills training, the extension of social protection, developing and strengthening micro-insurance, assistance in the formation of self-help groups and business and workers associations. Other policy interventions include securing property rights, providing credit, improving access to physical infrastructure, providing legal assistance, improving commercial and business regulations and the strengthening of linkages with the formal sector. All of these amount also to dealing with informality and in a way to facilitating the movement of informal workers and enterprises into the formal economy.

The Role of the Nigerian Church in Promoting Decent Work for Poverty Alleviation

The role Nigerian Church has to play towards promoting the decent work agenda for poverty alleviation in the nation will be better understood by viewing the

Church not as a transcendental institution but simply as a "Church in the world"; as an earthly institution with a divine mandate that cuts across the spiritual and the temporal realms. She has the mandate not only to teach but also to act in favour of the downtrodden and be a beam of light that shows the way. The discussion here will be limited to the roles of the Nigerian Church as a promoter of a just society, as an exemplary economic actor and as an advocate and supporter of the poor.

Towards Building a Just Society

As earlier observed, building a just society that will enhance poverty alleviation in Nigeria requires efforts that would lead to the dismantling of unjust structures and the establishment of just systems that guarantee equitable distribution of resources and equal participation in the processes of wealth generation in the nation. Both the laity and the hierarchy of the Church have a duty to contribute to the building of such a just society. The hierarchy of the Nigerian Church has particularly the duty to teach and authoritatively interpret the moral laws and precepts that apply in this matter.[841] In fulfilling the teaching mission, bishops and priest must commit themselves to spreading of the Gospel and the social doctrine of the Church. This should be directed towards guiding people's behaviour and consequently inspiring people to commit themselves more to the course of justice, according to each individual's role, vocation and circumstances. The Church does not have the power to formulate policies but by virtue of the mission which she received from Jesus Christ, the Church possesses a peculiar power to reach the innermost heart and conscience of those who formulate policies, build structures and establish systems in the community. In other words, the Church can lead people to the conversion of heart that must reflect itself in the social life in form of action that will upturn the unjust structures that have brought untold hardships to the working people and generated poverty in the entire nation. For this reason, the Nigerian Church must intensify her efforts in speaking out in social matters affecting the well-being of the citizens, acting at the same time as moral watchdog and guard-fly of the nation by identifying and vehemently condemning social ills and injustice in the system. She must speak out particularly against the alarming rate of poverty growth in the nation and the marginalization of the working people.

The church cannot afford to stand aloof and watch politicians and policy and law makers establish systems and structures that would further marginalize the already marginalized poor citizens. The poor always look forward to the Church to make clear statement that would trigger off structural changes capable, for instance, of correcting the structural imbalances in economic and political life. A good case at hand is the enduring controversy over a just minimum wage in the nation. In this issue, the Church is expected to come up with a strong statement that would help to ensure that justice is done; that those who work are justly remunerated so that they will be able to meet their personal needs and those of their family members.

841 Cf.: Paul VI, Encyclical, Populorum Progresio, 81.

Those called to exercise the teaching mission of the Church in Nigeria should therefore consider it a constant duty to call government's attention to the dignity and rights of those who work, to the situations in which that dignity and those rights are violated, and to the need to reorder and adjust the structures of the modern economy and the distribution of work.[842]

As we saw in the sixth chapter of this work, the Nigerian Church has in many ways, especially through the Bishops' Conference, endeavoured to make her voice heard in defence of the poor in general. The incessant rise of poverty incidence in the nation points, however, to the need for the Church to seek better ways of making the Gospel Message to take a deeper root in the socio-economic life of the society

The Nigerian Church is endowed with a solid structure and a wide position of influence. The Church is fully present at the grassroots and is perceived at the state and national levels as a formidable player in moral issues and a respectable voice of the poor. She is therefore in a comfortable position to intervene on behalf of workers and in so doing, contribute to the improvement of their working conditions, enhancement of their productivity and earnings and assist them to stay out of poverty.

In acting as an advocate of poor workers, the Church can exert enormous pressure on the Government to remove unnecessary regulations and to design favourable policies for the benefit of those in the informal economy. She can also assist in dealing with harassment from regulatory authorities. And through her development cooperation, the Church can offer awareness creation and legal advice and embark on campaign programmes targeting the improvement of labour laws and compliance to regulations.

In seeking to contribute more meaningfully to the elimination of the unjust and oppressive structures responsible for human misery in Nigeria, the Nigerian Church must adopt what has been described as the "incarnational discipline"[843] by which the teaching and the various interventions of the bishops would go beyond mere social analysis, pastoral exhortations and subtle appeals to the oppressors to being contextually applied for the structural changes that would liberate the poor masses from the dungeons of poverty. The Nigeria Church must also come up with a clear socio-ethical vision that would act as a guideline in the fight against poverty, while at the same time engaging herself in constructive dialogue and collaborative work with other religious bodies and other community-based Organizations for more effectiveness.

The lay faithful on their part have a duty, through initiatives and concrete actions, to infuse a Christian spirit into the laws and structures of the civil community. It is their duty to bring changes into the social, economic and political fabrics of the community. The laity can initiate the needed changes and bring about improvement by initiating transformations that are permeated with the spirit of the

842 Cf. John Paul II, Encyclical, Laborem Exercens, 1.

843 George Omaku Ehusiani, The Prophetic Church, op. cit., p. 103.

Gospel. They are particular urged to offer their skills and earnest assistance to public and private organizations, and also to working together to solve the social problems that deny people the opportunity to have decent work and so generate more poverty. They should spare no effort in ensuring that just and fair laws are instituted, based on sound moral precepts.[844]

The Church as Economic Actor

The role the Nigerian Church is expected to play as an economic actor stems from the fact that all her members are economic actors not only in their individual lives but also united together as a Church. At the parish and diocesan levels, the Church through her agencies and institutions employs many people; she also has investments and extensive properties for worship and mission.

As an investor, owner of economic units and employer of labour, the Nigeria Church is not only bound by all the moral norms and principles that govern the just operation of any economic enterprise but is also expected to be exemplary in the observation of these norms and principles. This challenge which the Church should never loose sight of is aptly worded by the Synod of Bishops way back in 1971: "While the Church is bound to give witness to justice, she recognizes that anyone who ventures to speak to people about justice must first be just in their eyes. Hence, we must undertake an examination of the modes of acting and of the possessions and lifestyle found within the Church herself."[845] This is also a strong reminder to the Nigerian Church that as an institution that stands for social and economic justice, she must endeavour to eliminate and purge herself of all forms of "indecency" in employment relationships and in her socio-economic life in general. This imposes on the Church the noble task of ensuring that labour of all the workers in the "Lord's vineyard" are justly remunerated. This includes especially those the Church has engaged as worker in her institutions such as schools and hospitals and also those who work in parish houses, bishop's courts and convents as domestic staff. No excuse in this regard should be entertained, as this would mean giving a bad example to other employers of labour that are always looking for excuses to justify their incessant and scandalous abuse of the rights of workers thereby increasing the incidence of "non-decent work" and "non-decent employment."

It must be acknowledged that in the area of job creation, the Church in Nigerian has been making some remarkable contributions but the quality and conditions of jobs she creates leave much to be desired. In recent times some commendable discussions have been going on in some quarters of the Church on how to improve the quality of work in the Church. It is however regrettable that despite the efforts being made, irregular employment relationships and poor conditions of work continue to thrive in the economic life of the Nigerian Church.

844 Paul VI, Encyclical, Populorum Progresio, 81.

845 World Synod of Catholic Bishops, 1971, Justice in the World, 40.

Although there may be no documentations on the state of labour within the Church, it is however a well known fact that many workers in the Church are not enrolled in any form of social security scheme, do not belong to any labour organization and enjoy very few rights at work. Some of them do not even know what their rights are, as there was never any contract signed, stipulating the terms of employment. Most employment relationships started with: "You are now employed, go and start working." The reply from the newly employed is often, "thank you Sir" and never "under what conditions?" In a situation like this, basic rights at work such over-time allowance, medical leave are usually granted as favour and no more as rights. Retirement or the termination of job contract often implies automatic loss of the source of livelihood for the affected worker.

With regard to wages and salaries, there is hardly any institution or agency of the Nigerian Church that can boost of paying the prevailing official minimum wage in the nation. This, of course, is an ugly side of the Church that needs urgent attention. The argument that the Church cannot afford to pay such a minimum wage should be handled with some degree of transparency.

There have also been repeated cases of arbitrary dismissal and job insecurity that often occur as a result of changes in the administration or management of Church institutions. Unhealthy working environment, irregular working hours, disrespect, intimidation and harassment of workers are gradually becoming common features of labour in the Nigerian Church.

A good number of church workers are employed on a temporary basis mostly because they have lost their jobs or could not find gainful employment elsewhere. While such gestures of benevolence are commended, care should however be taken to ensure that the remuneration received by such workers is commensurate to the work done and that what is due to them in justice is not given in charity. The Church in Nigeria must therefore take constructive steps to correct any noticeable neglect of workers' rights that would amounts to social and economic injustice on the part of those who employ labour on her behalf.

In order to effectively check such abuses, the Church should establish a system of coordinating and supervising employment either at the national level through the Catholic secretariat or at the provincial and diocesan levels through any other suitable Church organ. This is a veritable tool for ensuring, for example, that the labour of the many cooks, house boys, drivers and other domestic workers in Bishops' Courts and parish houses is well remunerated and that the rights of these workers are duly respected. The same is applicable to the workers and staff in diocesan secretariats, parish offices, Catholic schools and hospital and other Church establishments and of course the catechists and religious instructors who expressly are not engaged in free and voluntary services. Such a system of coordination and supervision should also be effectively utilized to ensure that employment relationships and working conditions, especially salaries and wages are not fixed unilaterally and arbitrarily by individual agents of the Church but in compliance with some clearly established regulations of the Church and the State.

The regulatory system should also sensitize Church workers on their rights and provide them with the opportunity to legitimately and without molestation seek redress when unjustly treated by those who directly deal with them on behalf of the Church. The rights of Church worker would however be better protected when they are encouraged and assisted to form their own associations and cooperative societies or to join the statutory labour unions and cooperative societies. The better remuneration and conditions of work enjoyed today by the catechists compared to some other Church workers in their category can, to a greater extend, be attributed to the high bargaining power they have been able to galvanize through their own associations in many dioceses in the nation. In the same way, having felt the need for effective organization, the personal drivers of the Nigerian bishops have recently formed their own association. The plenary meetings of the bishops provide them the opportunity to hold their own meetings and discuss issues of common interest and of course seek ways of supporting one another. Such an endeavour is a welcome development that should not only be encouraged but also given official recognition.

Supporter of the Working Poor

As Provider of social Services, the Church can contribute immensely to the generation of more decent work and alleviation of poverty among poor workers by providing and facilitating credit facilities for informal enterprises, organizing training programmes for informal workers, and assisting in introducing modern technologies and in establishing associations of informal workers. The trust and confidence the Church enjoys among government officials put her in a good position to act as a reliable channel through which the government can direct assistance, such as credit and training, to entrepreneurs and workers in the informal economy. On her own, the Church can also organize and provide soft loans and micro-finance schemes for poor workers and entrepreneurs in the informal economy. Through the Justice Peace and Development Commission JDPC, the Church has been making some remarkable achievements in this area. There are however other means yet to be exploited. For example, the different groups in the church, especially the Basic Christian Communities[846] in the villages, provide a good and reliable framework for organizing and dispensing loans and for providing micro-finance services. They prove to be reliable in ensuring minimal failures in

846 The basic Christians communities also known as small Christian communities are community-based or neighbourhood support organizations of Christians. They embark on communal task and have the Bible and prayers as their basis. As innovative social forms, they exhibit some contextual character with regard to daily living, socio-cultural situations and traditional social forms. They can also be described as self-organized groups with co-operative elements, participatory structures and community-oriented focus. The "Bible-sharing" activity offers them the opportunity to discuss some options for action that could be drawn from the Bible texts they read. They take special recognition of social problems and seek ways of solving them collectively. They undertake, for example, the mending of bad roads in the villages, and render some assistance to the sick and weak people in the community.

terms of paying back loans granted to their members. The leaders of these organizations should be supported with training packages and information towards, for example, enhancing their capacity for securing external support and for assisting their members in polling their resources together to assist one another and to boost their business activities. The organizations can also be encouraged to do more in terms of mobilizing themselves to confront, in more concrete ways, the unjust structures in the society that suppress the poor.

In the area of education, although the Church has done creditably well, there is however the need to look into the possibility of providing the education that is suitable, affordable and relevant to the working poor. To this end, the educational programmes offered by the Church should be so designed not only to provide certificates but so as to empower people with relevant skills and technical know-how that will enable them to free themselves from misery and degradation as well as work for their own well-being. The Church can commit herself to this type of education, through appropriate vocational training, adult literacy and public enlightenment programmes; education in fundamental human rights, rehabilitation of the handicapped and conventional schools with a sound religious and moral base.[847] It must also be borne in mind that the education that has more impact on poverty alleviation is the education that offers the poor the opportunity to acquire knowledge and skills, develop their capabilities and become more economically and socially active, especially through decent jobs in the formal economy. The church should therefore concentrate on building schools not for the rich who already have better chances in the society but for the poor to enable them to gain access to decent job opportunities. The Church should also find better ways of incorporating the catholic social teaching into the school curriculum as a mean of sensitizing people to the needs for social justice and how they as social and economic actors can contribute towards building a just society.

Apart from the conventional education and training opportunities that are provided, the Church should, from time to time, organise some training and skill acquisition programmes that would enable those that must enter the informal economy due to lack of job opportunities in the formal economy and workers and entrepreneurs already in it to acquire new skills or up-date their skills. For instance, young girls leaving primary and secondary schools, with little or no prospect of gainful employment, can be giving home economics courses in home-making, health, hygiene, child-care, family welfare, family economies, budgeting, marketing, gardening, poultry rearing, textiles, laundry work, foods and nutrition. In addition to these, home economics courses, vocational training courses in pre-nursing, pre-teaching, commercial training, machine knitting and professional dressmaking can also be offered to young people in general. Such courses will help these young people to be adequately prepared to make the best use of their talents. They will also enable them to avail themselves more easily of opportunities that may be available to them, for example, in further training in teaching and nursing, or in competing

847 CBCN, The Church in the Face of our Nation in Distress, Lagos, March 7-10, 1995.

openly in dress-making or machine work in a free market either for self-employment or for paid employment. The courses will also assist school leavers to integrate themselves more actively into the future progress and development of their own locality and help to stem the tide of urban migration. These young people should also be assisted and introduce to different possibilities for organizing themselves and working together to find better ways of making their needs known and of securing their rights.

In order to better appreciate and effectively play her role, the Nigeria Church must first and foremost change her perception of and her attitude towards the economic life of the people, especially the faithful. It must not "be supposed that the solicitude of the Church is so preoccupied with the spiritual concerns of her children as to neglect their temporal and earthly interests."[848] The notion that there is a divorce between religion and economics; that they run on parallel lines like darkness and light and have nothing in common, must therefore be corrected. Issues concerning the economic life of the people should not be seen as taboo-topics in the church or as a profane enterprise that leads to syncretism and perdition, as they are often conceived, after all the Church partakes of the fruits of the economic activities of the people. If the second Vatican Council should be taken seriously when it declared in article one of the *Gaudium et Spes* that "the joy and hope, the grief and anguish of the men of our time, especially of those who are poor and afflicted in any way, are the joy and hope, the grief and anguish of the followers of Christ as well"[849] then the Nigerian Church must not neglect the fears and hope of the people in their places of business and work, especially the working poor who have been robed of the right to "Decent Work".

848 Leo XIII, Encyclical, Rerum Novarum, 28.

849 Gaudium et Spes, 1.

SELECTED BIBLIOGRAPHY

Papal Documents

BENEDICT XVI, Encyclical, *Caritas in Veritate*, Vatican City: Libreria Editrice Vaticana, June 29, 2009.

JOHN XXXIII, Encyclical *Pacem in Terris*, Vatican City: Libreria Editrice Vaticana, April 11, 1963.

_____, Encyclicyl, *Mater et Magitra*, Vatican City: Libreria Editrice Vaticana, May 15, 1961.

JOHN PAUL II, Address to Business Men and Economic Managers (Milan, May 22, 1983) in L'Osservatore Romano, weekly edition in English, June 20, 1983.

_____, Encyclical, *Centesimus Annus,* Vatican City: Libreria Editrice Vaticana, May 1, 1991.

_____, Encyclical, *Fides et Ratio,* Vatican City: Libreria Editrice Vaticana September 15 1998.

_____, Encyclical, *Laborem Exeecens,* Vatican City: Libreria Editrice Vaticana, September 14, 1981.

_____, Encyclical, *Sollicitudo Rei Socialis,* Vatican City: Libreria Editrice Vaticana, December 30, 1987.

_____, *Message to the Secretary-General of the United Nation, on the occasion of the thirtieth anniversary of the Universal declaration of Human Rights*, 2nd December, 1978.

LEO XIII, Encyclical, *Rerum Novarum*, Vatican City: Libreria Editrice Vaticana, May 15, 1891.

PAUL VI, Apostolic Letter *Octogesima Adveniens*, Vatican City: Libreria Editrice Vaticana, 14 May 1971.

_____, Encyclical, *Populorum progression*, Vatican City: Libreria Editrice Vaticana, Macrh 26, 1967.

PIUS XI, Encyclical, *Quadragesimo Anno*, Vatican City: Libreria Editrice Vaticana, 15 May 1931.

PIUS XII, *Radio Message on he fiftieth anniversary of Rerum Novarum*, 1 June 1941.

Documents of National and Regional Episcopal Conferences

Catholic Bishops' Conference of England and Wales, *The Common Good and the Catholic Church's Social Teaching*: A statement by the Catholic Bishops' Conference of England and Wales, 1996.

Catholic Bishops' Conference of Nigeria, *Current Unrest*, Lagos, February 13, 1975.

_____, *For Peace and Progress*, a communiqué issued at the end of the meeting on June 13, 1982.

_____, *Healing the Wounds of the Nation*, Abuja: February, 2002.

_____, *Peace through Justice and Love*, Lagos, February, 1989.

_____, *The Catholic Church in an Independent Nigeria*: Joint Pastoral Letter of the Nigerian Hierarchy. October 1st, 1960.

_____, *The Church and Nigerian Social Problems: Memorandum of the Catholic Bishops' of*

Nigeria, February, 1972.
_____, *The Church in the Face of our Nation in Distress*, Lagos, March 7-10, 1995.
_____, *The Jubilee and National Reconciliation*, Lagos March, 2000.
_____, *The trust Shall make us Free*, Jos, September, 1992.
_____, *The Wind of Change in Nigeria*, Lagos, March, 1990.
_____, *Year of Destiny, of Election and of Holy Redeemer*, February, 1983.
German Bishops' Conference, The *many faces of globalization: Perspectives for a humane world order*, Study of the Groups of Experts "World Economic and Social Ethics" and the church agencies Adveniat, Caritas International, Misereor, Mission Aachen, Missio München and Renovabis, Bonn: Deutche Kommision Justitia et Pax, 2000.
SECAM, *Justice and Evangelization in Africa*, Statement of Episcopal Conference of Africa and Madagascar 1981.
U.S. Catholic Bishops, *Economic Justice for All*, Pastoral Letter on Catholic Social Teaching and the U.S. Economy, 1986.
_____, *A Place at the Table: A Catholic Recommitment to Overcome Poverty and to Respect the Dignity of All God's Children*, a Pastoral Reflection of the U.S. Catholic Bishops, 2002, at: http://www.usccb.org/bishops/table.shtml

Other Ecclesiastical Documents

Pontifical Council for Justice and Peace, *Compendium of the Social Doctrine of the Church*, Vatican City: Libereria Edtrice Vaticana, 2004.
Vatican Council II: The Conciliar and Post Conciliar Documents, *Gaudium et Spes,* Austin Flannery, (Ed.), Dublin: Dominican Publications, 1988,
The Catechism of the Catholic Church, Vatican City: Libreria Editrice Vaticana, 1993.
The Code of Canon Law, London: Collins Liturgical Publications, 1983.
World Synod of Catholic Bishops, 1971, *Justice in the World.*

Newspapers and Magazines

Daily Independent (Lagos), *Nigeria: Giving Fillip to Agric Sector*, 15 March, 2011.
Daily Trust, *Nigeria: Permanent Secretary Calls for Strengthening of Decent Work Country Programme*, a report put together by Francis Okeke, at: http://allafrica.com/stories/201003250669.html
Vanguard, *Informal Sector Accounts for 90 Percent of New Jobs in Country*. A report put together by Victor Ahiuma-Young and Ashiat Adeniyi, 15 September 2008.

ILO Documents

ILO, *A Global Agenda for Employment: Discussion paper,* Geneva, International Labour Office, 2001.
_____, *A global Agenda for Employment: Summary,* Global Employment Forum, Geneva, 1-3 Nov. 2001.
_____, Conclusions Concerning Human Resources Training and Development, Geneva: International Labour Office, 2000.
_____, *Conclusions concerning social security*, International Labour Conference, 89th

Session, Geneva, 2001.
_____, ILO Constitution, at: http://www.ilo.org/ilolex/english/constq.htm
_____, *Decent work and the informal economy,* Report VI, International Labour Conference, 90th Session, Geneva, 2002, Geneva: International Labour Office, 2002.
_____, *Decent Work and Poverty Reduction Strategies A reference manual for ILO staff and constituents*, Geneva: International labour Office, 2005.
_____, *Employment, Incomes and Equality: A Strategy for Increasing Productive Employment in Kenya*, Geneva: International Labour Office, 1972.
_____, *Economic security for a better world,* Geneva: International Labour Office, 2004.
_____, *Global Employment Trends 2004*, Geneva: International Labour Office. 2004 at: http://kilm.ilo.org/GET2004/DOWNLOAD/trends.pdf
_____, *Global Employment Trends 2004: Overview*, Geneva: International Labour Office, 2004.
_____, *Global Employment Trends: 2011: The challenge of a jobs recovery*, Geneva: International Labour Office, 2011.
_____, *Global Employment Trends Brief, January 2007*, Geneva: International Labour Office, 2007.
_____, *Global Employment Trends: January 2008,* Geneva: International labour Office, 2008.
_____, *Global Employment Trends: January 2010*, Geneva: International Labour Office, 2010.
_____, *Guidelines concerning a statistical definition of informal employment*, endorsed by the Seventeenth International Conference of Labour Statisticians, November-December 2003.
_____, *Job quality: It's just good business,* Turin: International Training Centre of the ILO, 2001.
_____, *Key Indicators of the Labour Market*: Poverty, working poor and income distribution KILM 20
_____, *Key Indicator of Labour Market: Working Poverty*, Table 20b, Working poverty (national estimates), at: http://kilm.ilo.org/KILMnetBeta/default2.asp
_____, *Promoting gender equality: A resource kit for trade unions, Booklet 4: Organizing the* unorganized: Informal economy and other unprotected workers, Geneva: International Labour Office, 2001.
_____, *Reducing the decent work deficit: A global challenge*, Report of the Director-General, Geneva: International Labour Office, 2001.
_____, *Report of the Director-General: Decent work*, Geneva: International Labour Conference, 1999.
_____, *Report of the Director-General*, Geneva: International Labour Office, 1935.
_____, *Resolution concerning decent work and the informal economy* ILC90-PR25-292-En.Doc.
_____, *Resolution concerning statistics of employment in the informal sector*, adopted by the Fifteenth International Conference of Labour Statisticians, January 1993.
_____, Social-Economic Security Programme, *Definitions: What we mean when we say*

"economic security", at: http://www.ilo.org/public/english/protection/ses/download/docs/definition.pdf

_____, *Statistical Report on the working poor in the Caribbean,* a report by the Labour Market and Poverty Studies Unit, Department of Economic, The University of the West Indies St. Augustine, Trinidad and Tobago, Geneva: International Labour Office, 2006.

_____, *Strengthening the ILO's Capacity to Assist its Members' Efforts to Reach its Objectives in the Context of Globalization*, Geneva, International Labour Office, 2007.

_____, *The Decent Work Agenda and Poverty Reduction*: ILO Contribution to IMF/World Bank Comprehensive Review of Poverty Reduction Strategy Process Washington 14-17 January 2002

_____, *The dilemma of the informal sector*, Report of the Director-General (Part 1), Geneva: International Labour Office, 1991.

_____, *Trade unions and the informal sector: Towards a comprehensive strategy*, background paper for the International Symposium on Trade Unions and the Informal Sector, Geneva, International Labor Office, 1999.

_____, *World Employment Report 2004–05: Employment, Productivity, and Poverty Reduction,* Geneva: International Labour Office, 2005.

_____, *Women and Men in the Informal Economy: A statistical picture,* Geneva: International Labour Office, 2002.

_____, *Working out of Poverty*, Report of the Director-General, International Labour Conference, 91st Session, Geneva: International Labour Office, 2003.

_____, *World Employment Report 1998-99: Employability in the global economy – How training matters,* Geneva, International Labor Office, 1998.

_____, *World Labour Report 1997-98: Industrial relations, democracy and social stability,* Geneva, International Labour office, 1997.

ILO/UNDP, *Elements of an Employment Framework for Poverty Reduction in Ghana* – A report of a joint ILO/UNDP mission prepared by James Heintz.

Documents by Other Authors

ABDULKADIR, M. S., *Poverty Alleviation in Northern Nigeria: C. 1900 – 1960.* In: Mustapha C. Duze et al. (Eds), Poverty in Nigeria: Causes Manifestations and Alleviation Strategies, London: Adonis & Abbey Publishers Ltd, 2008.

ABUMERE, I. et al, *Informal sector in Nigeria's Development Process*, Ibadan, Nigeria: Development Policy Centre, 1998.

ACQUAAH, N. E. and JUURIKKALA, O., *Savings in the Absence of Functioning Property Rights*, in: Institute of Economic Affairs 27(1), 71 – 75, March, 2007, London: Institute of Economic Affairs, 2007.

ADEDIPE, B., *The Impact of Oil on Nigeria's Economic Policy Formulation,* a paper presented at the conference on Nigeria: Maximizing Pro-poor Growth: Regenerating the Socio-economic Database, organized by Overseas Development Institute in collaboration with the Nigerian Economic Summit Group, 16th / 17th June 2004.

ADEYEMI, K.S., *Economic Policy Reforms in Nigeria: Achievements and Challenges*, at:

http://www.valuefronteira.com/vf/images/UnionBank/economic%20policy%20reforms%20in%20nigeria.pdf

ADEYINKA, S. A. et al., *An Evaluation of Informal Sector Activities and Urban Land Use Management in South West Nigeria,* at: www.fig.net/pub/fig2006/papers/ts35/ts35_02_adeyinka_etal_0641.pdf

ADU-AMANKWAH, K., *Trade unions in the informal sector* in: "Trade union in the informal sector: Finding their bearings: Nine country papers," (ILO, Labour Education, No. 116).

AJAKAIYE, D. O. and ADEYEYE, V. A., *Concepts, Measurement and Causes of Poverty*, CBN ECONOMIC & FINANCIAL REVIEW, VOL. 39 N0. 4.

Ali-AKPAJIAK, S. C.A. and PYKE, T., *Measuring Poverty in Nigeria*, Oxford: Oxfam GB, 2003.

AMOAKO-TUFFOUR, J., Forging links between formal and informal financial sectors: emerging practices in Ghana, The African Finance Journal, 4(1): 1-31, 2002.

ANHEIER, H. K., *Economic Environments and Differentiation: A Comparative Study of Informal Sector Economies in Nigeria*, in: "World Development", Vol. 20. No. 11, pp. 1573-1585, Great Britain: Pergamon Press Ltd, 1992.

ARIMAH, B. C., *Nature and Determinant of the Linkages between Informal and Formal Enterprises in Nigeria*, Oxford: Blackwell Publishers, 2001.

ARYEETEY, E., *Informal finance for private sector development in Africa*, background paper prepared for the *African Development Report 1998*.

ARYEETEY, E., *Recent Developments in African Financial Markets: Agenda for Further Research, Journal of African Economies*, 12(supp 2): ii111-ii152, 2003.

ASHE, J. *The PISCES II experience: local efforts in micro-enterprise development*, Washington: USAID, 1985.

BECKER, K. F., *The Informal Economy: Fact Finding Study,* Stockholm, Sweden: Swedish International Development Agency, 2004.

BELL, S. and NEWITT, K., *Decent Work and Poverty Eradication: literature Review and Two Country Study,* a study for the Decent Work and Labour Standards Forum, London: Ergon Associates Limited, 2010.

BELLO, M. O., *Accessibility of Land as a Tool for Empowering the Low income Earner of the Informal Sector in Nigeria*, at: www.fig.net/pub/fig2007/papers/ts_7a/ts07a_01_bello_1282.pdf

BONNER, C. and SPOONER, D., *Organizing in the Informal Economy: A Challenge for Trade Unions*, at: http://library.fes.de/pdf-files/ipg/2011-2/08_a_bonner.pdf

CARR, M. and CHEN, M. A., *Globalization and the Informal Economy: How Global Trade and Investment Impact on the Working Poor*, WIEGO, 2001, at: http://www.wiego.org/papers/carrchenglobalization.pdf

Central Bank of Nigeria, *Agricultural Credit Gu arantee Scheme Fund (ACGSF) Self Help Group Linkage Banking,* at: http://www.cenbank.org/devfin/selfhelp.asp

Central Bank of Nigeria, Enugu Zone, *A Profile of Regional/Zonal Poverty in Nigeria: The Case of Enugu Zone*, in: Measuring and Monitoring Poverty in Nigeria, Proceedings of the Seventh Annual Conference of the Zonal Research Units, 1998.

CHARMES, J., *Estimations and Survey methods for the Informal Sector*, Versailles, France: University of Versailles, 2002.

_____, J., "*Women working in the informal sector in Africa: new methods and new data,*" Paper prepared for the United Nations Statistics Division, the Gender and Development Programme of the United Nations Development Programme (UNDP) and the project "Women in Informal Employment: Globalizing and Organizing" (WIEGO), 1998.

CHEN, M., et al., *Counting the Invisible Workforce: The Case of Home-based Workers*, "World Development", Vol.27, No.3, 1999.

CHEN, M., et al, *Informality, Gender and Poverty: A Global Picture*, in: *Economic and Political weekly,* May 27, 2006, at:
http://www.wiego.org/publications/EPW/Chen%20Vanek%20Heintz%20Informality%20Gender%20and%20Poverty.pdf

CHEN, M. A. et al, *Mainstreaming Informal Employment and Gender in Poverty Reduction: A handbook for Policy-makers and Other Stakeholders*, London: Commonwealth Secretariat, 2004.

CHEN, M. A. et al., *Progress of the World's Women* 2005: *Women, Work and Poverty*, (New York: UNIFEM, 2005.

CHEN, S. and RAVALLION, M., *The Developing World Is Poorer Than We Thought, But No less Successful in the Fight against Poverty*, Washington D.C.: World Bank, 2008.

COLCLOUGH, C. and MANOR, J. (Eds.), *States* or *Markets? Neo-liberalism and the Development Policy Debate,* Oxford: Clarendon Press, 1991.

CORBETT, T. J. "*Poverty*," in: *Microsoft Student* 2006 [DVD]. Redmond, WA: Microsoft Corporation, 2005.

COUDOUEL, A. et al., *Poverty Measurement and Analysis,* Poverty Reduction Strategy Paper, Washington, D.C.: The World Bank, 2004.

CYPHER, J. M. and DIETZ, J. L., *The Process of Economic Development*, London, New York: Routledge, 1997.

DADA, J. O., *Harnessing the Potentials of the Informal Sector for Sustainable Development: Lessons from Nigeria*, at: http://unpan1.un.org/intradoc/groups/public/documents/AAPAM/UNPAN025582.pdf

DAVIDSON, B., *Africa: History of a Continent*, New York: Macmillan, 1972.

DEBERRI, E, P. et al., *Catholic Teaching: Our Best Kept Secret, fourth revised and expanded edition*, Maryknoll, New York: Orbis Books, 2003.

DELANCY, V., *The Economies of Africa.* In: Understanding Contemporary Africa, Gordon and Donald L. Gordon, (Ed.), London: Lynne Reinner Publishers, Inc. 2007.

DELVAUX, E., *The challenge of the informal economy.* In: 'Unprotected Labour: What role for union in the informal economy,' ILO: Labour Education 2002/2, No 127.

DERCON, STEFAN., *Income Risk, Coping Strategies and Safety Nets*, Background paper for *World Development Report 2000/2001,* Washington D.C.: World Bank 1999.

DFID, *What is Pro-Poor and Why Do We Need to Know?* Pro-Poor Growth Briefing Note, February 2004.

DIKE, E. *Economic Development, Urban Labour Absorption and the Informal Sector in Nigeria, mimeograph*, 1992.

DOLLAR, D. and KRAAY, A. *Growth is Good for the Poor*, in: Journal of Economic Growth vol. 7, no. 3, September 2002.

EGUZOZIE, B., *How Sovereign Wealth Fund Can Drive Nigeria's Growth, Infrastructure Development*, a newspaper article in "Businessday", 16 May, 2011.

EHUSANI, G. O., *A Prophetic Church*, Ede: Provincial Pastoral Institute Publication, 1996:

EKPO, A. H. and UMOH, O. J., *The Informal Sector*, at: http://www.onlinenigeria.com/economics/?blurb=495

FALOLA, T., *Economic Reforms and Modernization in Nigeria: 1945-1965*, Kent, Ohio: The Kent State University Press, 2004.

FARBMAN, M. and LESSIK, Adam., *The impact of classification*, in: Antoinette Gossens et al., *Small enterprises, new approaches,* proceedings of the Workshop "Small Enterprise Development, in search of new Dutch approaches, Ministry of Foreign Affairs/Dept. of Netherlands Development Cooperation, 1989

Federal Republic of Nigeria, National Poverty Eradication Programme (NAPEP): A Blueprint for the Schemes, NAPEP Secretariat, Abuja, 2001.

FEIGE, E. L., *The Underground Economy and the Currency Enigma*, in G. Fiorentini and S. Zamagni, (Eds.), The Economics of Corruption and Illegal Markets, The International Library of Critical Writings in Economics, Cheltenham, UK: Edward Elgar Publishing Limited, 1999

FORASTIERI, V., *Implementation of Working Conditions and Environment in the Informal Sector through Safety and Health Measures,* Geneva: International Labour Office, 1999.

FORASTIERI, V., *Implementation of Working Conditions and Environment in the Informal Sector through Safety and Health Measures* at, http://www.ilo.org/public/english/protection/safework/sectors/informal/inform1.htm#wcond

_____, *Implementation of Working Conditions and Environment in the Informal Sector through Safety and Health Measures,* a discussion paper, Geneva: International Labour Office, 1999.

GALLIN, D., *Organizing in the Global Informal Economy* at: http://www.globallabour.info/en/2007/09/organizing_in_the_global_infor.html

GINNEKEN, W. van, *Social protection for workers in the informal economy: New challenges for Asia and the Pacific,* report to the Twelfth ISSA Regional Conference for Asia and Pacific, Bangkok, 20-23 Nov. 2000.

Global Labour Institute: Informal Work: Notes on Trade Unions and the Informal Sector 1999, at:
http://www.globallabour.info/en/2007/09/notes_on_trade_unions_and_the_1.html

GREY-JOHNSON, C., *The African Informal Sector at the Crossroads: Emerging Policy Options*, Africa Development, 1992, Vol. XVII.

GROSH, M. and GLEWWE, P., (Eds)., *Designing Household Survey Questionnaires for Developing Countries: Lessons from 15 Years of the Living Standards Measurement Study,* Washington, D.C.: World Bank, 2000.

HAAN, H. C., *Training for Work in the Informal Sector: New Evidence from Eastern and Southern Africa*, Turin, Italy: ILO International Training Centre, 2001.

HADDAD, L and KANBUR, RAVI., *Are Better-off Households More Unequal or Less Unequal?* Policy Research and External Affairs Working Paper 373, Washington, D.C.: World Bank, 1990.

HART, K. *Informal Income Opportunities and Urban Employment in Ghana*, The Journal of Modern African Studies, 1973, Vol.11, No.1.

HAUGHTON, J., *Handbook on Poverty and Inequality*, Washington, D.C.: World Bank, 2009.

HODGES, A., *Children's and Women's Rights in Nigeria: A Wake-up* Call, Situation Assessment and Analysis, Lagos: UNICEF/National Planning Commission, 2001.

HOLZMANN, R., and JORGENSEN, S. L., *Social Protection as Social Risk Management: Conceptual Understandings for the Social Protection Sector Strategy Paper*, Social Protection Discussion Paper 9904, Washington, D.C.: World Bank, 1999.

HOWARD WHITE and EDWARD ANDERSON, *Growth vs. Redistribution: Does the Pattern of Growth Matter*? Development Policy Review 19(3): 167–289, 2001.

HUSSMANNS, R., *Defining and measuring informal employment,* a paper prepared for the United Nations Economic and Social Council, 18-20 February 2004, Bangkok, at: http://.unescap.org/stat/sos1/sos1_11e.pdf

_____, *Informal Sector and Informal Employment: Elements of a Conceptual Framework*, a paper presented at the Fifth Meeting of the Expert Group on Informal Sector Statistics, Delhi, September 2001.

_____, *Statistical definition of informal employment*, guideline endorsed by the Seventh International Conference of Labour Statisticians.

_____, and MEHRAN, F *Statistical definition of the informal sector: International standards and national practices*, at: http://www.gdrc.org/informal/huss0772.pdf

IDOGUN, E., *Nigeria: 'Small Scale Enterprises Can Drive the Economy'*, an interview granted to "Vanguard" on 26 March 2011.

IJAIYI, G. T. and UMAR, C. A., *The Informal and Formal Sector Inter-linkage and the Incidence of Poverty in Nigeria: A Case Study of Ilorin Metropolis,* African Development, Vol. XXXIX, No 3, 2004.

International Confederation of Free Trade Union, *International Recognised Core Labour Standard Review of the Trade Policies of Nigeria,* Geneva, 11 and 13 May, 2005.

IMF: *International Financial Statistics Yearbook, various issues*, cited in Oxfam, *Rigged Rules Double Standards,* Oxford: Oxfam International, 2002.

International Monetary Fund, *Joint Staff Advisory Note on the Progress Report for the* National Economic Empowerment and Development Strategy (NEEDS), Washington D.C.: IMF Publication Service, 2007.

_____, *Memorandum on Economic and Financial Policies of the Federal Government of Nigeria for 1999,* at: http://www.imf.org/external/np/loi/1999/022299.htm

_____, *Poverty Reduction Strategy Paper—National Economic Empowerment and Development Strategy*, IMF Country Report No. 05/433Nigeria, Washington, D.C. International Monetary Fund Publication Services, 2005.

International Trade Union Confederation, *Decent Work for All: A Key Objective for Economic and Social Development*, Statement to the 46th Session of the UN Commission for Social Development, New York, 6-15 February, 2008.

ISHENGOMA, E, K. and KAPPEL, R., *Economic Growth and Poverty: Does Formalisation of Informal Enterprises Matter?* Hamburg, Germany: GIGA German Institute of Global and Area Studies, 2006.

ISLAM, R., *The Nexus of Economic Growth, Employment and Poverty Reduction: An Empirical Analyses*. Geneva: ILO – Recovery and Reconstruction Department, 2004.

ISLAM, R., *The nexus of growth, employment, and poverty reduction: an empirical analysis*, Geneva: International Labour Office, 2004.

JOSEPH, R., *Economic Transformation and Developmental Governance in Nigeria: The Promise of the Obama Era,* Paper present at the Inaugural BusinessDay Scholars in Society Forum in Lagos, Nigeria in May 2909.

KAKWANI, N. and PERNIA, E. M., *What is Pro-Poor Growth?*" in: *Asian Development Review* 18(1): 1–16, 2000.

KALU, U.K., *Poverty and its Alleviation in Colonial Nigeria*, in: A. Oyebade, (Ed), *The Foundations of Nigeria*, Trenton and Asmara: African World Press, 2003.

KANBUR, R., and Vine, D., *The World Bank and Poverty Reduction: past, present and future*, in: Christopher L. Gilbert and David Vines (Eds), *The World Bank: Structure and Policies*, Cambridge: Cambridge University Press, 2000.

KAPPEL, R. and ISHENGOMA E. K., *Economic Growth and Poverty: Does Formalisation of Informal Enterprises Matter?* A working paper written for GIGA Research Program: Transformation in the Process of Globalization, Munich, April 2006, at: http://mpra.ub.uni-muenchen.de/1456/

KAPSOS, S., *Estimating growth requirements for reducing working poverty: Can the world halve working poverty by 2015*? Employment Strategy Papers 2004/14, Employment Trends Unit, Employment Strategy Department Geneva: International Labour Office, 2004.

KAPUR, D, Lewis J. P. and Webb, R., *The World Bank: Its First Half Century*, vol. I, Washington D.C.: Brooking Institution Press, 1997.

KHAN, A. R., *Growth, employment and poverty: An analysis of the vital nexus based on some recent UNDP and ILO/SIDA studies,* DESA Working Paper No. 49 ST/ESA/ 2007/DWP/49, New York: United Nations Department of Economic and Social Affairs, 2007.

KUZNETS, S., *Economic Growth and Income Inequality*, in: American Economic Review, 45 (1): 1 – 28.

LABEODAN O. A., *Women in the Informal House-Building Industry in Nigeria,* in: Habitat International, vol. 16, No. 1, Great Britain by Pergamon Press Ltd, 1992.

LAMB, M. L., *Solidarity*, in: Judith A Dwyer, "The New Dictionary of Catholic Social Thought" Collegeville, Minnesota: Liturgical Press, 1994.

LEE, E., *The Asian Financial Crisis: The Challenges for Social Policy* Geneva: International Labour Organization, 1998.

LIM, L. *Highlights of the ILC conclusions*, presentation to the Turin Workshop on the Follow-up to the ILC Conclusions on Decent Work and the Informal Economy, ILO International Training Centre, Turin, 10-12 February, 2003.

LINDBERG, C. H., *Property, poverty and the Poor,* in: Encyclopaedia Britannica 2005, Deluxe Edition CD-Rom.

Little, I.M.D., *Economic Development: Theory, Polity and International Relations*, New York: Basic Books, 1992.

MAJID, N., *The size of the working poor population in developing countries*, an Employment Paper 2001/16 for the employment sector of the Employment Strategy Department, ILO, 2001.

MALUMFASHI, S. L., *The concept of poverty and its Dimensions*, in: Mustapha C. Duze et al. (eds), Poverty in Nigeria: Causes Manifestations and Alleviation Strategies, London: Adonis & Abbey Publishers Ltd, 2008.

MAY, J. D. and STAVROU, S. E., *The Informal Sector: Socio-Economic Dynamics and Growth in the Greater Durban Metropolitan Region*, Working Paper No.18, Durban: Centre for Social and Development Studies, Durban, University of Natal, 1989.

MAYNE, R, J., *Europe, history of: The human condition,* in: Encyclopaedia Britannica 2005, Deluxe Edition CD- Rom

MEAGHER, K. *Crisis, Informalisation and the Urban Informal Sector in Sub-Saharan Africa*, Development and Change, Vol. 26, 1995.

_____, *Identity Economics: Social Networks & the Informal Economy in Nigeria*, (African Issues), Woodbridge, Suffolk, UK: James Currey, 2010.

_____, *Manufacturing Disorder: Liberalization, Informal Enterprise and Economic 'Ungovernance' in African Small Firm Clusters*, in: "Development and Change",volume 38, Issue 3, pages 473–503, May 2007.

MEAGHER, K. and YUNUSA, M. B., *Passing the Buck: Structural Adjustment and the Nigerian Informal Sector*, UNRISD discussion paper, United Nations Research Institute for Social Development, 1996.

METZ, H. C. (Ed), *Nigeria: A Country Study*, Washington: GPO for the Library of Congress, 1991, at: http://countrystudies.us/nigeria/51.htm

MOGENSEN, G. V., et al., *The informal economy in Denmark: Measurement and results*, Study no. 3, Copenhagen: The Rockwool Foundation Research Unit, 1995.

MUKTAR, M., *Poverty Alleviation as a Machinery for Economic Reconstruction in Nigeria*, in: Mustapha C. Duze et al. (Eds.), *Poverty in Nigeria: Causes Manifestations and Alleviation Strategies*, London: Adonis & Abbey Publishers Ltd, 2008.

National Poverty Eradication Programme (NAPEP), http://www.napep.gov.ng/whatwedo.php

NeLL-BREUNING, O. Von, *Baugesetze der Gesellschaft: Solidarität und Subsidiarität*, Freiburg: Herder Verlag Gmbh, 1990.

Nigeria Labour Congress, *Demand for the Review of the National Minimum Wage and General Wage*, 2009, at: http://www.nlcng.org/minimum%20wage.pdf

_____, *Economic Crises and Credible Electoral Reforms: Mobilizing for Positive Change*, 2009 May Day Speech by Nigerian Labour Congress.

_____, *History of the Nigeria Labour Congress*, at: http://www.nlcng.org/history.php

_____, *Policy Document*, at: http://www.nlcng.org/policydoc.pdf

_____, *Press Conference on the New National Minimum Wage Addressed by the President of the Nigeria Labour Congress, Comrade Abdulwahed I. Omar after the Meeting of the Central Working Committee of Congress at the Main Auditorium of Labour House on Friday January 14, 2011.*

NURUL AMIN, A.T.M., *The Informal Sector in Asia from Decent Work Perspective*, a working paper on the informal economy, Geneva: International Labour Office, 20002.

NWAKA, G. I., *The Urban Informal Sector in Nigeria: Towards Economic Development, Environmental Health and Social Harmony*, Global Urban Development Volume 1 Issue 1 May 2005.

NWOYE, M. I., *Small Business Enterprises: (How to start and succeed)*, Benin-City, Nigeria: Benin Social Science Series for Africa, 1994.

OBADAN, M. I. *Poverty Reduction in Nigeria: The Way Forward*, CBN, Economic and Financial Review, vol. 39, No. 4.

OBADAN, M. FAJINGBESI, A. A. and UGA, E. O. (Eds), *Integrating Poverty Alleviation Strategies* into Plans and Programmes in Nigeria, Ibadan: NCEMA, 2003.

ODEY, J. O., *The Parable of a Wasted Generation*, Enugu: Snaap Press, 2000.

OGWUMIKE, F. O., *An Appraisal of Poverty Reduction Strategies in Nigeria*, CBN Economic & Financial Review. Vol. 39 No. 4.

_____, *Poverty and Basic Needs: An Approach to Development in Nigeria*, unpublished Ph.D.Thesis, Department of Economics, University of Ibadan, 1987.

_____, *Poverty Alleviation Strategies in Nigeria*, in: Measuring and Monitoring Poverty inNigeria, Proceedings of the Seventh Annual Conference of the Zonal Research Units of CBN, 1998.

_____, *The Effects of Macro-level Government Policies on Rural Development and Poverty Alleviation in Nigeria*, Ibadan Journal of the Social Sciences, Vol. 1, N0. 1, 1995.

OKOJIE, C.E.E., *Women Entrepreneurs: Opportunities and Challenged in Nigeria*, in: F.O. MCOLIVER et al. (Ed.) Entrepreneurship Development: The Nigerian Experience, Benin-City, Nigeria: Mareh Publishers, 2006.

OKONJO-IWEALA, N. and OSAFO-KWAAKO P., *Nigeria's Economic Reforms: Progress and Challenges*, a working paper, Washington, DC: The Brookings Institution, 2007.

OKOROMA, L. I., *Nigeria: Mass Suffering - Will Social Security End It?* Leadership (Abuja), 30 August, 2009, at http://allafrica.com/stories/printable/200908311201.html

OKPE I. J., and Abu, G.A., *Foreign Private Investment and Poverty Reduction in Nigeria (1975 to 2003)*, in: Journal of social Sciences: Interdisciplinary Reflection of Contemporary Society, vol. 19, No. 3, May, 2009.

OLADEJI, S. I. and ABIOLA, A. G. *Poverty alleviation with economic growth strategy: prospects and challenges in contemporary Nigeria*, in: Journal of social development in Africa, vol. 15, No. 2. July, 2000.

ÖNIS, Z. and ŞENSES, F., *Rethinking the Emerging Post-Washington Consensus: A critical Appraisal*, ERC Working Papers 03/09 ERC – Economic Research Centre, Middle East Technical University, November, 2003.

Organization for Economic Cooperation and Development, *Rising to the Global Challenge: Partnership for Reducing World Poverty,* Statement by the DAC High Level Meeting in Paris. April 25–26 2001.

OSALOR, P., *The Informal Economy and Entrepreneurial Development*, at: http://www.articlesbase.com/economics-articles/the-informal-economy-and-entrepreneurial-development-3015678.html#ixzz1JrLsdsRI

OYERANTI O. and OLAYIWOLA, K., *Policies and Programmes for Poverty Reduction in Rural Nigeria*, an Interim Research Report Submitted to the African Economic Research Consortium (AERC), Nairobi for the Second Phase Collaborative Poverty Research Project, 2005.

POGGE, T., *Wachtum is gut! Nur welches*, in: Beatrice Weder di Mauro (ed.), "Chancen des Wachstums: Globalen Perspektiven für den Wohlstand von morgen", Frankfurt: Campus Verlag, 2008.

PRESTON, P. W., *Development Theory: An Introduction*, Oxford: Blackwell, 1996.

RADDA, S. I. *The Millennium Development Goals (MDGS) and Poverty in Nigeria: An Appraisal,* in: Mustapha C. Duze et al. (Eds), Poverty in Nigeria: Causes Manifestations and Alleviation Strategies, London: Adonis & Abbey Publishers Ltd, 2008.

RAVALLION, M. and CHEN, S., *China's (Uneven) Progress Against Poverty*, The World Bank, Policy Research Working Paper No. 3408, 2004.

RAVALLION, M. and CHEN, S., *What Can New Survey Data Tell Us about Recent Changes in Distribution and Poverty? The World Bank Economic Review* 11(2): 357–82, 1997.

ROWNTREE, B. S., *Poverty: A Sturdy of Town Life*, London: Macmillan and CO., 1901.

SCHÄFERS, M., *Prophetische Kraft der kirchlichen Soziallehre? Armut, Arbeit, Eigentum und Wirtschaftskritik*, Münster – Hamburg – London: Lit Verlag, 1998.

SCHNEIDER, F., *Size and Measurement of the Informal Economy in 110 Countries around the World*, a paper presented at a Workshop of Australian National Tax Centre, ANU, Canberra, Australia, July 17, 2002.

SCHUCK, M. J., *Modern Catholic Social Thought*. In: Judith A Dwyer ed., "The New Dictionary of Catholic Social Thought," Collegeville, Minnesota: Liturgical Press, 1994.

SEIBEL, H. D. *Coping with Scarcity:Microenterprise Strategies in Nigeria,* Saarbrücken: Verlag für Entwicklungspolitik, 1996.

SEN, A., *Development as Freedom,* New York: Oxford University Press, 1999.

SETHURAMAN, S. V. The Urban Informal Sector in Developing Countries: Employment, Poverty and Environment, Geneva: International Labour Office, 1981.

SHRESTHA, A., *Social Protection in the Informal Economy*, a paper presented in the National Consultation Workshop "Identifying Challenges of Informal Economy for Trade Unions" organised by DECONT on 15-16, May 2004 at Lalitpur, at: http://www.nepaldemocracy.org/institutions/Informal_Economy.htm

SILVA S. de, *The informal economy: Issues and challenges*, unpublished paper in: ILO: *Decent* Work and Informal Economy, Report VI, International Labour Conference, 90th Session, Geneva, 2002, Geneva: International Labour Office, 2002.

SINHA, S., and Lipton, M., *Damaging Fluctuations, Risk and Poverty: A Review*, Background paper for *World Development Report 2000/2001,* Washington, D.C., Brighton: Sussex University, Poverty Research Unit and World Bank, 1999.

SMITH, J.D., *Market motives in the informal economy*, in: Gaertner, W. and Wenig, A. (Eds.): *The economics of the informal economy*, Heidelberg: Springer Publishing Company, 1985. Social Security Programmes throughout the World: Africa – Nigeria. http://www.ssa.gov/policy/docs/progdesc/ssptw/2006-2007/africa/nigeria.pdf

SOMAVIA, J., *Perspectives on decent work,* Geneva: International Labour Office, 2000.

SOTO, H. de, *The mystery of capital: Why capitalism triumphs in the West and fails everywhere else,* New York, Basic Books, 2000.

STIGLITZ, J., *More Instruments and Broader Goals: Moving Toward the Post-Washington Consensus*, a paper presented at the second annual Lecture of the World Institute for Development Economics Research (WIDER), Helsinki: U.N. University Press 1998.

STIGLITZ, J. E., *The Post Washington Consensus*, a power Point presentation, August, 2005, at: http://www.policyinnovations.org/ideas/policy_library/data/01232

STIGLITZ, J., *The World Bank Research Observer;* Aug 1996; 11, 2; ABI/INFORM Global.

SUSANNA, A., *Competence Utilisation and Transfer in Informal Sector Production and Service Trades in Ibadan/Nigeria*, Munster, Hamburg: LIT Verlag, 1995.

SADC, Swiss Agency for Development and Cooperation, *Decent Work: a target to achieve the MDGs Fact sheet*, Berne: Employment and Income Division, 2008.

TENNSTEDT, F., *Sozialgeschichte der Sozialpolitik vom 18. Jahrhundert bis zum Ersten Weltkrieg*, Göttingen: Vandenhoeck & Ruprecht 198.

TOKMAN, V., (Ed,), *Beyond Regulation: The Informal Economy in Latin America* Boulder, Colorado, Lynme Riermer Publishers, 1992.

TREBILCOCK, A., *Decent Work and the Informal Economy*, Discussion Paper No. 2005/04, Helsinki: EGDI and UNU-WIDER 2005.

_____, A., *Decent Work and the Informal Economy*, discussion paper No. 2005/04 presentedat the EGDI–WIDER Conference on Unlocking Human Potential – "Linking the Informal and Formal Sectors" in Helsinki, 17-18 September 2004.

UN Secretary-General: *Road map towards the Implementation of the United Nations Millennium Declaration,* New York: United Nations, 200, also at: www.un.org/millenniumgoals/ and www.developmentgoals.org

UNDP, *About the MDGs: Basics (What are the Millennium Development Goals?*), at: http://www.undp.org/mdg/basics.shtml

_____, Methodology for the Participatory Formulation of Local Government Economic Empowerment & Development Strategy (LEEDS) in Local Government Areas (LGAs) in Nigeria, at: http://www.ng.undp.org/publications/poverty/LEEDS_Methodology.pdf

UNICEF-Nigeria, The Nigerian situation, at: http://www.unicef.org/nigeria/1971_2199.html

UNITED NATIONS, *A Better World for All,* New York: United Nations 2000.

_____, *Programme of Action of the World Summit for Social Development,* http://www.un.org/esa/socdev/wssd/text-version/agreements/poach2.htm

_____, *Report on the World Situation 2005, The Inequality Predicament,* at: http://www.sustainable-design.ie/sustain/un2005_ReportWorldSocialSystem.pdf
_____, *Report of the World Summit for Social Development, Copenhagen, 6-12 March 1995*, A/CONF.166/9 19 April 1995.
_____, *Report of the World Summit for Social Development*, Copenhagen, 1995.
_____, *The Inequality Predicament*, report on the world situation 2005, at: http://www.sustainable-design.ie/sustain/un2005_ReportWorldSocialSystem.pdf
_____, *The Millennium Development Goals Report 2009,* New York: United Nations, 2009.
_____, – Department of Economic and Social Affairs, *The Employment Imperative: Report on the World Social Situation 2007*, New York: United Nations Publications, 2007.
UNDP, *Human Development Report 1990*, New York: Oxford: Oxford University Press, 1990.
_____, *Human Development Report 1997,* New York: Oxford University Press, 1997.
_____, *Nigeria Human Development Report 2000/2001Millennium Edition*, Lagos: UNDP, 2001
_____, *Human Development Report 2001*, New York: Oxford University Press, 2001.
_____, *Human Development Report 2007/2008, Technical note 1*, New York: Oxford University Press, 2008.
_____, *Human Development Report Nigeria 2008 – 2009 Achieving growth with equity*, (Abuja, Nigeria: Development Programme, Nigeria, 2009).
United Nations Economic and Social Council, *Ministerial Declaration*, Official Records of the General Assembly, 61st Session, Supplement No. 3 (A/61/3/Rev.1).
United Nations Economic and Social Council, *Poverty and the Informal Sector: Measurement Issues*, (E/ESCAP/CPR(3)/2)/14 November 2006.
United Nations, Economic and Social Council, *Poverty and Informal Sector: Role of the* Informal Sector in Poverty Reduction, E/ESCAP/CPR(3)/1 2 October 2006.
United Nations Systems, *Nigeria: common Country Assessment*, Abuja: United Nations Systems, 2001.
United States Library of Congress - Federal Research Division, Country Profile: Nigeria, July 2008, at: http://memory.loc.gov/frd/cs/profiles/Nigeria.pdf
USAID/IMPACT Associates, *Micro- and small enterprises in Uganda: report of the National Baseline Survey*, consultancy report prepared for USAID, Kampala 1995.
UPPAL, J. S., *Informal Sector in Third World Countries,* Journal of Developing Societies, vol. V., 1989.
VARGHA, C., *Case Study on international labour standards and micro-enterprises promoted by the project URT/88/007 – Employment promotion in the informal sector,* Geneva, International Labor Office, 1992.
VERICK, S., *The Impact of Globalization on the Informal Sector in Africa*, Adis Ababa, Ethiopia: Economic and Social Policy Division, United Nations Economic Commission for Africa (ECA) And Institute for the Study of Labor (IZA).
_____, *The Impact of Globalization on the Informal Sector in Africa*, at: http://tradeinservices.mofcom.gov.cn/upload/2008/08/14/1218702966828_170237.pdf

WADE, R. H., *Winners and losers: the global distribution of income is becoming more unequal: that should be a matter of greater concern than it is*, in: *The economist*, 359 (8219), 2001.

WILLIAMSON, J., *Did the Washington Consensus Fail? Outline of Remarks at CSIS*, Washington DC: Institute for International Economics, 2000.

WILLIAMSON, J., *What Should the World Bank Think About the Washington Consensus?*

World Bank Research Observer, Washington, DC: The International Bank for Reconstruction and Development, Vol. 15, No. 2, August 2000.

World Bank's Doing Business website and online database: www.doingbusiness.org

World Bank, *Introduction to Poverty Analysis: Poverty Manual, All, JH Revision*, Washington, D.C.: World Bank Institute, 2005.

World Bank, *Nigeria: Country Brief*, at: http://web.worldbank.org/WBSITE/EXTERNAL/COUNTRIES/AFRICAEXT/NIGERIAEXTN/0,,menuPK:368906~pagePK:141132~piPK:141107~theSitePK:368896,00.html

World Bank, Poverty in the Midst of Plenty: The Challenge of Growth with Inclusion: A World Bank Poverty Assessment, World Bank, Population and Human Resources Division Western Africa Department Africa Region, 1996.

_____, *Pro-Poor Growth in the 1990s: Lessons and Insights from 14 Countries*, Washington D.C.: International Bank for Reconstruction and Development, 2005.

_____, *World Development Report 2000/2001: Attacking Poverty*, New York: Oxford University Press, 2001

_____, *World Development Report 2000/2001: Consulting with the poor, Nigeria: Voice of the Poor* – A country synthesis report. Nigeria.

World Bank and the International Monetary Fund, *Review of the Poverty Reduction Strategy Approach: Balancing Accountabilities and Scaling up Results* prepared by the Staffs of the World Bank and International Monetary Fund September 2005.

World Commission on the Social Dimension of Globalization, *A Fair Globalization: Creating Opportunities for All*, Geneva: International Labour Office, 2004.

_____, *A Fair Globalization: The Role of the ILO*, Report of the Director-General to the

World Commission on the Social Dimension of Globalization, Geneva: ILO, 2004.

World Trade Organization,, *Trade Policy Review: Body Trade Policy Review, Nigeria: Report by the Secretariat*. WT/TPR/S/39 27 May 1998.

_____, *Trade Policy Review, Nigeria: Report by the Secretariat*. WT/TPR/S/39 27 May 1998.

_____, *Trade Policy Review, Nigeria: Report by the Secretariat*. WT/TPR/S/147, 13 April 2005.

_____, *Trade Policy Review: Report by Nigeria*, WT/TPR/G/147 13 April 2005.

XABA, J. et al., *The informal Sector in Sub-Saharan Africa*, Geneva: International Labour Office, 2002.

YUNUS, M., *Eliminating poverty through market- based social entrepreneurship*, published by The Global Urban Development Magazine on the website: http://www.globalurban.org/Issue1PIMag05/Yunus%20article.htm

FSC
www.fsc.org
MIX
Papier | Fördert gute Waldnutzung
FSC® C083411

Kolibri 360 GmbH
Ferdinand-Jühlke-Straße 7
99095 Erfurt, Deutschland
produktsicherheit@kolibri360.de